THE LAW OF CONSUMER REDRESS IN AN EVOLVING DIGITAL MARKET

This book advances the emerging of a new sub-field of study, the Law of Consumer Redress, which encompasses the various dispute resolution processes for consumers, their regulations, and best practices. The book argues that the institutionalisation of alternative dispute resolution (ADR) bodies are expanding their functions beyond dispute resolution, as they are increasingly providing a public service for consumers that complements, and often replaces, the role of the courts. Although the book focuses on ADR, it also analyses other redress methods, including public enforcement, court adjudication and business internal complaints systems. It proposes a more efficient rationalisation of certified redress bodies, which should be better co-ordinated and accessible through technological means. Accordingly, the book calls for greater integration amongst redress methods and offers recommendations to improve their process design to ensure that, inter alia, traders are encouraged to participate in redress schemes, settle early meritorious claims and comply with outcomes.

PABLO CORTÉS is Professor of Civil Justice at Leicester Law School. He has advised the European Commission during the drafting of legislation on consumer ODR and ADR, and has been invited to write reports and to participate in expert meetings, inter alia, by the UN Commission on International Trade Law, the European Commission and the European Parliament. He serves on the advisory board of the ODR Civil Justice Council and the International Mediation Institute, and he has worked as a consultant for a number of organisations. He is fellow of the European Law Institute, the National Centre for Technology and Dispute Resolution (UMass) and in 2012 he was a Gould Research Fellow at Stanford University.

THE LAW OF CONSUMER REDRESS IN AN EVOLVING DIGITAL MARKET

Upgrading from Alternative to Online Dispute Resolution

PABLO CORTÉS
University of Leicester

CAMBRIDGE
UNIVERSITY PRESS

CAMBRIDGE
UNIVERSITY PRESS

University Printing House, Cambridge CB2 8BS, United Kingdom

One Liberty Plaza, 20th Floor, New York, NY 10006, USA

477 Williamstown Road, Port Melbourne, VIC 3207, Australia

4843/24, 2nd Floor, Ansari Road, Daryaganj, Delhi – 110002, India

79 Anson Road, #06–04/06, Singapore 079906

Cambridge University Press is part of the University of Cambridge.

It furthers the University's mission by disseminating knowledge in the pursuit of education, learning, and research at the highest international levels of excellence.

www.cambridge.org
Information on this title: www.cambridge.org/9781107079007
DOI: 10.1017/9781139940900

First published 2017

Printed in the United Kingdom by Clays, St Ives plc

A catalogue record for this publication is available from the British Library.

Library of Congress Cataloging-in-Publication Data
Names: Cortés, Pablo, author.
Title: The law of consumer redress in an evolving digital market : upgrading from alternative to online dispute resolution / Pablo Cortés, University of Leicester.
Description: 1 Edition. | New York : Cambridge University Press, 2017. | Includes bibliographical references and index.
Identifiers: LCCN 2017020804 | ISBN 9781107079007 (hardback) | ISBN 9781107437296 (paperback)
Subjects: LCSH: Online dispute resolution. | Consumer protection–Law and legislation. | BISAC: LAW / General.
Classification: LCC K2400 .C674 2017 | DDC 343.08/1–dc23
LC record available at https://lccn.loc.gov/2017020804

ISBN 978-1-107-07900-7 Hardback

Para Myriam

CONTENTS

FOREWORD

This is an important and forward-thinking book which makes a significant contribution to scholarship on justice and redress for consumers by adopting an international and multidisciplinary approach. Consumer protection – whether achieved though law, regulation, standards or ethics- is crucial to the proper functioning of our society and to the economy. As this work identifies, there are perhaps two, inter-related aims: inspiring, embedding and enforcing good practice on the one hand and the provision of appropriate redress in cases of breach on the other. The ability of the wronged consumer to rely on and assert his or her rights and to obtain appropriate redress is an inherent feature of justice. Moreover, the ability to obtain redress plays an integral part in enforcing good practice. That said, justice does not always have to be dispensed in a courtroom.

Due to the many and varied consumer transactions that take place on a daily basis – from buying online goods to obtaining routine legal advice – the potential number of disputes that could result is great. Often, the disputes that arise are of low or modest value, such that it would be disproportionate to retain lawyers to litigate in the traditional manner. Proportionality aside, many consumers would, in any case, simply be unable to afford legal advice or representation.

Alternatives to traditional litigation which are able to provide meaningful redress are, therefore, of critical importance. This book ably reviews and analyses various alternative dispute resolution options (ADR) and, more importantly, the greater use of and move towards online dispute resolution (ODR). Whether industry- or platform-specific, ADR/ODR options can provide such meaningful redress. This work goes further, and considers international issues, harmonisation, and system design.

However, the rapid development of extra-judicial redress schemes does not mean that the courts will become redundant for such disputes, provided that the courts can provide a means of redress that is simple, proportionate, just and effective. In England and Wales, wide-ranging reforms to the manner in which justice is delivered are under way. In particular, and as this work discusses, the creation of an "Online Court" – which, on current planning, will share many features of the ODR systems considered – will ensure that consumers can continue to access justice through the courts, but in a simpler, speedier and more user-friendly way.

I look forward to a future edition of this work, which details the developments in the law of consumer redress, any changes in the relationship between judicial and extra-judicial dispute resolution, and the role the Online Court has played in England and Wales. Until then, I warmly commend this first edition to anyone who wishes to understand this important subject and the potential for its development.

The Rt Hon. The Lord Thomas of Cwmgiedd
Lord Chief Justice of England and Wales

1 June 2017

ACKNOWLEDGEMENTS

As a cautionary note, I must admit that my analysis on consumer redress may be a bit biased as it has been influenced by my involvement in the drafting process of the Alternative Dispute Resolution (ADR) Directive and Online Dispute Resolution (ODR) Regulation, as well as by my participation in a number of ODR working groups – including the United Nations Commission for International Trade Law (UNCITRAL Working Group III), the Civil Justice Council, the National Center for Technology and Dispute Resolution and the International Mediation Institute. I have also served as a consultant for the European Commission and the European Parliament, and I have participated in the board of advisors of Youstice and NetNeutrals. My views have therefore been enriched and influenced deeply by these interactions. As a result I firmly believe that consumer redress, especially effective ADR techniques underpinned by ODR technology, can, and should, play an important role in the civil justice system, delivering greater access to justice to consumers. In addition, if properly designed, consumer redress can assist in increasing consumer trust, promoting market competition.

I am grateful to all the interviewees who kindly took the time to share their views with me. Their insights help me to have a much better understanding of the evolving nature of dispute resolution and technology. The writing of this book was possible due to the generous support of a grant from Nuffield Foundation, which is an endowed charitable trust that aims to improve social well-being in the widest sense. It funds research and innovation in education and social policy and also works to build capacity in education, science and social science research. The Nuffield Foundation has funded this project, but the views expressed are those of the author and not necessarily those of the Foundation.

I would like to express my deepest gratitude to the Lord Chief Justice for finding the time out of his busy schedule to read the manuscript and write the Foreword. I would also like to thank the academic mentors that helped me over the years. Especially, I would like to extend my sincere gratitude to Professors Chris Hodges and Cosmo Graham. Their leadership and selfless support for younger colleagues are truly inspiring.

I would like to thank my wife Anne-Marie for her unwavering support and love, and to my children Tristan, Alice and Ruben for making sure I get up early every morning with a big hug.

I would like to dedicate this book to the foremost academic in the family, my sister Myriam, who is currently the *rectora* and president at Pontifical University of Salamanca. She was my first academic mentor and the springboard that enabled me to further my studies at University of Limerick. Without her assistance at this crucial time, I would not have pursued a career in academia and this book may never have been written.

INTERVIEWEES

1. Julia Hörnle, Queen Mary University of London
2. Amy Schmitz, Colorado University
3. Caroline Mitchell, Financial Ombudsman Service
4. Enrico Maria Cotugno, AGCOM Italy (CORECOM)
5. Darin Thompson, Attorney at Ministry of Attorney General BC
6. Graham Ross, Modria
7. Carlo Pilia, University of Cagliari
8. James Tallack, Civil Aviation Authority
9. Nick Mawhiney, Civil Aviation Authority
10. Roberta Regazzoni, ResolviOnline
11. Mark McLaren, Which?
12. Steven Gould, Ombudsman Association
13. David Pilling, Ombudsman Services
14. Valentina Filippini, Onfconsumatori
15. Fernando Esteban de la Rosa, Universidad de Granada
16. Colin Rule, Modria
17. Vikki Rodgers, Pace Law School
18. Giuseppe de Palo, ADR Center/UN ombudsman
19. Chris Gill, Queen Margaret University Edinburgh
20. Iñaki Paredes, European Consumer Center Spain
21. Roberto Liscia, Netcomm
22. Imma Barral, Universidad de Barcelona
23. Alberto Elisavetsky, ODR Latinoamerica
24. Stefaan Voet, Lueven University
25. Amada Arley, Universidad Nacional Autónoma de México
26. Zbynek Loebl, Youstice
27. Iveta Havlova, Youstice
28. Ethan Katsh, National Centre for Technology and Dispute Resolution
29. Leah Wing, National Centre for Technology and Dispute Resolution
30. Peter Causton, Pro Mediate

31. Juan Bueso, ECC-Ireland
32. Cosmo Graham, University of Leicester
33. Elisabetta Sciallis, ECC-UK
34. Christoph Decker, European Commission
35. Richard Kirkham, University of Sheffield
36. Jin Ho, HiiL
37. Maria Pisano, ECC-Italy
38. Margaret Doyle, UK Administrative Justice Institute
39. Vincent Tilman, bMediation
40. Christopher Hodges, CSLS Oxford University

Introduction

The Law of Consumer Redress

In recent years the digital world has established itself as a convenient market for people, consumers and businesses, who come together and practice the essential actions of a functioning economy: selling and buying goods and services. Consumer expenditure represents the majority of the Gross Domestic Product (GDP). In the European Union (EU) consumer expenditure accounts for 56 per cent of the total GDP,[1] while in the UK the consumer GDP is 60 per cent,[2] and in the USA is over 70 per cent[3] (though different techniques are employed to arrive at these figures).

A growing level of regulation in the field of consumer protection is taking place in the EU – a body of law which is commonly known as *Consumer Acquis*. The rationale behind consumer regulation is supported by the view that a degree of consumer protection is required for a market to function more effectively.[4] Although it is possible to argue that the EU has adopted a paternalistic or interventionist approach with the expansion of consumer protection rights, in practice, however, these rights are as significant as the consumers' ability to enforce them, which is particularly challenging in the cross-border context. Consequently, legal certainty and consumer trust in the market can only be achieved when there are mechanisms that ensure compliance with the consumer protection legislation, and thus their legitimate expectations

[1] Communication from the Commission to the European Parliament, the Council, the Economic and Social Committee and the Committee of the Regions, 'A European Consumer Agenda – Boosting Confidence and Growth' COM(2012) 225 final p. 1.

[2] Consumer Council of Northern Ireland, 'Back to Business: Are Businesses Getting Consumers' Rights Wrong?' (December 2013) p. 3.

[3] Federal Reserve Bank of St. Louis, 'Personal Consumption Expenditures (PCE)/Gross Domestic Product (GDP)' (2013). Available at https://fred.stlouisfed.org/graph/?g=hh3.

[4] M. Armstrong, 'Interactions between Competition and Consumer Policy' (2008) 4(1) *Competition Policy Int* 97–147.

can be met.[5] The existing formal and informal processes (and their regulations) that consumers use to achieve compensation and justice are what this book refers to as the *Law of Consumer Redress*. Hence, this book deliberately merges concepts of justice and redress when examining different consumer redress systems.

When consumers and traders have unresolved disputes, they are understandably reluctant to consider formal judicial proceedings as a forum for finding redress, especially so when the loss is relatively small, as litigation is costly, slow and stressful.[6] Additional reasons include the perceived complexity of a court process and unclear legal advice – as legal representatives can rarely assure consumers on the outcome of a judgment, who then face the risk of having to pay legal costs without the guarantee of obtaining redress.[7] As a result, many organizations, including the EU and national governments, have decided to invest in and promote out-of-court redress options. Extrajudicial redress is often the preferred option for most disputes as it can provide informal resolution in an independent, fast and effective manner. This is why many consumer disputes are increasingly been channelled directly through Alternative Dispute Resolution (ADR) schemes, which are replacing courts in many jurisdictions as the main redress providers in areas such as financial matters and utilities.[8]

Consumer ADR systems differ significantly from traditional out-of-court processes employed between commercial parties – i.e. namely commercial arbitration and mediation processes. For that reason, leading academics have even referred to Consumer ADR (CADR) to distinguish it from traditional ADR models, or Consumer Dispute Resolution (CDR) to emphasize that for the great majority of consumer disputes judicial redress is not an option.[9] Thus, consumer ADR is very different from

5 European Commission Staff Working Paper, Impact Assessment Accompanying the document of the Proposal for a Directive on Alternative Dispute Resolution for Consumer Disputes and the Proposal for a Regulation on Online Dispute Resolution for Consumer Disputes SEC(2011) 1408 final (hereinafter Impact Assessment) p. 5.

6 Ibid. See also S. Weatherill, *EU Consumer Law and Policy* ([AU: Add Place for publishers? PC: I have followed throughout the manuscript the new OSCOLA that does not add the place]: Edward Elgar, 2014) p. 283.

7 University of Lincoln, Lincoln Law School, 'Representative Actions and Restorative Justice' (2008). Available at www.bis.gov.uk/files/file51559.pdf. Hereinafter, last accessed 12 January 2017.

8 C. Hodges, 'Consumer Ombudsmen: Better Regulation and Dispute Resolution' (2015) 16 *ERA Forum* 14.

9 See C. Hodges, I. Benohr and N. Creutzfeldt-Banda, 'Consumer-to-Business Dispute Resolution: The Power of CADR' (2012) 13 *ERA Forum* 199.

traditional ADR processes employed for resolving civil and commercial disputes. While traditional ADR is seen as an alternative to the court system, where parties may compare what they might get in court to what is being offered in a settlement,[10] consumer ADR often presents itself as the only resort for the consumer to find redress in a cost-effective and proportionate manner. Another defining feature of consumer ADR models is that given that most consumers do not obtain legal advice prior to contacting the ADR scheme, many procedures (especially ombudsman schemes) provide consumers with some level of advice and with processes that operate a triage or diagnosis stage that filters cases based on eligibility criteria. Lastly, while commercial ADR schemes are privately run and decisions are largely confidential, many consumer ADR schemes are either run by public regulators or closely controlled by them.

This book examines what I describe as the emerging Law of Consumer Redress, which encompasses the regulation affecting processes that enable consumers to resolve disputes and obtain compensation from traders, including dispute resolution procedures, best practices and the certification of providers. In so doing, this book discusses the regulatory transformation that this field is experiencing in the EU and elsewhere in the context of an evolving digital market. Dispute system design analysis takes place in order to identify best practices that can inform the regulation and design of consumer redress policies and processes.[11] It must be acknowledged that the terminology in this field can be confusing as it adopts different meanings for those that use it. The meaning of consumer redress adopted by this book includes ADR or out-of-court processes when used for consumer disputes (i.e. what has been termed as CADR or CDR) as well as regulatory and judicial processes in so far as these schemes have been designed for consumer cases in mind. Although the Law of Consumer Redress may be used as an umbrella term to describe the policy and the regulation affecting public and private enforcement options as well as judicial and ADR redress, the main purpose of this book is to contribute to the analysis of the transformation of consumer ADR techniques, increasingly underpinned by Online Dispute

[10] M. Moffitt, 'Three Things to Be against ("Settlement Not Included")' (2009) 78 *Fordham Law Rev* 1203–1245, 1207.

[11] Dispute System Design has been established as a field of its own. See Robert C. Bordone, Introduction to Dispute Systems Design, Presentation at Harvard DSD Symposium (7 March 2008).

Resolution (ODR) technology as these schemes are expected to become the main redress option for the digital consumer.

Technology as the Vehicle for Resolving Consumer Disputes in the Digital Era

Currently, around half of EU consumers shop online.[12] Conflicts arising from a typical purchase online (e.g. a tablet or a photographic camera that never arrives or that is damaged) are almost never resolved in the courts because the cost of bringing such claims outweighs the value of the dispute, especially when parties are located in different jurisdictions. Hence, the use of traditional face-to-face dispute resolution methods for settling disputes arising in this forum are nearly always impractical, time-consuming and expensive, particularly for settling low-value cross-border disputes.[13] Despite this, the growth of online purchasing is still increasing, so is the number of disputes between online consumers and suppliers. The European Commission observed that the lack of available out-of-court redress mechanisms for resolving effectively low-value disputes triggers buyers' mistrust of sellers, which in turn constrains competition and limits the growth of the digital market.[14]

Consumer redress is not only a topic of theoretical significance, but it is also a topic of high practical relevance, especially for the digital consumer. According to Which?, a UK-based charity defending consumer rights, nearly half of UK consumers (46 per cent) who bought goods online over the past two years had a problem with their purchase.[15] The three most common problems are deliveries arriving

[12] N. Mimica, EU Commissioner for Consumer Policy, 'EU Consumer Summit 2014: Ensuring that Consumers Reap the Benefits of the Digital Economy' Press Release IP/14/353 (1 April 2014). In the EU the proportion of consumers engaging in e-commerce has grown significantly in recent years. According to Consumer Scoreboard, 20 per cent of consumers participated in e-commerce in 2004, but this figure rose to 45 per cent by 2012. See http://ec.europa.eu/consumers/consumer_research/editions/docs/9th_edition_scoreboard_en.pdf.

[13] P. Cortés, *Online Dispute Resolution for Consumers in the EU* (Routledge, 2011) and R. Susskind, *Tomorrow's Lawyers: An Introduction to Your Future* (Oxford University Press, 2013), chapter 10.

[14] Impact Assessment n. 5.

[15] Which?, 'Millions Experience Problems with Online Purchases' (7 March 2014). Available at www.which.co.uk/news/2014/03/millions-experience-problems-with-online-purchases-357861/.

late (19 per cent), goods arriving faulty or damaged (13 per cent) and goods not arriving at all (12 per cent).[16] It has been estimated that approximately 3 per cent of all online transactions end up in a dispute, which is an impressive number if we consider that there are billions of online transactions a year.[17]

A society that is increasingly interacting online[18] would prefer to take advantage of an online forum for resolving their grievances. Indeed, statistics in many sectors show that the preferred vehicle of communication is the Internet.[19] This is even more predominant in those countries, such as in the USA, UK and the Netherlands, where there is a high level of Internet penetration with over 90 per cent and where the majority of the population uses Internet services, such as online banking. In the UK this figure was already set in 2013 at 83 per cent of households, where 73 per cent of adults were accessing the Internet every day and around half used online banking.[20] But even in those countries where the Internet penetration is relatively low, such as in Greece with just over 40 per cent, the figure grows every year.[21] The growth rate is exponential with regards to online access via smartphones – while in 2015 the number of smartphones in the world was estimated to be over 2 billion, this figure is expected to double to 4 billion by 2020.[22]

Similarly, online retail is growing very fast, even when brick-and-mortar retail is going down in the wake of economic crises. According to the Centre for Retail Research in 2013, online retailing in Europe grew in one year by a weighted average of 21.1 per cent to £111.2 billion, which was around 12 times faster than conventional outlets.[23] The British Retail

[16] Ibid.

[17] C. Rule, 'How the Internet Is Changing the Way Disputes Are Resolved' *Wire Innovation Insights* (24 June 2014). Available at http://insights.wired.com/profiles/blogs/how-the-internet-is-changing-the-way-disputes-are-resolved#axzz39bcSIGVK.

[18] According to Pew Research, 85 per cent of Americans use the Internet. See K. Zickuhr 'Who's Not Online and Why' (25 September 2013) www.pewresearch.org/fact-tank/2013/11/08/whos-not-online-5-factors-tied-to-the-digital-divide/.

[19] For tax claims in the property sector see W. Sapp, 'Creating an Online Property Guide and Resolution Center', Fair & Equitable (April 2014) p. 3.

[20] UK Office for National Statistics, 'Statistical Bulletin: Internet Access – Households and Individuals, 2013' www.ons.gov.uk/ons/rel/rdit2/internet-access–households-and-individuals/2013/stb-ia-2013.html.

[21] Special Eurobarometer 381 'E-Communication Household Survey' (June 2012).

[22] 'The Truly Personal Computer' *The Economist* (28 February 2015).

[23] Centre for Retail Research, 'Online Retailing: Britain, Europe and the US 2014'. Available at www.retailresearch.org/onlineretailing.php.

Consortium found that around 20 per cent of all non-food spending is through online shopping, and this figure is expecting to increase.[24]

Digital consumers are interacting increasingly through online marketplaces that enable transactions between consumer and businesses, such as eBay or Amazon, as well as through what is known as the Shared Economy, services such as Airbnb and Uber, which essentially allow users to sell services to consumers. These new business models are affecting (and often threatening) traditional brick-and-mortar businesses, which are either transforming to the online sphere or disappearing. Traditional brick-and-mortar businesses, such as DVD rentals, sale of CDs, travel agencies and broadsheet newspapers, are gradually moving online.

At the same time, the Internet has empowered consumers with information about their rights that previously was only available to them via professionals.[25] Although the notion of empowering consumers is increasingly becoming central to the EU consumer policy strategy, not all consumers are the same, with some being more vulnerable than others. Vulnerable consumers are mostly those who are the oldest, the least educated and those who do not know or have access to computers.[26] The definition of a vulnerable consumer in the EU led to a definition of an average consumer,[27] which became the benchmark for the majority of individuals. The Court of Justice defined an average consumer as someone who is reasonably well informed and reasonably observant and circumspect.[28] An added challenge is that the concept of consumer varies from country to country. Whereas some jurisdictions, notably within the EU, are adopting a more expansive consumer concept for instance including legal persons, other countries, such as the USA, have adopted a more restrictive approach.[29]

[24] Online Retail Monitor, British Retail Consortium (2016). Available at www.brc.org.uk/bis/default.asp?main_id=7.

[25] J. MacFarlane, 'ADR and the Courts: Renewing our Commitment to Innovation' (2012) 95(3) *Marq Law Rev* 927, 930.

[26] This is a heterogeneous group 'comprised of persons who, on a permanent basis, are considered as such because of their mental, physical or psychological disability, age, credulity or gender'. See European Parliament Resolution of 22 May 2012 on a Strategy for Strengthening the Rights of Vulnerable Consumers (2011/2272(INI)).

[27] J. Davies, 'ADR/ODR: Too Much Optimism in the Promotion of Cross-Border Trade?' in B. Hess, M. Bergstrom and E. Storskrubb (eds.), *EU Civil Justice: Current Issues and Future Outlook* (Hart, 2016) p. 43.

[28] Green Swann C-299/12.

[29] US federal courts have often restricted the application of consumer state law under the use of free services. For instance, while Facebook users were not considered consumers

Consumer expectations about redress are also moving online. Currently, the vast majority of consumer redress mechanisms use some type of distance means of communication. These can be as basic as emails and telephone communications to deal with consumer queries and the various aspects of the complaint. Dispute resolution processes that allow for distance communications are frequently referred as Online Dispute Resolution (ODR). ODR, originally an off-shoot of Alternative Dispute Resolution (ADR), offers online access to extra-judicial conflict settlement methods, such as negotiation, mediation, arbitration, complaint boards and ombudsmen schemes. ODR takes advantage of the speed and convenience of the Internet and online case management tools, making it the best (and often the only) option for providing redress to consumer grievances, strengthening consumer trust in a more reliable e-commerce.[30] ODR technology changes the paradigm of traditional redress procedures as it can support or replace the role of the neutral third party – for example enabling direct party-to-party negotiations through software that encourage settlement. This role has been termed as the fourth party in the dispute resolution process given its key role as facilitator in managing and framing the information exchange.[31]

The design of consumer redress mechanisms has two interlinked goals. Firstly, it increases access to justice by providing consumers, even vulnerable ones, with an easier pathway, than, for instance, the courts in

under Californian law, they were considered consumers by the French court of Cassation because Facebook users were considered an important source of funding due to the advertising schemes operating in Facebook. *In Re Facebook Privacy Litigation* 791 F. Supp. 2d 705 (2011) (N.D. Cal. 5 May 2011). Available at http://leagle.com/decision/In%20FDCO%2020110516720.

791 F.Supp.2d 705 (2011); D. Martic, 'Redress for Free Internet Services Under the Scope of the EU and UNCITRAL's ODR Regulations' (2014) 10 *Revista Democracia Digital e Governo Electrônico*, 360–373; C. Hoofnagle and J. Whittington, 'Free: Accounting for the Costs of the Internet's Most Popular Price' (2014) 61 *UCLA Law Rev* 606–670; A. Cunningham, 'Caveat Consumer? Consumer Protection and Cloud Computing – Part I' Queen Mary School of Law Legal Studies Research Paper, n. 130, pp. 1–29, January 2013.

30 Cortés, n. 13. E. Katsh and J. Rifkin, *Online Dispute Resolution: Resolving Conflicts in Cyberspace* (Jossey-Bass, 2001); G. Kaufmann-Kohler and T. Schultz, *Online Dispute Resolution* (Kluwer Law International, 2004); J. Hörnle, *Cross-border Internet Dispute Resolution* (Cambridge University Press, 2009); M. Wahab, E. Katsh and D. Rainey, *Online Dispute Resolution: Theory and Practice* (Eleven International Publishing, 2012).

31 Katsh and Rifkin, ibid., pp. 93–116.

small claims procedures, to meet their legal needs.[32] Secondly, effective redress mechanisms enhance consumer trust and contribute towards building a more competitive market. The success of large online market places that provide effective ODR technology has been exemplified by the eBay dispute resolution paradigm, which acts as the neutral third (and fourth) party, and claims to resolve over 60 million disputes a year between its buyers and sellers.[33] This is a significant number, particularly if we take into account that English courts receive around 1.5 million civil claims every year. Effective ODR tools have the potential to impact on the willingness of consumers to raise complaints reflecting sub-standard transactions, leading to higher trading standards.

Yet, there are still too many unresolved consumer disputes for which a redress option is needed. The European Commission believes that in the EU the usage of ADR is well below its potential. In 2015 the European Commission reported that only around half of the retailers (54 per cent) knew about ADR schemes for consumers, either in their sector or in another sector – the breakdown of this percentage was as follows: 30 per cent of traders were willing or legally required to use it, 16 per cent said there was no ADR in their sectors and the remaining 8 per cent declared their unwillingness to use it.[34] Moreover, empirical data shows very low consumer ADR use.[35] The European Commission estimated that consumer disputes amount to financial losses estimated at 0.4 per cent of the EU's GDP and that a well-functioning and transparent ADR for these disputes could save around €22.5 billion a year, corresponding to 0.19 per cent of EU GDP.[36] Consequently, the EU passed legislation that aimed to promote consumer ADR: the Directive on consumer ADR and the

[32] H.W. Micklitz, 'The Future of Consumer Law – Plea for a Movable System' (2013) 2(1) *J Eur Consum Mark Law* 5–11 and C. Hodges, I. Benohr, N. Creutzfeldt-Banda, *Consumer ADR in Europe* (Civil Justice Systems) (Beck/Hart, 2012) pp. 367–453.

[33] N. Rogers, R. Bordone, F. Sander and C. McEwen, Designing Systems and Processes for Managing Disputes (Kluwer, 2013) pp. 24–25; S. Smith and J. Martinez, 'An Analytical Framework for Dispute System Design' (2009) 14(4) *Har Negot Law Rev* 1401–1446; L. Del Duca, C. Rule and Z. Loebl, 'Facilitating Expansion of Cross-Border E-Commerce-Developing a Global Online Dispute Resolution System' (2012) 1(1) *Penn St J Law Int Aff* 59.

[34] DG Justice and Consumers, European Commission, Consumer Conditions Scoreboard (2015) p. 47. See http://tinyurl.com/hrbltnl.

[35] DJS Report 'Understanding consumer experiences of complaints and redress' Citizens Advice (June 2016). Available at http://tinyurl.com/gljmkv6.

[36] Impact Statement, n. 5.

Regulation on consumer ODR, which have transformed the foundations of consumer redress in the EU.[37] The ADR Directive requires Member States to ensure the availability for consumers of quality ADR entities that observe procedural standards,[38] while the ODR Regulation establishes a pan-European website, called the ODR platform, which redirects consumer complaints arising from online contracts to nationally approved ADR entities. These two innovative regulatory initiatives have initiated a process institutionalizing and professionalizing consumer ADR, which is becoming the main pillar of the Law of Consumer Redress.

Contribution of This Book to the Academic Debate and Methods

This book examines the emerging legal framework for consumer redress in the digital era. In so doing it examines how this field is evolving while it tries to identify best practices and regulatory recommendations that help to achieve the policy aim of designing and promoting the use ADR and ODR methods that assist in invigorating e-commerce. Accordingly, the main theme that acts as a thread to this book is a shift in consumer redress, which is changing the priorities of policy makers; their focus is no longer on guaranteeing the protection of consumers by their national judicial processes and public enforcement bodies, but there is an emerging layer of ADR and ODR structures that provide a public service helping consumers to obtain accessible and tangible redress. This book seeks to identify best practices for redress schemes that offer consumers both effective individual redress and better compliance with consumer protection law, thus raising industry standards.

The book critically discusses the socio-legal developments in this field and argues, inter alia, that consumer redress is more effective when complemented with incentives that encourage parties to participate in these out-of-court processes, settle meritorious claims early and ensure extrajudicial enforcement of final outcomes. This book calls for a more

[37] Directive 2013/11/EU on Alternative Dispute Resolution for Consumer Disputes OJ L165/63 (hereinafter the ADR Directive) and Regulation 524/2013 on Online Dispute Resolution for Consumer Disputes OJ L165/1 (hereinafter the ODR Regulation). See also P. Cortés (ed.), *The New Regulatory Framework for Consumer Dispute Resolution* (Oxford University Press, 2016).

[38] Arts. 6–11 ADR Directive.

holistic approach to consumer redress that integrates through technology consumer ADR techniques and other redress options, including the courts, regulators and public enforcement bodies, moving upstream from dispute resolution to dispute prevention and providing consumers with greater protection.

While there are already some important socio-legal studies on best practices for consumer ADR schemes in Europe,[39] most of these studies have not examined the impact of the ADR Directive and the use of technology in the field of consumer ADR, which remains a fairly unarticulated subject.[40] Furthermore, there is not empirical work on how technology and economic incentives can be pivotal in ensuring the success of voluntary extrajudicial schemes.[41] Hence, this book hopes to fill this gap by contributing to our understanding on the impact that recent legal developments and best practices in ODR techniques could have in transforming traditional ADR redress schemes into more accessible and efficient online redress mechanisms.

This book summarizes some of the key findings of a research project funded by the Nuffield Foundation to identify how consumer redress schemes are being transformed. The research project focused on the regulatory and technological changes affecting consumer redress in the EU. It examined a range of reports, opinions and insights that can help to inform about best practices and strategic developments in the field of consumer ODR. The research has identified a number of challenges (such as consumer lack of awareness and the voluntary nature for traders) and opportunities (to improve consumer redress for non-complainants) facing these emerging redress systems. Consequently, it has called for policy makers, competent administrative authorities, regulators and individual redress bodies to develop their strategic aims in response. It is hoped that this book can provide a helpful reference point in that context.

[39] See, e.g., J. Stuyck, E. Terryn, V. Colaert, T. Van Dyck, N. Peretz, N. Hoekx and P. Tereszkiewicz, *Study on Alternative Means of Consumer Redress Other Than Redress Through the Ordinary Judicial Proceedings* (Catholic University of Lueven, 14 January 2007); and Hodges et al., n. 32.

[40] P. Cortés, n. 13 and M. Stürner, F. Gascón Inchausti and R. Caponi, *The Role of Consumer ADR in the Administration of Justice – New Trends in Access to Justice under EU Directive 2013/11* (Selp, 2015). In the Spanish language, see for example, F. Esteban de la Rosa, *La protección del consumidor en dos espacios de integración: Europa y América* (Tirant lo Blanch, 2015).

[41] See a first approximation of this topic at P. Cortés, 'A New Regulatory Framework for Extra-Judicial Consumer Redress: Where We Are and How to Move Forward' (2015) 35(1) *Legal Stud* 114–141.

This book evaluates the main consumer redress schemes in the EU with a particular focus on those operating in Italy, Spain and the UK. These schemes are currently adapting their processes to the European legislation and to a society progressively interacting in the digital sphere. The book notes that the consumer redress landscape is diverse and often incoherent; consequently, identifying issues that will be equally relevant to all types of schemes is not always possible as national traditions and narrow sectorial pressures heavily influence the need for a 'menu of process pluralism'[42] in consumer redress. Thus, recommendations are often made on an *ad hoc* basis rather than for the whole field of consumer redress.

This book seeks answers to the following research questions: first, how are traditional redress schemes adopting ODR technology into their processes (Chapters 1 and 3); second, what is the impact of the new regulation on consumer redress on ADR schemes (Chapters 4 – 6); and third, how redress processes, and in particular ADR schemes, are designed to, inter alia, increase access to redress while discouraging unmeritorious claims, facilitate voluntary compliance of final decisions and encourage traders to tackle causes of complaints as well as consequences (Chapters 7 and 8).

The field of consumer redress is multidisciplinary as it draws concepts inter alia from law, sociology, political science, economics and psychology. Accordingly, the main methods used throughout this book have been doctrinal, normative, comparative and socio-legal approaches. The doctrinal method, sometimes referred as the black-letter approach,[43] has been described by Richard Posner as 'not a field with a distinct methodology, but an amalgam of applied logic, rhetoric, economics and familiarity with a specialized vocabulary and a particular body of texts, practices, and institutions'.[44] This method is employed to examine legislation and policy rules. The analysis often adopts a normative approach critically examining how the legislation ought to be in order to provide an effective and holistic redress structure for consumers. The comparative method is employed when national rules and traditions are

[42] C. Menkel-Meadow, L. Love, A. Schneider and J. Sternlight, *Dispute Resolution: Beyond the Adversarial Model*, 2nd edn (Aspen, 2011).

[43] M. Doherty and P. Leighton, 'Research in Law: Who Funds It and What Is Funded? A Preliminary Investigation' (2004) 38(2) *Law Teach* 182.

[44] R. Posner, 'Conventionalism: The Key to Law as an Autonomous Discipline' (1988) 38 *Univ Tor Law J* 333, 345.

contrasted. Although this book has a distinctive EU approach, the analysis often draws comparisons with practices in the United States, and it compares the national approaches adopted in various EU jurisdictions (though the most in-depth analysis within the EU is limited to Italy, Spain and the UK).

Last, but not least, the socio-legal approach is employed to examine consumer redress models in their social context and in seeking to influence government policy in the provision of consumer redress. Thus, to inform and contrast the views expressed in this book, I have conducted qualitative research through interviews with stakeholders representing the academia, ADR schemes, ODR providers, consumers, businesses and policy makers, in order to extract best practices that inform consumer redress. Accordingly, a total of forty qualitative interviews were carried out to establish a detailed understanding of the transformation in this sector. Most of the qualitative fieldwork was conducted between February and December 2015.[45] The interviews lasted around one hour and were carried out on the phone and face to face to enable participants to express their views on these changes. This generated valuable insights into the challenges and opportunities facing consumer redress. However, the views expressed here are those of the author, and while these views have been informed by those interviewed, unless otherwise stated they do not necessarily express interviewees' own views.

Structure of This Book

This book examines best practices on consumer redress schemes, with a particular focus on ADR processes as the primary route of consumer redress and on the impact of technology in the dispute resolution process. The book is divided into eight chapters.

Chapter 1 contrasts the role of public enforcement bodies and pan-European Networks in seeking traders' compliance with consumer law, with the role of processes ADR schemes typically offering consumers with individual redress. This chapter calls for greater collaboration between public enforcement bodies and ADR schemes in order to ensure that more consumers (and not only complainants) have access to redress. It argues that effective data exchange will lead to more effective redress as

[45] See list of interviewees at the beginning of this book.

well as dispute prevention strategies and higher industry standards, thus meeting the goal of increasing consumer trust in the market.

Chapter 2 considers the state of play of technology in consumer dispute resolutions and the challenges that they face in their growth. It analyses how ADR has been adapted to meet the needs of consumer disputes, the concept of ODR and its main processes. It notes that the new online paradigm changes the dynamics of traditional face-to-face ADR procedures and it evaluates the main obstacles slowing down the expansion of ODR.

Chapter 3 discusses developments in the field of civil procedure to resolve consumer disputes. In so doing it examines the interplay and potential synergy that the European Small Claims Procedure (ESCP) and collective redress mechanisms have (or could have) with extrajudicial redress options. These two types of court procedures lend themselves to be complemented with technology and ADR. This chapter proposes new strategies to better integrate court processes with ADR/ODR techniques and explores specific pathways of collaboration. It calls for the provision of procedural pathways that promote settlements and for an online uniform process that facilitates the enforcement of judgments.

Chapter 4 analyses the core regulation of the Law of Consumer Redress, which is the new EU legal framework for consumer out-of-court redress: the ADR Directive and ODR Regulation. This chapter critically examines the two pioneered legislative European initiatives and proposes a number of functions in the design and revision of the European ODR platform, such as an online negotiation tool to encourage early settlements. However, this chapter notes that the present legal framework will not meet its policy-stated aims of improving redress and increasing cross-border e-commerce in so far it does not meet the objectives of closing the gaps in consumer ADR, ensuring quality of ADR processes and raising awareness about their availability. This chapter argues that these objectives will only be met if national governments ensure that traders inform and participate in ADR/ODR and if these entities are properly monitored to ensure that they comply with the quality requirements set in the regulatory framework.

Chapter 5 discusses consumer redress in three completely different jurisdictions: Italy, Spain and the UK. Accordingly, it examines the implementation of the ADR Directive and the impact it had on the main nationally approved ADR entities in these three jurisdictions. This chapter offers a picture of three radically different dispute resolution traditions that reflect three diverse redress cultures in the EU. Currently, the main redress models in Italy are mediation and 'representative negotiations or joint conciliations' (where representatives of consumers and businesses resolve disputes on their behalf), while Spain has a public arbitration system and the UK relies mainly on sectorial ombudsman schemes. This chapter recommends making business adherence mandatory in the regulated sectors, facilitating access through a national ODR platform and ensuring that national competent authorities provide adequate supervision, in particular to ensure that traders comply with the information obligations and that certified ADR entities remain independent and impartial.

Chapter 6 evaluates the Technical Notes developed by the UNCITRAL Working Group III (ODR) for e-commerce disputes which are characterized by being cross-border and of low value. The Notes envisage a three-stage online procedure that starts with automated negotiation between the parties without a human neutral, and is followed by conciliation and finally by either an arbitration process or a recommendation, which may be complemented by self-enforcement mechanisms. The main thrust behind the UNCITRAL initiative was to establish an internationally accepted and trusted, normative framework for ODR. This chapter argues that although this initiative was the most important international legal effort in the field of consumer redress, it fell short to establish a new legal framework due to incompatible views that the United States and the European Union had on pre-dispute arbitration. This chapter contrasts the discussions carried out in the UNCITRAL Working Group III with the EU initiatives in consumer ODR. It submits that the legally binding nature of arbitral awards will not guarantee their out-of-court enforcement, that the confidentiality of the awards may let market abuses go undetected. Hence, in order to ensure transparency this chapter calls for adequate monitoring by accreditation agencies and for the publication of binding awards.

Chapter 7 examines when and why traders participate in consumer redress. In some regulated sectors traders have a statutory obligation; in the remaining sectors they decide to opt in either voluntarily or as a part of belonging to a trade association. This chapter argues that the new information obligation set in the ADR Directive should be complemented with a residual mandatory ADR scheme (or a truly accessible online court or tribunal that incorporates ADR techniques) that encourages traders to opt in membership to a specialized ADR entity. The chapter also examines how ADR entities can ensure an adequate coverage in the provision of consumer redress by fleshing out the procedural grounds upon which ADR entities can refuse complaints. This chapter argues that even though the Directive assures the availability and awareness of quality ADR entities, it does not ensure that traders participate in these processes, which poses the risk of undermining consumer trust in the whole redress system. This risk will be augmented if traders, who can often choose and pay for these ADR entities, engage in forum shopping, especially if procedural restrictions contained in the Directive are not adequately monitored by the competent authorities.

Chapter 8 looks at the dispute system design used in consumer redress; in particular, this chapter discusses two essential elements for a successful consumer redress scheme: a high level of settlements and out-of-court compliance with final outcomes. It argues that the online forum offers the possibility to design multi-tiered procedures that promote early settlements and facilitate out-of-court compliance with outcomes. It submits that since consumer ADR models are providing a public service, they must incorporate appropriate governance structures that favour dispute avoidance strategies. This is indeed a feature of some statutory ADR schemes that collaborate with regulators (such as certain ombudsman schemes underpinned by sectorial legislation), which, in addition to offering dispute resolution services, provide consumers with advice and the industry and the regulator with intelligence data that help to prevent future disputes.

The book concludes summarizing the findings and arguing that if these dispute system design features are spread into other consumer redress processes, they will deliver greater benefits for the society at large, thus realizing the often-overstated policy aims of consumer ADR/ODR: that is, increasing access to justice and boosting market competition through efficient consumer protection policies.

1

Consumer Redress

From Public Enforcement to Alternative Dispute Resolution

1.1 Introduction

There are a number of ways in which consumers may obtain redress when facing a dispute with a business. Normally consumers first attempt to settle disputes directly with the business or trader in question. If this is not possible, then some consumers may stop dealing with the business and some may even voice their complaint in a social network or review site. Consumers may also bring their claims to the attention of a public enforcement body or a consumer organization if they need further information on how to purse a satisfactory resolution to their grievances. But, it will only be the most determined and best informed of consumers, who as a matter of principle or because the value or nature of the dispute is significant to them, will decide to pursue the matter further, through a public authority, an Alternative Dispute Resolution (ADR) scheme, or the court system.

In terms of consumers pursing individual redress in courts they typically rely on ordinary litigation (if they can afford it or have a legal protection insurance) or in a small claims procedure, if this is an available and user-friendly option. In some countries, notably in the USA, collective redress in the form of class actions may be offered when a high number of consumers have been affected by the same traders' breach of contract. Similarly, public enforcement and regulatory bodies may investigate a business that infringed the law and as a result damaged the rights of many individuals, but they rarely provide restorative justice to individual consumers. Moreover, given the high cost of litigation and the limited resources of enforcement bodies and consumers, judicial redress for consumer matters are only employed in exceptional circumstances, unless, as discussed in Chapter 3, consumer claimants can join a collective action or have access to a small claims procedure.

In practice, in many jurisdictions, the majority of disputes that are not settled directly with the trader are increasingly being resolved with the assistance of an independent consumer ADR scheme. The Introduction of this book has already noted that consumer ADR schemes are different from commercial ADR schemes. While commercial parties may compare what they might get in court to what is being offered in a settlement,[1] (what is commonly known as the best alternative to a negotiated agreement or BATNA),[2] consumer ADR often presents itself as the only pathway to find redress in a proportionate manner.[3]

This chapter is divided into four parts. First it discusses how public authorities monitor and cooperate within the EU to ensure traders' compliance with consumer law. Secondly, it examines the main rules and features of the most common consumer ADR processes – namely, mediation, arbitration, ombudsman systems and complaint boards. Thirdly, it discusses chargebacks and escrow system as an important consumer redress option. Lastly, it calls for more cooperation between public enforcement bodies and ADR schemes.

1.2 Public Enforcement and Consumer Cooperation Schemes

1.2.1 The Role of Public Enforcement Bodies

In the context of consumer law, regulators and enforcement authorities are public bodies entrusted with the correction of market abuses.[4] In doing so, they have the role of monitoring, investigating and enforcing consumer law as consumers themselves do not often have the resources to do so. Their rationale is to ensure regulatory compliance by protecting the general interest of consumers in asymmetric relationships with traders.[5] Their main purpose is thus to change business behaviour by

[1] M. Moffitt, 'Three Things to Be against ("Settlement Not Included")' (2009) 78 *Fordham Law Review* 1203–1245, 1207.

[2] W. Fisher and M. Ury, *Getting to Yes: Negotiating Agreement Without Giving In* (Penguin, 1981).

[3] C. Hodges, I. Benohr, N. Creutzfeldt-Banda, 'Consumer-to-Business Dispute Resolution: The Power of CADR' (2012) 13 *ERA Forum* 199.

[4] An earlier version of this section appeared in P. Cortés, 'Enforcing EU Consumer Policy More Effectively: A Three-Pronged Approach' in S. Drake and M. Smith (eds.), *Effective Enforcement of EU Law and Policy* (Edward Elgar, 2016).

[5] C. Hodges, 'The Consumer as Regulator' in D. Leczykiewicz and S. Weatherill (eds.), *The Images of the Consumer in EU Law* (Hart, 2015) pp. 245–246.

providing guidelines,[6] issuing administrative sanctions and, in the most egregious cases, requesting injunctions and bringing prosecution to chase rogue traders and scammers.[7]

Normally public enforcement bodies do not offer compensation to individual consumers, which is the main goal of private enforcement (including ADR), but sometimes they may provide collective redress by distributing the proceeds from a business infringement to groups of consumers affected. An interesting model has been recently developed by Ofgem, which is the energy regulator in the UK. If an energy provider is found in breach of the law for, say incorrect billing or misselling, regulators and the offending business can reach a settlement whereby a payment is made to eligible consumers who have been affected by the breach, or it is given to an energy trust or charity which assists vulnerable consumers, especially those who are more likely to have been affected by the breach.[8] Similarly, in Italy, the telecom regulator ('Autorità per le Garanzie nelle Comunicazioni (AGCOM)) has set up an automatic compensation scheme whereby in case of suspension of service for administrative reasons or when there is a delay in the activation of the line, the regulator monitors that telecoms pay compensation to all those affected.

It must be noted that the approaches to correct infringements to consumer laws vary from country to country. Whereas some jurisdictions put greater emphasis on public enforcement actions, others rely more on private enforcement. Thus, some jurisdictions, typically in the EU, rely more on the role of public enforcement authorities (e.g. Trading Standards Services and the Competition Market Authority in the UK), other countries, notably the USA, rely more on private class actions and ADR. This is notwithstanding that also the USA has enforcement bodies that monitor business compliance with consumer law (e.g. the Federal Trade Commission). Hodges notes that 'enforcement of EU

[6] See, for example, in the context of providing guidelines for online reviews, Competition and Markets Authority, UK Presidency of ICPEN Report: 1 July 2015–June 2016 (30 June 2016). Available at www.gov.uk/government/publications/cma-icpen-presidency-report-2015-to-2016/uk-presidency-of-icpen-report-1-july-2015-to-30-june-2016.

[7] Directive 2009/22/EC of 23 April 2009 on Injunctions for the Protection of Consumers' Interests [2009] OJ L110/30, Arts. 1–3.

[8] See Ofgem, 'Enforcement Guidelines' (2014). Available at www.ofgem.gov.uk/ofgempublications/89753/enforcementguidelines12september2014publishedversion.pdf. For an overview of this system see M. Canto-Lopez, 'Ofgem's Recent Trends in Enforcement: Settlements, Redress and the Consumer's Interest' (2016) 21(2) *Utilities Law Rev* 65–70.

consumer law is a mixture of enforcement by public authorities, self- or co-regulatory bodies, private enforcement through litigation and increasingly also through consumer ADR'.[9] However, he observes that the enforcement of competition law in the EU is wholly focused on public enforcement; this approach contrasts with that taken in the USA, where class actions are the main tool to correct breaches.[10]

Nonetheless, there are EU countries that rely more than others on private enforcement options. An effective and innovative example of private enforcement used in Germany is the *abmahnung* procedure. This legal figure empowers private individuals with the role of monitoring traders' compliance with certain consumer laws, such as unfair trade practices, and asks for financial compensation when there is a breach. Thus, for instance, if a trader fails to comply with their duty of information, a lawyer can send a letter or email to the offending trader. This letter must contain three documents: proof of breach (e.g. screenshots of the trader's terms and conditions), a contract that sets out the compensation to be paid if there are further breaches and an invoice with the lawyer's fee for sending the letter. This system is very successful in Germany and it is often used against breaches of traders established in Austria too. In a way, the German *abmahnung* resembles the 'cease and desist' letters employed in the UK and the USA, but it has the defining characteristic that such a letter is accompanied by an important incentive, the legal fee that the trader must pay in order to avoid legal action. Therefore, for this technique to work well it is essential to have an accessible and efficient judicial system.

However, typically, in the EU there are a number of legislative texts that commend the compliance and enforcement of the consumer protection provisions to public authorities. Examples of these legal provisions can be found in the Directive on unfair terms in consumer contracts,[11] the Directive on misleading advertising,[12] and the Directive on unfair commercial practices.[13] These are often areas where individual redress would not be suitable and where public enforcement bodies can deploy this task more effectively.[14] But, the effectiveness of public enforcement bodies varies significantly, as do their powers, which are

[9] C. Hodges, 'Collective Redress: A Breakthrough or a Damp Squib?' (2014) 37 *J Consum Policy* 67–89, 70.

[10] Ibid. [11] Directive 13/93/EC. [12] Directive 2006/114/EC.

[13] Directive 2005/29/EC.

[14] S. Weatherill, *EU Consumer Law and Policy* (Edward Elgar, 2014) pp. 299–301.

delimited by national law. As already noted, they are allowed to prosecute traders who have breached consumer laws, but they cannot order traders to compensate consumers.[15] Even when they have acquired the competence to do it, they may not have the resources to pursue all breaches.[16]

The normal modus operandi of public enforcement bodies is to resolve breaches in consumer regulations informally by first notifying traders of the breach and sometimes settling through compensations or fines when there is no criminal conduct. Indeed, this 'soft' enforcement power can be very effective in requesting businesses to cease activities that damage consumers' interests.[17] If businesses do not comply with the requests made by the public enforcement bodies, then they can bring an injunction as a last resort measure requiring a trader to stop engaging in a particular conduct.[18] Though, they do not often have the power to bring individual compensation to consumers who have suffered a loss as a consequence of the trader's breach.[19] Moreover, given their limited budgets these bodies have to prioritize some actions and industries over others.[20]

1.2.2 European Networks for the Compliance of EU Consumer Law

In the EU one of the main challenges to effective enforcement by national public authorities is the territorial limitation of their competence, which

[15] Although these restrictions have started being lifted in some jurisdictions – see, for example, in the UK the Consumer Rights Act 2015 including the ability of enforcers to seek additional remedies, including compensation to affected consumers, when taking an action under the Injunctions Directive. See also The European Consumer Organisation (BEUC), 'Improving Enforcement Cooperation – BEU Response to the Consultation on the Review of Consumer Protection Cooperation (CPC) Regulation' BEUC-X-2014-005 (3 February 2014) p. 2.

[16] This is especially so when national economies have to implement austerity measures, and while enforcement bodies acquire greater competences, these are not always matched with an increment in their budgets. This situation is also happening in the private sector where there is an increasing demand to offer more services with fewer resources, what Susskind refers as 'the more-for-less challenge'. R. Susskind, *Tomorrow's Lawyers* (OUP, 2012) pp. 4–5.

[17] See C. Hodges, 'Ethical Business Regulation: Understanding the Evidence' Better Regulation Delivery Office, Department for Business Innovation & Skills (February 2016).

[18] Art. 5 of the Directive 2009/22 on Injunctions for the Protection of Consumers' Interests OJ 2009 L110/30 and Regulatory Enforcement and Sanctions Act 2008 in the UK.

[19] University of Lincoln, Lincoln Law School, 'Representative Actions and Restorative Justice' (2008). Available at www.bis.gov.uk/files/file51559.pdf.

[20] I. Ramsay, *Consumer Law and Policy*, 3rd edn (Hart, 2012) p. 88.

does not correspond with the economic liberalization of the Single Market, let alone the Digital Market.[21] Consequently, there is a growing need to build and enhance existing enforcement structures that enable a more effective cooperation between national enforcement bodies and consumer associations; such cooperation can lead to a more effective tracking of market abuses that increasingly operate cross-border. In the context of EU consumer policy, there is a legal framework for promoting this collaboration, which establishes two pan-European networks: the Consumer Protection Cooperation Network (CPC Network) for national enforcement authorities and the European Consumer Centres Network (ECC-Net) for consumer organizations. These two networks are examined next.

Consumer Protection Cooperation (CPC) Network

The CPC Regulation[22] provides the legal framework for the establishment of a network encompassing all the national consumer authorities of the EU Member States and the European Economic Area (EEA) partner countries.[23] It also cooperates with a number of international organizations.[24] The CPC Network members cooperate in the investigation of breaches of EU law that affect consumers in two or more EU Member States.[25] The goal of the CPC is to safeguard consumers' collective interests across the EU. This is mainly achieved by sharing information and enforcing consumer protection law across borders,[26] which in effect requires the use of the administrative resources of one country of the Network to favour the interests of consumers residing in another country. The CPC Regulation sets out the provisions which enable the Commission to coordinate the enforcement activities of the

[21] Ibid., p. 4.

[22] Regulation (EC) 2006/2004 on Cooperation between National Authorities Responsible for the Enforcement of Consumer Protection Laws (CPC Regulation) [2006] OJ L 364. See also the Decision 2007/76/EC setting out the details on the cooperation [2007] OJ 2007 L32/192.

[23] The EEA partner countries are Iceland, Liechtenstein and Norway.

[24] Currently, the CPC cooperates closely with the following organizations: the International Consumer Protection and Enforcement Network (ICPEN), the Organisation for Economic Cooperation and Development (OECD) and the US Federal Trade Commission (FTC).

[25] European Commission, 'Report on the Functioning of Regulation (EC) 2006/2004 on Cooperation Between National Authorities Responsible for the Enforcement of Consumer Protection Laws (CPC Regulation) COM(2014)' 439 final p 1.

[26] CPC Regulation, Art. 8.

competent national authorities, especially when tackling a particular sector on an EU-wide basis.

One of the ways that the CPC Network operates is through sweeps of websites,[27] whereby the national public authorities that form the network assess whether the websites investigated comply with the EU law in areas such as app purchases, online games and car rentals.[28] For instance, a sweep in 2013 found that 382 out of 552 websites checked did not respect consumer law.[29] The sweep led to enforcement action by first requesting traders to cease unfair commercial practices that breached EU law. This enforcement action in turn led 62 per cent of these websites to bring voluntarily their business practices in line with the consumer law.[30] This type of soft enforcement action, which has been replicated with app purchases,[31] is effective because it leads to a high level of voluntary compliance. It also helps to inform the European Commission on how to develop guidelines to further facilitate voluntary compliance by traders.[32]

There are however some important limitations in the operation of the CPC Network.[33] The European Commission noted that the main hurdle is the coordination framework established in the Regulation, which is too vague on the obligations that enforcement bodies have to cooperate with their counterparts in other Member States;[34] the current alert system, which notifies all the Network members, is inefficient because only the national enforcement bodies can use it, whilst the Commission and consumer organizations are currently not allowed to use it.[35] Furthermore, the competent national authorities forming the CPC Network have very different forms of autonomy. Whilst some are fully independent and autonomous, others are under the supervision of judicial or governmental authorities, requiring them to request permission before taking certain actions. This can obstruct cooperation amongst these national

[27] Sweeps of websites is the random selection of websites to check their level of compliance with the applicable law. More than 3,000 websites operating in the EU have been screened to check their compliance with EU law. European Commission Report, n. 25 and CPC Regulation, Art. 9.

[28] European Commission Report, n. 25, p. 4 and CPC Regulation, Art. 9.

[29] The lack of compliance was due to various problems, such as lack of mandatory information on the trader's indemnity, lack of information on how to complain and the lack of opt-out options for price supplements. See European Commission, 'Co-ordinated Enforcement Action Leads to Greater Compliance with Consumer Rights on Travel Websites' IP/14/436 (14 April 2014).

[30] Ibid. [31] European Commission Report, n. 25, p. 2.

[32] See, e.g., http://tinyurl.com/o8893au. [33] Ibid. [34] Ibid., 8. [35] Ibid., 9.

enforcement bodies.[36] Lastly, the Commission has argued that there is a need for a well-functioning pan-European IT platform to share enforcement expertise and infringements of consumer protection laws.[37] An effective platform will lead to better and quicker enforcement by enhancing the coordination action of public enforcers to target infringers of consumer laws.

Some of these hurdles have been recently addressed in a welcome legislative proposal which intends to amend the CPC Regulation with the view of developing more efficient cooperation.[38] The proposal would give new powers to national authorities, which could check if websites geo-block consumers from other Member States, or if they do not comply with EU consumer protection rules. They would be also able to order the taking down of websites that have scams, and they could request information to domain name registrars and banks to identify infringing traders. Importantly, where the legal breach occurs on an EU-wide basis, the European Commission would have the power to coordinate common action with the national enforcement authorities to stop the breach. The Commission has also published an updated guide for unfair commercial practices which seeks to respond to the changes brought by the digitalization of consumer transactions.[39]

European Consumer Centres Network (ECC-Net)

The ECC-Net was created in 2005 as a result of a merger between the network for the extrajudicial settlement of consumer disputes (EEJ-Net),[40] which advised on ADR schemes, and the European Consumer Information Centres (the Network of Euroguichets), which informed consumers about their legal rights. The main objective of this Network is to support the cooperation of Member States concerning information, advice and appeals in consumer protection matters.

Alongside the ECC-Net is FIN-Net, which carries out the same role in the financial sector. The ECC-Net also cooperates with other European networks, namely SOLVIT (internal market) and the European Judicial Network on civil and commercial matters. The ECC-Net is co-financed

[36] Ibid., 10. [37] Ibid., 13.

[38] Proposal for a Regulation on Cooperation between National Authorities Responsible for the Enforcement of Consumer Protection Laws COM(2016) 283.

[39] See also Guidance on the application of the Unfair Commercial Practices Directive SWD (2016) 136.

[40] The EEJ Network was created following a Council Resolution of 25 May 2000.

through grants by the EU (Department for Justice) and by each of the participating States, which are the 28 EU countries, as well as in Norway and Iceland. Each participating country has a point of contact and at least one office.[41] The aim of ECC-Net is to provide consumers entering into cross-border transactions with information about their rights and obligations, and it also helps them to resolve disputes as a result of these transactions without having to bring legal proceedings.

Each national ECC responds and advises consumers on their queries about cross-border transactions. Questions are often submitted via their website or by email. In the event of a complaint, the ECC will help and support consumers in their contacts with the trader – hence, in effect the ECC-Net operates as a first-tier ADR. The process starts by a consumer passing a complaint to its national ECC contact point, which, unless they think the complaint is manifestly unfunded, will liaise with their partner contact point at the other Member State, who in turn will contact the trader with the objective of reaching an amicable solution. If parties through their national ECC contact points cannot reach a settlement, then the consumer may be advised to take legal action or consider ADR options if these are available.

According to the 2015 annual report the ECC-Net dealt with more than 93,000 consumer contacts for information, which led to over 37,000 complaints across the EU,[42] which is a relatively modest figure suggesting that the majority of EU consumers are not aware of their existence. Nonetheless, the ECC-Net carries out a relevant role in the enforcement of consumer policy. This includes assisting consumers to resolve complaints, informing consumers about their rights and producing annual reports and ad hoc studies which inform regulators and public bodies on what regulatory changes may be necessary to facilitate compliance and improve enforcement options.

Overall, enforcement bodies and pan European networks play a role in improving consumer redress by informing businesses and consumers about their rights, passing feedback to regulators, chasing rogue traders and in some cases helping to provide individual redress. However, the cooperation between national enforcement bodies and ADR is largely underdeveloped as only a few referrals occur in practice.

[41] The list of national contacts is available online at http://ec.europa.eu/consumers/ecc/contact_en.htm.

[42] The European Consumer Centres Network, '10 Years Serving Europe's Consumers Anniversary Report 2005–2015'. Available at http://tinyurl.com/zuxz4ch.

1.3 The Regulation of the Main Consumer ADR Processes

The most common ADR processes that consumers use to settle complaints with businesses are mediation, arbitration, complaint boards and, increasingly more, ombudsman processes. The following section examines the main features and their regulatory frameworks.

1.3.1 *Mediation*

Mediation is a process where a neutral third party, the mediator, assists the consumer and the trader to reach an amicable settlement. The role of the mediator is to help parties to communicate by pointing out their common objectives and encouraging them to agree a settlement. The mediator has little or no authoritative decision-making power. Unlike a judge or an arbitrator, a mediator will try to focus parties' minds in how to move forward reconciling their competing interests by finding a mutually satisfactory resolution.

The mediation process can be facilitative, where the mediator simply helps parties to communicate in a constructive manner, or evaluative (sometimes referred as conciliation), where the mediator takes a more hands-on approach providing parties with his or her assessment of the dispute and suggesting proposals for settlement. In the consumer context, as well as in other asymmetric relationships such as in employment disputes, the evaluative approach is more common. The mediation process is characterized for being informal (i.e. where there is no need for legal representation) and confidential. It requires empathy and compromise from both parties. Settlements normally take the form of a binding contract, where parties have complete autonomy to decide the terms of their settlement.

Mediation can be used in multi-tier processes as a prior step to adjudication. In the UK, as well as in many other jurisdictions, there are ombudsman schemes, which use mediation and conciliation techniques as a core part of their dispute resolution processes. Indeed, disputes are resolved in this mediation stage in the majority of cases. The mediation process is usually very informal and it is frequently carried out through caucus discussions over the phone. Mediation can be used as part of the med-arb technique. Indeed, this is the main consumer redress procedure used in Portugal and Spain.[43] Also mediation techniques for consumer

[43] See Chapter 5. See also C. Marques Cebola, 'The Implementation of the Consumer ADR Directive in Portugal: The Necessary Reform or Missed Opportunity?' and F. Esteban de

disputes are employed in court-annexed processes, such as the Small Claims Mediation offered by English county courts,[44] which offers one-hour telephone mediation and resolves around 10,000 disputes a year.[45]

In the EU some procedural elements of mediation are regulated by the Mediation Directive.[46] The implementation of this Directive varies greatly from country to country. While some countries, such as the UK, has taken a *de minimis* approach, implementing the Directive only for cross-border complaints,[47] other EU Member States have implemented the Directive through a national law that regulates both domestic and cross-border mediation. The Directive contains five substantive rules:

i. It encourages voluntary Codes of Conduct for mediators and training.[48] A requisite to be a certified mediator is that applicants adhere to a code of conduct, which at least must comply with the EU Code of Conduct for Mediators.[49]
ii. It empowers judges with the right to invite the parties to a dispute to attempt mediation.
iii. It provides that agreements resulting from mediation can be rendered enforceable if both parties so request. This can be achieved, for example, by way of approval by a court or certification by a public notary.[50]
iv. It ensures that mediation takes place in an atmosphere of confidentiality.[51] It provides for the 'without prejudice' nature of

la Rosa, 'Challenges for the Implementation of the Consumer ADR Directive in Spain' in P. Cortés (ed.), *The New Regulatory Framework for Consumer Dispute Resolution* (OUP, 2016).

44 S. Prince, 'Mediating Small Claims: Are We on the Right Track?' (2007) 26(2) *Civil Justice Q* 328–340.

45 Lord Justice Briggs, Interim Report, Civil Courts Structure Review (December 2015).

46 Directive 2008/52/EC. In the UK it was implemented by the Cross-Border Mediation (EU Directive) Regulations 2011/1133 and provisions in the Civil Procedure Rules encouraging mediation. See for instance the Pre-Action Protocols and CPR r. 14(2)(e).

47 In fact there is no Act regulating mediation in the UK, nor is there State control for the training and appointment of mediators. Instead, the legal framework of mediation has been developed through piecemeal judicial decisions in individual cases and sector-specific regulation encouraging the use of ADR.

48 Art. 4.

49 The EU Code of Conduct for Mediators 2014 can be found at http://ec.europa.eu/civiljustice/adr/adr_ec_code_conduct_en.htm. See, for example, the requirements set in England and Wales by the Civil Mediation Council, available at www.civilmediation.org.

50 Art. 6. In Italy it can be done by the lawyers of the parties. See C. Pilia, P. Cortés and P. Vargiu, 'The Implementation of the Consumer ADR Directive in Italy' in P. Cortés, *The New Regulatory Framework for Consumer Dispute Resolution* (OUP, 2016).

51 Art. 7(2).

mediation, preventing Member States from compelling any information arising out of, or in connection with, a mediation process to be used as evidence in court or in arbitration, except where this is necessary for overriding considerations of public policy of the Member State concerned or where this evidence is needed for enforcing the agreement.[52]

v. It guarantees that the parties will not miss their possibility to go to court as a result of the time spent in mediation. In other words, time limits for bringing an action before the court are suspended during the mediation.[53]

At the international level the United Nations Commission on International Trade Law (UNCITRAL) has developed an international framework for conciliation and mediation processes, which is the Conciliation Rules and the Model Law on International Commercial Conciliation.[54] Yet, unlike in the field of arbitration, it has not produced a convention that would assure a uniform approach to enforcement of the settlement agreements. In 2014, UNCITRAL Working Group II started working on an instrument to address enforcement of conciliated settlement agreements.[55] The proposed instrument aims to put conciliated and mediated settlement agreements on the same footing as arbitral awards to provide the users with greater legal certainty. Although presently the discussions exclude consumer mediation, it would inevitably inform the legal approach that can be taken in the consumer field.

1.3.2 Arbitration

Arbitration can be defined as an adjudicative procedure whereby the parties agree on a neutral third party (called the arbitrator) to resolve their disputes. Some of the most common features of arbitration are the following: the process is confidential, the arbitrators have expertise on consumer issues, the awards are legally enforceable, there are restrictions on appeals, awards do not form binding precedents and the process is often more informal, faster and cost-efficient than a court process.

52 Art. 7(1).

53 When the limitation period has expired during the mediation process, Art. 8 the Regulations in England has extended the limitation period by eight weeks after the end of mediation.

54 Conciliation Rules 1980 and Model Law on International Commercial Conciliation 2002.

55 See www.uncitral.org/uncitral/en/commission/working_groups/2Arbitration.html.

Most statutes on arbitration are based on the Model Arbitration Law adopted in 1985 by UNCITRAL. They also implement the New York Convention 1958 on the Recognition and Enforcement of Foreign Arbitral Awards, which makes enforcement quasi-automatic by the courts; indeed, arbitral awards are more easily enforced than judgments from foreign jurisdictions. Enforcement will only be prevented in cases where there has been an important procedural breach (i.e. one affecting rt. 6 of the European Convention of Human Rights) or under grounds of public policy.

The defining feature of the arbitration process is the principle of party autonomy, whereby parties agree on the terms of the process. This principle is however undermined in consumer contracts, as consumers do not have bargaining power to negotiate the contract – in fact, consumers rarely read them. As a result, there are significant differences in the way the law regulates consumer arbitration depending on the jurisdiction, particularly in terms of enforcing pre-dispute arbitration clauses. It must be remembered that an arbitration clause establishes the forum for resolving a contractual dispute as well as the procedure that will be employed. The validity of these clauses varies significantly depending on the jurisdiction. A notable difference in the legal approach is found between the USA and the EU.

In the USA, the majority of consumer contracts contain arbitration clauses, regulation of which falls within the same legal framework of commercial arbitration – i.e. the Federal Arbitration Act (FAA) 1925.[56] Although most States have enacted laws restricting arbitration agreements, these laws have been pre-empted by section 2 of the FAA, which provides the validity of arbitration clauses. In *AT&T Mobility* v. *Concepcion*, the Supreme Court stated that 'the principal purpose' of the FAA is to 'ensur[e] that private arbitration agreements are enforced according to their terms'.[57] These clauses will be valid, even if they are contained in a void or illegal contract that on its face violates state law;

[56] Federal Arbitration Act (FAA) 1970, 9 United States Code ss. 201–208, 301–307 (implementing the New York Convention under ss. 201–208 and the Panama Convention under ss. 301–307); C. Drahozal, 'New Experiences of International Arbitration in the United States' (2006) 54 *Am J Comp L* 233; J. Bucilla II, 'The Online Crossroads of Website Terms of Service Agreements and Consumer Protection: An Empirical Study of Arbitration Clauses in the Terms of Service Agreements for the Top 100 Websites Viewed in the United States' (2014) 15 *Wake Forest Law Rev* 102, 133–149. Exceptionally an arbitration clause may be considered as 'substantially unconscionable'. See *Bragg* v. *Linden Research* 487 F Supp ed 593 (E D Pa 2007).

[57] 131 S. Ct. 1740.

that was what happened in the case of *Buckey Check Cashing* v. *Cardegna*, where a pay-day loan contract was void under Florida law.[58] Moreover, it is important to note that in the USA, the majority of consumer arbitrations are initiated by traders and proceed on a default basis.[59]

Unlike in the USA, the doctrine of competence/competence[60] in the EU is subject to European law, chiefly the Unfair Terms Directive, which restricts the validity of pre-dispute arbitration clauses in consumer contracts and in the case law developed by the Court of Justice of the European Union.[61] Whether an arbitration clause (or other standard contract term in a consumer contract) is unfair depends on whether the clause would cause a significant imbalance in the parties' rights and obligations to the detriment of the consumer and contrary to good faith,[62] and this depends on the precise circumstances of the case to be determined by the national courts.[63]

In terms of the case law, there are two key cases: *Claro*[64] and *Asturcom.*[65] These cases in effect transfer the competence/competence rule from the arbitral tribunal to the courts, which have the power to decide over the legality of the arbitral proceedings.[66] Furthermore, the court held that, if a pre-dispute arbitration clause is held to be unfair by the national court, the award has to be annulled, even if the consumer has failed to raise the unfair nature of the term during the arbitration proceedings.[67]

[58] In this case the Supreme Court stated three propositions that had been accepted in previous precedents: 'First, as a matter of substantive federal arbitration law, an arbitration provision is severable from the remainder of the contract. Second, unless the challenge is to the arbitration clause itself, the issue of the contract's validity is considered by the arbitrator in the first instance. Third, this arbitration law applies in state as well as federal courts.' See 546 U.S. 440.

[59] S. McGill, 'Consumer Arbitration after *Seidel* v. *TELUS*' (2011) 51 *Can Bus Law J* 187, 209.

[60] According to this doctrine it is the arbitral tribunal who has the power to determine the validity and the extent of the arbitration clause, including its own jurisdiction over the matter at dispute.

[61] See Unfair Terms Directive 13/93, CJEU, 26 October 2006, Case 168/05 E.M.M. *Claro* v. *Centro Movil Milenium* [2006] ECR I-10421 and CJEU, 6 October 2009, Case 40/08 *Asturcom Telecomunicaciones* v. *Christina Rodrígues Noguera* [2009] ECR I-9579.

[62] Art. 3 (1) of Directive 93/13/EC. [63] C-168/05 *Claro* para. 22 [64] Ibid.

[65] C-40/08 *Asturcom.*

[66] N. Reich, 'A "Trojan Horse" in Access to Justice – Party Autonomy and Consumer Arbitration in Conflict in the ADR-Directive 2013/11/EU' (2014) 10(2) *ERCL* 258–280, 270.

[67] C-40/08 *Asturcom* para. 39.

Moreover, in the EU, the ADR Directive allows the Member States to refuse the certification of ADR entities that provide arbitration services – e.g. Germany has made this restriction. In those Member States where certification may be awarded to arbitration providers, the ADR Directive requires the consumer to be informed about the binding nature of the process and to accept this specifically.[68] According to Reich, it would require being in a durable medium, and it would not be sufficient to include through a hyperlink, in the general terms of the contract or in a click-wrap clause.[69] However, it must be noted that when the trader commences the arbitration process, then the ADR Directive is not applicable.[70]

National law can also restrict the use of arbitration. According to the UK Arbitration Act, an arbitration agreement concluded with a consumer (whether pre- or post-dispute)[71] is considered to be unfair, and hence unenforceable,[72] where a modest amount of money is sought, which has been set at £5,000.[73] Furthermore, the Act states that the consumer provisions apply to natural and legal persons, such as a business, that obtains goods and services for purposes outside its trade or profession.[74] Thus, under UK law, if the amount in dispute is no more than £5,000, an arbitration clause is automatically not binding on consumers, so there is no need to apply any of the tests set out in the Unfair Terms Directive.[75] If the amount in dispute exceeds £5,000, the significant imbalance test applies on a case-by-case basis to assess whether the arbitration clause is binding on the consumer.

The Annex to the Directive lists as an example of unfair term a clause which purpose is 'excluding or hindering the consumer's right to take legal action . . . particularly by requiring the consumer to take disputes exclusively

[68] Art. 10(2). The ADR Directive 2013/11/EC is discussed in further detail in Chapter 4.

[69] Reich, n. 66, p. 273. [70] Art. 2(2)(g).

[71] Arbitration Act 1996, s. 89(1): For this purpose 'arbitration agreement' means an agreement to submit to arbitration present or future disputes or differences (whether or not contractual).

[72] Such an arbitration clause would not be binding on the consumer, but could be used by the consumer against a business supplier (clause is unilaterally void): Unfair Terms in Consumer Contract Regulations 1999 (SI 1999/2083), reg. 8(1).

[73] Unfair Arbitration Agreements (Specified Amounts) Order 1999 (SI 1999/2167). J. Hornle and P. Cortés, Draft Report for the ODR Advisory Group, Working Paper on Legal Issues in Online Dispute Resolution (July 2014) p. 5.

[74] S.90 of the Arbitration Act 1996. See also *Heifer International* v. *Christiansen* [2007] EWHC 3015 (TCC) paras 226, 250.

[75] Directive 93/13/EC, implemented in the UK by the Unfair Terms in Consumer Contracts Regulations 1999 (SI 1999/2083).

to arbitration not covered by legal provisions'.[76] The meaning of this provision has been interpreted by the courts as private arbitration, which is different from public or statutory forms of arbitration, such as the small claims procedure or an ombudsman procedure.[77] The English courts have found an arbitration clause for a high-value dispute valid when the consumer has previously obtained legal advice.[78] Yet, the implementation of this unfair term varies from country to country. For instance in Ireland, the Arbitration Act 2010 states that a consumer arbitration agreement will be unfair, and hence invalid, if each party is required to bear its own costs.[79]

1.3.3 Ombudsman

An ombudsman is a neutral third party which investigates consumers' complaints against a trader. This ADR model first appeared in the Scandinavian countries before they spread across Europe and the USA. Originally their remit was limited to oversee public bodies, so typically it was an independent office that dealt with individual complaints against public institutions. Currently they operate in a number of sectors where they have technical expertise. The name and role of the ombudsman is protected in some jurisdictions which require the approval of competent authorities to safeguard public trust in high standards for this ADR model.[80] Creutzfeldt observes the heterogeneous composition of ombudsman schemes noting that:

> There is a multitude of ombudsmen bodies across Europe and, although they share the same title, they have varying powers, mandates and decision-making authorities. Generally speaking, private sector ombudsmen can issue binding decisions on member businesses, whereas public sector ombudsmen make recommendations but cannot issue binding decisions.[81]

[76] Annex I [q].

[77] Landgericht Krefeld Case 6 O 186/95. Judgment of 29. April 1996 [1997] ILPr 716; *Picardi* v. *Cuniberti* [2002] EWHC 2923 (QB) para. 102; *Heifer* paras. 231–232 and *Mylcrist Builders Ltd* v. *Mrs G Buck* [2008] EWHC 2172 (TCC) para. 54.

[78] *Allen Wilson* v. *Buckingham* [2005] EWHC 1165 (TCC) para. 43; *Westminster Building Company* v. *Beckingham* [2004] BLR 508 (QB) para. 45.

[79] See European Communities (Unfair Terms in Consumer Contracts) Regulations 1995 and 2000.

[80] For England and Wales see s. 56 of the Companies Act 2006, sch. 1 pt. 1 of the Company, Limited Liability Partnership and Business Names (Sensitive Words and Expressions) Regulations 2014 and annex A of the Companies House guidance.

[81] N. Creutzfeldt, 'Ombudsman Schemes – Energy Sector in Germany, France and the UK' in P. Cortés, *The New Regulatory Framework For Consumer Dispute Resolution* (OUP, 2016).

The organization of an ombudsman generally comprises three types of staff. The first line of contact is the enquiry staff, who deal with enquiries mostly over the phone and via email. They do provide some advice, helping consumers to articulate their complaint, and supply them with information. If the complaint is eligible then they encourage the consumers to escalate it. The second type of staff is the case-handlers or adjudicators, who receive the complaints, talk to the parties and request the necessary information to make a decision. Using their experience and authority they will always try to help parties to settle the case at the earliest possible stage. They will act as conciliators or evaluative mediators, encouraging parties to settle and informing them about the merits of their claims. Although adjudicators settle the majority of the complaints, there are a small percentage of cases, generally the most novel or complicated ones, which escalate to the last tier, the ombudsmen. This third tier of the ombudsmen review the cases dealt by the adjudicators. Normally ombudsmen and adjudicators will make preliminary decisions giving the parties the opportunity to respond to and challenge the arguments before a final decision is made.

The ombudsman model works particularly well where there is a significant imbalance of power between the parties in terms of information and resources. The asymmetry situation between the parties lends itself to inquisitorial and conciliatory models where the case handler or investigator assists the complainant in pursuing and settling a meritorious claim – he or she investigates and judges the dispute. The enabling role of the ombudsman means that consumers are not required to find a legal basis to support their complaint; indeed, consumers are even assisted in the formulation of their complaint.

Ombudsman schemes are informal, and therefore they do not treat evidence in the same way as a court. Similarly, the informality of the procedure means that an ombudsman cannot take evidence under oath, compel witnesses or cross-examine an individual. If they receive complaints that are better heard by a court (e.g. when there are allegations of fraud), then it is expected that they refer the cases to the competent authority. There is no formal appeal of an ombudsman, but if it is a statutory scheme run public body, their decisions may be challenged by a judicial review process,[82] which in practice happens only rarely.

[82] In the financial year of 2012/2013, courts received 31,029 requests for judicial review of decisions of the Financial Ombudsman Service – this number is relatively small if we compare with the number of complaints received by FOS was over half of a million. See

Ombudsman schemes are expected to feedback information to businesses, and if they operate in regulated sectors, they also feedback to the regulator. Hence, ombudsman schemes are not simple dispute resolution bodies, they also perform an important function in advising consumers and sharing learning with businesses and regulators.[83] This is done by identifying patterns of disputes and formulating guidelines that seek to improve the standards of the industry where they operate and avoid future disputes.

The largest ombudsman scheme in the world is the Financial Ombudsman Service (FOS), which was created in the UK by statute in 2000 as the mandatory ADR entity for the financial sector.[84] It has jurisdiction to deal with consumer complaints against financial institutions based in the UK. FOS receives a high volume of complaints (around half of a million a year) and resolves these at a distance through either telephone or written communications. Adjudicators have expertise and training in the sector where they work (mortgages, etc.). Adjudicators also have access to a database with previous cases, which are now published online. Adjudicators (sometimes referred as 'case handlers') attempt first to resolve the complaints informally by discussing the dispute with the parties separately. Adjudicators will then write to the parties with their view on what is fair and reasonable for the case at hand. This often prompts the parties to settle the case based on the recommendation, but either party can disagree and request the case to be escalated to a senior adjudicator ('ombudsman') for a final decision – typically only around 6 or 7 per cent of complaints go to an ombudsman. The outcome is not legally binding on the consumer, but if the consumer accepts the recommendation, then it becomes binding for the business.

1.3.4 *Complaints Boards*

The term 'complaints boards' normally refer to ADR schemes that are established by either legislation or a trade association with the purpose of resolving consumer disputes by a board that is composed by a collegial

C. Mitchell, 'The Ombudsman as a Form of Dispute Resolution for Consumers' Workshop on Consumer Arbitration, Brunel Law School (3 September 2014).

[83] C. Hodges, 'Consumer Ombudsmen: Better Regulation and Dispute Resolution' (2015) *ERA Forum* 3. See also R. Kirkham, 'Regulating ADR: Lessons from the UK' in P. Cortés (ed.), *The New Regulatory Framework for Consumer Dispute Resolution* (OUP, 2016).

[84] See www.financial-ombudsman.org.uk/.

body with equal representation from trade and consumers associations. These boards are popular in Nordic countries, such as in Denmark, Sweden, Finland, Norway and Iceland.[85] The Netherlands also operates a well-functioning complaints board. These often incorporate sectorial expertise so they are able to provide resolutions in an expeditious manner taking into account the sectorial law and industry guidelines. Complaints boards, like ombudsman schemes, require consumers to elevate first the complaint directly to the trader.

The outcomes of the boards may be recommendations, such as the case in the Swedish model, or binding, as it is the case in the Netherlands. An advantage of the Swedish ADR model is that it can process complaints against traders who have not opted into the ADR system. Although the recommendation is not binding, it is followed in 80 per cent of the cases. This is partly because the ADR is independent and respected, and partly because it publishes the names of those businesses that do not comply online and in a consumer magazine twice a year.[86] Simple issues in which the trader has not responded to the consumers are frequently settled by the secretariat, who simply contacts the trader after receiving a complaint. The Dutch ADR system has over 50 complaints boards and issues contractually binding decisions, but it only covers complaints against traders who are opted into the complaint board, which is normally a requirement for members of a trade association or by a requirement of the sectorial legislation.[87]

In addition, as it is further examined in Chapter 5, there are other ADR processes, such as the Spanish arbitration boards and the Italian joint conciliations, which procedural features would fit in the classification of complaints boards. The Spanish arbitration boards are set up by national legislation and they have a collegial composition for claims

[85] Nordic Council of Ministers 'A Study on Alternative Dispute Resolution and Cross-border Complaints in Europe' (TemaNord, 2002) p. 27.

[86] See The National Board for Consumer Disputes called the Allmänna reklamationsnämnden (ARN) available at http://arn.se/other-languages/english-what-is-arn/. In addition, other sectors have their own separate board, such as The Board for Legal Protection Insurance Issues, www.forsakringsnamnder.se/Footer-meny/English, and the Swedish Funeral Association Complaints Board available at www.begravningar.se/english. The list of non-complying traders with the recommendation from the complaint board is also available online at www.radron.se/svarta-listan.

[87] See De Geschillencommissie at www.degeschillencommissie.nl. See also E. Verhage, 'The Implementation of the Consumer ADR Directive in the Netherlands' in P. Cortés (ed.), *The New Regulatory Framework for Consumer Dispute Resolution* (OUP, 2016).

over €300.[88] One member is appointed by a trade association, a second member is chosen by a consumer association and the third member is the chair, which is a civil servant in charge of setting up the arbitration panel. Although the Spanish arbitration board has a very broad scope, in practice the majority of complaints fall within the categories of universal services, for which it is feasible to benefit from the sectorial expertise of the panellists. Similarly, in Italy, the use of joint conciliations shares some of the features of complaint boards. These joint conciliations (known as *conciliazione paritetica*) are composed of one representative from a consumer association and one representative from a business association. These schemes are established by ad hoc agreements through Memoranda of Understanding between consumer associations and large traders or trade associations. The ADR process consists of representatives carrying out a negotiation over the complaint without the participation of the consumer and agreeing on proposals of settlements which are later passed on to the consumers, who can accept or reject such proposals, though in the vast majority of the cases these proposals are accepted by the consumers.

1.4 Chargebacks and Escrow Services

Chargebacks are a remedy commonly used by consumers to reverse transactions made with credit cards when a fraudulent use has occurred, or when there is a certain violation of the contract terms, such as when goods have not been delivered, or when they are defective. They intend to balance the inequality of power between consumers and businesses. In this sense they are regarded as a very efficient tool for consumers because of the speed, accessibility and lack of charge for consumers, who just have to notify their banks, card issuers or online payment providers to cancel a transaction.

Although chargebacks are not an ADR scheme service per se, they do provide redress to consumers who used credit cards (and sometimes debit cards, such as in Denmark) to pay for goods or services. Chargebacks offer one single remedy (the return of the payment), even though not all disputes relate to a breach of contract or fraud. It must be highlighted that a chargeback does not affect the validity of the contract; it simply reverses the payment back to the consumer.

[88] Real Decreto 231/2008.

When consumers issue a chargeback, they are not required to give evidence for their request to cancel the payment, but before a consumer applies for a chargeback, it must first complain to the trader. The onus is on the business, who has the burden of proving that the merchandise or service was given according to the contract terms. Once this is proved, the bank makes effective the payment to the trader.

There is not a global chargeback system[89]; instead, chargebacks are subject to national and regional laws. In the UK consumers have rights to claim damages from the credit card issuer when the purchase value is within the range of £100–£30,000.[90] This would include when a UK consumer deals with a foreign business, which eliminates the need for the consumer to initiate a legal action in a foreign jurisdiction. Chargebacks are also an important remedy in the USA,[91] but they have two important restrictions: they do not offer remedies for pre-authorized payments and there is a 60-day limit to contest a billing statement under $50.[92]

In the EU, the chargeback system is regulated by the Directive on Payment Services and the Directive on Credit Agreements for Consumers.[93] These two Directives recognize three instances under which the consumer can request a chargeback: (i) when the card payment has not been authorized by the consumer, (ii) when the trader has not respected the consumer's right – e.g. the cooling off period and (iii) in the case of bankruptcy.[94] There are also a number of restrictions. In the first scenario, when a payment has not been authorized, the consumer will have to carry out the loses to a maximum of €150 when the credit card has been lost or stolen, or when someone has got access to it and its security features – i.e. when the cardholder was negligent in leaving the

[89] V. Rogers, 'Managing Disputes in the Online Global Marketplace: Reviewing the Progress of UNCITRAL's Working Group III on ODR' (2013) 19 *Disp Resol Mag* 21.

[90] Consumer Credit Act 1974 s. 75(3). The upper limit is increased under section 75(a) introduced in 2010 in cases where the consumer has explored other avenues for redress and remained unsuccessful.

[91] Chargebacks in the USA are regulated in the Truth in Lending Act and Regulation Z. See generally N. Peretz, 'The Single Euro Payment Area: A New Opportunity for Consumer Alternative Dispute Resolution in the European Union' (2008) 16 *Michigan State J Int L* 573.

[92] See 12 Code of Federal Regulations s 226.13(b)(1–3).

[93] Directive 2007/64/EC on Payment Services in the Internal Market and Directive 2008/48/EC on Credit Agreements for Consumers.

[94] See ECC-Net 'Chargeback in the EU/EEA' (2014) p. 6.

card together with the PIN number.[95] Although it varies depending on the national law, a common time limit to bring a chargeback is 90 days counting from the moment the time of the transaction.[96] When the trader has gone bankrupt, or is unable to pay, most national laws allow consumers to exercise the chargeback against the credit card issuer.

Purchases with debit cards are not covered by the EU law, but they can be covered by national law or by the card companies' operating rules. Thus one important limitation of chargebacks is that, saved for some exceptions, they only apply to credit card payments. Another criticism is that there is a lack of transparency since in most countries credit card providers do not publish the procedures or the number of cases.

If a European consumer has not succeeded when seeking the refund of the payment through a chargeback process, the consumer can still pursue the claim through an ADR scheme. The aforementioned Directives require all Member States to ensure the availability of ADR schemes,[97] but while some Member States, such as Italy, make it mandatory for banks and financial intermediaries to opt into these schemes and follow decisions, other Members States, such as in Spain, have made compliance with ADR decisions voluntary for the banks.[98]

Similar to chargebacks, escrows systems and online payments such as PayPal can reverse payments when challenged by consumers. An escrow is an online payment option which for a small fee maintains accounts for online buyers that want to make deposits via electronic money transfers. The money is transferred to the seller once the buyer receives and approves the purchased item, after an agreed inspection period.[99] If the parties disagree over the facts, the escrow service decides who keeps the transaction money by acting as an adjudicator. In a way escrows operate as an insurance mechanism as the buyer has to pay a fee for its use.[100] Accordingly, some consumers are reluctant to use escrow services, partly because

[95] Art. 61 of the Payment Service Directive 2007/64/EC. In order for this restriction to kick in, the payment service provider must prove that the cardholder acted fraudulently or with gross negligence (Art. 59(2)).

[96] ECC-Net, n. 94, p. 12.

[97] Art. 24 Directive 2008/48/EC on Credit Agreements for Consumers and Art. 83 Directive 2007/64/EC on Payment Services.

[98] See Italian Law on Banking (Testo Unico Bancario Article 128-bis (introduced by Law 262/2005 on savings) and Spanish Law 44/2002 of 22 November on Reforming the Financial System Arts. 29–30.

[99] www.escrow.com.

[100] C. Riefa, *Consumer Protection and Online Auction Platforms* (Ashgate, 2015) p. 249.

they cost money and complicate the otherwise quick buying process.[101] Escrow services are popular in Asia and it is often used for the payment of online auctions to help avoiding the problem of fraudulent sales.[102]

Bitcoin uses an escrow system as it holds the payment until both parties are satisfied with a transaction. In the event of a dispute, Bitcoin decides who keeps the payment.[103] The system works through the use of encrypted payments requiring multi-signatures (one held by the buyer, one by the seller and one by the trusted agent). The money can only be released when two keys are used, so if the buyer and seller are not in agreement, the escrow adjudicates for a fee who keeps the money and gives the key to that party.[104]

1.5 The Need for Greater Cooperation between Enforcement Bodies and ADR Schemes

Both public enforcement bodies and ADR schemes seek to provide better compliance with consumer rights, but while the enforcement bodies' main role is to ensure regulatory compliance and collective redress, ADR schemes' main function – the same as chargeback and escrows – is to provide individual redress. This chapter has discussed the ongoing efforts from pan-European networks to improve the collaboration amongst national enforcement bodies (i.e. the CPC Network) as well as through the establishment of an ad hoc ADR Network for cross-border matters (i.e. the ECC-Net). In the same vein, the ADR Directive encourages ADR entities to participate in cross-border ADR networks, especially those that operate in specific economic sectors, such as FIN-Net for ADR entities dealing with financial disputes. ADR entities are also required to exchange best practices and collaborate with other ADR entities vis-à-vis cross-border and domestic disputes.[105] This role is

[101] P. Ortolani, 'Self-Enforcing Online Dispute Resolution: Lessons from Bitcoin' (2015) *Oxf J Legal Stud* (advance publication) pp. 1–35.

[102] C. Rule, *Online Dispute Resolution for Businesses* (Jossey-Bass, 2002) p.102.

[103] Bitrated holds a public reputation system that uses trusted agents who decide who keeps a Bitcoin payment made in a disputed transaction. See www.bitrated.com/.

[104] See G. Prisco, 'Bitrated Unveils Reputation System and Multisig Escrow' (24 February 2015) https://bitcoinmagazine.com/articles/bitrated-unveils-reputation-system-multisig-escrow-1424750534. See also R. Koulu, 'Blockchains and Online Dispute Resolution: Smart Contracts as an Alternative to Enforcement' (2016) 13(1) *Scripted* 41–69, and Ortolani, n. 101.

[105] Art. 16 of the ADR Directive.

expected to be taken by sectorial networks, such as the European Network for Energy (NEON),[106] and by ADR organizations such as the Ombudsman Association in the UK and Ireland.[107]

However, there is very limited evidence of collaboration between public enforcement bodies and ADR bodies. This situation is now starting to change as a result of the ADR Directive, which requires competent authorities (which are often interconnected with public enforcement bodies) to certify ADR schemes that comply with the requirements set in national law that transposes the ADR Directive.[108] Furthermore, ADR entities are now required to cooperate with enforcement bodies by providing them with feedback on recurring problems in the sector where they operate.[109] For instance, if an ADR discovers that a trader has overcharged many consumers, they cannot ask him to compensate those who have not claimed, but what they can do is inform the regulatory authority to investigate that trader.

ADR entities can now also request information to enforcement bodies when they consider that such additional information is necessary to resolve individual disputes.[110] This type of collaboration could include a request for information made by an ADR entity to the regulator or an enforcement body on the interpretation of a particular legal provision, especially if such interpretation may affect a large number of complaints. It is submitted that these expert options from enforcement bodies and regulators should be made publicly available as they could assist in bringing greater consistency in the decision making of ADR entities. Naturally these publications will need to comply with the national rules on professional secrecy and other duties of confidentiality that Member States may have established for enforcement bodies and ADR entities.

Another potential area where there is the possibility of greater collaboration between enforcement bodies and ADR entities is providing assistance in ensuring that traders comply with the outcomes of ADR entities within a reasonable period of time. ADR entities could refer decisions that have not been complied with by the trader within a reasonable period of time (e.g. after one month) to the public enforcement bodies, who should enquire of traders on the reason for the delay.[111]

[106] See www.neon-ombudsman.org/.
[107] See www.ombudsmanassociation.org/.
[108] See Chapters 4 and 5 of this book.
[109] Art. 17(1) of the ADR Directive.
[110] Art. 17(2) of the ADR Directive.
[111] This and other related issues are explored further in Chapter 8.

In addition, a key function of enforcement bodies is to ensure that traders comply with the information requirements, which as further discussed in Chapter 4, include the obligations that traders have to inform about (but not necessarily to participate in) certified ADR entities, obligations that have been extended to the CPC Network.[112] This role in monitoring compliance with information requirements could also be shared with private enforcement mechanisms, as was already mentioned with the example of the German *abmahnung*.

Yet, as noted earlier, in most cases consumers do not have the resources to go to court and public enforcement bodies do not provide individual redress. Indeed, in the EU the tendency is to separate the roles of enforcement from that of individual redress. What is however missing is a greater effort from many enforcement bodies to ensure that traders operating in their sectors provide consumers an avenue of independent redress through ADR entities, and from these private ADR entities to feedback regulators. Indeed, there is a mismatch between the reported levels of knowledge of ADR schemes by traders (52.7 per cent in the EU) and the percentage of traders who have used an ADR mechanism (6.7 per cent)[113] – though this figure seems to be growing (and sometimes even displacing the role of public enforcement bodies).[114] And this is despite the fact that the majority of traders (82 per cent) who have used an ADR scheme said that they would be willing to use it again.[115] Yet, by and large traders' adherence to ADR is voluntary, which is an important obstacle for consumers seeking to obtain redress.

In order to overcome this lack of redress, it is proposed that regulators, in addition to their enforcement role, provide a residual ADR scheme with competence to process complaints against those traders that are not members of a certified ADR entity. An interesting example to follow, which is further discussed in Chapter 7, has been developed by the Civil

[112] Recital 57 and Art. 21 of the ADR Directive 2013/11/EC. See also Annex to the Proposal on Cooperation between National Authorities Responsible for the Enforcement of Consumer Protection Laws.

[113] European Commission, 'The Consumer Conditions Scoreboard – Consumers at Home in the Single Market' (9th edn) July 2013, p. 50.

[114] Previous surveys consistently showed that as little as 3 per cent of consumers with unresolved disputes with traders go to ADR schemes that offered mediation, conciliation or arbitration services. European Commission, 'Consumer Attitudes towards Cross-Border Trade and Consumer Protection. An Analytical Report' Flash Eurobarometer 299 (March 2011) p. 45.

[115] European Business Test Panel Survey – Alternative Dispute Resolution p. 2. Available at http://ec.europa.eu/yourvoice/ebtp/consultations/2010/adr/report_en.pdf.

Aviation Authority (CAA) in the UK. The CAA has a residual ADR system (Passenger Advice and Complaints Team (PACT)) which issues non-binding recommendations on consumer complaints made against airlines which have not joined a certified ADR entity. Although the complaint system run by the CAA is free of cost for consumers, it has recently started charging £150 to airlines for each processed complaint. Conversely, certified ADR entities issue decisions that are contractually binding on the airlines and they are allowed to charge a nominal fee to consumers (of up to £25) – but this fee must be refunded to consumers in the event of upholding a claim, even if the outcome is an apology to the consumer. It is thus not a great surprise that two-thirds of airlines have joined an ADR entity only a few months after this policy was put in place.[116]

1.6 Conclusion

The chapter has examined how public enforcement authorities monitor and cooperate within the EU to ensure compliance with the consumer protection legislation. It has noted that while public enforcement bodies seek legal compliance and deterrence through sanctions, individual redress for a legal breach is typically left to private enforcement initiatives, including ADR. Moreover, the role of public enforcers remains very important not only for chasing rouge traders but also when using their soft powers of notifying non-compliant traders. This chapter has discussed the need for greater cross-border cooperation within the CPC Network and how the ECC-Net operates de facto as a first-tier ADR scheme for consumers with cross-border disputes.

The processes and the regulation applicable to the main consumer ADR models (namely arbitration, mediation, ombudsman and complaint boards) and chargebacks were also examined. In so doing, this section analysed the applicable regulation of the different ADR models and observed that evaluative mediation or conciliation is increasingly used as a prior step in adjudicative schemes, including in arbitration and ombudsman schemes. It also noted the different models of the complaints boards and their common features, such as their collegial

[116] Civil Aviation Authority, 'Alternative Dispute Resolution' (September 2016). Available at www.caa.co.uk/Passengers/Resolving-travel-problems/How-the-CAA-can-help/Alternative-dispute-resolution.

composition, sectorial expertise and the requirement for consumers to attempt first to resolve their dispute directly with the trader.

Finally, this chapter noted that there is a growing need to increase the collaboration between public enforcement bodies and ADR schemes. This collaboration should be routed in exchanging information on market problems and ensuring that consumers have access to individual redress either through an independent certified ADR entity or through a residual ADR scheme operated by the regulator. The collaboration between public enforcement bodies and ADR entities is now more easily achieved through the framework of the ADR Directive and the increased use of technology, which helps to capture and analyse high volume of cases. Also courts and tribunals could play an important role in closing the gaps in consumer redress. To these issues turns the analysis in the next two chapters.

2

Upgrading from Alternative to Online Dispute Resolution

2.1 Introduction

Technology is gradually being embedded in the everyday life of a society increasingly interacting using electronic means, and it is now catching up with consumer redress schemes, which, when they are accessible online, are often collectively referred to as Online Dispute Resolution (ODR).[1] The Alternative Dispute Resolution (ADR) Directive requires that consumers in the EU must be able to communicate with the trader and the

[1] R. Bordone, 'Electronic Online Dispute Resolution: A System Approach - Potential, Problems, and a Proposal' (1998) 3 *Harv Negot Law Rev* 175; E. Katsh and J. Rifkin, *Online Dispute Resolution: Resolving Conflicts in Cyberspace* (Jossey-Bass, 2001); C. Rule, *Online Dispute Resolution for Businesses* (Jossey-Bass, 2002); G. Kaufmann-Kohler and T. Schultz, *Online Dispute Resolution* (Kluwer Law International, 2004) p. 7; L. Ponte and T. Cavenagh, *Cyberjustice, Online Dispute Resolution for E-Commerce* (Parson Prentice Hall, 2005); G.-P. Calliess, 'Online Dispute Resolution: Consumer Redress in a Global Market Place' (2006) 7(8) *German L J* 647; M. Conley Tyler and J Bornstein 'Accreditation of On-line Dispute Resolution Practitioners' (2006) 23(3) *Conflict Resol* Q 383; O Rabinovich-Einy, 'Technology's Impact: The Quest for a New Paradigm for Accountability in Mediation' (2006) 11 *Harv Negot Law Rev* 253; D. Larson, 'Technology Mediated Dispute Resolution (TMDR): A New Paradigm for ADR' (2006) 21(3) *Ohio St J Disp Resol* 629; R. Morek, 'The Regulatory Framework for Online Dispute Resolution: A Critical View' (2006) 38 *Univ Tol Law Rev* 163; J. Hörnle, *Cross-border Internet Dispute Resolution* (CUP, 2009) p. 75; P. Cortés, *Online Dispute Resolution for Consumers in the European Union* (Routledge, 2010) pp. 52–54; A. Lodder and J. Zeleznikow, *Enhanced Dispute Resolution through the Use of Information Technology* (CUP, 2010) pp. 75–85; C. Hodges, I. Benohr, N. Creutzfeldt-Banda, *Consumer ADR in Europe* (Civil Justice Systems) (Beck/ Hart, 2012) pp. 367–453; L. Del Duca, Rule and Z. Loebl, 'Facilitating Expansion of Cross-Border E-Commerce-Developing a Global Online Dispute Resolution System' (Lessons Derived from Existing ODR Systems - Work of the United Nations Commission on International Trade Law) (2012) 1(1) *Penn St J Law Int Aff* 59; M. Wahab, E. Katsh and D. Rainey, *Online Dispute Resolution: Theory and Practice* (Eleven International Publishing, 2012); A. E. Vilalta Nicuesa, *Mediación y Arbitraje Electrónicos* (Aranzadi, 2013); P. Cortés and F. Esteban de la Rosa, 'Building A Global Redress System For Low-Value Cross-Border Disputes' (2013) 62(2) *Int Comp Law Q* 407.

ADR entity through electronic means.[2] In other words, it requires ADR entities to employ ODR techniques. This is because the use of distance means of communication is the only feasible manner for settling low-value (and often medium-value) consumer disputes, let alone if these are cross-border disputes.[3] It is for that reason that the ODR Regulation has set up an ODR platform, which is in essence a website that operates as a central hub where consumers can identify a nationally certified ADR entity where to submit their complaints online. ADR entities process complaints when the trader has agreed to it or is legally required to do so. The EU ODR platform is examined in Chapter 4.

ODR is generally understood as ADR processes conducted at a distance through the use of Internet communications technology that enables parties to send and store the information online. In practice however there is an increasingly blurred distinction between ODR and ADR schemes, as the latter are gradually incorporating technology into their processes. ODR technology can be used for resolving e-commerce disputes as well as those that arise from brick-and-mortar transactions. The software can help to analyse legal problems, assist in the negotiation and in the decision making and sometimes even make decisions (or proposals for settlements) without the assistance of a neutral third party. The level of technology varies depending on the ODR provider.

This chapter first looks at the definition of ODR and the impact that technology has in the dispute resolution process. It then examines the main types of ODR processes and it offers examples of the main providers. Finally, this chapter evaluates the main obstacles behind the expansion of ODR.

2.2 The Concept of Online Dispute Resolution

The concept of ODR has been discussed by many scholars and has been included in legal and policy documents that adopted a meaning tailored to the aims and objectives of such instruments.[4] In general terms ODR is referred to as the use of technology to carry out the dispute resolution process. Although it can include court processes, these may be also referred to as e-Justice, while ODR is often referred to as the synergy

[2] Art. 5(2)(d) Directive 2013/11/EU on Alternative Dispute Resolution for Consumer Disputes OJ L165/63.

[3] R. Susskind, *Tomorrow's Lawyers: An Introduction to Your Future* (Oxford University Press, 2013), chapter 10.

[4] See n. 1.

between ADR and Information and Communications Technology (ICT). Ethan Katsh has defined ODR as a process for resolving disputes that employs electronic communications, information processing technology or both.[5] Colin Rule, also a leader in the ODR field, argues that ODR can be taken to mean any use of technology to complement, support or administer a dispute resolution process.[6] However, perhaps, the most common operation of ODR is through a web-based platform which allows parties to upload information about their dispute and to communicate between themselves and the neutral third party.

Fowlie distinguishes between two main types of ODR models.[7] In the first model he includes technology-based schemes where technology plays an instrumental part in the ODR process by for example automatically generating proposals for settlement or reaching decisions.[8] An example of this type of technology is the eBay Resolution Center, which is discussed later. In the second model he puts technology-assisted schemes, which support traditional ADR processes, for instance allowing for online submission of claims and using a case management tool to store information and facilitate the interactions between the parties. This basic technology is often common in consumer redress, and it simply supports distance means of communications. An example of this category would be the ODR system for domain names, which is also discussed later. But first this section notes the references to ODR made by a number of international, regional and national bodies as part of their legal texts or as a means to justify them.

2.2.1 Definitions of ODR in Legal and Policy Documents

UNCITRAL Working Group III, which as discussed in Chapter 6 developed Technical Notes on ODR for resolving low-value e-commerce disputes, defines ODR as an 'online dispute resolution which is a mechanism for resolving disputes facilitated through the use of electronic communications

[5] Katsh and Rifkin, n. 1. [6] Rule, n. 1.

[7] F. Fowlie, 'Online Dispute Resolution and Ombudsmanship' in M. Wahab, E. Katsh and D. Rainey (eds.), *Online Dispute Resolution: Theory and Practice* (Eleven International Publishing, 2012) pp. 313–314.

[8] See for instance Ross Intelligence at www.rossintelligence.com; See also C. Schoenberger, 'Computers' Reasoning Skills to Equal Humans by 2029' (26 June 2012). Available at http://tinyurl.com/zza2btj and J. Suquet, P. Casanovas, X. Binefa, O. Martínez, A. Rui and J. Ceballos, 'CONSUMEDIA. Functionalities, Emotion Detection and Automation of Services in an ODR Platform' (in file with author).

and other information and communication technology'.[9] In Canada, the Civil Dispute Resolution Tribunal Act defines ODR thus:

> online dispute resolution services means dispute resolution services that are provided by way of electronic communication tools and are intended to assist parties in resolving a dispute by agreement without direct assistance from a tribunal officer or person engaged or retained by the tribunal to provide facilitated dispute resolution services.[10]

The EU does not define ODR in its legislation. The ODR Regulation simply notes the convenience of using ODR techniques in consumer ADR schemes, stating that 'ODR offers a simple, efficient, fast and low-cost out-of-court solution to disputes arising from online transactions'.[11] The Regulation also sets out the functions of the EU ODR platform.[12]

In the UK, the Civil Justice Council (England and Wales) Report by the Advisory Group on ODR discussed its definition in the context of a proposal for an online court that integrates ADR techniques, in the following terms:[13]

> Our conception of ODR is broader than that of many specialists in online dispute resolution. When we speak of ODR we are referring to the use of IT and the Internet to help resolve disputes (other than the computerization of the current court system). Our exclusion in brackets means we do not consider, for example, that conducting court hearings across video links or online tracking of the progress of trials to be ODR.

Hence, there is no universally accepted definition of ODR. Indeed, since the field is evolving very quickly there is a high risk that any rigid definition would quickly become outdated. ODR is therefore often defined for what it can offer and how it functions in specific contexts.

2.2.2 The Impact of Technology in the Redress Process: The Fourth Party

Ethan Katsh, as noted in the Introduction of this book, called the role of technology in the dispute resolution process the fourth party,[14] which is something more than mere software. In addition to the two parties in

[9] Art. 2 (1).
[10] Art. 1 Canadian (British Columbia) Civil Dispute Resolution Tribunal Act 44–2012.
[11] Whereas 8 ODR Regulation (EU) 527/2013.
[12] See Art. 5(4). See further analysis in Chapter 4.
[13] Civil Justice Council Advisory Group, 'Online Dispute Resolution for Low Value Civil Claims' (February 2015) paras. 1.5–1.7.
[14] Katsh and Rifkin, n. 1, pp. 93–116.

dispute and the neutral third party (e.g. the mediator or the arbitrator), the technology in well-designed ODR platforms can play a very important role in resolving consumer complaints. It shapes the way parties interact in a similar way as a neutral third party does. For instance, it can perform a diagnosis or triage function, identifying whether a particular claim is worth pursuing; it can help parties to frame their claims and focus their minds on finding a common remedy; it can inform parties about their legal rights and how similar disputes have been resolved in the past. Sometimes the fourth party substitutes the neutral third party in an online negotiation while other times the fourth party simply replaces some of the administrative roles that the third party had to do manually, such as informing parties about the procedural rules, setting up meetings, notifying parties when the documentation is completed, etc.[15]

The use of technology in the dispute resolution process can bring advantages to traders and consumers alike. The most obvious benefit is that ODR techniques offer flexibility so parties can participate in a place and at a time that is convenient for them. Also, asynchronous communications provide consumers with time to cool down and translate information when necessary. Importantly, the applicable law and the contract is often clear in low-value consumer disputes, and more notably, with high volumes of disputes the types of disputes are similar, so an online tool can identify patterns and streamline the process by categorizing complaints and providing useful information to consumers, traders and regulators.

Accordingly, ODR techniques offer the opportunity to widen consumer access to redress and to build strategies leading to dispute prevention. Yet, ODR is no panacea, and for some consumers, particularly those belonging to vulnerable groups (i.e. the older, the less educated, the disabled, etc.) can find technology a hindrance.[16] For that reason ODR technology must acknowledge its limits, and in so far that is possible to do so, establish safeguards that help vulnerable consumers to access redress options, by for instance providing online or telephone support, allowing for hard-copy submissions[17] and

[15] Ibid., p. 94.

[16] Council of Europe Committee on Legal Affairs and Human Rights 'Access to Justice through Online Instruments' Introductory Memorandum, Rapporteur: Mr J. Xucla (23 September 2014).

[17] Art. 5(2)(d) of the ADR Directive allowing for submission by post when one party cannot use the online process. The Court of Justice of the EU held that when the consumer does not have access to technology or the Internet, he or she should be able to have an

enabling public access points where consumers can get assistance to participate in the online process.[18]

2.3 Types of Online Dispute Resolution Processes

There are many different types of ODR processes, but broadly they can be categorized as consensual and adjudicative processes. Within consensual processes in the context of ODR there are three main types: automated negotiation, assisted negotiation and online mediation.

Automated negotiation allows parties to analyse their bargaining positions; this is done by evaluating and prioritizing their bids, which are kept hidden during the negotiation. The bids are only disclosed when both parties reach a settlement; that is why this type of negotiation is also called a double-blind bidding negotiation. Normally, there is an algorithm that evaluates bids from the parties, and settles the case if the offers are within a prescribed range. The negotiation commences when one party invites the other to negotiate the amount of money in dispute. The other party is notified via email and invited to participate in the online negotiation. They can usually submit up to three offers, and if the bids of both parties come within a predetermined range or a given amount of money, then the technology automatically settles the dispute at the mid-point of the two offers. An example using this model is SmartSettleOne.[19]

Assisted negotiation involves processes designed to improve parties' communications through the assistance of software which frames parties' communication in a way that promotes settlement. In fact, it can be said that assisted negotiation is just a different type of mediation, but with the difference of using software – the ODR platform – as the moderator. Examples of this ODR model are eBay Dispute Resolution Centre, Modria, The Rechtwijzer, Youstice and Resolver.

Online mediation basically replicates the face-to-face mediation process online. The procedure is agreed by the parties, and it may be in written form, if parties communicate through text submissions to the mediator, or one that is supported by telephone or video-conferencing. The mediator can hold joint or caucus meetings with the parties. In ombudsman schemes, case handlers act as conciliators proposing

alternative offline avenue to access a mandatory conciliation process. See joined Cases *Rosalba Alassini and Others* v. *Telecom Italia* C-317/08.

[18] JUSTICE, 'What Is a Court?' (2016) Available at http://tinyurl.com/jfxh3mn.

[19] See www.smartsettle.com/home/products/smartsettle-one.

settlements or recommendations, which parties may or not accept. Most ODR schemes for consumers use this technique as part of their dispute resolution processes. Examples are also Modria and Youstice.

In terms of online adjudication, like in mediation, it mostly replicates the offline processes. This process is usually a written one, where the applicant initiates the process and uploads supporting documentation while the respondent provides feedback and evidence. Within this category we can include online processes that employ ombudsman processes, arbitration or a tribunal where an independent third party issues or imposes a decision. Examples are the Canadian Civil Resolution Tribunal, the English Traffic Penalty Tribunal and the dispute resolution model for domain names.

There are also online processes where a number of peers or experts are invited to share in an ODR platform their views on a particular dispute. These processes are often referred to as case appraisal and crowd-sourced dispute resolution. They normally vote on which party in a dispute should win the case and, depending on the ODR platform, the majority vote will be binding (e.g. the eBay Community Court in the Netherlands for feedback disputes) or not binding (e.g. the i-Court House).[20]

Typically the process is supported by an online platform that includes a case management tool, which allows parties to submit the claim and response as well as all the supporting documents online. The case handler or third party (e.g. an adjudicator) is able to access all the information through a website platform, and can require parties to submit additional information. The case handler may or may not have a video-conferencing hearing. The outcome can be issued online and it may be binding to one or both parties.

2.4 Examples of ODR Providers

2.4.1 Private ODR Providers

eBay's Dispute Resolution Centre

The world's most well-known ODR system for consumer disputes is eBay's Dispute Resolution Centre. The eBay online auction house and market place enables millions of transactions on a daily basis. A huge

[20] See C. Rule and C. Nagarajan, 'Leveraging the Wisdom of Crowds: The eBay Community Court and the Future of Online Dispute Resolution' *AC Resolution Magazine* (Winter 2010).

number of transactions inevitably correlates to a high number of disputes. Initially eBay ignored complaints from its users on the basis that eBay's role was only to act as an intermediary, and buyers and sellers should simply rely on the feedback exchanged. However, it quickly realized that providing a process to adjudicate grievances will increase users' trust in eBay. Furthermore, eBay realized that its platform and business model offers a natural forum for resolving disputes online.

There are a number of reasons that explain why eBay and more generally online marketplaces lend themselves to incorporate ODR technology. First, disputes are often of low value, so it would not be cost-effective to resolve these disputes face to face, let alone in the courts. Second, sellers are instructed to ship items only after they have received the payment from the buyer. Hence, both parties have strong incentives to participate in a dispute resolution process because the buyer wants compensation and the seller wants to obtain positive feedback in order to remain competitive in the eBay market. Third, the disputes that arise from eBay can be classified into a small number of issues. In addition to fraud alerts, the rest of complaints are classified as either 'item not received', 'item not as described' or 'unpaid item'.[21] This allows the development of software that recognizes disputes and proposes automatically fair solutions to the litigants. eBay has thus categorized the great majority of claims in a *numerus clausus* list. The limited types of claims have permitted eBay to design fast-track and cost-effective ODR processes.[22] Last, but not least, in most cases eBay controls the money used in the transaction through its collaboration with PayPal, so it can reverse payments from sellers to buyers.

eBay's Resolution Centre resolves the majority of disputes, though in some jurisdictions, such as in the USA, eBay has separate ODR schemes for a number of categories of purchases, such as vehicles and business equipment.[23] The advantage of dealing with a large number of disputes is that the same issues arise many times, so it is possible to divide the disputes into different sections. The ODR process starts when a buyer

[21] See http://resolutioncentre.ebay.co.uk/

[22] L. Del Duca, C. Rule and K. Rimpfel, 'eBay de Facto Low Value High Volume Resolution Process: Lessons and Best Practices for ODR Systems' (2015) 4 *Penn St J Law Int Aff* 242.

[23] See eBay Motors Vehicle Purchase Protection at http://pages.motors.ebay.com/buy/purchase-protection/ and eBay Business Equipment Protection at http://pages.ebay.com/help/buy/business-protection.html. For instance NetNeutrals is an ODR provider for motor vehicle claims. See www.netneutrals.com/About-Us.aspx.

or seller files a complaint. To do so, the claimant is asked to fill in a web-based standard claim form to identify the type of dispute and to present a list of common solutions, from which the claimant has to select the ones to which he or she would agree.[24] The other party is then contacted via email.

The respondent then files the reply and selects resolution options. If both parties agree on the same resolution, the dispute is resolved; if an agreement is not reached, then the parties are put into a negotiation environment. eBay's Resolution Centre employs a web interface that shapes communications into a constructive and polite negotiation. This is achieved with software tools that limit the free text space, encourage the proposition of agreements, set deadlines and even shape the tone of exchanges. This software is the key element of the process because it takes over some of the expertise of the neutral third party; thus this process could be defined as 'technology-mediated negotiation'. eBay has concentrated its ODR tool on a reduced number of recurring issues such as delays, bad descriptions and negative feedback. eBay software uses a precedent system that recognizes patterns of common sources of problems. This information is then used not only to streamline the dispute resolution process by encouraging parties to negotiate a settlement based on options chosen by disputants in previous similar disputes, but also to build a dispute prevention strategy which targets causes of problems.

When disputes cannot be resolved directly between the buyer and seller through eBay's ODR platform, then the claim can be escalated to the Resolution Services team, which is managed by eBay's Customer Support section.[25] The Resolution Services team will examine the claim and the supporting information provided by the parties and will make a decision on whether the claim (or part of it) is upheld. eBay's decision is based on its own rules, so one can say that eBay has developed its own substantive norms.[26] For instance, as part of eBay's Money Back Guarantee policy, which applies when a buyer does not receive an item or the item is not as promised, the buyer has the right to file an online complaint within 30 days of the latest estimated delivery date. The seller then has three business days to respond.[27] Sellers are required

[24] Rule, n. 1, p. 103. [25] Del Duca, et al., n. 22.

[26] E. Katsh, J. Rifkin and A. Gaitenby, 'Ecommerce, E-disputes, and E-dispute Resolution: In the Shadow of "eBay Law"', (2000) 15(3) *Ohio St J Disp Resol* 705–734.

[27] eBay, 'Ebay Money Back Guarantee' http://pages.ebay.com/help/policies/money-back-guarantee.html last visited 9 July 2015.

to cover the cost of return postage on items which are faulty or not as described.[28] The economic threshold recoverable is limited to the price of the item, so buyers cannot recover for consequential damage, the amount of which can only be recoverable in a judicial forum.

Modria

The ODR director of eBay and PayPal from 2003 to 2011, Colin Rule obtained a license from eBay that helped him, together with Chittu Nagarajan and others, to develop software in order to set up his own company: Modria.[29] The aim of this company is to provide ODR technology to ADR schemes and businesses' internal complaints systems, for the resolution of both low-value as well as high-value disputes. Its technology is used to handle cases ranging from consumer e-commerce to divorce, landlord–tenant, insurance, patents and tax disputes. Modria has developed a tiered procedure which contains a number of modules.[30]

i. First is the 'diagnosis module', which identifies the issues in dispute. This stage has a triage function as it assists in filtering complaints.
ii. The next level offered by Modria is a 'negotiation module', which summarizes the issues, requires parties to make proposals for settlement and allows the software to suggest settlements that parties are free to accept. This module seeks to resolve the majority of low-value disputes.
iii. Unresolved disputes move upstream to the next phase, the 'mediation module', where a neutral third party will be appointed with the aim of facilitating an amicable agreement.
iv. The final stage is arbitration, where the neutral party will adjudicate the dispute. Modria claims that, like with eBay, the majority of disputes will be resolved in the first two stages without human intervention, though for that to operate effectively parties will need strong incentives to cooperate.

[28] The eBay money back guarantee only functions for 'purchases that are usually sent by post' and excludes vehicles, real estate, businesses for sale and digital content, intangible items and services. See generally C. Riefa, *Consumer Protection and Online Auction Platforms* (Ashgate, 2015) 252–253.

[29] B. H. Barton, 'The Lawyer's Monopoly – What Goes and What Stays' (2014) 82 *Fordham Law Rev* 3067–3090, 3075–3076. Modria, Inc. www.modria.com last visited 14 October 2015.

[30] See 'Our Modular Dispute Resolution System' Modria. Available at www.modria.com/resolution-center.

Thus far, Modria has assisted in the development of various ODR platforms for resolving disputes between taxpayers and national tax offices. In effect the ODR platform, called the Online Resolution Center, allows taxpayers, who consider that the tax of their property has been miscalculated, to submit a claim online.[31] The platform is an online communication tool which enables taxpayers to submit questions, issues or assessments about their property tax to the tax office. The objective of these platforms is to provide taxpayers with some information on how the tax is calculated, and if they still think that it has been miscalculated, then they can submit the claim and follow the case online. The online platform appears to be user-friendly and eliminates unnecessary paperwork.

In addition, Modria has provided services to the American Arbitration Association (AAA) to build an ODR platform to manage AAA's New York No Fault case load. The platform manages over 100,000 cases on an annual basis, including document management, production of forms and analysis. Although it does not include a module of online mediation, the software already exists and can be added at a later stage. The platform, established in 2014, provides claimants and their lawyers with a secure website to submit online claims and to manage those claims through the platform.[32]

The Rechtwijzer

The Dutch Legal Aid Board first developed in 2007 a website called the Rechtwijzer (meaning 'signpost to justice' or 'conflict resolution guide'), the role of which was to assist people in conflicts to find a lawyer and other legal support. A new version of Rechtwijzer was launched in 2014, through a joint project by the Dutch Legal Aid Board and HiiL,[33] though Modria has been drafted to advise on the technology and dispute system design. The new platform is based on a 2.0 technology that operates not only as a diagnosis and referral tool, but also as a fully fleshed dispute resolution tool. The new platform allows parties with problems as diverse as family separation and consumer disputes to communicate by distance

[31] W. Sapp, 'Creating an Online Property Guide and Resolution Center' *Fair and Equitable* (April 2014) pp. 3–7.

[32] C. Rule, ODR News April 2014, 'AAA Chooses ODR for Its Largest Volume Case Load' (2014) 1(1) *Int J Online Disp Resol* 97.

[33] See www.hiil.org/project/rechtwijzer.

means. Parties can request an online mediator to get involved, and if a settlement cannot be reached, then a judge can get into the online process. The online process can be divided in the following stages:

i. Diagnosis and information, which is intended to be offered free of cost.
ii. Intake, which is fee based (a flat fee of approximately €500). This stage allows parties to use the platform to resolve their dispute with or without the involvement of a third party. The fee covers online and telephone support.
iii. Dialogue between the parties; this is free of cost, but the rest of the steps involve a third party and require the payment of a fee.
iv. Trialogue, which entails the hiring of an online mediator for a fee through a pay-as-you-go system.
v. External online review.
vi. Online adjudication by a judge if required by the parties.
vii. After-care stage: this tool allows parties to come back to the process if a dispute re-emerges.

The whole process is settlement orientated, and it seeks to set the parties mind on reaching an amicable agreement while taking into considerations what are the alternatives of not doing so – i.e. their BATNA.[34]

Youstice

Youstice is an ODR platform which was launched in April 2014.[35] The focus of this platform is the assistance in the resolution of low-value, high-volume consumer complaints. The platform is accessible from a number of shops' websites, allowing unsatisfied buyers to submit complaints directly to the traders. Youstice manages the workflow of the discussion, allowing parties to negotiate their disputes and agree on a resolution. If a settlement cannot be reached, then parties can escalate their dispute to a neutral ODR provider accredited by Youstice. It thus offers two levels of dispute resolution:

i. Negotiation through friendly and intuitive online forms, and
ii. Third-party review or adjudication carried out by certified external ODR providers.

[34] W. Ury and R. Fisher, *Getting to Yes* (Penguin, 1981). [35] See http://youstice.com/en/.

It offers a trustmark to those online shops that reach a direct agreement with the complainant in at least 80 per cent of cases and that implement at least 98 per cent of the agreements or recommendations delivered by the neutral third party (though they are now considering to increase the compliance requirement to 100 per cent). If a consumer confirms that a settlement has not been implemented within 30 days, then Youstice assumes the cost of the compensation.

The business model is the trustmark and negotiation tool that is linked to Youstice-accredited ODR providers. The fee starts at €100 euros p.a. for small shops, €500 for small to medium size, €1,000 for medium to larger size, and it has a negotiable fee with the largest retailers. Furthermore, parties will have to pay the ODR provider (and not to Youstice) a small fee (which often is around €25) per case that is escalated to the third-party reviewer. This fee is blocked and it may be returned to the complainant if the reviewer decides that the fee should be paid by the seller. Presently Youstice deals with disputes arising out of the general sale of goods (electronics, furniture, cosmetics, etc.) and has recently moved to provide their services in specific sectors such as car rental, energy and gambling. Youstice collaborates with other trustmarks and with consumer associations. The latter can use the platform to provide advice to consumers by replying to their queries. They can choose to forward a consumer complaint, assign it to a retailer or invite the retailer to Youstice if the retailer is not already registered.

This platform has been partly inspired by eBay's ODR system, though Youstice offers its services to any consumer or trader who wishes to use it. Consumers can initiate the ODR process by using the option of 'report a problem' from the businesses website where the consumers have bought the goods. The process starts by asking the complainant to determine the type of claim according to one of the following categories, which are accompanied by an iconic pictogram: (i) not delivered goods, (ii) received later, (iii) damaged or defective goods or (iv) problem with the payment. Then the complainant is prompted with a list of options (also accompanied by iconic pictograms) on how to resolve the claim: (i) refund, (ii) price reduction, (iii) reimburse costs of transport, (iv) let the retailer propose the resolution or (v) replacement. Each time one party has completed an action, the Youstice platform will send a notification via email requiring the other party to click on the link and log in at the Youstice platform.

Resolver

Similar to some of the services provided by Youstice, Resolver[36] is a free assisted complaints management system for consumers. Consumer complaints are categorized in different fields ranging from restaurants and legal services to energy or telecom suppliers. Once the consumer decides to bring a claim to the business, then Resolver assists the consumer in the process. Its complaint process is set out in five stages:[37]

i. It explains the consumers' rights.
ii. It helps consumers to draft a complaint letter or email.
iii. It records all written (and phone) communications between the consumer and the business.
iv. It creates a case file accessible to the consumer at all times.
v. It provides consumers with useful information on how to escalate a complaint, including to an independent ADR entity.

Resolver is free of cost for consumers, who only have to register to use its services, but Resolver assures that they will not pass the registration information on to anyone without the consumers' permission. Resolver's business model rests on informing businesses what consumers complained about, while keeping data anonymous. Resolver covers more than 2,000 organizations from different sectors, including energy, water, telecoms, motoring, insurance, retail companies, restaurants, gyms, energy efficiency, National Health Service (NHS) and leisure activities. It also contains the contact information of the complaints departments of all these organizations.

Dispute Resolution Scheme for Domain Names

This adjudicative scheme has been established by the Internet Corporation for Assigned Names and Numbers (ICANN), which holds the registration of the entire generic top-level domain name system (i.e. all the .com, .net, .org, etc.). In 1999, ICANN developed the Uniform Domain Name Dispute Resolution Policy (UDRP). The UDRP is legally a mandatory administrative procedure that resembles a documents-only arbitration, but it does not follow the arbitration laws; panels are unaccountable and decisions are not legally binding,

[36] See www.resolver.co.uk. [37] Ibid.

allowing parties to initiate a legal action at any time during the UDRP procedure. Parties adhere to the UDRP through a clause in their contract, which is formed between the registry (ICANN) and the registrar (the Internet Service Provider) and between the registrar and the registrant (domain-name holder).[38] The contractual clause states that certain egregious trademark breaches (cyber-squatting claims) by registered domain names will be resolved by one of ICANN's approved dispute resolution providers.[39] Currently, there are five approved providers:

i. World Intellectual Property Organisation (WIPO) Arbitration and Mediation Centre;[40]
ii. National Arbitration Forum (NAF);[41]
iii. Asian Domain Name Dispute Resolution Centre (ADNRC);[42]
iv. Czech Arbitration Court (CAC);[43] and
v. Arab Center for Domain Name Dispute Resolution (ACDR).[44]

The defining feature of the UDRP is that it operates within its own ecosystem.[45] First, the participation in the process is mandatory for the parties in exchange for their right to register a domain name. It thus ensures the participation of the parties by requiring users, i.e. domain-name holders, and complainants, i.e. trademark owners, to use the ODR process to resolve their disputes over the trademark breach. The beauty of this system is that it controls the enforcement since ICANN has the power of deciding who keeps a disputed domain name.

38 UDRP Policy, para.1.

39 P. Cortés, 'An Analysis of the UDRP Experience: Is It Time for Reform?' (2008) 24(4) *Computers Law and Security Report* 349–359 and 'The UDRP Reviewed: The Need for a "Uniform" Policy' (2008) 14(6) *Comput Telecommun Law Rev* 133–139.

40 WIPO was approved by ICANN on December 1, 1999. It is based in Geneva, Switzerland. See www.wipo.int/amc/en/domains.

41 NAF was approved by ICANN on December 23, 1999. It is based in Minneapolis, Minnesota. See http://domains.adrforum.com/.

42 ADNDRC was approved by ICANN on February 28, 2002. It has two offices in Beijing and Honk Kong. See www.adndrc.org/adndrc/index.html.

43 CAC was approved by ICANN on January 23, 2008. See Preliminary Report for the Special Meeting of the ICANN Board of Directors, available at www.icann.org/minutes/prelim-report-23jan08.htm.

44 See http://acdr.aipmas.org/?lang=en.

45 T. Schultz, 'Private Legal Systems: What Cyberspace Might Teach Legal Theorists' (2007) 10 *Yale J Law Tech* 159.

2.4.2 *Public ODR Providers*

The English Traffic Penalty Tribunal

In common law jurisdictions, in addition to courts there are tribunals, which are specialist courts that typically adjudicate disputes between citizens and a governmental body. In the UK there are over 70 tribunals dealing with matters as varied as social security, employment, health, education, tax, immigration and parking. Although one of the key features of tribunals is that the procedure is designed to be used by citizens acting as claimants without legal representation,[46] in practice tribunals may not be as user-friendly as one might expect.

In the UK there are a number of tribunals that are incorporating ODR technology in their processes, allowing parties to submit online claims and deciding most of their caseloads through e-decisions. An example of that in England and Wales is the Traffic Penalty Tribunal, which is a statutory body that considers appeals against parking fines.[47] These tribunals often offer parties the possibility of submitting their claims in paper form.

The Traffic Penalty Tribunal operates in England and Wales and it uses an ODR platform to process appeals against parking fines issued by the county councils.[48] Around half of the appeals a year are resolved by issuing online decisions. The platform enables parties (i.e. the driver complainant and the county council) to file the appeal and the response, to upload evidence, to follow the case online and even to participate in telephone hearings while examining the same interface of the ODR platform. Appellants create an account and receive notifications via email, while the local authorities use a dashboard to follow their appeals. These dashboards display the status of each case and they prompt messages when there is new information or when an action is required.

The Canadian Civil Resolution Tribunal

The Civil Resolution Tribunal is an online tribunal launched in 2016 in British Columbia, Canada.[49] This is a public scheme regulated under the Civil Resolution Tribunal Act 2012, which offers litigants with small

[46] See Sir Leggatt, *Tribunals for Users: One System, One Service* Report of the Review of Tribunals by Andrew Leggatt (2011) para. 1.9.

[47] See www.parking-appeals.gov.uk/olappeals.

[48] See www.trafficpenaltytribunal.gov.uk/how-to-appeal.

[49] Bill 44 – 2012 Civil Resolution Tribunal Act.

claims an online dispute resolution option.[50] The online tribunal is available as an alternative pathway to the courts for resolving small claims through a more convenient and cost-effective process. It deals with claims under 25,000 Canadian dollars related to debts, damages, recovery of personal property and certain types of condominium disputes, but excluding disputes affecting land. The online tribunal encourages amicable settlements at the earliest possible stage. Its procedure is inspired in the multi-stage procedure drafted by the UN for online dispute resolution and on the eBay dispute resolution model. It has three stages:

i. The tribunal's process requires parties first to engage in the tribunal's online negotiation platform, which is subject to short timelines and templates that support the negotiation process.
ii. If a settlement is not reached within a certain period of time, then a tribunal case manager is appointed to assist the parties to settle their dispute through a mediation process that takes place online and over the telephone. When parties do not settle in the mediation, they are invited to agree to a third and final stage: adjudication.
iii. The adjudicator contacts the parties via the online platform, over the phone and when necessary through video-conferencing, in order to make a decision that is final and binding.

The Proposal for an Online Court for England and Wales

The proposal for an Online Court for England and Wales seeks to incorporate ADR techniques in a bespoke online procedure for litigants in person (i.e. self-represented parties). The forthcoming online court follows two landmark reports from the Judiciary published in January and July 2016 (*Civil Courts Structure Review* by Lord Justice Briggs), whose main recommendation (to overcome the disproportionate costs of paying for legal representation when litigating low- and medium-value civil disputes) was the introduction of an Online Court by 2020.[51] These reports in turn follow the proposals made by the Civil Justice Council (a public advisory body)[52] and by JUSTICE (a human rights

[50] See www.civilresolutionbc.ca.

[51] Lord Justice Briggs, *Civil Courts Structure Review* Interim Report (December 2015), and Final Report (July 2016). Hereinafter, Briggs Interim Report and Final Report respectively.

[52] Civil Justice Council Online Dispute Resolution Advisory Group, 'Online Dispute Resolution for Low Value Claims' (February 2015).

NGO).[53] These reports noted the need to invest in technology and in court-annexed ADR schemes, especially in order to assist litigants in person with civil and commercial disputes of low and medium value. Inevitably, many consumer disputes could fit within this category.

The proposal for the Online Court became doable when the Lord Chancellor's Autumn Statement in November 2015 committed £732 million to digitalize the court system, making the launch of the Online Court unquestionable. The proposed procedure for the Online Court follows closely the Canadian online Civil Resolution Tribunal. It will resolve the majority of monetary civil disputes under £25,000 (though a soft launch may start initially at £10,000) where full legal representation is normally disproportionate. The online court will thus offer a new multi-tier dispute resolution procedure designed for litigants in person.[54]

Lord Justice Briggs in his Interim Report noted that 'the true distinguishing feature [of the Online Court] . . . is that it would be the first court ever to be designed in this country, from start to finish, for use by litigants without lawyers'.[55] However, this is not entirely accurate, as tribunals as well as the small claims procedure were also originally designed to operate without lawyers in response to consumer demand in the early 1970s.[56] The main risk of the new Online Court would be similar to the shortcomings of the existing tribunals and small claims procedures. After all, it is a court procedure, which may remain only accessible to highly educated consumers with medium- or high-value disputes.

An important novelty of the Online Court will be its departure from the traditional adversarial process, operating instead an online tiered procedure, with new procedure rules, which will contain three main stages that are similar to those used by the Civil Resolution Tribunal in Canada.

i. Stage one will consist of a fully automated triage process, where parties fill in the claim and are offered simple commoditized online advice.
ii. In Stage two the unresolved claims will pass to an officer who will provide case management support and recommend parties to attempt a settlement (through telephone mediation, judicial early neutral

[53] JUSTICE, 'Delivering Justice in an Age of Austerity' (April 2015).
[54] Briggs Interim Report. [55] Ibid., para. 6.5.
[56] R. Smith, Response for the Legal Education Foundation to the Interim Report on the Civil Courts Structure Review (2016) para. 8.

evaluation or ODR). This stage hopes to settle the majority of claims. Decisions from a case officer, which may be called a case lawyer since they are expected to have legal training, could be appealed to a judge by either party.[57]

iii. In the final Stage three the remainder of the claims will be sent to a judge for final determination on the documents (and when necessary via telephone, video or exceptionally using face-to-face hearings).

Briggs proposed a final fourth stage to join up and streamline the enforcement of judgments throughout the county court system. This ambitious reform seeks to deliver a court system which is accessible, transparent and operates at a proportionate cost. Susskind has suggested the implementation of stages three and two first, as the design of stage one would be the most difficult since it would require the building of 'diagnostic rule-based expert systems'.[58] But Briggs recommended that work should be undertaken to launch the three stages at the same time. In any event, as it was discussed elsewhere, a key factor for the success of the Online Court will be embedding the right incentives to ensure the claims are channelled through the most appropriate dispute resolution option, which is hoped to be for most cases stages one and two.[59] Hence, the effective design of these stages is paramount to its success, yet the history of ODR demonstrates that the design of technology and dispute resolution is far from easy.

2.5 Challenges to the Growth of ODR

Despite the existence of effective dispute resolution technology, the overall success of ODR has been very limited. This is particularly so if we consider that technology has permeated our lives in many ways, from the way we communicate at social level, to how we conduct business and interact with the government. Although the first ODR initiatives date back to the 1990s, the development of ODR since then has been rather slow. The following paragraphs examine three key factors that explain the low use of ODR techniques, namely: the lack of awareness, the lack of incentives for traders to participate in ODR schemes and the cost of

[57] Final Report 7.35.

[58] R. Susskind, ODR Group Response, Civil Justice Council (31 March 2016) paras. 5–6.

[59] P. Cortés, 'The Online Court: Filling the Gaps of the Civil Justice System?' (2017) 36(1) *Civil Justice Q* 54–71. See also Chapter 7 in this book.

technology.[60] This section notes the extent to which these factors have been addressed by the recent European regulatory framework, which is then examined more broadly further on in Chapter 4.[61]

2.5.1 *Lack of Awareness*

First and foremost, as with ADR, there is a high level of unawareness of ODR tools. Consumers with unmet legal needs do not know where to go after an online transaction has gone sour. This may be partly because the lack of information and the unavailability of ODR providers that can be trusted as independent bodies to resolve consumer grievances.

In order to identify trusted ODR bodies, it is necessary to have an accreditation system that ensures minimum due process compliance. Indeed, up till recently in the EU there were only soft laws that recommended procedural standards.[62] Yet, without monitored standards through an accreditation system, potential users may distrust compliance with due process guarantees, which has a knock-on effect on the trust that potential users have in private ODR providers. This is why one of the main aims of the ADR Directive has been to include a list of the minimum legal standards and a certification system carried out by the competent authorities of the EU Member States. Certified ADR/ODR entities must be independent, impartial, have expertise in consumer redress, effective, transparent, fair, and respect the principles of liberty and legality.[63] What remains to be seen during the next few years is how rigorous is the monitoring carried out by the national competent authorities.

[60] An earlier version of these factors were discussed in P. Cortés and A. Lodder, 'Consumer Dispute Resolution Goes Online: Reflections on the Evolution of European Law for Out-Of-Court Redress' 21(1) (2014) *Maastricht J* 17–20.

[61] See the Impact Statement of the ADR Directive and ODR Regulation justifying the need to provide a legal framework in the field of consumer ADR/ODR. Commission staff working paper, Impact Assessment, SEC(2011) 1408 final. An earlier version of this discussion appeared in P. Cortés and A. Lodder, 'Consumer Dispute Resolution Goes Online: Reflections on the Evolution of European Law for Out-Of-Court Redress' (2014) 21(1) *Maastricht J* 14–38. See also Chapter 4 of this book.

[62] See Commission Recommendation 98/257/EC of 30 March 1998 on the Principles Applicable to the Bodies Responsible for Out-of-Court Settlement of Consumer Disputes (O.J. 1998, L 115); Commission Recommendation 2001/310/EC of 4 April 2001 on the Principles for the Out-of-Court Bodies Involved in the Consensual Resolution of Consumer Disputes (O.J. 2001, L109/56).

[63] See Arts. 6–11 of the ADR Directive. See also Chapter 4 in this book.

Moreover, the ADR Directive tries to remedy the lack of awareness by information requirements of all traders with unresolved disputes.[64] In effect, traders are required to notify consumers before they enter into a contract if they are adhered to a certified ADR entity, which must be accessible online.[65] But importantly, even if they are not, once a dispute with a consumer cannot be resolved directly with the trader, then, the trader has the obligation to inform consumers about the existence of ADR entities operating in their business sector, and clarify whether or not the trader is willing to participate.

Moreover, pursuant to the ODR Regulation, all traders operating online, as well as all online market places (such as eBay and Amazon), must provide a link to the European ODR platform in an easily accessible place on their websites and in their emails they send to consumers with contractual offers.[66] In addition to the link, traders offering online contracts must include an email address, so they can receive the complaints submitted by consumers in the ODR platform. As discussed in Chapter 4, the EU ODR platform enables all certified ADR entities to process consumer disputes online through the platform. However, this hurdle can only be overcome if traders and market places comply with these information requirements (which many have yet to do) and if ADR entities offer their services online (which surprisingly not all do since some still require the physical presence of the parties or their legal representatives).[67]

2.5.2 *Lack of Incentives to Participate*

A second factor that constrained the development of ODR is the lack of incentives to participate in an ODR process outside the courts. This is further discussed in Chapter 7 of this book. For now, what it is relevant is to note here that many traders are reluctant to use and pay for ODR due to the lack of incentives. It seems logical that if a trader has dismissed a complaint from a consumer, then that trader is likely not to be interested in escalating that complaint to an ADR/ODR process, especially if the consumer is unlikely to take legal action.

The success of the eBay redress system stems from eBay's realization that it was in their own interests that conflicts between their users were

[64] Art. 13 of the ADR Directive. [65] Art. 5 of the ADR Directive.
[66] Art. 14 of the ODR Regulation.
[67] See the procedure requirements of the dispute resolution bodies listed in the ODR platform. Available at https://webgate.ec.europa.eu/odr/main/index.cfm?event=main.adr.show.

resolved efficiently.[68] As already noted, sellers in eBay as well as those of other online marketplaces such as Amazon are keen to resolve disputes because they rely on reviews and feedback to continue selling. However, for other traders (as opposed to those who operate in a third-party auction site where unhappy buyers leave negative feedback that impact on the subsequent sales of traders)[69] it is more difficult to motivate them to participate in ODR systems. It appears that the new information requirements set in the ADR Directive do not incentivize most traders into using ODR,[70] partly because many do not comply with it, so it is largely unknown. A key incentive, discussed in Chapter 7, is how effective is the alternative redress option, such as a mandatory residual ADR entity or an online court.

A related factor is the lack of the enforceability of agreements to use ODR and final outcomes. When dealing with consumer disputes, even those having an enforceable outcome (such as an arbitral award or a recognized mediated settlement), the often low value of the outcome may not justify the cost and resources of going to court to seek enforcement. This is why, as discussed in the previous section, most ODR schemes are either based on consensual processes where enforcement is often not an issue or employ a process where self-enforcement is built in the design as exemplified earlier with the UDRP and the Bitcoin system. Therefore, consumer redress schemes must be designed in a manner that ensures extrajudicial compliance of outcomes. As will be further discussed in Chapter 8, technology opens up a number of innovative ways to incentivize compliance with final outcomes. These include tools such as trustmarks, reviews and feedback systems, and passing the enforcement to the payment intermediaries.

2.5.3 The Cost of Using ODR Technology

The growth of ODR is intrinsically associated with the use of ADR. It has been argued that ADR is not always cheaper than going to court, in

[68] L. Edwards and A. Theunissen, 'Creating Trust and Satisfaction Online: How Important Is ADR? The eBay Experience' (2007) 5 *Web J Curr Legal Issues*.

[69] L. Webb, 'International BBB Ratings á la eBay: A Proposal for an Improved Online Better Business Bureau to Facilitate International Business Transactions' (2004) 35 *Calif West Int Law J* 127.

[70] P. Cortés, 'A New Regulatory Framework for Extra-Judicial Consumer Redress: Where We Are and How to Move Forward' (2015) 35(1) *Legal Stud*, 114–141.

particular if a small claims procedure is available.[71] Indeed, the dispute resolution process in the court may be cheaper for a trader when compared to the cost of funding the ADR process (especially if the latter is not publicly funded and the consumer does not pay a fee to use it) since leaving the courts as the only dispute resolution forum helps to discourage the number of consumer complaints.

Furthermore, investment in ad hoc ODR technology is costly, in particular for the development of bespoke ODR software. It must be noted that while online ADR may be based on already existing software (such as email, Skype and so on), generic software will not offer the full potential of ODR in, for example, embedding algorithmic analysis that recognizes patterns of conduct and leads to the settlement of disputes without the intervention of a neutral third party.[72] Indeed, the development of ODR software that is user-friendly and effective is far from easy.[73] Against this background, the European Commission has decided to offer the benefits of economies of scale and develop a so-called ODR platform. This is a web-based ODR platform with an online case management tool, available to nationally certified ADR entities. But, as it will be examined in Chapter 4, the EU ODR platform does not include algorithms that generate settlement proposals.

Overall, it appears that consumer redress schemes are incorporating technology in an organic manner, but most ADR schemes seem reluctant to invest heavily in technology as this can be expensive and they operate in a very competitive market that is moving quickly and cannot assure quick returns. Instead, many ADR schemes are processing individual claims that they receive by phone or via email or the web through their own internal case management tool. They are also relying on the use of the EU ODR platform and the services licensed by technology providers, such as Modria and Youstice.

2.6 Conclusion

This chapter has examined the concept of ODR, which varies depending on the context where it is used and the main types of processes employed.

[71] H. Genn 'Civil Mediation: A Measured Approach? (2010) 32(2) *J Soc Welf Fam Law* 195–205.

[72] Rabinovich-Einy, n. 1.

[73] G.A.W. Vreeswijk and A.R. Lodder, 'Gearbi: Towards an Online Arbitration Environment Based on the Design Principles Simplicity, Awareness, Orientation, and Timeliness' (2005) 13(2) *Arti Intell Law* 297–321.

It noted the impact that technology has on the dispute resolution processes. Accordingly, this chapter argued that adequate ODR technology can have a transformative impact on the ADR process. It can even change the paradigm of dispute resolution, altering the users' perception and transforming the role of the third party, which is then shared with the ODR technology (i.e. the fourth party).

This chapter has examined the processes of the most important private ODR providers, namely, the eBay Dispute Resolution Centre, Modria, Youstice, Resolver, Rechtwijzer and the ODR process for domain names. It has also analysed how ODR technology is being adopted by tribunals and courts. Thus, this chapter discussed the processes employed by the English Traffic Penalty Tribunal, the Canadian Civil Resolution Tribunal and the proposal for an Online Court for England and Wales.

Lastly this chapter has noted some of the main obstacles behind the slow expansion of ODR models, especially when compared with how technology has pervaded other social and economic sectors. These obstacles were briefly examined in the context of regulatory changes in the EU. These issues will be further examined throughout the rest of this book, but first, the role of the courts is explored.

3

Judicial Redress for Consumer Disputes – The Need for Collaboration between Courts and Extrajudicial Schemes

3.1 Introduction

There is an increasing corpus of consumer protection laws that stem from national and European norms. Substantive European rules in consumer protection were initially limited to minimum requirements,[1] but they are now moving towards legislative instruments based on maximum harmonization principles[2] as well as on the creation of horizontal instruments.[3] In addition to regulators, national courts are expected to play an important role in enforcing these emerging consumer protection laws. However, access to courts is relatively more costly for a consumer than a trader, which is evidenced by the fact that most claims in court are brought by traders against consumers.[4] Moreover, the low probability of consumers suing businesses incentivizes traders not to comply with costly regulations. It has been observed that many traders 'prefer (quite systematically) not to honour even the most obvious claims against them because non-compliance costs them less'.[5]

In order to achieve a more effective enforcement for consumer laws, the EU is developing judicial procedures that have the double aim of achieving increased access to justice and a more integrated European market. In so doing the EU faces the difficult task of building civil justice mechanisms while respecting national cultures and procedures. In this regard Weatherill observes that:

> Creating an integrated market lies at the heart of EU's objectives, but there is no intent to set aside the existence of different legal jurisdictions.

1 E.g. Directive 84/450/EEC on misleading advertising and Directive 93/13/EEC on unfair terms.
2 E.g. Directive 2005/29/EC on unfair business to consumer commercial practices.
3 E.g. Directive 2011/83/EU on consumer rights.
4 D. Leczykiewicz and S. Weatherill, 'Images of the Consumer in EU Law' in D. Leczykiewicz and S. Weatherill, *The Images of the Consumer in EU Law* (Hart, 2015) p. 16.
5 S. Grundmann, 'Targeted Consumer Protection' in D. Leczykiewicz and S. Weatherill, *The Images of the Consumer in EU Law* (Hart, 2015) p. 239.

> This presents a challenge to the promotion of an effective system of access to justice for the consumer in Europe.[6]

At the same time, new forms of communications are demanding accessible redress models that are better suited to an increasingly digital consumer. In this respect, our civil justice system is given two routes: (i) to radically modernize the court system making it more accessible through technology, ADR techniques, collective redress and legal aid or (ii) to promote more informal extrajudicial ODR processes which lessen the burden of the courts. These two options however do not have to be mutually exclusive, and indeed they should complement each other if a holistic approach is adopted between judicial and extrajudicial avenues.[7] This chapter argues that there are in particular two types of judicial processes that lend themselves for this type of collaboration: collective actions and small claims. These processes often deal with many individual consumer disputes which are of low value, so they would benefit from the efficiencies that technology and ADR processes can offer.

This chapter thus examines the regulation of these two main routes for resolving consumers' disputes in court: collective actions and small claims. In recent years there have been important efforts at the EU level to promote the use of these court options, notably through a Commission Recommendation requiring Member States to set up collective redress mechanisms and amending the European Small Claims Procedure (ESCP). This chapter evaluates these new legal developments for which the use of technology in the dispute resolution process appears to be particularly suited, especially when consumers encounter small and cross-border claims. This chapter proposes strategies to better integrate court processes with ADR/ODR techniques and explores possible pathways of collaboration.

3.2 Collective Redress

3.2.1 The Background

Consumers with low-value disputes do not have the resources or the motivation to pursue litigation against a trader, unless they can join their

[6] S. Weatherill, *EU Consumer Law and Policy* (Edward Elgar, 2014) p. 283.

[7] C. Hodges, 'The Need for a Holistic Review of the Dispute Resolution Landscape in England and Wales' (2017) *Legal Stud* forthcoming.

similar claims into one. The European Commission describes collective redress and its rationale as follows:[8]

> Collective redress is a procedural mechanism that allows, for reasons of procedural economy and/or efficiency of enforcement, many similar legal claims to be bundled into a single court action. Collective redress facilitates access to justice in particular in cases where the individual damage is so low that potential claimants would not think it worth pursuing an individual claim. It also strengthens the negotiating power of potential claimants and contributes to the efficient administration of justice, by avoiding numerous proceedings concerning claims resulting from the same infringement of law.

An entity representing a group of consumer claimants can go to court and seek either injunctive relief,[9] where cessation of the unlawful practice is sought, or compensatory relief, through a collective action (also referred as a group or class action) aimed at obtaining compensation for damage suffered. Cappelletti observed that collective actions break from the traditional litigation in a number of ways, notably, allowing standing to a claimant who has suffered a small fragment of the loss to sue on behalf of the other claimants.[10] This can be done on an opt-in or opt-out basis and it may require the court's approval for its operation. The right to have standing is extended in collective actions to a number of nationally qualified entities, such as certain consumer associations and public enforcement bodies. Interestingly, Hodges notes that the origin of collective actions was not to improve access to justice, but to provide more cost-effective procedures for judges who were faced with the management of multiple similar claims, such as the Spanish scandal on contaminated oil and a series of product liability cases in England.[11]

However, it must be noted that collective actions are not a silver bullet of consumer redress as they have shortcomings too.[12] For instance, there are conflicts of interest between lawyers and consumers, and often the

[8] European Commission Communication, 'Towards a Coherent European Approach to Collective Redress' COM(2013) 401 final para 1.2.

[9] See Directive 2009/22 on injunctions for the protection of consumers' interests [2009] OJ L 11/30.

[10] M. Cappelletti, 'Alternative Dispute Resolution Processes within the Framework of World-Wide Access-to-Justice Movement' (1993) 56 *Mod Law Rev* 282–296, 285.

[11] C. Hodges, 'Collective Redress: A Breakthrough or a Damp Squib?' (2014) 37 *J Consum Policy* 67, 82.

[12] L. Mullenix, 'Ending Class Actions As We Know Them: Rethinking the American Class Action' (2014) 64 *Emory Law J* 399.

litigation costs can drain the compensation obtained in a judgment.[13] Also a lengthy court process carry the risk of more delays in enforcing a judgment where the compensation could even be further restricted by an insolvent defendant who may have to pay first secured creditors.[14] Under these circumstances, settlement can offer a better redress option for consumers and other stakeholders.[15]

The European Parliament and the Commission are considering ways of developing and encouraging judicial and extrajudicial collective redress. Indeed, the term 'collective redress' has been used as opposed to 'collective action' in order to encapsulate extrajudicial mechanisms, particularly voluntary models such as ombudsman schemes.[16] The EU appears resolute to avoid replicating the US model for class actions, which has been criticized for providing excessive economic incentives to lawyers (with the counterpart of a significant lower recovery for consumers) and for promoting unmeritorious claims that can even lead to blackmailing defendants into settling cases. The European Commission has noted that punitive damages and pre-trial discovery procedures fuel class actions in the USA into what they termed a 'toxic cocktail' that should not be introduced in the EU.[17] In fact the US model would not work in the EU because the US system relies on important economic incentives: namely, the American costs rule,[18] the widespread use of contingency fee agreements[19] and extensive third-party funding.[20]

However, contractual clauses that seek to waive consumers' rights to collective actions will be regarded as unfair in the EU, if, as one would expect, they create imbalance between the rights and obligations of the parties to the detriment of the consumer.[21] This position contrasts with that taken by the US Supreme Court, which has upheld a contractual

[13] Geroge Rutherglen, 'Wal-Mart, AT&T Mobility, and the Decline of the Deterrent Class Action' (2012) 98 *Va Law Rev Brief* 24, 25–27.

[14] C. Hodges and A. Stadler, *Resolving Mass Disputes – ADR and Settlement of Mass Claims* (Edward Elgar, 2013) p. 6.

[15] Ibid. [16] Ibid., 72. [17] MEMO/08/741, p. 4.

[18] US plaintiffs losing a case will not have to pay the legal costs of the successful respondents.

[19] Also known as damage-based agreements. This is when the legal costs of the claimant are agreed as part of the recovery made in the court judgment or in a settlement.

[20] This is where a third-party funding company provides a litigant with funding to bring the litigation in exchange for a percentage of the settlement. See C. Hodges, 'Collective Redress in Europe: The New Model' (2010) 29(3) *Civil Justice Q* 373.

[21] Unfair Terms Directive 13/93/EC.

waiver of consumers to join a class action when an arbitration scheme appears to offer an adequate avenue for consumers to pursue their claims individually.[22]

3.2.2 The EU Soft Laws

In 2012 the European Parliament issued a Resolution supporting a horizontal framework of national procedural laws for collective actions to avoid fragmentation, while respecting the different legal traditions of the Member States.[23] The Parliament has been very clear that safeguards should be put in place to avoid the use of collective redress for unmeritorious claims.[24] A year later, the Commission issued a Recommendation requiring all the EU Member States to establish collective redress mechanisms.[25] The Recommendation contains a series of common principles for collective redress mechanisms and requires Member States to introduce a generic collective action procedure within four years. The Commission reported in 2013 that 16 Member States out of the 28 already had such systems.[26] This figure is changing rapidly.

For instance, France passed a new law in 2014 allowing for collective actions.[27] Under the new legislation a number of government-approved consumer associations (initially 16 gained the public accreditation) can bring a class action on behalf of consumers for disputes that arose in the last five years. The French law allows for two procedures: an opt-in system (where the claimants make clear that they want to join the collective action) that operates by default and an opt-out system (where the court decides who the claimants of the class are, unless the named claimants expressly disagree). A simplified procedure can be carried out when the

[22] *AT&T* Mobility v. *Concepcion*, 563 U.S. 321 (2011). As this case demonstrates the US Supreme Court has gone as far as invalidating State laws that attempted to protect consumers' right to access the courts. Thus, while many States have enacted laws to restrict arbitration agreements, these laws they have been preempted by the application of the Federal Arbitration Act by the US Supreme Court.

[23] European Parliament Resolution of 2 February 2012 'Towards a Coherent European Approach to Collective Redress' 2011/2089(INI).

[24] European Parliament Resolution (2011) supra para 20.

[25] Commission Recommendation on Common Principles for Injunctive and Compensatory Collective Redress Mechanisms in the Member States Concerning Violations of Rights Granted under Union Law (11 June 2013).

[26] For the consultation process in the EU see generally http://ec.europa.eu/consumers/archive/redress_cons/collective_redress_en.htm.

[27] Art. L. 423–17 of the French Consumer Act (*loi Hamon*) of 13 February 2014.

court can identify the claimants, and when they have suffered damages for the same amount. An example of the latter was the first collective action submitted in the French courts, *UFC-Que Choisir* v. *Foncia*, for charging tenants a monthly fee for sending them the bills for the rent.[28]

According to the Commission Recommendation, redress procedures should be available to enforce the areas 'where EU law grants rights to citizens and companies, notably in the areas of consumer protection, competition, environment protection and financial services'.[29] Although the Commission supports a horizontal framework on consumer redress in the Recommendation, it states that it does not intend to harmonize Member States' national procedures, at least for the time being.[30] The rationale of developing a horizontal instrument is 'in order to avoid the risk of uncoordinated sectorial EU initiatives and to ensure the smoothest interface with national procedural rules'.[31] It is thus not clear yet whether the Commission will introduce a hard law instrument, like a Directive or a Regulation, as that will depend on how satisfactory will be the national regulation. The stated rationale for developing a horizontal instrument is 'to avoid the risk of uncoordinated sectorial EU initiatives and to ensure the smoothest interface with national procedural rules'.[32]

After the European Commission passed the role of enforcement of competition matters to national competition authorities, it quickly realized that the limited resources of the national authorities should be complemented by allowing private enforcement to stop infringements of EU competition laws,[33] such as abuse of a dominant position or cartels. This led to the approval of a Directive on Antitrust Damages Actions, which requires Member States to set up collective redress procedures before the end of 2016.[34] In the UK these cases are processed in the Competition Appeals Tribunal, which under the Consumer Rights

[28] See France 24 'UFC-Que Choisir vs Foncia: L'action de Groupe Loin de la "Class Action"' (1 October 2014). Available at www.france24.com/fr/20141001-ufc-que-choisir-foncia-action-groupe-class-action-difference-loi-hamon-proces-france-etats-unis-associations-justice/.

[29] Ibid.

[30] Commission Recommendation on Common Principles for Injunctive and Compensatory Collective Redress Mechanisms in the Member States Concerning Violations of Rights Granted under Union Law (11 June 2013).

[31] Communication, para. 4.

[32] European Commission Communication, n. 8, para. 4.

[33] See C. Petrucci, 'Collective Redress and Competition Law' in in S. Drake and M. Smith, *Effective Enforcement of EU Law and Policy* (Edward Elgar, 2016) 202–230.

[34] Directive 2014/104/EU on Antitrust Damages Actions OJ L349/1. The implementation deadline is 27 December 2016.

Act can allow opt-out cases. A recent high profile case has been filed against Mastercard, where the damages claimed for illegal commissions charged to traders and consumers amount to 16 billion GBP.[35]

3.2.3 *Characteristics of the EU Model on Collective Redress*

The European Commission published a Communication on collective redress (beyond competition matters), which sets out the various debates on collective redress in the EU and acts as a response to the European Parliament's Resolution.[36] In the Communication, the European Commission established the issues that in their view should be included within a horizontal legal framework:

i. Distinction between public enforcement and private collective redress: The Commission observes that while public enforcement seeks legal compliance and deterrence through sanctions, private enforcement's main goal is to obtain compensation for a legal breach.[37] These two roles complement each other and remove the need for punitive damages in collective redress.
ii. Admissibility: Collective actions should only be brought when certain admissibility conditions are fulfilled, empowering the courts to assess whether the national criteria is met.
iii. Standing: In representative actions it should be ensured that the representative entity acts genuinely in the best interests of the group represented.
iv. The 'opt-in' model is preferred, but since some Member States already have 'opt-out' mechanisms, that approach should be 'duly justified by reasons of sound administration of justice'.[38]
v. Effective provision of information to potential claimants: It is noted that while broad advertising could be an effective tool to identify claimants, these techniques must be balanced with the adverse impact on the reputation of the defendant.

[35] '£14bn damages claim filed against MasterCard' The Law Society Gazette (8 September 2016).

[36] European Parliament Resolution of 2 February 2012 'Towards a Coherent European Approach to Collective Redress', 2011/2089(INI).

[37] See W. van Boom and M. Loos (eds.), *Collective Enforcement of Consumer Law: Securing Compliance in Europe through Private Group Action and Public Authority Intervention* (Europa Law Publishing, 2007).

[38] Communication, para. 3.4.

vi. Interplay with public enforcement: In certain areas (competition, environment and data protection), public enforcement plays a major role, which must not be put in jeopardy by litigation being commenced before the conclusion of the public investigation. The Commission proposes that this can be achieved by rules restricting public access to documents obtained or produced by the public authority and by suspending limitation rules.
vii. Effective cross-border enforcement: The Commission does not recommend the introduction of a specific rule for collective claims beyond the existing rules of international private law.
viii. Availability of collective consensual dispute resolution: Consensual ADR is recognized to provide effective redress for collective actions, even more effectively than the courts.[39]
ix. Funding of collective action: The Commission believes that third-party financing (including contingency fee agreements) should be restricted in so far that it brings a 'risk of stimulating abusive litigation or litigation that does little to serve the best interests of litigants'.[40] The Commission does not find it necessary to recommend direct support from public funds and stated that the 'loser pays' principle, which is well established in the EU, should also apply to collective redress.

According to Hodges, 'The Commission's claim that its safeguards present a firm barrier against abuse cannot be sustained. Firstly, the safeguards in the Recommendation themselves contain too many exemptions'.[41] In his view, depending on how Member States adopt these exceptions, 'the result is that certain national contexts will fuel, or chill, litigation'.[42] He concludes noting that the EU only wishes to encourage collective actions but for the most meritorious cases, and that it is still too early to refer to an EU model for a collective action as there are very different national models.[43]

3.2.4 *Collective Redress and ADR*

The Commission Recommendation encourages parties to use collective ADR at both pre-action and during the judicial process. Accordingly, it recommends that collective actions should be accompanied by collective

[39] Hodges and Stadler, n. 14. [40] Communication, para. 3.9. [41] Hodges, n. 11, p. 78.
[42] Ibid. 79. [43] Ibid. 83.

ADR. The Commission's view is that it should be encouraged before and during the judicial process (putting a halt to the limitation period while parties seek a settlement), but remain voluntary; yet judges should not be prevented from inviting parties to seek a consensual solution. Where a consensual solution is reached, the court should verify the legality of the outcome and confirm it.

This approach is in line with the Mediation Directive, which empowers courts to invite parties to use mediation. The ADR Directive refers to collective redress in the context of nationally certified ADR entities,[44] but it does not require its provision in the Member States, nor does it offer minimum procedural requirements. It must be noted that the majority of ADR entities either do not have, or have a very limited, provision of collective redress;[45] moreover, existing collective ADR procedures are slow and complex, and their operation is employed at the discretion of the ADR entity.[46] Thus, the majority of ADR processes do not allow consumers to join an existing claim, and consequently it may not be effective in ensuring that a trader stops an illegal conduct – for that consumers would need to go to the regulatory enforcement body or seek judicial redress.

Conversely, some ADR providers already offer these services for consumer and competition matters.[47] For example, some national ADR entities, especially those with statutory backing, such as the Financial Ombudsman Service in the UK, may identify a test case that is identical or very similar to other cases. They send this sample case for the determination to a senior ombudsman or to the courts and, in the meantime, all similar cases are halted. Although the decision from the court or the ombudsman does not form a precedent as such, it is used as a guideline for the other cases.[48] Similarly, there a number of ADR bodies, such as the Spanish consumer arbitration system,[49] that recognize the possibility of grouping cases which are based on the same claim – yet, the decision

[44] Recital 27 Directive 2013/11/EC.

[45] For a study of consumer ADR in the UK example see C. Graham 'Collective Consumer Redress' in P. Cortés, *The New Regulatory Framework for Consumer Dispute Resolution* (OUP, 2016).

[46] Civic Consulting, European Parliament Study Cross-border Alternative Dispute Resolution in the EU (2011).

[47] Graham, n. 45.

[48] C. Hodges, I. Benohr, N. Creutzfeldt-Banda, *Consumer ADR in Europe (Civil Justice Systems)* (Beck/Hart, 2012) 272 et seq.

[49] Real Decreto 231/2008 on Consumer Arbitration.

or arbitral award only affects those who brought the claim. In a way, this is equivalent to the opt-in system used by most national courts in the EU, and therefore it does not compensate consumers as a class, but only those who were aware and brought their claims.

It is likely that the use of collective actions will increase as consumer rights and the use of technology in ADR processes increase. But, it is unlikely that collective arbitration will grow as arbitration continues to have a contractual nature. This restriction is clearly observed in the USA, where businesses unanimously refuse to opt for collective arbitration as they would face higher claims for financial compensation. However, it seems more likely that one of the following two models will develop in the EU. One option is arbitration mandated by law, such as exists in Portugal for essential services, although this option may be challenged on the principle of access to justice.[50] On the other hand, new ADR models may be created, such as the Anglo-Saxon or Nordic ombudsman system, which are able to process collective consumption claims while also allowing appeals in court. Nevertheless, it should be noted that currently these ADR systems rarely deal with collective actions. Therefore, the most likely option for collective redress may remain with the courts, while at the same time consumers may be offered the possibility of a faster ODR option, but one that is not collective. Another option, as discussed earlier with the Financial Ombudsman in the UK, would involve an ADR entity submitting a test case to court, then resolving the remaining pending cases by following the approach of the judgment.

3.3 The European Small Claims Procedure

It is pertinent to examine small claims procedures as these procedures provide a middle ground between formal litigation and ADR methods, where low-value disputes can be resolved in courts through a less formal and expeditious judicial procedure.[51] Furthermore, for these processes

[50] E.g. The Spanish Constitutional Court ruled that compulsory arbitration in transport was unconstitutional given that it breached the right to access to justice. See Judgment 174/1995 of 23 November 1995.

[51] The analysis of the European Small Claims Procedure presented in this chapter is an elaboration of a paper presented in: Workshop for the JURI Committee on 'Cross-Border Activities in the EU – Making Life Easier for Citizens', In-Depth Analysis 'European Small Claims Procedure and the Commission Proposal of 19 November 2013' (February 2015) pp. 249–279. Available at www.europarl.europa.eu/RegData/etudes/STUD/2015/510003/IPOL_STUper cent282015per cent29510003_EN.pdf. Earlier versions of this

the use of cost-efficiencies through online access is particularly important in order to deliver a redress option at a proportionate cost, especially in cross-border matters. This section examines the European Small Claims Procedure (ESCP), and it calls for greater interactions with ADR and ODR techniques.

The ESCP is intended to be a user-friendly procedure that allows parties to resolve cross-border low-value civil and commercial disputes up to €5,000 through a simplified procedure without the need for legal representation.[52] This procedure is designed to be carried out entirely in writing, using standard forms available online in all languages.[53] The ESCP is available to parties as an alternative to the procedures existing under the laws of the EU countries.[54] In particular, domestic small claims tracks in civil procedure exist and are being frequently resorted to in England and Wales, Ireland,[55] Sweden and Poland.

Member States determine which national courts have jurisdiction to offer the ESCP, but it is also subject to the rules of the Brussels Ia Regulation,[56] since the ESCP Regulation is silent on this issue. Subject to the exceptions laid down in the Brussels Ia, the *actor sequitur forum rei* principle applies, meaning that defendants shall normally be sued in the courts of the Member State where they are domiciled. An important

section appeared in P. Cortés and R. Manko, 'Developments in European Civil Procedures' in P. Cortés, *The New Regulatory Framework of Consumer Dispute Resolution* (OUP, 2016) and in P. Cortés, 'The Need for Synergies in Judicial Cooperation and Dispute Resolution: Changes in the European Small Claims Procedure' in X. Kramer and B. Hess (eds.) *From Common Rules to Best Practices in European Civil Procedure* (Hart, 2017) forthcoming.

52 Regulation (EC) 861/2007 of the European Parliament and of the Council of 11 July 2007 establishing a European Small Claims Procedure, O.J. 2007 L 1999/1. Hereinafter, ESCP. The ESCP Regulation was amended on 16 December 2015 and it will enter into application on 14 July 2017 – see Regulation (EU) 2015/2421.

53 P. Cortés, 'Does the Proposed European Procedure Enhance the Resolution of Small Claims?' (2008) 27(1) *Civil Justice Q* 83–97.

54 M. Tulibacka, 'Europeanization of Civil Procedures: In Search of a Coherent Approach', *Common Mark Law Rev* 46 (2009): 1527–1565, p. 1544; R. Mańko, 'European Small Claims Procedure: Commission proposal to remedy weaknesses in the current system', *EPRS In-Depth Analysis*, PE 542.137 (November 2014), p. 7.

55 See P. Cortés, 'Small Claims in Ireland and the EU: The Need for Synergy between National Courts and Extrajudicial Redress' in N. Neuwahl and S. Hammamoun (eds.), *The European Small Claims Procedure and the Philosophy of Small Change* (Les Éditions Thémis, 2014).

56 Regulation (EU) No 1215/2012 of the European Parliament and of the Council of 12 December 2012 on jurisdiction and the recognition and enforcement of judgments in civil and commercial matters.

exception applies to consumers, who in many cases are given the option of bringing claims to their national courts.[57] Member States must allow the submission of claims and other documents by post or via electronic means, removing the need to travel to another country. Oral hearings can only be required in exceptional circumstances, and they are encouraged to be held using distance means of communication in order to obviate the parties' need to travel to the hearing.

Moreover, the main advantage of the ESCP is that judgments can be enforced without the need for an intermediary procedure to declare their enforceability – i.e. the *exequatur*. Even following the abolition of *exequatur* in general by the Brussels Ia regulation, the conditions of enforcing judgments under the ESCP still remain more favourable to creditors seeking enforcement. This is because the grounds of the 'reverse *exequatur*' procedure, as defined in Brussels Ia, are broader than those allowed under the ESCP.[58]

3.3.1 *An Analysis on the Performance of the ESCP*

The Commission reported that on average the ESCP has reduced the cost of litigating cross-border cases up to 40 per cent and the duration from 2 years and 5 months to only 5 months.[59] This is a significant improvement, but it is still too expensive and too long for many consumer claims, which could benefit from quicker and more informal resolution. Two-thirds of those who used it were overall satisfied with the procedure.[60]

[57] Art. 15 Brussels I Regulation allows consumers to use their own jurisdiction when the business activity had been directed to the consumers' domicile. See generally, N. Marchal Escalona, 'La Protección del Consumidor en los Litigios Transfronterizos de Escasa Cuantía en la Unión Europea y en América Latina' in F. Esteban de la Rosa (ed.), *La Resolución Alternativa de Litigios de Consumo en los Estados Miembros de la UE: Impacto del Nuevo Derecho Europeo* (2015, Tirant) and R. Miquel Sala, *El Proceso Europeo de Escasa Cuantía* (Aranzadi, 2009) 81–85.

[58] P.A. Nielsen, 'The New Brussels I Regulation', *CMLR* 50 (2013): 503–528, pp. 505, 524–528; R. Mańko, 'Europeanisation of Civil Procedure: Towards Common Minimum Standards?' *European Parlaimentary Research Service In-depth Analysis*, PE 559.499 (June 2015), p. 17.

[59] European Commission, Report from the Commission to the European Parliament, the Council and the European Economic and Social Committee on the application of Regulation (EC) 861/2007 of the European Parliament and the Council establishing a European Small Claims Procedure COM(2013) 795 final. Hereinafter, the Commission Report.

[60] Special Eurobarometer 395, European Small Claims Procedure (April 2013). Hereinafter, Eurobarometer 395. Available at http://ec.europa.eu/public_opinion/archives/ebs/ebs_395_en.pdf.

Some of the most obvious advantages are that the ESCP offers claimants a fast-track process with strict deadlines that is, in principle, the same in every Member State.

The Regulation removes the parties' requirement to have legal representation – though in practice one-third of users had to employ a lawyer.[61] This feature of the Regulation has affected the national small claims procedures.[62] In addition, the claim and response forms are available online in all the EU languages, and just over half of the users (62 per cent) found them easy to fill in.[63] The ESCP thus attempts to facilitate self-representation; accordingly, it does not require parties to make any legal assessment to support their claims. Nevertheless, it is obvious that submitting a claim presupposes that claimants are at least aware of their legal rights.[64] It must be noted that while discouraging legal representation may keep costs down, making the process more proportionate to the value of the claim, it could also raise access to justice concerns when only one party has legal representation. This situation may be common in consumer disputes, where consumers as claimants are more likely to be self-represented, which could undermine the principle of equality of arms if adequate procedural safeguards are not put in place.

Great expectations have been put on the ESCP to increase access to justice for European litigants with cross-border claims.[65] However its use has been very low – an estimated 3,500 cases in the year 2012.[66] The three

[61] Ibid.

[62] For instance, in Spain the requirement to have legal representation was increased for claims over €900 to claims over €2,000, which was the original limit of the ESCP. Arts. 23, 31 and 539 Ley 1/2000 de Enjuiciamiento Civil. See generally, J.C. Ortiz, 'La Aplicación en España de los Procesos Europeos Monitorio y de Escasa Cuantía: La Reforma de la Legislación Española en Virtud de la Ley 4/2011, de 24 d Marzo' (2011) 24 *Revista General de Derecho Procesal* 2.

[63] Also 16 per cent of users reported difficulties in filling in the forms. See Commission Report, p. 6.

[64] M. Loos, 'Individual Private Enforcement of Consumer Rights in Civil Courts in Europe' Centre for the Study of European Contract Law Working Paper Series No. 2010/01. p. 4.

[65] The European e-Justice Portal is a single point of entry to all relevant information about the ESCP. Forms to be used in the European Small Claims Procedure can be accessed at https://e-justice.europa.eu/content_small_claims_forms-177-en.do and to find out which court has jurisdiction over the ESCP see http://ec.europa.eu/justice_home/judicialatlascivil/html/sc_courtsjurisd_en.jsp#statePage0.

[66] In many countries, the average number of ESCP cases filed yearly was, on average, actually less than 50, with as little as 2 cases filed yearly in Slovenia, 3 in Bulgaria, 8 in Portugal, 15 in the Netherlands or 48 in Poland. The only notable exception has been

main obstacles identified by the Commission were: (i) the lack of awareness about the ESCP; (ii) disproportionate costs and time in litigating small claims and (iii) the lack of transparency about the costs of litigation and the methods of payment.[67] Research carried out in the EU concluded that there was a significant lack of awareness,[68] where only 12 per cent of EU citizens are aware of the ESCP. More surprisingly, only half (53 per cent) of the judges and courts of the Member States are aware of the ESCP; out of those courts that are aware, many are not fully informed about the ESCP.[69] The other two obstacles identified are related to the unpredictability of costs and time employed for resolving a cross-border claim of small value. Parties often face uncertainty about the potential costs related to translations, travelling and lawyers' fees, and there is a lack of clarity about the details of the procedure.[70] As a result, not only vulnerable consumers but a large portion of society may not see the ESCP as an accessible redress option, which explains why research shows that the ESCP is rarely used.[71] This situation contrasts with that of some national small claims procedures and ADR processes which are proving to be more effective.[72]

Another key obstacle for the success of the ESCP that neither the Commission nor the Deloitte report mentioned, is that, unlike in ADR processes, EU citizens still find the judicial procedure too complicated and they do not feel confident to start it on their own.[73] Accordingly, it is

Spain with over 1,000 cases filed yearly on average. Deloitte, 'An Assessment of the Socio-Economic Impacts of the Policy Options for the Future of the European Small Claims Regulation' Final Report (19 July 2013) p. v. Hereinafter, the Deloitte Report.

67 Deloitte Report, ibid., p. v.

68 Ibid. and ECC-Net, European Small Claims Procedure Report (September 2012). Hereinafter ECC-Net. Available at http://ec.europa.eu/consumers/ecc/docs/small_claims_210992012_en.pdf.

69 European Commission, Impact Assessment of the Proposal for a Regulation of the European Small Claims Procedure SWD(2013) 460, p. 24. Hereinafter, Impact Assessment.

70 F. Alleweldt et al., 'Cross-Border Alternative Dispute Resolution in the European Union' IMCO (June 2011) IP/A/IMCO/ST/2010-15, pp. 52–63; ECC-Net (2012) pp. 3–6.

71 Eurobarometer 395 p. 82; Hodges et al., n. 48, pp. 127, 397; European Parliament, Cross-border ADR Final Report (2011) IP/A/IMCO/ST/2010-15. pp. 52–63. Previous research has already noted that national small claims procedures generally only benefit well-informed and articulate individuals. J. Balwin, 'The Small Claims Procedure and the Consumer' (1995) Office of Fair Trading, London. See also F. Cownie, A. Bradney and M. Burton, *English Legal System in Context* (5th edn, OUP, 2010) 208.

72 ECC Ireland, The Development of Alternative Dispute Resolution in Ireland – An Analysis of Complaints, Best Practices and Future Recommendations, 2008.

73 Eurobarometer 395, p. 79.

important that research is carried out to find out who the beneficiaries of the ESCP are – as currently it is unclear whether these are consumers, Small and Medium Enterprises (SMEs) or others – and which steps, if any, can be taken to make the procedure more user-friendly, faster and more cost-effective. However, existing research suggests that the ESCP is hardly used by consumers, and the rationale behind the expansion of scope by the Commission is to increase redress avenues for traders and not so much for consumers.[74]

As discussed later in this chapter, both, the Eurobarometer and the Deloitte report found that there were no problems with the enforcement of judgments.[75] This finding clearly suggests that the ESCP is mainly used by businesses which have legal representation and are often required to sue in the defendant's forum. Hence, it is not used by consumers in their own jurisdictions, because if they used it, then they would surely have found great difficulties in seeking the enforcement of judgments in a different language and through a foreign enforcement procedure – let alone finding and contacting the relevant enforcement authorities. This is why the ECC-Net and many other consumer bodies have observed that the main obstacle to the effectiveness of the ESCP is the enforcement.[76]

3.3.2 *An Analysis of the Amendments of the ESCP Regulation*

Increasing the Economic Ceiling for Small Claims

The formality of a judicial process can in itself be a barrier for small claims. The Commission noted that 45 per cent of businesses would not take a case to court because the cost of doing so was disproportionate in terms of costs and lengthy proceedings.[77] Similarly, most consumers are also unlikely to go to court for a small claim, especially if it is one under €786.[78] For that reason, as noted later, litigants dealing with small claims should be offered more informal means of dispute resolution when these are available.

The amended Regulation increased the economic threshold from €2,000 to €5,000.[79] This increase is a welcome reform as lifting the

[74] C. Hodges, 'The Consumer as Regulator' in D. Leczykiewicz and S. Weatherill (eds.), *The Images of the Consumer in EU Law* (Hart, 2015) p. 248.

[75] Eurobarometer 395, p. 8 and Deloitte Report, n. 66, p. v.

[76] ECC-Net, 'European Small Claims Procedure Report' (2012) p. 22.

[77] Commission Report p. 3. [78] Eurobarometer 395. [79] Article 2(1) of the ESCP.

economic threshold does not necessarily increase the cost of litigating higher-value disputes. In fact, the estimated cost of litigating a cross-border claim of €5,000 is very similar (and sometimes the same) to the cost of litigating a claim of €10,000,[80] which may justify another increase when regulation is revised again in five-years time, which is expected to happen in 2021.

Greater Use of Electronic Communications

With the aim of promoting the use of electronic communications the amended Regulation states that electronic services should be the preferred option when the technical means are available and it is compatible with the national procedure. It is regrettable that the electronic communications are not imposed, but only recommended. In general, service will remain subject to the requirements laid down by the law of the addressee's location, though a national law can impose the duty to accept electronic service.[81]

High court fees may be a factor for citizens' decision not to pursue legal action.[82] The fees and the methods of payment are set by the Member States and they vary significantly depending on the jurisdiction. While some national courts require the payment of the court fees in their premises, in others it has to be done in cash, with cheques or by lawyers – these obstacles add more hurdles, making claims unworthy to pursue.[83] Although the amended Regulation does not cap the court fees, it requires fees not to be disproportionate to the value of the claim and not to be higher than fees charged in a simplified domestic procedure.[84] Member States are allowed to levy a reasonable minimum fee, as well as a separate fee for filing an appeal. The amended text also provides that a Member State must offer at least one of the three options of distance means of payment: bank transfer; credit or debit card payment; direct debit from the claimant's bank account.

The ESCP is essentially a written process, but in exceptional circumstances, when the competent court considers it would not be possible to reach a judgment based on paper submissions, it may require an oral hearing, which must be conducted by the distance means of communications available to the court. It must be noted that even while the original Regulation encouraged the use of electronic communications

[80] Deloitte Report, n. 66, p. x. [81] Art. 13 of the ESCP. [82] Impact Assessment p. 3.
[83] Ibid. [84] Art. 15(1a) ESCP as amended.

for the oral hearing,[85] the majority of the hearings still required the presence of the parties, witnesses and experts. According to the Commission, travel costs to attend an oral hearing (which are often non-recoverable) were between €400 and €800, which discouraged low-value claims as the costs for these claims would be disproportionate.

Consequently, the amended Regulation allows national courts, whenever the applicable law of civil procedure permits it, to gather written evidence *ex officio* in order to avoid holding a hearing. However, parties retain their right to appear in court if they decide to do so.[86] This is in line with the interpretation of the right to a fair trial (article 6 of the European Convention of Human Rights and article 47 of the EU Charter of Fundamental Rights), which requires that access to a hearing should be incorporated at least at an appeal or review route. Furthermore, the decision to grant or refuse a request for an oral hearing will remain. If a person to be heard is domiciled or habitually resident abroad, the court will have to hear that person by distance communication technology (e.g. video- or teleconference) when such technology is available at the court, unless the use of such technology would not be appropriate for the fair conduct of proceedings. Thus, Member States will not be legally obliged to ensure that courts are actually equipped with such technology due to concerns over the financial aspects of installing such technology. Nevertheless, Member States are strongly encouraged to install appropriate devices, and the amended Regulation presumes that, as a rule, courts will have access to video-conferencing technology.

Extension of the Information Obligations

The 2007 ESCP Regulation already required Member States to provide information on a number of issues, such as the competent courts, valid means of communications, the possibility of appeals, the accepted languages for the enforcement, the competent enforcement authorities and the availability of practical assistance to litigants for filling in the forms;[87] though in practice the latter information was not often available. The Commission reported that 41 per cent of Member States do not provide such assistance to the parties.

[85] Arts. 8 and 9.1. Cf. F. Gascón Inchausti, 'Algunas Reflexiones Acerca de la Oralidad y la Prueba en el Proceso de Escasa Cuantía' (2006) VI *Anuario Español de Derecho Internacional Privado* 285–308, 307 (noting that the restrictions of oral hearings may lead to unfair judgments).

[86] Art. 8(2). [87] Arts. 11 and 25 ESCP.

The amended Regulation extends the information obligations in respect of court fees, methods of payment of court fees and the availability of assistance in filling in the forms. It also requires Member States on one hand to provide practical assistance in filling in the standard forms provided for the ESCP, and on the other hand general information on the scope of the ESCP and the competent courts – the latter can be provided in brochures, handbooks, national websites or the European e-Justice Portal, or by reference to appropriate organizations, such as the ECC-Net.

It remains unclear whether a party who has to submit the claim or a defence in another jurisdiction would be able to obtain this assistance in their local court. Moreover, there are no information obligations regarding the enforcement process, which is subject to national law. Although nothing in the amended Regulation impedes this assistance, it is regrettable that the amended text did not spell out the extension of these obligations to assist individuals who have to submit a claim or a defence, or are seeking enforcement in another Member State.

Member States are however not obliged to provide for legal aid in addition to what is provided by the Legal Aid Directive,[88] or assess specific cases, but are required only to provide general information to citizens. Under the amended text, parties are entitled to free assistance in filling in the forms and general information about the procedure, but Member States are not required to provide for legal aid or for legal assistance in the form of a legal assessment of cases, notwithstanding the generally applicable rules of national law implementing the Legal Aid Directive.

Challenges in the Enforcement Process

Judgments from an ESCP are enforceable in any Member State (with the exception of Denmark)[89] without the need of going through the formal mutual recognition procedure for judgments.[90] When a judgment is served on a defendant based in another Member State other than that of the court seized, the service must be done in a language that the defendant understands or in the language of the Member State where

[88] Council Directive 2002/8/EC of 27 January 2003 to improve access to justice in cross-border disputes by establishing minimum common rules relating to legal aid for such disputes (OJ L 26, 31.1.2003, pp. 41–47).

[89] Art. 2(3) ESCP. [90] Art. 18 ESCP.

the service is affected.[91] Hence, a translation is often required for an effective service. Accordingly, a party who seeks to enforce a judgment will need to produce an original copy of the judgment and a certificate contained in Form D – the amended Regulation limits the translation requirement to Section 4.3 of the form, which contains the substance of the judgment.[92] Similarly, a court settlement approved or concluded before a court in the course of the ESCP shall be recognizable and enforceable under the same conditions as an ESCP judgment.[93] These are welcome amendments as they would cut down on the costs of those seeking the enforcement.

The enforcement is subject to the national procedure – in other words, national court orders will be enforced in the same manner as those coming from other Member States.[94] A key issue in the enforcement stage is finding the appropriate court in the enforcing Member State. For example, Irish courts refer consumers who seek to enforce an order in their favour outside Ireland to the Irish ECC, which assists claimants through their ECC partners to identify the enforcement authorities in the country where the respondent is based.[95]

Research findings on the effectiveness of the enforcement of the ESCP seem to be very contradictory. The study carried out by Deloitte for the Commission found that there were no difficulties in the enforcement of judgments, with 97 per cent of judgments enforced (23 per cent of respondents said that the defendants complied voluntarily while 74 per cent obtained a successful enforcement order).[96] This information led the Deloitte Report to state that there were no difficulties with the enforcement,[97] and consequently, the Commission did not take measures to tackle this problem. However, the Deloitte study also stated that in more than four out of ten cases (42 per cent) the case was still ongoing, without clarifying for how long these cases have been opened. A key element would be to assess which percentage of these cases was in the enforcement stage and who the parties were. Indeed, the argument for lack of obstacles in the enforcement contrasts with the ECC-Net Report, which stated that 'a much bigger problem than the lack of awareness and other issues described before is the question concerning the enforcement of

[91] Regulation (EC) 1393/2007 on the Service in the Member States of Judicial and Non-Judicial Documents in Civil or Commercial Matters.
[92] Art. 26 ESCP. [93] Art. 23a ESCP as amended. [94] Art. 21(1) ESCP.
[95] ECC-Net, European Small Claims Procedure Report (September 2012) p. 27.
[96] Eurobarometer 395, p. 35. [97] Deloitte Report, n. 66, p. 65.

judgments'.[98] This is because the difficulty with the enforcement mainly arises when it is the consumer who uses the ESCP in his or her country of residence and then needs to enforce the judgment in a different Member State.[99] The enforcement stage will often be in a different language and subject to a foreign national procedure.

Empirical research should distinguish between those applicants who find out about the process of enforcement (when, for instance, the enforcement takes place in the same jurisdiction of the court which issued the judgment, or when the applicant has hired a lawyer) to those cases where applicants do not seek enforcement because of the lack of information and resources. Accordingly, the first group is unlikely to face difficulties in the enforcement, but those in the consumer sector will inevitably find greater difficulties. It is difficult to prove this empirically, but one could reasonably suspect that the reported lack of problems in the enforcement is because consumers do not use the ESCP.

Practical measures to facilitate the enforcement would be if consumer applicants have the support from the ECC-Net (which normal remit excludes support in judicial processes) as they do in Ireland; if the enforcement procedure is accessible through distance means of communications; and if applicants can contact lawyers who can assist them with the enforcement process – a good tool for this task would be the database 'Find a Lawyer', which is offered by the e-Justice Portal in most EU Member States.[100]

The obstacles in the enforcement process have been recently noted by LJ Briggs in a recent landmark report that reviews the structure of the civil courts in England and Wales.[101] The report, which was discussed in the previous chapter, proposes an online court for small claims and calls for the centralization, automation and digital access to the enforcement process. LJ Briggs summarized his findings as follows:

> I am advised that many litigants experience problems in completing the forms that underpin modes of enforcement. Inter-active online forms can

[98] ECC-Net, 'European Small Claims Procedure Report' (2012) p. 22.

[99] Research found that only a minority of ESCP judgments made in the consumer's jurisdictions in the UK are enforced in a different Member State. See A. Bradney and F. Cownie, 'Access to Justice?: The European Small Claims Procedure in the United Kingdom' in N. Neuwahl and S. Hammamoun (eds.) *The European Small Claims Procedure and the Philosophy of Small Change* (Les Éditions Thémis, 2014) p. 118.

[100] See https://e-justice.europa.eu/content_find_a_lawyer-334-en.do,

[101] L.J. Briggs, 'Civil Courts Structure Review: Interim Report (December 2015). Available at www.judiciary.gov.uk/wp-content/uploads/2016/01/ccsr-interim-report-dec-15-final1.pdf.

> assist the parties through preventing errors in its completion. Work has already been undertaken in this respect in the field of Accelerated Possession and has proved successful.
>
> Significant judicial time is spent on checking these forms and granting interim orders. Digitisation renders this work more administrative and . . . It may even prove suitable for a measure of automation, where routine checking is done by computer.[102]

Furthermore, the report observes that in most cases an enforcement process simply requires the 'routine completion and checking of forms, rather than the making of judicial decisions involving legal principle or discretion, [and] that there is much that ought to be able to be done to streamline them'.[103] The report acknowledges that there are cases where the ownership of the debtor's assets or bank accounts affects the interests of third parties. Although these cases may require judicial determination, such issues are always separate from the issues in the original proceedings, so they can be decided by a centralized body. Consequently, Briggs argued that there are 'real advantages in creating an enforcement platform for the enforcement of all civil judgments'.[104]

Although it might be still too early to launch a pan-European platform for the enforcement of cross-border judgments, it would be beneficial to identify the existing processes and best practices across the EU. The European Commission could then issue a Green Paper followed by a Recommendation on the collected best practices and in due course a Regulation enabling an online single point of entry for enforcing cross-border claims through the e-Justice portal, which in turn should provide seamless connection with national platforms.

3.4 A Model of Cooperation between the Alternative Dispute Resolution and the Courts

It has already been noted that access to justice can be achieved not only via the courts, but also through extrajudicial schemes, especially in the consumer context as these processes can often offer the most appropriate option to resolve consumer disputes of low value. Insofar that ODR provides a redress option where there was none before it contributes to a better compliance with consumer law. In a similar vein Hodges argues that

[102] Ibid., p. 115. [103] Ibid., p. 114. [104] Ibid., p. 116.

> both small claims mechanisms and aggregation of individual claims in collective actions can now be seen as disappointingly empty mechanisms that consumers do not find attractive because they do not satisfy the criteria of user-friendliness, speed, low cost, and effective outcomes.[105]

By contrast out-of-court options can meet these criteria. The European Commission acknowledges that there is a need to complement court access to justice with more effective and informal out-of-court redress options.[106] Accordingly, the Commission has even recognized its commitment to see the courts as the last resort and to promote settlements when this is possible.[107] Although, as noted earlier, the Commission Recommendation on collective redress encouraged the use of ADR pre-action and during the court process, neither the ESCP nor the ADR Directive and the ODR Regulation[108] have articulated channels to complement these judicial and extrajudicial redress options. This section attempts to identify pathways of collaboration between ADR/ODR and the courts (using the ESCP as an example) with the goal of assisting in the design of a strategy that delivers a more holistic approach to access to justice and consumer redress.

3.4.1 Procedural Requirement to Consider the Suitability of Pre-Action ADR/ODR

It is important for consumer disputes to be channelled through the most appropriate redress process, which should typically be the most cost-effective of those available to the parties. If this line of argument is to be followed, then it would be desirable for the ESCP and other court processes to encourage more clearly the use of ADR/ODR. Although there is limited empirical research comparing the small claims processes with extrajudicial or ADR options, it appears that the latter, when

105 Hodges, n. 74, p. 248.

106 European Commission Staff Working Paper, Impact Assessment Accompanying the document of the Proposal for a Directive on Alternative Dispute Resolution for Consumer Disputes and the Proposal for a Regulation on Online Dispute Resolution for Consumer Disputes SEC(2011) 1408 final.

107 Viviane Reding, Vice-President of the European Commission and EU Commissioner for Justice 'Towards a More Coherent Enforcement of EU Consumer Rules' (19 March 2013). Available at http://europa.eu/rapid/press-release_SPEECH-13-237_en.htm.

108 Directive 2013/11/EU on Consumer Alternative Dispute Resolution OJ L165/63 and Regulation (EC) 524/2013 on Consumer Online Dispute Resolution OJ L165/1.

available, is a more informal and cost-effective option that offers a higher degree of satisfaction amongst its users.[109]

Courts should have jurisdiction in two instances: first, when at least one litigant chooses the judicial forum, but courts should clearly discourage straightforward cases that could be resolved by an extrajudicial body, especially in consumer cases where there are certified ADR/ODR bodies; second, where there are reasons that make the courts the first forum for the resolution of a claim – for example when there is a matter of public interest, a need to clarify the law or any other reasonable justification.[110]

Judicial and ADR options (saved for arbitration) are often not mutually exclusive, but they complement each other. Consequently, courts should be seen as a dispute resolution forum of last resort, performing a supervisory function rather than the default redress option for most consumer disputes. Some countries, such as the UK, expect their litigants to explore more informal and cost-efficient redress options before embarking on a judicial process, and thus settle more efficiently those claims that are ripe for early resolution. Other national procedural laws should be amended to require parties to consider extrajudicial options before submitting and responding to a claim. The same is recommended for national and cross-border cases. Yet, courts should encourage, not compel (at least for the time being), parties to attempt out-of-court options where this is available.

It is regrettable thus that the recent amendment of the Regulation did not include a provision ensuring that parties are well-informed and able to identify the most suitable method to resolve their disputes. However, the amended Regulation granted the European Parliament with the power to amend the standard forms (prior consultation with the Council) using the delegated legislation procedure. It is submitted that the European Parliament should consider changing the claim and response forms in order to require litigants to consider the suitability of extrajudicial options for resolving their disputes. Hence, claimants should be asked in the Claim Form A whether an extrajudicial scheme was attempted, and if it was not attempted, the next question should ask whether they would like to try it if this is available as part of a court-annexed programme. Respondents should be asked the same questions,

[109] DG Justice and Consumers, European Commission, Consumer Conditions Scoreboard (2015) p. 47.

[110] Hodges et al., n. 11, p. 452.

and in the event that both parties agree to it, then an out-of-court settlement should be attempted.

3.4.2 *Court-Annexed ADR during the Litigation*

Currently, the only reference to ADR is made in ESCP Regulation, which simply states: 'Whenever appropriate, the court or tribunal shall seek to reach a settlement between the parties.'[111] There is no evidence of national courts using this option unless a court-annex programme is used. Furthermore, the ADR Directive has left out any connections between the courts and ADR – this may be in part due to its legal basis, which does not fall within the pillar of judicial cooperation.[112] The only meaningful cooperation between the ADR and judicial processes is implied in the ODR Regulation, which states that when a consumer complaint submitted to the EU ODR platform cannot be resolved through an ADR entity, then a national contact point may inform about 'other means of redress',[113] which for low- and medium-value claims could only be the national small claims procedure, and for cross-border claims would be the ESCP.

The use of extrajudicial processes should be offered to the parties not only at the time of submitting their claim and response, but also during the court process. Litigants should be able to request the court to stay proceedings for a short period of time (e.g. up to 30 days) while they attempt to settle their case.

In addition, courts should be able to recommend parties to attempt ADR when they consider that it may be beneficial for them, especially if these ADR processes are inexpensive, quick and can be carried out by distance means of communication.[114] In consumer disputes, courts can let the parties choose, or in case of disagreement appoint a nationally

[111] Article 12(3).

[112] The ADR Directive is based on Arts. 114 and 169 TFEU, and not Article 81 TFEU. See generally G. Rühl, 'Alternative and Online Dispute Resolution for (Cross-Border) Consumer Contracts: A Critical Evaluation of the European Legislature's Recent Efforts to Promote Competitiveness and Growth in the Internal Market' (2015) 38 *J Consum Policy* 38–456.

[113] Article 7(2)(a)(v) ODR Regulation.

[114] In this regard the CJEU held that judicial protection was secured as long as electronic means are not the only means of accessing a settlement procedure for those parties without access to those means. *Rosalba Alassini* v. *Italia Telecom SpA* (C-317/08) para. 60.

certified ADR entity. This approach follows the line of the Mediation Directive and the EC Recommendation on Collective Redress as both recommend parties to attempt mediation and other extrajudicial processes before and during the judicial process. The Mediation Directive empowers judges to recommend mediation during the judicial process,[115] though this power is rarely used in practice unless a court-annexed ADR/ODR scheme has been set up.

Furthermore, in compliance with the European principles of equivalence and effectiveness, the offer of court-annexed ADR schemes should be extended to cross-border procedures, such as the ESCP, when these schemes are available for domestic disputes, e.g. the one-hour free telephone mediation in England or the conciliation stage of the online court,[116] or the registrar's informal facilitation in Ireland.[117] When settlements cannot be reached, cases should automatically return to the competent judge.

In order to deal effectively with cross-border claims, these extrajudicial processes should be offered by specialized third parties (i.e. facilitators) that in addition to their own national languages can also offer their services in English or in another major EU language. These facilitators should rely on the use of distance means of communications, such as the use of telephone and online case management tools complemented by translation software. If adequate resources were allocated, national European Consumer Centres would be able to carry out this role of facilitators for settling consumer disputes. Similarly, cross-border disputes falling within the scope of other EU wide networks, such as FIN-Net for financial matters and SOLVIT for the incorrect application of European Law by public bodies, could support the provision of such an out-of-court scheme, which would necessarily need to be coordinated on a pan-European basis, and presumably through the e-Justice portal.

3.4.3 Cost Incentives

When out-of-court processes are not mandatory, parties should be economically incentivized to consider ADR/ODR in favour of the alternative, more expensive and formal judicial adjudication. Cost incentives may help to achieve this objective in consumer disputes, especially when

115 Art. 5(1).
116 Lord Justice Briggs, 'Civil Courts Structure Review' Final Report (July 2016).
117 Cortés, n. 51, pp. 272–273.

a business has unreasonably refused to participate in an available ADR entity. These incentives could be allocated at the start of a court procedure or at the end when allocating the legal costs.

First, national laws could impose court fees on business defendants who refused to participate in ADR without a valid justification. The fee may be refundable in the event of succeeding in the defence or when there is a valid justification for refusing to resolve a consumer claim through ADR. Secondly, a business refusal to participate in ADR should be taken into account over the decision on who is responsible for costs during the court action. Thus, a further financial penalty should be imposed to a business when the court has considered that a business has behaved unreasonably in rejecting a suitable offer to settle or to participate in an ADR process.[118] These sanctions should be proportionate and only imposed when the business did not have a justifiable reason for preferring the judicial forum (e.g. there is a need to clarify a point of law or set up an enforceable precedent).[119]

3.4.4 *Referral from ADR to the Courts*

There should be four types of referrals from ADR bodies to the courts: when traders refuse to participate or settle a claim, when there is evidence of certain crimes, when there is a point of law that needs to be clarified, and when enforcement is necessary.

When Traders Do Not Settle a Claim

Consumers with cross-border disputes can now invite traders to participate in an out-of-court process through a request sent via the EU ODR platform. Accordingly, the platform can be instrumental in increasing consumers' access to justice as it could divert those consumers with cross-border disputes that could not have been resolved through ADR processes to the competent national courts. The EU ODR platform should incorporate a plug-in to e-Codex,[120] which is a pilot that currently enables litigants and the courts to communicate through electronic

[118] P. Cortés, 'A Comparative Review of Offers to Settle – Would an Emerging Settlement Culture Pave the Way for their Adoption in Continental Europe? (2013) 32(1) *Civil Justice Q* 42–67.

[119] See F. Sander and S. Goldberg, 'Fitting the Forum to the Fuss: A User-Friendly Guide to Selecting an ADR Procedure' (1994) 10(1) *Negot J* 49–68, 54.

[120] For more information on e-Codex and the pilot project for the ESCP, see www.e-codex.eu/pilots/small-claims.html.

means using the e-Justice Portal. In order for parties to use it, they will need to identify themselves with either an electronic signature or another electronic ID. Once the competent court receives the claim, it serves the respondent normally via regular post, but it is a question of time before electronic service becomes mainstream.

Furthermore, the EU ODR platform could be helpful in raising awareness about ongoing collective actions as well as on small claims processes that are not often used by consumers. Last, but not least, a central online platform, such as that developed by e-Codex, could be a very useful instrument for the public authorities to monitor the types of cases that go to the courts. This information, if adequately captured, would be useful to the European Commission when developing legal responses to improve trade in the Internal Market. Monitoring frequent disputes will help to identify patterns upon which to build regulatory and practical responses that can lead to avoiding the arrival of new disputes. This strategy will be more effective than resolving disputes as isolated events.

Evidence of Criminal Offences

Out-of-court schemes are normally bound by confidentiality of their processes, but these have some limits when there are public policy considerations. The Mediation Directive states that confidentiality in a mediation process can only be waived to seek the implementation of the settlement and 'where this is necessary for overriding considerations of public policy of the Member State concerned, in particular when required to ensure the protection of the best interests of children or to prevent harm to the physical or psychological integrity of a person'.[121] The public policy consideration frequently means that mediators are required to keep the discussions during the mediation confidential, except when there are matters affecting the safeguard of the children, and when there is evidence of money laundering. Importantly, information about any other crime, no matter how hideous, is protected by the privileged discussions, in the same manner as would be about crimes heard over confession to a Catholic priest.

In the consumer context, other issues, such as fraud or serious allegations of environmental or health damage may arise – for instance, a claim of car clocking (i.e. reducing the mileage that a vehicles marks on its

121 See in article 7(1) (a). Also Article 7(2) states that 'nothing in paragraph 1 shall preclude Member States from enacting stricter measures to protect the confidentiality of mediation'.

odometer). Private ADR providers are unlikely to report these types of breach. A different scenario may occur with public ADR schemes,[122] because statutory bodies have closer ties with regulators and public enforcement bodies, which could in turn carry out an investigation if there are concerns about the infringements of consumer law. Policy makers and ADR associations should review and clarify under which circumstances the confidentiality issue should be set aside requiring ADR bodies to report crimes to the relevant public authorities.

When a Point of Law Needs to Be Considered

A drawback in processing claims through ADR processes is that it could undermine the constitutional role of the courts in assisting in the development and clarification of the law.[123] Indeed, the role of ADR should not be to clarify legal points, but to resolve complaints by applying 'established law to factual disputes'.[124] Hodges et al. argue that courts should refer cases to consumer ADR if 'it involves application of fixed law and it is proportionate for a CADR body to process it. This will usually be the case in mass cases'.[125]

Referrals could also be sent to the regulator. Currently when there is an important point of law to be clarified, a business and the ADR body (or the public enforcement body or the regulator) may agree to take the case to court.[126] As already mentioned, the Financial Ombudsman Service in the UK has referred test cases to the courts. Similarly, there has been for instance an agreement between banks and the Office of Fair Trading (OFT) to seek clarification in court on the unfair terms regulation.[127] In a similar vein, more recently, parties agreed to take the case to court pro-bono and without claiming for legal costs in order to clarify the legality of parking fines on whether these amounted to illegal penalty clauses.[128]

Indeed, the role of courts would be more relevant if national procedural law enables ADR entities to refer test cases to designated national courts in the form of preliminary references in order to clarify statutory interpretation when necessary and assure greater consistency in the

[122] A certified ADR entity carries out public functions. In the UK for instance there are a number of private ombudsman that carry out statutory roles in various sectors, such as energy and financial services.

[123] H. Genn, *The Hamlyn Lectures 2008: Judging Civil Justice* (CUP, 2010).

[124] Hodges et al., n. 48, p. 453. [125] Ibid. [126] Ibid., p. 279.

[127] *Office of Fair Trade (Respondent)* v. *Abbey National plc & Others (Appellants)* [2009] UKSC 6.

[128] *ParkingEye Ltd (Respondent)* v. *Beavis (Appellant)* [2015] UKSC 67.

decision making. However, in order to avoid ADR from referring too many questions to national courts, it would be possible to follow the example of the Court of Justice of the EU (CJEU) and declare that a particular point of law is already clear or has already been resolved – this is what the CJEU terms as *acte clair* and *acté eclairé*.[129] Moreover, a national court could in turn elevate this consultation to the CJEU.

Fast-Track Enforcement

Finally, courts can carry out an important role as a stopper for those cases in which the trader refuses to comply with the outcome of an ADR decision. Hence, after a period of time, such as a month, where the trader has not complied with a final decision or settlement, the ADR entity should refer the case automatically to either the court or the enforcement body. The mere existence of such a fast-track system to facilitate the enforcement would speed up compliance with outcomes.[130] The collaboration between courts and extrajudicial bodies in the enforcement of outcomes is further developed in Chapter 8.

3.4.5 Appeals and Reviews of ADR Decisions

In appropriate cases, national courts should consider appeals and reviews from ADR/ODR bodies, but there should be a suitable filter that balances access to justice with proportionate costs in redress. This is because most consumer disputes are of low value, so by their nature would be disproportionate to allow appeals from extrajudicial decisions.[131] That said, as noted earlier, there are cases where a court decision would be necessary to set a precedent as well as in order to allow compliance with the right to fair trial contained in articles 6 European Convention of Human Rights (ECHR) and 47 of the Charter of Fundamental Rights of the European Union.[132] The right to a fair trial must be considered in conjunction to the right to an effective remedy (Art. 13 ECHR). The right

[129] On this point see M. Loos, 'Consumer ADR after the Implementation of the ADR Directive: Enforcing European Consumer Rights at the Detriment of European Consumer Law' Amsterdam Law School Legal Studies Research Paper No. 2015–42, pp. 13–14.

[130] Hodges et al., n. 48, pp. 252 and 452. [131] Ibid., p. 452.

[132] See the Irish experience with Financial Service Ombudsman (*Ulster Bank Investment Funds Ltd* v. *FSO* [2006] IEHC 323 and *Molloy* v. *FSO* [2010] IEHC 182.

to a fair trial embraces the use of appropriate redress[133] and expeditious justice.[134] It even allows the States to make the use of ADR mandatory before resorting to the courts as long as these court restrictions are considered to be legitimate and proportionate under article 6 as the European Court of Human Rights found in favour of decisions made by administrative authorities.[135] Its only requirement is the subsequent control by a judicial body.[136]

Naturally, the rights to access to court under article 6 can be waived by the parties, provided that the waiver is unequivocal, there is no constraint and it is 'attended by minimum safeguards commensurate to its importance', including impartiality of the neutral third party.[137] In practice, consumers can decide whether or not to use ADR, and often in mediation or ombudsman processes consumers can choose whether or not to accept a final decision, but traders may be compelled to accept an outcome agreed by the consumer in an ombudsman process. By contrast, if consumers refuse a recommendation, then they can still pursue the matter in court – though in practice they rarely do so.[138]

In the UK and Ireland, save for a few exceptions, such as the Pension Ombudsman,[139] the Scottish Legal Complaints Commission[140] and the Irish Financial Service Ombudsman,[141] which allow appeals processes in the High Court, the rest of statutory ADR bodies only allow judicial reviews. These reviews typically consider the facts of ADR decisions as

[133] Council of Europe Committee on Equality and Non-Discrimination 'Equality and Non-Discrimination in the Access to Justice' Report Doc 13740, Rapporteur: Mr V. Riceard Badea (31 March 2015) para. 10.

[134] Council of Europe Committee on Legal Affairs and Human Rights 'Access to Justice through Online Instruments' Draft Report, Rapporteur: Mr J. Xucla (2 November 2015) para. 13.

[135] ECtHR, *Le Compte, Van Leuven and De Meyere* v. *Belgium* Appl. no. 6878/75 and 7238/75, Judgment of 23 June 1981, para. 51. See also the view of the Court of Justice of the EU in the joined Cases C-317/08 to C-320/08, *Rosalba Alassini and Others* v. *Telecom Italia SpA and Others* (18 March 2010).

[136] ECtHR, *Zumtobel* v. *Austria*, Appl. no. 12235/86, Judgment of 21 September 1993, para. 29–32.

[137] Ibid., pp. 617–618. ECtHR, *Osmo Suovaniemi and others* v. *Finland*, Appl. no. 31737/96, Judgment of 23 February 1999 and ECtHR, *Pfeifer and Plankl* v. *Autria*, Appl. no. 10802/84, Judgment of 25 February 1992.

[138] See the restrictions to appeal OS decisions at www.ombudsman-services.org/resolving-complaints.html.

[139] www.pensions-ombudsman.org.uk/guidance/appealing-a-determination/.

[140] www.scottishlegalcomplaints.org.uk/making-a-complaint/unhappy-with-a-decision.aspx.

[141] www.financialombudsman.ie/faq/findings.asp.

proven, and only consider (i) whether the application of the law was manifestly inadequate, (ii) where there is no evidence to support a particular finding or when in the light of the evidence the finding appears to be unreasonable and (iii) whether there was a clear breach of the procedural rights of one of the parties. Thus, national courts play a role in ensuring that ADR bodies apply the consumer law correctly and maintain adequate procedural standards.[142]

A more permissive approach has been adopted by the Canadian Civil Resolution Tribunal,[143] whereby a party who objects to a decision of the tribunal will be able to ask a court to hear the matter within 30 days, which will examine the case *de novo*, though applicants have to pay the deposit equivalent to the amount awarded by the tribunal. A similar system is that used by the dispute resolution process used for domain names. A trademark owner can submit a claim for cybersquatting against a domain name holder whose register domain name is breaching the trademark. Parties are free to choose the courts to resolve these issues, but almost never do so because the out-of-court process is a much more cost-effective forum to resolve these cases. What it is important to note is that respondents (i.e. domain name holders) are forced to participate in the process unless they take the case to court. Under this procedure parties can also challenge the outcome in court, which will examine the case *de novo*, but again, given the high costs of litigation, they rarely do so.

3.5 Conclusion

The European Commission believes that a more integrated civil justice system will deliver a more effective internal market, noting that 'the current redress systems have their strengths and weaknesses and no single mechanism is ideal for all types of claims'.[144] In this vein, the European Commission has begun shifting its policy, at least in the consumer context, by moving their efforts from promoting court redress to encouraging also out-of-court options. This chapter argues that there should be more interconnection between these two seminal redress options, leaving the judicial avenue as the last resort for consumer

142 H. Edwards, 'Alternative Dispute Resolution: Panacea or Anathema?' (1985) 99 *Harv Law Rev* 668, at 671 (referring more generally to the supervisory role that courts have over ADR schemes).

143 See ss. 54–56 of the Civil Resolution Tribunal Act 2012.

144 European Commission, MEMO/08/741 (27 November 2008) p. 3.

matters, only used when out-of-court options are unavailable or inadequate. This approach would clearly favour a preference for voluntary settlement, either through a court-annexed scheme or as a filter before claims are filed in court.

Whether judicial or not, new forms of dispute resolution methods are enriching the toolbox of the Law of Consumer Redress, which is increasingly characterized by being more accessible and supported by technological means. Amongst judicial processes, this chapter has examined the European developments in collective redress, especially the Commission Recommendation, and the recent amendment of the ESCP, and it noted that consumers rarely use these judicial redress tools. It is argued that for the ESCP to become a more effective redress tool, it needs to be more user-friendly, consumers need greater guidance, it needs to be truly accessible online and it should integrate mechanisms that facilitate the enforcement of judgments in a Member State different to where the consumer is residing.

This chapter has argued that judicial processes will benefit from collaborating with ADR processes. Accordingly, this chapter proposed the following types of interactions between extrajudicial fora and national courts. First, national laws should change their procedural laws to require parties to consider out-of-court options before submitting and responding to a claim. Similarly, the European Parliament should amend the ESCP standard claim and response forms requiring parties to explain the previous efforts to settle claims and their willingness to participate in out-of-court schemes. Second, parties should be offered to participate in court-annexed ADR during the litigation process when these schemes are available (and they should also be extended to cross-border processes with the support of pan-European organizations). Third, the design of judicial processes should use economic incentives as a leverage to encourage settlements and the participation in ADR processes when appropriate. Fourth, ADR and ODR bodies should refer cases to a competent court when a trader refuses to participate or settle in an ADR process, when there is manifest evidence of certain criminal offences or there are other public policy concerns, when a point of law needs to be clarified, and when there is a need to enforce an outcome or decision. Lastly, appeals and reviews of ADR decisions should be allowed, though not encouraged, thus ensuring that extrajudicial bodies apply their legal standards correctly.

4

Out-of-Court Consumer Redress

The European Law on ADR and the Re-design of the ODR Platform

4.1 Introduction

The previous chapters observed that Alternative Dispute Resolution (ADR) methods, when coupled with online communications, seem to offer normally the most suitable approach for resolving consumer grievances arising from e-commerce. These techniques (notably, automated and assisted negotiation, online mediation, online arbitration, as well as online ombudsmen bodies) provide a more efficient communication between disputants, and are collectively known as Online Dispute Resolution (ODR).

Although it is believed that ODR is generally the best, and frequently the only, option for increasing individual consumer redress,[1] the European Commission noted that its full potential has not yet been realized as its growth lags behind e-commerce.[2] In 2013 the Commission stated that only 4 per cent of European consumers had used an ADR body in the past, while around a quarter of European consumers had experienced a dispute in the previous year.[3] The European Commission found that there are various factors that can stimulate online purchases across borders. According to a recent study by the Commission, improving

[1] See OECD Conference on Empowering E-consumers Strengthening Consumer Protection in the Internet Economy, Background Report DSTI/CP(2009)20/FINAL, Washington DC, (8–10 December 2009) p. 29. European Commission, EU Consumer Policy Strategy 2007–2013, COM(2007) 99 final p.11.

[2] European Commission Staff Working Paper, Impact Assessment Accompanying the Document of the Proposal for a Directive on Alternative Dispute Resolution for Consumer Disputes and the Proposal for a Regulation on Online Dispute Resolution for Consumer Disputes SEC(2011) 1408 final p. 5.

[3] Duch-Brown and Martens, 'Barriers to Firms' Cross-Border E-commerce in the EU Digital Single Market', JRC/IPTS Digital Economy Working Paper (2015). See also European Commission Staff Working Document, 'A Digital Single Market Strategy for Europe – Analysis and Evidence' SWD(2015) 100 final.

security of payments can increase the number of sales by 5 per cent; a similar increase would result out of improving language skills; furthermore, lowering the costs of resolving disputes would increase online purchases by 12 per cent.[4] Hence, the European Commission has the firm belief that effective redress mechanisms is necessary to boost competition and growth in e-commerce, which is expected to play a key role in increasing economic growth in the Internal Market.[5] However, as noted in previous chapters, public enforcement and judicial options are, on their own, insufficient to provide most consumers with redress.[6] Conversely, extrajudicial avenues, such as ADR and ODR, can provide consumers with more effective redress options.

Yet, unlike public enforcement and judicial processes, consumer ADR has been largely unregulated. This situation is now changing in the EU, where the ADR Directive and the ODR Regulation have triggered the regulation,[7] and thus the institutionalization and professionalization, of what is increasingly becoming the main avenue of consumer redress. It is thus submitted that this new regulatory framework on consumer ADR forms the main pillar of what this book refers to as the Law of Consumer Redress.

The European Commission stated that the new regulation seeks to tackle three main deficiencies in the provision of extrajudicial redress in the EU:[8] (i) the absence of quality standards;[9] (ii) the low levels of

[4] Ibid., p. 9. [5] See Impact Assessment, n. 2, p. 5.

[6] S. Weatherill, *EU Consumer Law and Policy* (Edward Elgar, 2014) p. 296.

[7] Directive 2013/11/EU of the European Parliament and of the Council of 21 May 2013 on alternative dispute resolution for consumer disputes and amending Regulation (EC) No 2006/2004 and Directive 2009/22/EC, [2013] OJ L165/63 and Regulation (EU) No 524/2013 of the European Parliament and of the Council of 21 May 2013 on online dispute resolution for consumer disputes and amending Regulation (EC) No 2006/2004 and Directive 2009/22/EC, [2013] OJ L165/1.

[8] Communication on Alternative Dispute Resolution for Consumer Disputes in the Single Market COM(2011) 791; Civic Consulting, European Parliament Study Cross-Border Alternative Dispute Resolution in the EU (2011) pp. 9, 31 and 49; ECC-Net Cross-Border Dispute Resolution Mechanisms in Europe-Practical Reflections on the Need and Availability (2009) p. 57.

[9] This situation has been criticized extensively noting that soft laws, such as the EU Recommendations on ADR, were insufficient to ensure minimum quality standards for ADR entities. See Commission Recommendation 98/257/EC of 30 March 1998 on the Principles Applicable to the Bodies Responsible for Out-of-Court Settlement of Consumer Disputes (O.J. 1998, L 115); Commission Recommendation 2001/310/EC of 4 April 2001 on the Principles for the Out-of-Court Bodies Involved in the Consensual Resolution of Consumer Disputes ([2001] OJ L109/56). See Impact Assessment, n. 2.

consumer awareness on ADR schemes[10] and (iii) the availability of ADR in all sectors for the resolution of consumer complaints. The ODR Regulation sets an online platform that operates as a single entry point for resolving consumer complaints arising out of e-commerce. The ODR platform links disputing parties with nationally certified ADR schemes, which the legislation refers to as ADR entities. It must be noted that the basis for this legislation was article 114 TFEU. Furthermore, the proposals came from the formerly known as the Directorate General for Health and Food Safety (DG SANCO),[11] which demonstrates that the main goal behind this legislation was to strengthen the Internal Market. Although it can be argued that access to justice was also an important goal, the fact that DG JUST was not the department in charge of these initiatives illustrates how the priority was to stimulate the Internal Market, while increasing access to justice was seen as a secondary aim.

This chapter analyses the European regulatory framework for consumer ADR and the practical implications of the new regulatory regime, especially from the standpoint of digital consumers engaging in e-commerce. Accordingly, it critically examines the ADR Directive and ODR Regulation,[12] and it proposes a number of functions in the design of the European ODR platform with the aim of meeting the goal of increasing consumer trust in the Internal Market by increasing their access to effective redress.

[10] ADR national entities are more widely set up to resolve disputes in the fields of financial services, package travel and telecommunications. Identified gaps, where ADR is particularly inaccessible, include games of chance, food products, non-food consumer goods, construction and transport. See Civic Consulting Study for DG SANCO, 'Study on the Use of Alternative Dispute Resolution in the EU' (2009) Figure 14, p. 59.

[11] Proposal for a Directive on alternative dispute resolution for consumer disputes (Directive on consumer ADR) COM(2011) 793 final and Proposal for a Regulation on online dispute resolution for consumer disputes (Regulation on consumer ODR) COM(2011) 794 final.

[12] An early version of this analysis appeared in P. Cortés, 'The New Landscape of Consumer Redress: The European Directive on Consumer Alternative Dispute Resolution and the Regulation on Online Dispute Resolution' in P. Cortés, *The European Framework for Consumer Dispute Resolution* (OUP, 2016) and in 'Directive 2013/11/EU on Alternative Dispute Resolution for Consumers and Regulation (EC) 524/2013 on Online Dispute Resolution' in A. Lodder, A Murray and T. Wisman (eds.)*Commentary on the EU Regulation of Electronic Commerce and Information*, 2nd edn (Edward Elgar, 2016).

4.2 New Legal Standards for Consumer Dispute Resolution Processes: The Directive on Consumer Alternative Dispute Resolution

The expansion of e-commerce is limited by the traditional, court-based channels for resolving disputes. These systems are unable to resolve high volumes of low-value claims, let alone for disputes where parties are far from each other. Both the EU and UN, with the goal of enhancing cross-border trade, have recently recognized the need to promote extrajudicial consumer redress by promoting the use of ODR mechanisms. However, while UNCITRAL, as discussed in Chapter 6, has developed procedural guidelines for ODR providers,[13] the EU has designed a legal framework aimed at improving the availability, coordination and accessibility of certified ADR/ODR schemes. The following section examines the central piece of the new legal framework: the ADR Directive.

4.2.1 Scope of Application: The Obligation of the Member States to Ensure the Provision of ADR

The ADR Directive imposes an obligation on the EU Member States to ensure the provision of nationally certified ADR entities, which are accessible online, for consumer complaints arising from the sale of goods and the provision of services.[14] Contracts for the sale of property and tenancy agreements fall outside the scope as these contracts are not legally viewed as being a good or a service. It applies to all contractual disputes, domestic and cross-border, where a trader is established in the EU and a consumer is a resident of a Member State.[15] The national ADR infrastructure must cover contractual disputes when traders are established in their respective territories,[16] which includes when trades have a place of business (i.e. a branch, agency or another establishment), statutory seat or central administration. Member States may meet this obligation by either ensuring that private or public certified ADR entities are available in every economic sector, or by setting at least one residual certified ADR entity that operates in all the sectors where there is not

[13] UNCITRAL Working Group III (Online Dispute Resolution). See www.uncitral.org/uncitral/commission/working_groups/3Online_Dispute_Resolution.html.
[14] Art. 2(2).
[15] Art. 2(1). The definitions of the terms 'consumer' and 'trader' are identical to those provided in Art. 2 of the Directive 2011/83/EU on consumer rights OJ L 304.
[16] Art. 5(1).

already a certified entity.[17] Furthermore, a Member State may fulfil this obligation by relying on ADR entities established in another Member State;[18] but if that ADR entity ceases to operate, it is the responsibility of that Member State to replace it. Similarly, traders established in one Member State can be covered by ADR entities established in another Member State,[19] which allows traders to engage in forum shopping.

The ADR Directive seeks to ensure that consumers and businesses have available options to resolve their disputes without having to go to court. Yet, importantly, the Directive does not make the use of ADR mandatory in any economic sector, nor does it affect the existing regulation that makes its use mandatory in some specific sectors.[20] Indeed, as long as the right to access to justice is preserved,[21] through an appellate or review process for example, Member States can make participation in an ADR process compulsory.[22] It is thus questionable whether the consumer arbitration scheme in Portugal, which is mandatory for businesses offering essential services,[23] is breaching the traders' right to access to justice.

The scope of the ADR Directive covers consumer (but not trader) complaints arising from contracts of sales and services, both offline and online, including statutory obligations (e.g. statutory guarantee) and the provision of digital content for remuneration. The restriction of only allowing consumers to act as complainants is based not only on the likelihood that traders are in a better position, as they normally have already received the payment from the consumer and can more easily obtain redress, but also a desire on the part of governments not to upset the present ADR structure that accounts for weaker parties acting as complainants. Indeed, a large number of ADR entities are publicly funded and designed to protect consumer rights and interests by addressing the inequality of bargaining power between consumers and traders.

This is a Directive that does not require full harmonization; on the contrary, it only contains a minimum harmonization clause. Accordingly, while the Directive does not prevent Member States from creating

[17] Art. 5(3). [18] Art. 5(3). [19] Recital 26.

[20] E.g. Directives 2009/72/EC and 2009/73/EC concerning Common Rules for the Internal Market in Electricity and Gas.

[21] Art. 1. [22] *Rosalba Alassini and Others* v. *Telecom Italia* C-317/08.

[23] C. Marques Cebola, 'The Implementation of the Consumer ADR Directive in Portugal: The Necessary Reform or Missed Opportunity?' in P. Cortés, *The New Regulatory Framework for Consumer Dispute Resolution* (OUP, 2016) pp. 251–272.

ADR entities with the competence to deal with complaints from traders against consumers, it does not require this.

Conversely, the ODR Regulation simply sets up the infrastructure (i.e. the ODR platform) to make ADR processes accessible online for resolving e-commerce disputes. The Regulation permits traders to bring complaints against consumers within the ODR platform insofar as the legislation of the Member State where the consumer is habitually resident allows for this possibility.[24] The extension to business-to-consumer cases has occurred in Member States that mostly rely on mediation techniques, namely, Belgium, Germany, Luxemburg and Poland.[25]

The Directive applies to binding and non-binding ADR processes, and it describes ADR entities as adjudicative and consensual extrajudicial schemes created on a durable basis (i.e. not created on an ad hoc basis for a single dispute).[26] It thus includes a plethora of ADR processes, covering, inter alia, mediation, conciliation, arbitration, ombudsman procedures and complaint boards. However, it excludes direct negotiation, the internal complaint handling systems operated by the trader and judicial settlement.[27] Furthermore, Member States can decide whether the ADR entities established in their territories have the power to impose a decision[28] – in other words, a Member State may limit the accreditation to non-binding ADR entities, restricting the use of arbitration schemes (e.g. Germany), but it may not restrict the operation of a consumer arbitration entity established in another Member State that offers its services in the Member State with the restriction.

The Directive excludes services from sectors generally provided by the State, namely, non-economic services of general interest, health care and public providers of higher education.[29] The minimum harmonization clause of the Directive means that Member States can expand its application. For instance, the UK has extended its scope to disputes arising from public providers of higher education because most UK students of higher education self-finance their studies, so they are already covered by the consumer law.

[24] Art. 2(2) ODR Regulation.

[25] See www.webgate.ec.europa.eu/odr/main/index.cfm?event=main.home.show&lng=EN.

[26] Recital 20. [27] Art. 2(2).

[28] Art. 2(4). See generally N. Reich, 'Party Autonomy and Consumer Arbitration in Conflict: A "Trojan Horse" in the Access to Justice in the EU ADR Directive 2013/11?' (2015) 4(1) *Penn St J Law Int Aff* 290–232.

[29] Art. 2(2) (f) and (g).

ADR entities can extend or limit their own scope. For example, disputes between businesses and discrimination claims fall outside the scope of the Directive, but naturally ADR entities are free to extend their services and use the same procedures for these disputes. Indeed, although for these cases the ADR entities are not required to comply with the requirements set by the Directive, they should do so for reasons of consistency.[30]

It must be highlighted that certified ADR entities have a competitive advantage as they are subject to higher standards than those that are not certified, so consumers and businesses are likely to choose certified ADR entities. In addition, businesses and consumers are signposted towards certified ADR entities; hence, even when businesses have chosen to participate in a non-certified ADR body, they still have the legal obligation to notify consumers about the certified ADR entities.

4.2.2 Quality Criteria and Due Process Standards for Certified ADR Entities

According to the Directive, all certified ADR entities must comply with the quality standards established in Articles 5–12. It must be noted that the blueprint of many of these principles can be traced back to the standards contained in the Recommendations for consumer out-of-court processes.[31] The following paragraphs examine these minimum requirements contained in the ADR Directive.

Access to an ADR Entity

Certified ADR entities must accept both domestic and cross-border disputes, including those referred by the European ODR platform.[32] This requirement does not imply that certified ADR entities will be required to offer their services in all the European languages. In fact, they can restrict the languages in which they will process disputes, which in most cases will be the language of the trader. Since traders choose (and often pay for) the ADR entity, in cross-border disputes the most likely ADR entity will be one that is established in the Member State of the trader.

[30] Department for Business Innovation & Skills (BIS), 'Alternative Dispute Resolution for Consumers: Government Response to the Consultation on implementing the Alternative Dispute Resolution Directive and the Online Dispute Resolution Regulation' (November 2014) p. 11.

[31] See Recommendations 98/257/EC and 2001/310/EC.

[32] Art. 5(2)(e).

Accordingly, consumers in cross-border disputes will usually have to process their complaints in a foreign language. The EU ODR platform acknowledges this hurdle and it provides users with an automated translation tool, which is supported by a human assistant for the translation of outcomes or settlements. In addition, the ADR Directive requires Member States to assist their consumers in accessing ADR entities operating in another Member State. This assistance can be conferred to the European Consumer Centre Network.[33]

The ADR procedure must be available online and offline;[34] entities dealing with disputes arising from online transactions must provide a link on their website to the ODR platform;[35] and, they may, but they are not required to, conduct the whole procedure via the online case management tool offered by the ODR platform.[36]

All ADR entities must have a website which allows parties to access information about the ADR procedure and to submit complaints and supporting documents online. Parties cannot be required to have legal representation, though they can have it if they so choose.[37] Parties can request information on a durable medium[38] and submit a complaint offline by regular post if they wish to do so. The ADR procedure must be free or available at a nominal cost to the consumer[39] and must comply with the data protection law.

ADR entities can only refuse to process a complaint based on six procedural rules.[40] The refusal must be reasoned and communicated to the complainant within three weeks of receiving the complete complaint file. The six procedural grounds upon which a complaint may be

[33] Art. 14.

[34] Art. 8(a) ADR Directive. However, the EU ODR platform have listed, arguably in contradiction to the principle of accessibility, ADR entities that require the physical presence of the parties or their legal representatives. This requirement seems to be at odds with a digital cross-border society.

[35] Art. 14(5) ODR Regulation. [36] Art. 10(d) ODR Regulation.

[37] Art. 8(b) ADR Directive.

[38] Regulation 5 of the Consumer Contracts (Information, Cancellation and Additional Changes) Regulations 2013 states that 'durable medium means paper or email, or any other medium that – (a) allows information to be addressed personally to the recipient, (b) enables the recipient to store the information in a way accessible for future reference for a period that is long enough for the purpose of the information and (c) allows the unchanged reproduction of the information stored'.

[39] Art. 8(c) ADR Directive.

[40] Art. 5(4). These restrictions are discussed in greater detail in Chapter 7. See also P. Cortés, 'The Impact of EU Law in the ADR Landscape in Italy, Spain and the UK: Time for Change or Missed Opportunity?' 16(2) (2015) *ERA Forum* 125–147.

dismissed are: (i) when the consumer has not attempted to resolve the complaint directly with the trader, (ii) complaints are frivolous or vexatious, (iii) disputes have been considered by another ADR scheme or by a court, (iv) the value of the claim falls below or above a pre-specified monetary threshold, (v) complaints are over one year old and (vi) complaints would seriously impair the effective operation of the ADR entity – this could be the case where dealing with a complaint would tie up the ADR entity's resources with the effect that it is unable to handle its other complaints effectively.

When an ADR entity refuses a complaint it must be reasoned and communicated to the complainant within three weeks of receiving it. After this period, ADR entities are required to process the complaint. National legislators and competent authorities can flesh out these grounds in order to ensure that ADR entities do not reject viable complaints, making certain that new barriers to consumers' access to redress are not created.[41] Competent authorities must monitor ADR entities, ensuring that new barriers to consumers' access to redress are not created when allowing ADR entities to reject complaints.

Expertise, Independence and Impartiality

Neutral third parties (i.e. 'the neutrals') working for certified ADR entities must have adequate expertise, be impartial and have no conflict of interest. Collegial bodies (i.e. panels with more than one neutral third party) must have equal stakeholder representation for consumers and traders.[42] The independence of neutrals is also guaranteed by requiring their appointment for a term of office (i.e. three years) of sufficient duration to ensure their independence. During this period the ADR entities are not allowed to remove their neutrals without a just cause. Moreover, neutrals cannot work for the trader (or professional organization of which the trader is a member) for a period of three years after their role as neutrals has ended.

Neutrals do not have to be licensed legal practitioners, but they must have the necessary knowledge in the field of ADR or judicial resolution of consumer disputes, and a general understanding of law. In addition ADR entities are expected to provide training for their neutrals.

Trade associations can be approved ADR entities. Furthermore, one of the most controversial provisions in the Directive is that it allows for

[41] Ibid. [42] Art. 6.

ADR entities and their neutrals to be hired exclusively by one trader as long as this is permitted by the national law and ADR entities have obtained the approval of their certification bodies (i.e. the national competent authorities) and complied with a number of safeguards, such as ensuring that ADR entities have a separate budget[43] and that the remuneration of the neutrals is not linked to the complaints' outcomes.

The Principle of Transparency

The Directive sets a number of information requirements that ADR entities must make available on their websites and provide in a durable medium if requested by one of the parties. The information must include, inter alia, the ADR entity's contact details as well as their neutrals', their scope, the languages in which disputes can be submitted, the rules employed for resolving complaints, the fees if any, the average length of ADR procedures, the legal effect of the outcome and a link to the European Commission's website which lists all certified ADR entities.

ADR entities must include an annual activity report containing information about the number of disputes received, the types of complaints, the number of complaints rejected and discontinued, and observations of any systematic problems leading to disputes between traders and consumers. Also, every two years each ADR entity has to submit a report to its national competent authority with similar information to that provided in the annual activity reports.[44]

The Principle of Effectiveness

According to this principle, certified ADR entities must offer online and offline access to the procedure, be free of charge or at moderate cost to consumers regardless of the value of the complaint,[45] and ADR entities must decide in three weeks from the submission of the complaint whether they are competent to deal with a dispute; in such case the complaint should be resolved within 90 days of submission of the

[43] The requirement of a separate budget does not apply if there is an equal number of neutrals remunerated by the trade association of which the trader is a member, and neutrals appointed by consumer organizations.

[44] Art. 19(3) of the ADR Directive.

[45] Art. 8. The fact that the Directive does not allow CADR entities to charge market rate fees to consumers for high-value disputes has been criticized. See G. Ross, 'The Possible Unintended Consequences of the European Directive on Alternative Dispute Resolution and the Regulation on Online Dispute Resolution' (2014) 10 *Revista Democracia Digital e Governo Electrônico*, 206–221, 220.

complete complaint file – but, in exceptional cases of highly complex disputes, the ADR entity may extend the 90-day deadline and inform the parties of the expected delay.

It must be noted that this period may be too long for certain types of disputes, particularly in the context of low-value disputes arising from e-commerce.[46] If one compares the length of time taken by successful ODR providers such as eBay's Resolution Centre, then it appears clear that the ideal time frame for resolving low-value disputes is less than a week. Empirical research carried out in eBay over hundreds of thousands of users demonstrated that effective consumer redress schemes assisting buyers and sellers to resolve their disputes have a positive impact in the volume of trade of those users who benefited from ODR – in other words, those buyers who had disputes and were offered effective redress had subsequently entered into more transactions than those who did not have any disputes. However, there was one category of buyers with disputes resolved who subsequently entered into less transactions: when disputes took too long to be resolved – i.e. over six weeks.[47] This is because online users have the expectation of quick transactions and quick resolutions. Therefore, the 90-day period will be too long for online disputes of low value.

The Principle of Fairness

The principle of fairness requires parties to be given the opportunity to comment on the evidence and documents submitted by the other party. In adjudicative processes, such as in arbitration, the arbitrator must ensure that parties are aware of their rights and the consequences of participating in this procedure. In processes where the neutral imposes the outcome of the dispute, the neutral has to provide grounds for their decisions in order to strengthen the perception of the ADR process as a fair method of settling disputes. If there is a settlement, the agreement itself will constitute the ground on which the outcome is based.

In consensual processes consumers must be informed about their choice of whether to agree to a settlement, which could be less favourable

[46] Ibid.

[47] C. Rule, 'Quantifying the Economic Benefits of Effective Redress: Large E-Commerce Data Sets and the Cost-Benefit Case for Investing in Dispute Resolution' (2012) 34 *Univ Ark Little Rock Law Rev* 767. Colin Rule argues that if the marketplace or traders provide consumers with an effective redress option, then they will in turn provide greater loyalty to those traders.

to an outcome obtained in the courts, their right to obtain independent legal advice, the effect of the agreement, and their opportunity to reflect before deciding whether to consent to amicable solutions.[48] These safeguards aim to provide an extra layer of protection to consumers in order to avoid them being pressurized to settle complaints in a way that does not respect their full legal entitlements.

The Principle of Liberty

According to this principle, consumers cannot be required to agree on a legally binding process before the dispute has materialized.[49] Hence, if parties agree to go to arbitration provided by an ADR entity, which is common, for instance, in Spain and Portugal, the agreement between the parties must take place after the dispute arises. However, traders (but not consumers) can commit themselves to participate in the arbitration process before the dispute arises.

This principle respects the right to access the court and it is also enshrined in Article 47(1) of the Charter of Fundamental Rights of the EU and in Article 6(1) of the European Convention of Human Rights. The rationale is that when consumers enter into a contract they do not know if a dispute will arise, and even if they contemplated that option, they cannot know what would be at stake in such a dispute.

Furthermore, in line with the Mediation Directive, the limitation period for seeking action before the courts cannot be an obstacle for those who attempt to resolve a dispute through a consensual ADR entity.[50] Consequently, if a limitation period expires while the parties are participating in an ADR process, then this period is extended so that the parties have the opportunity to initiate judicial proceedings in relation to that dispute.

The Principle of Legality

This principle states that processes that impose a solution on the parties cannot result in the consumer being deprived of the rights that cannot be derogated from by agreement. This principle only applies to processes that replace the court option – i.e. arbitration – and it does not apply to consensual processes, such as mediation and conciliation schemes. The non-derogable rules must be respected even when decisions are awarded

[48] Art. 9. [49] Art. 10.
[50] Art. 12. See similar provisions in the Mediation Directive 2008/52/EC, Art. 8(1).

based on equitable principles, fairness or codes of conduct, which does not preclude the ADR entity from providing the consumer with greater protection than that afforded by the mandatory law.

Thus, in domestic disputes, the national mandatory consumer law must be respected. In cross-border disputes, Rome I Regulation applies, which means that the applicable law will often be the law of the consumers' habitual residence, particularly where the trader has actively targeted the consumer's jurisdiction by, for instance, offering goods in the language and currency of the consumer.[51] The rationale behind this rule is that since consumer expectations may be informed by their domestic legislation, meeting their expectations is important in order to achieve the legislative goal of increasing consumer confidence in cross-border trade.

4.2.3 *Information Requirements*

Participation by businesses in ADR entities remains voluntary in most economic sectors, but the ADR Directive requires traders to inform consumers about certified ADR entities on two occasions: (i) traders affiliated to ADR entities must provide this information before the conclusion of the contract, and (ii) in *all cases* traders must inform consumers after a complaint has not been processed by their internal complaints handling system.[52] The latter information requirement is particularly welcome since consumers very rarely read the terms and conditions when they enter into a contract, so it is useful for consumers to find out about ADR once a complaint cannot be resolved directly with the trader or its customer satisfaction department. Indeed, this is the most relevant legal change affecting all businesses established in the EU. It is then not surprising that some businesses with a high number of complaints, such as telecoms, have been very critical of this legal provision, since the information obligation could increase the number of complaints exponentially. Similarly, Member States, such as Spain, whose public purse fully funds the operation of ADR, had misgivings about this information requirement. In fact, Spain, despite its general support for ADR, abstained when voting in the European Council (COREPER) to approve the ADR Directive.[53]

51 See Art. 6(2) of the Rome I Regulation (O.J. 2008, L 177/6) and *Peter Pammer* (C-585/08).

52 Art. 13(3).

53 Statement by Spain on the 177795/11 CONSOM 196NI 616 JUSTCIV 339 CODEC 2242. Available at http://tinyurl.com/zlulx9z.

With regard to the first information requirement, businesses must provide the contact information of ADR entities on their websites and in their contract if they are affiliated to a ADR entity – this may be because they have opted in voluntarily, or because they are required to participate in ADR processes by the sectorial law or by the industry as part of their membership of a particular trade association.[54]

The other information obligation, as noted earlier, requires *all* businesses, regardless of whether they have joined an ADR, with unresolved consumer complaints to notify consumers in a durable medium about certified ADR entities operating in their sector, and clearly inform consumers whether or not they would participate in their ADR processes. This is normally carried out in a 'deadlock' letter where the consumer is informed that the complaint has not been upheld.

In addition, the ODR Regulation requires that online businesses that have agreed to use an ADR entity, either individually or because it applies to their sector, have to provide the link to the ODR platform when they make an offer via email, and they must include information about the platform in the terms and conditions of the contract.

Furthermore, *all* businesses operating online have to include a link on their website to the ODR platform.[55] This obligation is extended to those websites that act as intermediaries between sellers and buyers – well-known examples of these online marketplaces are eBay and Amazon.

Although it appears a bit strange that traders are legally required to inform consumers of ADR entities, even when they have no intention of using them, this obligation was included because it is believed that it will encourage traders to refer disputes to ADR entities by forcing them to consider in every unresolved complaint whether ADR is appropriate.[56] Yet, as will be discussed later and in subsequent chapters, traders' refusal to participate in ADR may inevitably lead to consumer confusion and loss of trust in the whole ADR infrastructure.

54 Examples of regulated sectors where the provision of ADR is often mandatory are the financial sector and some utility providers such as water, gas, electricity and telecoms.

55 Art. 14(1).

56 See Recital 49 noting that 'traders should be encouraged as far as possible to participate in ADR procedures'.

4.2.4 *Competent Authorities*

The ADR Directive requires each Member State to designate a national point of contact and at least one competent authority whose main role is to certify ADR entities and monitor their operations.[57] Appointed competent authorities, which are often the regulators, can provide additional guidelines or requirements to the ADR entities they supervise. In order to ensure effective compliance national competent authorities can issue proportionate penalties to traders and ADR entities that do not comply with the information requirements.[58] The penalties are regulated by the national laws, but typically they may lead a competent authority to seek enforcement action through the courts in order to ensure compliance. Lack of compliance could lead to fines and even imprisonment[59] – though the latter will be unlikely. Sanctions must be proportionate and enforcers are expected to use soft measures to increase compliance. Indeed, research has demonstrated that collaboration of enforcers with businesses providing information, guidance and advice is more effective than the mere deterrence of sanctions.[60]

Above all, what is important is that competent authorities adopt a proactive role, ensuring compliance with the information requirements. As an example of best practice one can look at the UK Civil Aviation Authority, which is the regulator and competent authority for the aviation sector.[61] They have contacted all the airlines established in the UK and requested the following information: (i) confirmation, or otherwise, that the airline has contracted a ADR entity, and its contact details; (ii) a sample copy of the 'deadlock' letter with the reference to a ADR entity and (iii) screenshots from the airlines' websites of terms and conditions with the reference to ADR bodies if applicable as well as screenshots of where the link is to the ODR platform.

ADR entities must cooperate with national consumer protection authorities and enforcement bodies.[62] Every two years ADR entities are required

[57] Arts. 18 and 20. [58] Art. 21.

[59] The UK law sets up to two years of imprisonment and unlimited fine for breach of its ADR Regulations. See Alternative Dispute Resolution, In-depth Guide. Available at http://tinyurl.com/gwfn797.

[60] C. Hodges, 'Ethical Business Regulation: Understanding the Evidence' Better Regulation Delivery Office, Department for Business Innovation & Skills (February 2016).

[61] Email from Matthew Buffey, Head of Consumer Enforcement, Civil Aviation Authority, 'Re. Alternative Dispute Resolution (ADR); Online Dispute Resolution (ODR) and notice provisions under Regulation (EC) 261/2004' (10 March 2016) (on file with author).

[62] Art. 17(1) of the ADR Directive. See also Chapter 1.

to submit a report to the competent authorities with information about their operation, which basically expands on the annual activity reports.[63] In turn, every four years competent authorities must provide a report to the European Commission with information on the performance of the ADR entities that they monitor.[64] National reports must include information on best practices, shortcomings and recommendations on how to improve consumer ADR. Also, every four years the Commission is required to submit a report to the Parliament, the Council and the Economic and Social Committee on the application of the Directive.[65] The implementation of the ADR Directive has started a process of seeking greater consistency in the ADR infrastructure. The first important steps to achieve this have been the transposition into national laws and the certification process, both at the national (across sectors) and EU level. The next step will take place in 2019 when the European Commission will decide whether to propose amendments to the ADR Directive.

4.3 The Foundation for a Pan-European ODR Platform: Regulation on Online Dispute Resolution

ADR processes, especially in the cross-border and e-commerce context, are not feasible without the enabling means of distance communications. As noted in Chapter 2, the role of technology in these online processes is so fundamental that it has been labelled as the 'fourth party' because it displaces, and sometimes even replaces, the role of the neutral third party.[66] The European Commission has thus realized that ADR processes should be complemented with technology; this led to the approval of the ODR Regulation as a complement to the ADR Directive. The ODR Regulation ensures the accessibility of ADR processes through an ODR platform that offers a means of distance communication between the parties and ADR entities. It is to this Regulation that we turn now in our analysis.

4.3.1 Scope of Application

The ODR Regulation establishes an EU-wide ODR platform that aims to facilitate the resolution of consumer disputes, domestic and cross-border, arising from online contracts for the sale of goods and provision of

63 Art. 19(3). 64 Art. 20(6). 65 Art. 26.

66 E. Katsh and J. Rifkin, *Online Dispute Resolution: Resolving Conflicts in Cyberspace* (Jossey-Bass, 2001) p. 93.

services. The first point to note is that its scope of application is therefore restricted to disputes arising from e-commerce. While an ODR platform seems the natural place to resolve e-commerce disputes, it is not entirely clear why its scope has been restricted to these disputes, as there will be many other disputes to be resolved that could benefit from this forum. It would thus be preferable if the access (and use of the case management tool) could be optional for ADR entities dealing with disputes arising outside the realm of e-commerce. An explanation for this restriction might be found in the need to narrow the scope in order to facilitate the design of complaint forms as well as to make the platform more manageable for the administrator. However, if the ODR platform becomes successful in resolving e-commerce disputes, that should lead to the expansion to other sectors, and even to commercial cases, especially where one party is a small business.

As noted earlier, the Regulation has an important difference in scope when compared with the Directive: traders may also bring complaints against consumers as long as the national law where the consumer has its habitual residence allows it. This option is more likely to occur when national models primarily follow mediation techniques.[67] For instance, Belgium allows businesses to bring claims against consumers using nationally certified ADR entities using both the EU and their national ODR platform (*Service de Médiation pour le Consommateur*).[68] These cases may be related to feedback reviews (e.g., where the consumer wants to avoid more costly defamation litigation) and money claims for unpaid goods or services. Given the nature of most consumer ADR entities, which are often publicly subsidized, this option has not yet been made available in most Member States.

4.3.2 *The ODR Platform*

The ODR platform[69] offers consumers a single online point of entry to send complaints arising from e-commerce to traders, and if they agree, to certified ADR entities.[70] Similarly, at the time of writing a number of Member States are developing national ODR platforms or help desks that signpost disputants to ADR entities, though their scope extends outside

[67] Art. 2(2).
[68] See Annual Report for 2015 at www.mediationconsommateur.be/fr/telechargements/rapport-annuel-2015-0.
[69] Art. 5(3). See link at https://webgate.ec.europa.eu/odr. [70] Art. 5(6).

the e-commerce realm. The features of these national platforms vary, but they act mostly as clearing houses at the national level, facilitating the communications between the parties, rather than resolving the dispute itself. The European Commission (DG JUST) manages the EU ODR platform, and for its implementation has allocated a budget of 4.5 million euros.[71] The platform offers an optional electronic case management tool to ADR entities, enabling them to conduct the dispute resolution procedure online via the ODR platform.[72]

As already noted, all online traders and intermediaries must include on their websites an 'easily accessible' link to the ODR platform. Traders must also provide an email address (so that consumers have a first point of contact) even when they do not intend to participate in an ADR process.[73] The expectation is that these links should be contained in the section of the website where traders have information on how to submit complaints. In addition, the link must be included by the ADR entities operating in the e-commerce sector, the European Consumer Centres Network, and by the consumer and business associations. Hence, while e-commerce complaints may be channelled through the ODR platform, the rest of consumer complaints (the offline ones) will only be able to rely on the support given by the ECC-Net when facing cross-border complaints, and by the national consumer bodies when facing domestic disputes.

Each Member State has designated a contact point that contains at least two ODR advisors, which in most cases are members of the national European Consumer Centres, as they already have expertise on cross-border disputes. Although the contact points must assist parties with cross-border disputes, they can also provide assistance to parties with domestic disputes. Their main functions are assisting in the submission of complaints; providing general information on consumer rights, the functioning of the platform and ADR procedures; and informing parties about other means of redress.[74]

The ODR platform has the functions of providing electronic standard complaint and response forms in all the languages of the EU, offering a translation tool, communicating the complaint form to the respondent, and when the latter agrees, forwarding the complaint to the competent ADR entities.[75]

[71] Art. 5(1); COM (2011) 794 final, p. 5. [72] Art. 9(d). [73] Art. 14. [74] Art. 7(2).
[75] Art. 5(4).

The weakest link is therefore that if parties do not agree on participating in an ADR process within 30 days, then the complaint will be dismissed. At this point, the ODR platform and the ODR advisors should notify the individual complainant about mandatory ADR entities, if there are any, or, in their absence, about other redress options, such as the availability of the small claims procedure.[76] But they can only do so if the consumer actively contacts the ECC or the ODR contact point and requests such information.

A feedback system has been integrated in the ODR platform to collect users' reviews (consumers and traders) about the platform. After the conclusion of the process ADR entities must inform the platform of the date of receiving the complaint, its subject matter, the date of conclusion and the outcome of the case.[77] Member States are required to issue effective, proportionate and dissuasive penalties for the infringement of the Regulation.[78]

The ODR platform is managed by the European Commission, which is in charge of its development, operation and maintenance. For the technical aspects, the Commission is assisted by an expert group, consisting of national authorities, ADR entities, business and consumer representatives and members from the European Disability Forum.

The Regulation has conferred the Commission with the power of delegated acts to flesh out the operation of the ODR platform.[79] These acts need first to be communicated to the European Parliament and the Council, and then they will enter into force if no objection is communicated within two months of their communication.[80] The Commission must report every year to the Parliament and the Council on the functioning of the platform, and every three years the Commission must submit to them a detailed report with proposals to reform the Regulation when necessary.[81]

4.3.3 *The Process to Submit a Complaint*

The ODR platform is reasonably user-friendly. The landing page asks the user to select first the language and state whether the user is a consumer or a trader. The latter will only be allowed to submit complaints when the consumer-respondents are based in a Member State where the national law allows for this option – namely, in Belgium, Germany, Luxemburg or

[76] Art. 9(3)(a) and 9(8). [77] Art. 10(c). [78] Art. 18. See also Hodges, n. 60.
[79] Regulations (EU) 2015/1051 (non-legislative act) L 171/1. [80] Art. 17. [81] Art. 21.

Poland.[82] The complaint form is based on a questionnaire that first checks that the claim is admissible by asking complainants to confirm that they live in the EU and that the claim relates to good or services bought online.[83]

When the claim is submitted by a consumer (or their representative) the complaint form has three steps that must be completed before the submission of the claim: trader details, description of the complaint and the personal information. Accordingly, the first step is for the consumer to introduce the details of the trader, which may represent an insurmountable hurdle if the consumer does not have access to all the traders' contact details, including the correct email address. The platform offers a search engine which assists in finding out the details of a few major traders, such as Apple, Ryanair or Barclays, but it does not include at the time of writing (January 2017) other major traders such as Samsung, EasyJet or Santander Bank. Improving this database, following the example of private providers, such as Resolver.co.uk, would make the platform more useful for consumers as it can be difficult for them to find out the adequate email address of the trader. Therefore, it is submitted that the platform should develop its list of available emails. The national contact points and ODR advisors should assist in the task of gathering this information.

The second step requires the consumer to describe the complaint proving details of the purchase. The consumer must first describe the type of good and service. The platform requires the consumer to choose from a drop-box one of the following options: consumer goods, education, energy and water, financial services, general consumer services, health, leisure services, postal services and electronic communications, transport services, and other. The second drop-box narrows down the category of the dispute. For instance, if a consumer selects leisure services, then the options available in the second drop-box are: hotels and other holiday accommodation, package travel, travel agency services, time-share and similar, restaurants and bars, services related to sports and hobbies, cultural and entertainment services, gambling and lottery, and other leisure services. The form requires to provide the date of the purchase, the price, the reference number and the type of the complaint with another drop-box with the following options: defective/caused damage, no conformity with the delivery, invoicing/billing, warranty/guarantee,

[82] See https://webgate.ec.europa.eu/odr/main/index.cfm?event=main.home.show&lng=EN.
[83] Ibid.

other. After that, the complaint form asks for details on the claim and the remedy sought in two free-text boxes. Lastly, the form contains three yes or no questions: 'Was the trader already contacted about the complaint?'; 'Was there an attempt to reach an out-of-court settlement or was the other party taken to court over the complaint?'; 'Does the trader want to use a specific dispute resolution body?' The answers to these questions do not preclude the complainant to progress to the last step.

Finally, step three requires complainants to insert their personal data: name, email address, phone number, postal address, as well as the detail of the representative if there is one. The claim form also allows claimants to choose the language in which they would like to receive messages from the ODR platform.

4.3.4 *Language, Assistance and Translation*

The language is a key challenge for many cross-border cases, particularly those of low value. Although the platform provides an electronic translation function supported by human intervention (only for the translation of settlements) assisting parties and ADR entities with the exchange of information,[84] the dispute resolution process is carried out in the language chosen by the ADR entity, which will often be the language chosen by the trader.[85] In spite of that consumers expect to participate in a dispute resolution process conducted in their own language or in the language of the transaction.[86]

While some consumers can manage in using a foreign language in an online transaction, the language level of many may not be sufficient to take part in an ADR process. Even though the Regulation designates ODR advisors as the intermediaries to assist parties' communications with the ADR entities,[87] their manpower is obviously very limited. It has been argued elsewhere that a more useful role for ODR advisors would be, inter alia, to manage an effective negotiation tool that can efficiently

[84] Arts. 5 and 6.

[85] P. Cortés and A. Lodder, 'Consumer Dispute Resolution Goes Online: Reflections on the Evolution of European Law for Out-of-Court Redress' 21(1) (2014) *Maastricht J* 26.

[86] Flash Eurobarometer Report Cross-Border and Consumer Protection (March 2011).

[87] The lingua franca is normally English for the ECC. The ECC Protocol on Case Handling IT Tool states that the problem description should be written in English by the Consumer ECC unless another language is agreed between the ECCs sharing the claim. See Art. 6.

assist parties in settling their disputes directly – without the intervention of neutrals.[88] This view is envisaged by UNCITRAL in its ODR guidelines for promoting the use of ODR methods in the resolution of e-commerce disputes arising from cross-border low-value transactions.[89]

However an important limitation of the design of the platform is that, due to data protection restrictions, ODR advisors can only access those cases where the parties (consumer, trader or ADR) have contacted them through the platform. The next section examines the functions of the platform.

4.4 The Functions of the ODR Platform

4.4.1 The Design of the ODR Platform Front Office

The front office has been designed with the aim to accommodate all types of users, taking into consideration the special needs of older people as well as young consumers. It takes into account the needs of disabled people by following the Web Accessibility guidelines,[90] which includes inter alia finding the right colour balance and ensuring the level of contrast between text and background is adequate.

The design has aimed to provide an easy navigation across multiple browsers and a wide range of devices from smartphones to desktop computers. The navigation intends to be intuitive with an explanation of the steps that parties must take. A good design should bring a clear and intuitive workflow that offers simple steps that parties can easily follow. It should also limit the number of choices that consumers have in order to avoid distraction, what in the IT jargon is known as noise. If consumers experience problems in the navigation they can consult the user manual and the frequently asked questions (FAQ) and reach out to an ODR advisor.

The consumer starts the process by going to the splash page and choosing the language of the platform. The welcome page enables the

[88] P. Cortés, 'A New Regulatory Framework for Extra-Judicial Consumer Redress: Where We Are and How to Move Forward' (2015) 35(1) *Legal Stud* 114–141.

[89] See Chapter 6. See also UNCITRAL Working Group III (Online Dispute Resolution). See www.uncitral.org/uncitral/commission/working_groups/3Online_Dispute_Resolution .html. See generally P. Cortés and F. Esteban, 'Building a Global Redress System for Low-Value Cross-Border Disputes' (2013) 62(2) *Int Comp Law Q* 407–440.

[90] See the guidelines at www.w3.org/standards/webdesign/accessibility.

user to proceed as a complainant, respondent, ADR entity, ODR advisor or the administrator (i.e. the European Commission).

The consumer follows the screening phase by first entering the traders' details, where the first hurdle can be found if for instance the consumer has not obtained the trader's contact address. The next step is for the complainant to introduce their complaint details. This is followed by a request for the complainant to provide their contact details and to submit the complaint. Consumers are able to save a draft complaint and complete it at a later stage.[91]

The trader is notified electronically via an email that contains a link to the platform. By pressing the link the trader is redirected to the platform where they can access the complaint and the supporting information. At this point, a trader that is not required to participate in the ADR process has three options: (i) it can contact the consumer to settle the matter directly, though these communications aiming at negotiating a settlement cannot take place through the platform; (ii) it can agree to have one of the approved ADR entities resolve the complaint, for which the trader is likely to be asked to pay a fee or (iii) it could do nothing, leaving the consumer waiting for 30 days until he or she receives an automated response by the platform stating that the case is closed. To the frustration of most consumers the latter is the most common outcome.[92]

4.4.2 *The ODR Platform Back Office*

The back office is accessible to the European Commission, the ADR entities dealing with complaints arising from online contracts and the ODR contact points, which will have at least two ODR advisors per Member State. The ODR advisors are able to access the cases when they receive queries submitted by the parties through the platform. To that end, the platform provides them with an internal search engine that helps them to navigate through a large volume of cases.

At the time of writing, a number of Member States, such as Belgium, already have,[93] or are in the process of developing, national online

[91] Art. 2 of the Commission Implementing Regulation (EU) 2015/1051.

[92] See J. Minor, 'European Priorities for Consumer Protection' Westminster Business Forum Keynote Seminar: The Future of Consumer Law and ADR in the UK' (London, 14 September 2016) Conference Proceedings p. 57.

[93] See Economie http://belmed.fgov.be and Service de Médiation pour le Consommateur www.mediationconsommateur.be.

portals, gateways or helpdesks, which act as clearinghouses signposting complainants to nationally approved ADR entities. The features of these national platforms vary, but they are increasingly interoperable with the European platform mainly through the use of XML format for web services communications.[94]

4.4.3 *The Translation Tool*

The complaint and response forms are available in all EU languages. Parties can use a translation tool that enables the translation of text that is included in the free text area, such as complaint description, messages exchanged, resolutions, etc. It accepts all types of documents, including Word doc, pdf (except images), Excel and PowerPoint. The user can come back to the original text.

Language is a key challenge for many cross-border cases, particularly those of low value. Consumers expect to participate in a dispute resolution process conducted in their own language or in the language of the transaction.[95] It must be noted that, while consumers may manage in using a foreign language in an online transaction, the language level of many may not be sufficiently nuanced to take part in the ADR process.

The Regulation designates ODR advisors as the intermediaries to assist parties' communications with the ADR entities,[96] but their resources are quite limited. Thompson notes, 'not only are human resources expensive, but they can also create bottlenecks that slow the justice process down'.[97] He argues that artificial intelligence (AI) can replicate the support given by humans in a more effective way through four possible functions: problem diagnosis, information, self-help and triage. Arguably, a more useful role for ODR advisors would not be to act as language interpreters, but as managers of a platform that offers an effective negotiation tool that can efficiently assist parties in settling their disputes directly – without the intervention of neutral third parties.[98]

[94] Connecting Europe Facility (CEF) Trans-European Telecommunications Networks, Work Programme 2015, p. 34.

[95] Flash Eurobarometer Report Cross-Border and Consumer Protection (March 2011).

[96] The lingua franca is normally English for the ECC. The ECC Protocol on Case Handling IT Tool states that the problem description should be written in English by the Consumer ECC unless another language is agreed between the ECCs sharing the claim. See Art. 6.

[97] D. Thompson 'Addressing 'Leveraging Technology in Civil Justice ODR' Society for Computers & Law (6 October 2014). Available at www.scl.org/site.aspx?i=ed38839.

[98] See Chapters 6 and 7 in this book.

4.5 Evaluation of the Design of the ODR Platform

During the testing period of the ODR platform, 120 representatives taken from all the EU Member States were chosen to form an expert group.[99] The participants were put in four groups representing consumers, traders, ADR entities and ODR contact points. The feedback provided by the expert group was passed to the designers, who tried to incorporate it during the several updates of the platform. For instance, one of the main issues is the quality of automated translation, which is not good enough for a number of language pairs and is still a work in progress.

In addition to the language issue, amongst the key findings were that those playing the role of consumers pointed out that the language used in the system needs to be less formal and legal. Initially what consumers need is advice on what are their rights and how they can pursue a claim. In order to do that it is important to develop a triage or diagnosis system that filters cases and explains to consumers about their dispute resolution options with a particular trader. Indeed, both groups representing consumers and traders requested clearer and advance information about the procedure.[100]

However, the first challenge that the consumer may encounter is to provide the trader's email address as this may not be the one sent to confirm the transaction (which often is a 'do not reply' email). If this proves to be an important hurdle, then enforcement authorities should require traders to use the same email address as that used in the transaction. Also, as noted earlier, the platform provides the email address of a small number of traders, but this list should be expanded, perhaps with the cooperation from ADR entities, which have the contact details of those traders that have signed up with them.

Another important finding came from the group representing traders, which recommended that the platform should allow parties to settle a case before it goes to an ADR entity.[101] A well-designed negotiation tool, especially one informed by AI, can prove very effective in resolving disputes. If the database of cases reveals that the platform receives high volumes of low-value complaints, and if these can be categorized into certain groupings, then it would be advisable to develop an online negotiation tool enhanced with algorithmic analysis enabling parties to

[99] European Commission, 'The Online Dispute Resolution Platform' Expert Group Meeting (Brussels, 12 December 2014) powerpoint on file with author.

[100] Ibid. [101] Ibid.

settle their disputes directly, without the need to involve ADR entities and neutral third parties. Other types of cases could be automatically forwarded to ADR entities, without the need for traders to agree to it.

Another major weakness of the current design is that consumers are not notified by the platform when a trader refuses to resolve a complaint, but only when the case is closed after 30 days of inactivity. A preferable design would be one whereby the ODR platform offers traders the possibility of clicking a link that confirms that they are not required and willing to participate in the dispute resolution process. This link should automatically trigger a communication via email to the consumer complainants, so they do not have to wait 30 days to know that their complaint will not be processed.

Similarly, the ODR platform does not automatically refer cases to ADR entities,[102] which is bewildering as this tool would enhance the effectiveness of the ODR platform. When the trader does not reply to a complaint, the consumer can reach out to the ODR contact point, which may inform the consumer about a mandatory ADR entity (if there is one) – this option adds a level of bureaucracy, which should be done automatically by the ODR platform. For the time being, the risk is that if the trader does not respond to the complaint then that complaint may be 'lost'. This would not occur if the consumer had gone directly to the mandatory ADR entity. It is submitted that when there are ADR entities (mainly complaints boards or ombudsman schemes) that have statutory power to receive consumer complaints, then the ODR platform should refer these complaints not only to the trader, but also to the mandatory ADR entity. This would be, for example, the case of the Swedish complaints board or that of some sectorial ombudsmen in the UK.[103] In a similar vein, Germany, Portugal and the Netherlands have mandatory ADR entities in certain sectors where there is a high risk of consumer detriment.

If there were proper monitoring of the cases that go through the ODR platform, the collected information would assist in designing strategies on dispute prevention and improving the design of the platform. There is

[102] ODR Regulation Art. 9.6 states that the ODR platform will refer the claim to an ADR entity when parties have agreed; Art. 9.8 states that if parties do not agree to an ADR entity, the claim will not be further processed.

[103] The ARN in Sweden processes complaints without the need for traders to opt into the process. In the UK there are statutory ombudsman, such as The Legal Ombudsman and The Financial Ombudsman Service. See Chapter 1.

the expectation that this first version of the EU ODR platform, which can be termed as 1.0, will be followed by upgrades, say the 2.0, which will enhance the functions and the interoperability of the EU ODR platform. The ODR platform should in time become available not only via the web but also through an app, so that the younger generation finds it more accessible through tablets and smartphones. Indeed, there are more smartphones than computers, and the number is growing exponentially, expecting to reach 4 billion and around 80 per cent of adults by the end of the decade.[104] Another design feature for the ODR platform that would truly increase trust in the Internal Market would be the use of a well-recognized trustmark for those traders that respond to the complaints sent through the ODR platform and agree to participate in processes offered by ADR entities.[105]

4.6 Proposal of Additional Functions for the EU ODR Platform

This part of the section provides a number of recommendations for the redesign of the EU ODR platform.[106] In doing so, this section proposes new functions for the ODR platform, arguing that its ultimate goal is not simply to enable consumers to submit complaints in their own language, or to help the parties in finding an adequate ADR entity, but to increase consumer trust in e-commerce. Accordingly, it is submitted that, on their own, neither the standardization of complaints nor identifying ADR entities achieve this goal. It is therefore proposed that the ODR platform should incorporate the following four interrelated functions: (i) problem diagnosis and conflict prevention, (ii) online negotiation, (iii) referral function and (iv) the monitoring function.

4.6.1 *Problem Diagnosis and Conflict Prevention Function*

The first function of the ODR platform should be to assist complainants to identify the type of dispute they have – i.e. the problem diagnosis or triage function. The ODR platform should provide relevant information to complainants helping them to understand what are their legal duties

104 'The Truly Personal Computer' *The Economist* (28 February 2015) p. 21.

105 See Chapter 8.

106 A first approximation to this topic appeared in P. Cortés, 'A New Regulatory Framework for Extra-Judicial Consumer Redress: Where We Are and How to Move Forward' (2015) 35(1) *Legal Stud* 114–141.

and rights. For instance, summaries of outcomes in similar cases or case studies can be helpful. A good information tool should tailor the content into different types of complaints, acting as a diagnosis or knowledge management tool that discourages unmeritorious complaints.

This function would be more effective if not only ODR advisors but also national advice centres were linked to the ODR platform. Also universities could provide support through their collaboration with advice centres, enabling consumers with difficulties to navigate through the ODR platform.[107] One benefit of dealing with a high volume of e-commerce complaints is that they can easily be categorized and resolved when parties agree to the facts as the applicable law on these disputes is often unequivocal.[108] Most disputes relating to the sale of goods usually concern the non-arrival or untimely delivery of the goods in question, or their non-correspondence with the description provided at the time of the transaction; while disputes about services will often relate to the quality of those provided, or whether they were provided at all, for example, in cases of flight cancellations. Indeed, relevant information is essential for parties to manage their expectations of what a reasonable outcome may be. To be effective, the information should be kept to a minimum and be practically orientated to the consumer's situation. Although these predictions would be relatively basic, in the future, a proper analysis of the data could provide very accurate information, obviating the need to escalate the complaint to an ADR entity. It can also provide useful information about ways on how to improve and refine the design of the complaint and response forms in order to make them more resolution-focused. Therefore, the collection of data can be a very valuable part of the ODR system.

An effectively designed ODR platform should play a key role in the prevention of future disputes.[109] Hodges et al. observe that effective consumer redress mechanisms should not only increase consumer protection, but also mandate behavioural consequences for markets and

[107] JUSTICE ' What Is a Court?' (2016) Available at http://tinyurl.com/jfxh3mn.

[108] E. Katsh, J. Rifkin and A. Gaitenby, 'E-Commerce, E-Disputes, and E-Dispute Resolution: In the Shadow of "eBay Law"' (2000) 15(3) *Ohio St J Disp Resol* 705, 709, and C. Hodges, I. Benohr and N. Creutzfeldtz-Banda, *Consumer ADR in Europe* (Hart, 2012), p. 453.

[109] See generally, S. Smith and J. Martinez, 'An Analytical Framework for Dispute System Design' (2009) 14(4) *Harv. Negot. Law Rev* 1401–1446. Hodges et al., n. 108, p. 1. R. Susskind, *The End of Lawyers? Rethinking the Nature of Legal Services* (OUP, 2008) 224.

traders.[110] To this end, the ODR platform should classify complaints into a systematic taxonomy so that once the information is processed it could be shared with traders and regulators, allowing for real-time information on what is happening in the markets.[111] This information would allow regulators and traders to give a quick response to market problems that need to be addressed. While regulators would be able to monitor legal compliance, reducing the cost of public enforcement, traders would obtain valuable information on disputes,[112] allowing them to improve trading standards and avoid future disputes.[113]

The key idea is to unlock the information contained in databases – this is what is commonly known as 'big data', which can be defined as 'things one can do at a large scale that cannot be done at a smaller one to extract new insights or create new forms of value, in ways that change markets, organizations, the relationship between citizens and governments, and more'.[114] eBay has appreciated the value of this information as it does not only handle over 80 per cent of disputes automatically, but it has integrated measures to avoid new disputes too.[115] Similar lessons have been learnt by more traditional service providers, such as Telecom Italia, which adapted its customer service system to deal with many complaints that previously had gone to external ADR entities.[116] Therefore, a tool that automatically breaks down and classifies the types of complaints received in the ODR platform can be a valuable asset for regulators and traders, particularly for those without sophisticated in-house systems. Appropriately processed data can be an effective mechanism for

[110] Hodges et al., n. 108, pp. 199, 200, 220. [111] Ibid.

[112] It is likely that the ODR platform will receive many complaints that are simple requests for information. According to the ECC-Net, in 2011, 40 per cent of the contacts were consumer requests for information that arose from cases where traders had unattended the requests. European Consumer Centres 'Network, Annual Report 2011 Getting Help Advice on your Purchases Abroad' (2012). Available at http://ec.europa.eu/consumers/ecc/ecc_annual_reports_en.htm.

[113] This important role was first envisioned by Ury, Brett and Goldberg in *Getting Disputes Resolved: Designing Systems to Cut the Costs of Conflicts* (Jossey-Bass, 1988).

[114] V. Mayer-Schonberger and K. Cukier, *Big Data, a Revolution That Will Transform How We Live, Work, and Think* (Houghton Mifflin Harcourt, 2013).

[115] C. Rule, 'Making Peace on eBay' ACResolution, (Fall 2008). O. Rabinovich-Einy and E. Katsh, 'Lessons from Online Dispute Resolution for Dispute System Design' in M. Wahab, E. Katsh and D. Rainey (eds.), *Online Dispute Resolution: Theory and Practice* (Eleven International Publishing, 2012) p. 42.

[116] The external ADR method previously used by Telecom Italia is 'joint conciliations', whereby a representative of the consumer met with a representative of the trader in order to settle a complaint.

recognizing patterns, which would enable traders and regulators to incorporate preventive measures. Hence, information on recurring complaints would aid traders and processes to move 'upstream' from dispute resolution to dispute prevention.[117]

However, it must be noted that the current design of many private ADR entities has the inherited risk of a fee model that charges on a case-by-case basis. This model has disincentives for dispute avoidance. Thus, close monitoring by competent authorities and other stakeholders, such as consumer associations, should ensure ADR entities' meaningful collaboration with regulators and enforcement bodies.[118] Moreover, ADR entities should adjust their funding models to align these with incentives for businesses to improve their trading standards.[119]

4.6.2 Online Negotiation

It is important that the ODR platform allows for early resolution, as this has proven to lead to higher consumer satisfaction in both traditional and e-commerce.[120] As already noted, this option has been pointed out in the feedback given by the expert group that tested the ODR platform.[121] Such a tool would be in accord with the UNCITRAL ODR model for settling of e-commerce disputes as efficiently as possible.[122] This omission may be explained if we consider that the ODR platform was preconceived by the European Commission not to resolve disputes,

117 Smith and Martinez, n. 109, p. 1434.

118 C. Hodges, 'The Way Forward: Policy Principles on the Role of Law and Interests in ADR' at the Fourth Annual Oxford Consumer ADR Conference on 18–20 April 2016.

119 See Chapter 8.

120 For instance, empowering delivery drivers to receive and resolve complaints related to delivery problems have proven greater consumer satisfaction than referring complainants to call centres. See 'Getting it Right, and Righting the Wrongs. Department for Communities and Local Government' 2010. Similarly, eBay found that buyers trading activity was higher when they were able to resolve complaints quickly in less than a week. See C. Rule, 'Quantifying the Economic Benefits of Effective Redress: Large E-Commerce Data Sets and the Cost-Benefit Case for Investing in Dispute Resolution' 34 (2012) *Univ Ark Little Rock Law Rev* 767–777.

121 See also D. Thompson, 'Online Dispute Resolution Expansion in the EU' (2012) 22(6) *Computers & Law* 31, 32; P. Cortés, 'Improving the EU's Proposals for Extra-judicial Consumer Redress' (2012) 23(2) *Comput Law* 27–28.

122 United Nations Commission on International Trade Law (UNCITRAL) Working Group III (Online Dispute Resolution) Twenty-Fifth Session, 'Online Dispute Resolution for Cross-Border Electronic Commerce Transactions: Draft Procedural Rules' New York, 21–15 May 2012. Draft Art. 5.

but to harness the national ADR infrastructure to do so. Yet, a timely and effective negotiation tool can be very useful in recurring complaints. Indeed, that is how eBay resolves the majority of its over 60 million annual disputes using the software, without human intervention.[123] An effective ODR platform should include a negotiation tool that proposes computer-generated settlements that are tailored to the complaints falling within the scope of application. This role is what Katsh called the 'fourth party' – that is, when technology shares (and sometimes even takes over) the role of the neutral third party in the dispute resolution process.[124]

As discussed in Chapter 2, it is possible to distinguish between two basic models of online negotiation: assisted negotiation and automated negotiation or blind-bidding.[125] The eBay and PayPal models employ assisted negotiation, categorizing disputes and matching them with solutions adopted by parties in similar past disputes. For example, when a buyer is dissatisfied with the purchase of a gadget, the solutions offered will be limited to returning the gadget (with or without paying the shipment), to obtaining a partial refund, or to being sent a new gadget by the seller. These three possibilities are automatically presented by eBay's ODR platform.[126]

The other negotiation model is known as automated negotiation or blind-bidding.[127] This technique may be used to reach settlements when liability is not challenged. Automated negotiation uses software that allows users to analyse their bargaining positions; it offers a space for evaluating and prioritizing offers and counter offers. Such offers are kept hidden during the negotiation, and are only disclosed when these offers match or enter into a pre-established range; hence the name of 'blind-bidding'.[128] The negotiation commences when one party invites the other to negotiate the amount of money in dispute. They can usually submit up to three offers, and if the bids of both parties come within a predetermined

[123] T. Schultz, 'The Roles of Dispute Settlement and ODR' in Ingen-Housz, *ADR in Business: Practice and Issues Across Countries and Cultures* (Kluwer, 2011) p. 135.

[124] O. Rabinovich-Einy, 'Technology's Impact: The Quest for a New Paradigm for Accountability in Mediation' (2006) 11 *Harv Negot Law Rev* 253. Cf. Katsh and Rifkin, n. 66, p. 36.

[125] A. Lodder and J. Zeleznikow, *Enhanced Dispute Resolution through the Use of Information Technology* (Cambridge University Press, 2010) pp. 75–85.

[126] N. Rogers, R. Bordone, F. Sander and C. McEwen, *Designing Systems and Processes for Managing Disputes* (Kluwer, 2013) pp. 24–25, 250.

[127] See Chapter 4. [128] See, e.g., Cybersettle.com and SmartSettle.com.

range or a given amount of money, the embedded algorithm automatically settles the dispute at the mid-point of the two offers. Although it is a simple dispute resolution technique, it effectively encourages the parties to reveal their 'bottom line' offers and demands, splitting the difference when the amounts are close, that is, when they fall within a specified range which may be from 5 to 30 per cent.[129]

For assisted negotiations to be effective it is important to constantly update the standard forms, taking into account previous cases, meaning that past experience informs and helps develop new generations of standard forms.[130] Although users should be able to access the form in their own language and fill in multiple-choice options, a standardized system will inevitably result in some restrictions in the communication between the parties. Such restrictions might even give rise to due process concerns, particularly if an arbitrator can take into account the online record of the unsuccessful negotiation when later issuing an arbitral award. The ODR platform should be designed in such a way that it automatically generates an agreement formalizing any settlement that has been reached. The agreement should inform claimants that they have voluntarily agreed to the settlement and that they can no longer pursue the enforcement of other legal rights related to the issues addressed in the ODR proceeding.

Conversely, if these ODR techniques are not employed, requiring each dispute to be resolved ad hoc by a neutral third party, then it is merely replication of traditional ADR processes. This type of redress system is inevitably more costly and less effective. In fact, the cost of resolving a consumer dispute on average through existing ADR is currently too high. By way of examples on average costs, the Consumer Arbitration Entity in Spain was reported to spend over €400 in resolving each case, while the Financial Ombudsmen Services in the UK reported £555 per case.[131] These costs are unsustainable for the majority of consumer complaints.

[129] See P. Cortés, 'A European Legal Perspective on Consumer ODR' (2009) 15(4) *Computer and Telecommunications Law Review* 92. See also Y. Gabuthy, 'Online Dispute Resolution and Bargaining' (2004) 17(3) *Eur J Law Econ* 353–371.

[130] This approach was taken first by SquareTrade and later by eBay and PayPal in order to promote settlement between the disputants. See S. Abernethy, 'Building Large-Scale Online Dispute Resolution and Trustmark Systems' in Online Dispute Resolution: Technology as the 'Fourth Party' (E. Katsh & D. Choi eds. 2003). Cf. O. Rabinovich-Einy 'Technology's Impact: The Quest for a New Paradigm for Accountability in Mediation' (2006) 11 *Harv Negot Law Rev* 253.

[131] C. Hodges, I. Benohr, N. Creutzfeldt-Banda, 'Consumer-to-Business Dispute Resolution: The Power of CADR' (2012) 13 *ERA Forum* pp. 199, 206 and 216. See also The Financial

Therefore, in order to realize the potential of a negotiation tool, the ODR platform should offer parties a list of possible remedies, encouraging the settlement of meritorious complaints. The more information the parties are able to obtain and exchange during the negotiation process, the more likely they will be in settling their dispute. Such negotiation will even be more effective when coupled with a subsequent ADR process that, if negotiations fail, is capable of progressing to a stage where, at least to some degree, a predictable decision would be proposed or imposed by a neutral third party in a quick and cost-effective manner.[132]

4.6.3 *Referral Function*

A referral function that the ODR platform should have is one that helps consumers to identify an effective redress system when the trader has not responded to the complaint. The type of referral will depend on where the parties are based and the sector where they operate. Accordingly, the ODR platform would be the best instrument to refer cases to more adequate forums, which can be the courts, enforcement bodies or mandatory ADR schemes.

Given that traders do not respond to the majority of complaints (55 per cent) submitted by consumers via the ODR platform,[133] it is clear that the invitation by the ODR platform to select an ADR entity is not successful. Hence, it is imperative for the platform to make referrals to other redress options, such as chargebacks, enforcement bodies and even the courts. Indeed, as discussed in the previous chapter, an important pathway should be to redirect consumers, when appropriate, to court processes, especially when the ESCP and collective redress options are available. In time, the ODR platform could also link to the e-Justice Portal, providing national courts with a simple and user-friendly

Ombudsman Service 'Annual Review 2010/11' Available at www.financial-ombudsman .org.uk/publications/ar11/foreword.html.

132 According the European Consumer Centres' Network, the ECCs could only find an amicable solution in settlement with the trader in 41.6 per cent of all cases and 56.2 per cent of disputes arose from e-commerce transactions. In 75 per cent of cases where no solution was found this was due to lack of agreement with the trader. ECC Network Annual Report 2010, p. 1; K. Henry, 'Med-Arb: An Alternative to Interest Arbitration in the Resolution of Contract Negotiation Disputes' (1988) 3(2) *Ohio St J Disp Resol* 385.

133 Minor, n. 92.

case-management tool. Such tools could assist parties and courts to communicate online when processing consumer claims. Their design would need to be tailored in order to allow for the interoperability between national courts and the ODR platform. Although it is acknowledged that the design of such tools will be challenging, if successful it would bring the benefits associated with economies of scale. In doing so, it will also facilitate the communications amongst national courts and, as a result, it could deliver a more expeditious and accessible judicial redress when other more informal and cost-effective ADR options are unavailable and when traders refuse to comply with a settlement.

The previous chapter noted that ADR bodies should refer cases to courts when the complaints they receive are not suitable to be resolved through an ADR process because there is evidence of certain crimes, there is an important point of law, or there is any other reason that makes it more suitable to be processed in the courts. A referral system could even include a system of preliminary reference between ADR bodies and enforcement bodies, which could in turn trickle up to national courts and subsequently even to the Court of Justice of the European Union when there is an important point of EU Law. These avenues would ensure a better application of consumer law, leaving the role of resolving most basic legal issues to sectorial enforcement bodies, and that of clarifying and developing the law to the courts, while allowing ADR bodies to operate more effectively in the 'shadow of the law'.[134]

The ODR platform could also help consumers to enforce the outcomes when the trader has not complied voluntarily. The first step would be to provide consumers with information on enforcement, and ODR advisors may be able to assist consumers on an ad hoc basis. In time however it would be preferable if consumers have access to a streamlined online process to request the enforcement of outcomes. As further discussed in Chapter 8, enforcement bodies, regulators and new technologies could provide useful assistance in speeding up the process without involving the courts.

4.6.4 Monitoring Function

ADR entities have an important limitation as they normally deal with individual disputes. For example, if there is a train or a flight delay and

[134] R. Mnookin and L. Kornhauser, 'Bargaining in the Shadow of the Law: The Case of Divorce' (1979) 88 *Yale Law J* 950.

the law states that all passengers are entitled to compensation, but only one consumer complains (first to the business, and then to the ADR entity), then it is likely that only that consumer will receive compensation, but not the rest of passengers, who even though they were equally entitled will not be compensated because they did not complain. Thus, the effective enforcement of consumer rights cannot rely exclusively on ADR entities.

In this regard, Hodges argues that the link between ADR entities and public regulatory entities has the important function of collecting aggregated data on consumer disputes, which can lead to more effective cooperation with public enforcement bodies, as they will be able to identify earlier market abuses and lack of compliance with consumer policies.[135] These exchanges of information are hoped to have a knock on effect in improving the coordination between public and private enforcement bodies.

Although the ADR Directive requires certified ADR entities to cooperate with national enforcement bodies,[136] as many ombudsman entities in regulated sectors already do,[137] the ODR Regulation does not require such cooperation between the EU ODR platform and other enforcement bodies. As noted earlier when discussing the conflict prevention function, the information contained in the platform, if appropriately shared, could improve the enforcement role of public regulators. This is because the use of technology in processing disputes can help to go beyond individual complaints, and provide information leading to redress to others entitled to it, but who have not complained (because they were not aware or did not have the time or resources to do so). Hence, this lack of cooperation between the platform and enforcers is an important shortcoming since the information captured by the platform can be instrumental to chase rouge traders and tackle market problems, so that action can be taken promptly.[138] It is therefore recommended that the EU ODR platform should incorporate clearly defined pathways that enable the coordination between the platform (as well as the ADR entities) and public enforcement bodies.

135 C. Hodges, 'Consumer Ombudsmen: Better Regulation and Dispute Resolution' (2015) *ERA Forum* 5.

136 Art. 17(1) ADR Directive.

137 This is often the case in the regulated sector. For instance, the Financial Service Ombudsman in the UK often shares complaints data with the regulator and enforcement body, the Financial Conduct Authority.

138 Ibid. 6.

A pathway should therefore be built to share information about complaints to national enforcement bodies and the CCP network, helping them to monitor problems with the enforcement of European consumer policy through recurring claims. The platform should be able to recognize when there is a pattern showing the lack of compliance with consumer rights as well as when there may be consumers who did not complain, but who would be entitled to compensation. Consequently, it is paramount that while respecting data protection legislation, enforcement agencies have access to the information submitted in the platform for the early identification of rogue traders and market failures.[139]

In terms of effective enforcement of consumer protection laws, a key concern is that increasingly using courts as a last resort, and moving disputes from public enforcement and courts to ADR entities could lead to an inadequate enforcement of the European consumer policy as ADR entities may not adjudicate based on the legal entitlements of the parties.[140] Consequently, it would be desirable that adjudicated decisions are published while maintaining confidentiality of personal data. This would in turn encourage traders to settle meritorious complaints.

It must be noted that most ADR entities operate consensual procedures (such as mediation techniques) that enable parties to reach amicable settlements. Arguably, if these settlements are not properly monitored, it could lead parties with asymmetric powers (i.e. consumer and businesses) to reach settlements that do not reflect effective enforcement of EU consumer law, where, to put it bluntly, the experienced trader could put pressure on consumers to settle for less than what they would be entitled (and thus with what would be recognized by a court of law). Such potential abuses could theoretically compromise the rule of law, particularly when cloaked under private and confidential settlements. Therefore, the more private ADR entities grow, the more need there is for greater transparency and for developing an effective mechanism to evaluate their performance.

The ADR Directive attempts to counterbalance this risk by requiring a high level of transparency to monitor certified ADR entities and imposing a supervisory role on the national competent authorities, whose role

[139] Hodges et al., n. 108, p. 220.

[140] See, for example, G. Wagner, 'Private Law Enforcement Through ADR: Wonder Drug or Snake Oil?' (2014) 51(1) *Common Mark Law Rev* 165–194 and H. Eidenmiller and M. Engle, 'Against False Settlement: Designing Efficient Consumer Rights Enforcement System in Europe' (2014) 29 *Ohio St J Disp Resol* 261.

is to ensure compliance by the certified ADR entities.[141] As noted earlier, these certified ADR entities have the obligation to cooperate with enforcement bodies and must publish periodical reports, which if rigorously carried out, are hoped to impact on a greater level of public scrutiny and accountability of ADR entities.

4.7 Conclusion

With the goal of stimulating the Internal Market, the EU has adopted legislation that aims to overcome the obstacles in consumer redress by promoting the use of ADR and ODR. The European Commission found that the three main obstacles to the growth of ADR/ODR were gaps in coverage, the absence of legal standards and a lack of awareness.[142] While the ADR Directive increases the availability of quality ADR for consumer disputes, the ODR Regulation creates an ODR platform that acts as a signposting service, directing contractual disputes from online sales to ADR entities. It is however difficult to conclude that these three obstacles have already been overcome.

The first obstacle was the gaps in the availability of ADR/ODR bodies. This chapter has noted that not much has changed in this regard, as while there may be ADR entities that have been certified to cover all types of consumer disputes, traders by and large remain reluctant to participate in ADR voluntarily, unless required by their sectorial regulations or by their trade associations. Moreover, the new regulatory framework requires traders to inform about ADR/ODR bodies, but in most cases they are not required to participate, leaving many (if not most of the) consumer disputes unresolved. The chapter highlighted that there is a counter-productive incongruity in the traders' obligation to inform (but not to participate) in ADR/ODR. Only an effective residual ADR body at the national level, or alternatively a judicial system that is truly easily accessible to consumers, would fill the gaps. This proposal is further expanded in Chapter 7 of this book.

The second obstacle was the absence of legal standards. This chapter noted that the ADR Directive has set minimum procedural standards, and in doing so, it has increased minimum due process guarantees for certified ADR entities. But, as discussed in the next chapter, the new legislation is transposed into national law, adjusting to the peculiarities of

[141] Art. 19 ADR Directive. [142] See EC Communication, n. 8.

the national ADR infrastructure. Consequently, domestic law has discretion, inter alia, to allow traders to bring disputes against consumers, and to certify ADR entities which are not independent of the traders' in-house complaint system as well as arbitration schemes that impose outcomes on the parties. This variety brings the inevitable risk of implementing these standards in an inconsistent manner; this risk is enhanced because each of the 28 Member States have their own different national competent authorities that assess the ADR entities' compliance with the national law. In order to achieve a more levelled playing field, the European Commission should appoint a single pan-European authority or working group to provide guidelines to a single national accreditation system. Furthermore, since in most economic sectors traders are able to choose amongst (and pay for) ADR entities that operate transparently, this will inevitably lead to forum shopping affecting the independence of ADR entities. These issues will be explored further in Chapter 8.

The third obstacle was the lack of awareness. This chapter observed that there is a low level of compliance amongst traders with their information requirements. Evidence of the lack of knowledge is that during the first three months of operation the ODR platform received around 5,500 complaints;[143] but only in those cases where the trader responded were they processed by certified ADR entities, which means that the majority were not processed. Moreover, the number of reported cases alone is hardly a high number of complaints for the whole of the EU, especially since all online traders have the legal obligation to carry the link to the platform in an accessible manner. Indeed, many, if not most, do not provide it, and when they do, they often bury it in their T&C and rarely include an email address. For that reason, the ODR platform should develop, with the assistance of the contact points (and the ADR entities), a database with the traders' email addresses – at least of those that are signed up with an ADR entity. Hence, the first step towards effective redress must be to ensure that when traders have agreed to participate in ADR, the ODR platform is able to send consumer complaints to the traders' correct email address.

Accordingly, in order to meet its objectives of closing the gaps, ensuring quality standards and increasing awareness, the ODR platform must be more than a mere referral site and offer the following functions. First, a problem diagnosis and conflict prevention function should promote

[143] Email from Olivier Micol, European Commission (18 May 2016) on file with author.

early resolution through the provision to consumers of automated bespoke information on their rights and obligations (including procedural obligations such as the prior attempt to settle a complaint directly with the trader). Second, the platform must include an online negotiation tool, which offers consumers and cooperative traders with a forum to settle complaints (and record their outcomes) before these escalate to ADR entities. Third, the platform should have a full referral function, which not only invite parties to select an ADR body, but it automatically refers cases to ADR bodies when the negotiation has failed and the trader is signed to an ADR process – in the remaining of cases, consumers should be assisted in escalating the complaint to a court process. Finally, the ODR platform should incorporate a monitoring function, which feedbacks enforcement bodies, so they can react quickly to market abuses.

It is recognized that these additional functions will require public investment, but without this additional level of support the current pan-European ADR/ODR system is doomed to fail. The aforementioned functions would make the ODR platform more effective and they will be instrumental to meet the policy aim of increasing consumer trust in the Internal Market. However, it is acknowledged that while the pan-European structure is increasingly important, the main infrastructure of consumer redress depends on how it is implemented in the national systems. Thus, the next chapter examines the transposition of the EU legal framework into the national legal systems.

5

Consumer ADR in Three Radically Different Jurisdictions

Italy, Spain and the UK

5.1 Introduction

The implementation of the ADR Directive has offered the possibility to re-assess the national ADR infrastructure of the EU Member States in order to improve the national provision of consumer redress. However, in practice, partly due to the limited time that Members States had to implement the ADR Directive (two years), the transposition has not been gold plated. Indeed, most Member States simply complied with the minimum legal requirements, as this was the less costly option to implement it in time.

The ADR Directive describes ADR entities as adjudicative and consensual extrajudicial processes created on a durable basis. A caveat should be noted when examining the terminology employed when referring to consumer redress models in different jurisdictions and economic sectors. Sometimes different terms are used to refer to similar redress models. For instance, the French *médiateur*, the UK ombudsman and the German conciliator have equivalent roles.[1] Similarly, the same concepts are given different meanings depending on the jurisdictions. For instance, while in Ireland 'facilitating an amicable solution' has been described as conciliation and 'procedures where the ADR scheme proposes a solution' as mediation,[2] the opposite view is adopted in the UK, where conciliation is mostly used in the context of employment

[1] N. Creutzfeldt-Banda, 'How Important Is Procedural justice for Consumer Dispute Resolution? A Case Study of an Ombudsman Model for European Consumers', (2014) 37(4) *J Consum Policy* 533.

[2] The Irish Department of Jobs, Enterprise and Innovation 'Consultation on the Implementation of the EU Directive on Consumer Alternative Dispute Resolution and the EU Regulation on Consumer Online Dispute Resolution' (June 2014) p. 2.

disputes.[3] By contrast, in Italy *conciliazione* is often referred to mediations carried out by a judge, as well as in the context of 'representative negotiations or joint conciliations' (*conciliazione paritetica*) where representatives of consumers and businesses resolve disputes on their behalf, which is in effect a form of representative negotiation.

When examining the ADR models in different jurisdictions one must be mindful also about the main motivations behind the promotion of ADR. Although the growth of ADR has been subject to similar motivations (including seeking a more proportionate, informal, private and cost-efficient dispute resolution model), the emphasis on these motivations has varied depending on the country. Whereas in Italy ADR is seen as a public priority to relieve the notoriously congested Italian courts from civil claims that take years to be resolved, in the UK the main motivation for encouraging ADR is the extremely high costs of litigation, even for low- or medium-value claims; lastly, in Spain, the civil procedure, even for low-value claims, is not suited for litigants without legal representation, and this has led the Spanish government to fund a public arbitration scheme for consumers.

This chapter analyses the main redress models operating in three radically different jurisdictions – namely Italy, Spain and the UK – which have organically developed their own redress models.[4] Currently, the leading redress model in Italy consists of mediation (pre-action mediation and the public mediation for telecoms) and 'representative negotiations', while Spain has a public arbitration system, and the UK relies mainly on sectorial ombudsman schemes. The aim of this chapter is to examine critically the ADR infrastructure in these three jurisdictions and the impact that the ADR Directive has had in order to make recommendations on how to improve these national redress systems.

5.2 Consumer Redress in Italy

In Italy, the two main ADR methods for resolving consumer complaints are mediation (which consideration of is now prerequisite to lodge a

[3] C. Hodges, I. Benohr and N. Creutzfeldtz-Banda, *Consumer ADR in Europe* (Hart, 2012) pp. xxix–xxx.

[4] An early analysis of the different ADR models in these three jurisdictions was presented at an ERA conference on Consumer ADR and it appeared in P. Cortés, 'The Impact of EU Law in the ADR Landscape in Italy, Spain and the UK: Time for Change or Missed Opportunity?' (2015) 16(2) *ERA Forum* 125–147.

claim in court) and representative negotiations (i.e. *conciliazione paripatetica* or joint conciliations). While pre-action mediation is normally used in civil and commercial disputes and in some sectors (notably in telecommunications and energy), representative negotiations are growing in many sectors through agreements, mainly between large businesses and consumer associations. In addition, there are a few ombudsman-like schemes, such as in the banking and financial sector.

5.2.1 Mandatory Mediation in Italy

The overloaded court system in Italy, with around 5 million pending lawsuits, operates at a snail pace, taking on average three years to process a civil claim in the first instance.[5] Furthermore, in Italy every individual has the right to appeal a judgment – unlike in the UK where individuals with civil claims do not have an automatic right of appeal, instead they are only entitled to have their request for appeal to be considered by the court.

The implementation of the Mediation Directive was seen as an opportunity to promote the use of mediation in Italy not only for cross-border but also for domestic disputes. The first national law enacted was the Legislative Decree 28/2010, which required claimants to invite defendants to attend a mediation information session (what in the UK is called a Mediation Information and Assessment Meeting or MIAM) before lodging a claim in court. The Italian Constitutional Court invalidated this law because it was implemented by governmental legislation without passing the statute required by Parliament.[6] Consequently, the Parliament passed the Legislative Decree No 69/2013, which presently regulates mediation in Italy.

The new law brought a number of changes. For instance, under the previous mediation law, parties were allowed to choose mediation providers from anywhere in the country. This situation led to a race to offer the lowest fees allowed by the law, which impacted on the standards applied and the quality of mediation. The new law requires parties to choose providers within the judicial district with competence to hear the case. The other important change was that under the new law parties are required to have legal representation during the mediation.

[5] OECD Economics Department Policy Notes 'What Makes Civil Justice Effective' (18 June 2013).

[6] Case 272/2012 of the Constitutional Court.

The advantage of this option is that a settlement reached during the mediation can be made enforceable by the signature of the lawyers without the need of judicial approval.

The statutory mediation has two phases: the mandatory MIAM and the optional mediation. Attendance to MIAMs is optional for defendants (but not for claimants), who in fact only attend in under half of the cases. If parties decide to proceed to mediation, the procedure can terminate with a settlement proposal, which may impact on the costs of a subsequent judicial case. Accordingly, if only one party accepts the proposal and the other does not achieve a more advantageous outcome at the end of the litigation, then the court may penalize the party who refused the settlement with a fine and all the legal costs.

Mandatory MIAMs apply for many civil cases, including consumer matters. The scope covers disputes related to matters about condominium, property rights, division, inheritance, family agreements, lease, loan, commercial rents, medical negligence, defamation, insurance, banking and financial services. It must be noted that in these cases the law does not classify claimants as consumers, but as private citizens entering into civil disputes. However, this classification is not justified under some of these categories, namely for loans, insurance, banking and financial services. This has recently led an Italian court in Verona to elevate a preliminary question to the Court of Justice of the EU asking whether the requirement of mandatory pre-action mediation with legal representation as a precondition for the bringing of legal proceedings in consumer matters is compatible with articles 1 and 2 of the ADR Directive.[7]

[7] Request for a preliminary ruling from the Tribunale Ordinario di Verona (Italy) lodged on 10 February 2016 – *Livio Menini and Maria Antonia Rampanelli* v. *Banco Popolare – Società Cooperativa* (Case C-75/16). The questions referred were the following two:

1. In so far as it provides that Directive 2013/11 (1) 'shall be without prejudice to Directive 2008/52', (2) must Article 3(2) of Directive 2013/11 be construed as meaning that it is without prejudice to the possibility for individual Member States of providing for compulsory mediation solely in those cases which do not fall within the scope of Directive 2013/11, that is to say the cases referred to in Article 2(2) of Directive 2013/11, contractual disputes arising out of contracts other than sales or service contracts, as well as those which do not concern consumers?
2. In so far as it guarantees consumers the possibility of submitting complaints against traders to appropriate entities offering alternative dispute resolution procedures, must Article 1 . . . of Directive 2013/11 be interpreted as meaning that it precludes a national rule which requires the use of mediation in one of the disputes referred to in Article 2 (1) of Directive 2013/11 as a precondition for the bringing of legal proceedings by the consumer, and, in any event, as precluding a national rule that requires a consumer

In addition, Italian courts have the discretionary power to order parties to attempt mediation even in the type of civil claims that fall out of the statutory requirement to engage in pre-action mediation. The Consumer Code also encourages consumer associations and consumers themselves to attempt mediation before initiating legal proceedings.[8]

In Italy traders are legally required to register with the Chambers of Commerce and to provide an email address. This facilitates the process of informing the respondent and setting up the MIAM within the 30 days required by the law. Save for the mandatory legal representation, the participation in the MIAM, which may last for up to one hour, is free of cost for the parties. Parties who proceed to a full mediation pay the statutory fees (which are lower than court fees) except for low-income parties (i.e. those receiving under €10,000 p.a.), whose fees are waived. In these cases the costs are covered by the mediation provider so they put financial pressure on the providers, especially when the number of cases progressing from the MIAM to an actual mediation is low. According to the national statistics for 2014, around 40 per cent of respondents that went to MIAMs agreed to go to mediation; of all those who went to mediation, around a quarter settled.[9]

Parties will only need to attend the MIAM in order to avoid cost penalties in a subsequent court case. Thus, when a party refuses to proceed to mediation, it forces the other party to start a legal action. Because Italian courts are very slow, the party who refuses to pay has an economic incentive to let the other party escalate the dispute in the hope that it will give up.

Overall, MIAMs have positive and negative elements. The main positive factors are that they have helped to raise awareness about mediation and settlements become enforceable when signed off by lawyers (i.e. without the need of a court approval). The negative elements are that claimants with frivolous claims can also use MIAMs, and that these MIAMs lack teeth in bringing defendants to the negotiation table when

taking part in mediation relating to one of the aforementioned disputes to be assisted by a lawyer and to bear the related costs, and allows a party not to participate in mediation only on valid grounds?

The questions are available at http://eur-lex.europa.eu/legal-content/EN/TXT/PDF/?uri=CELEX:62016CN0075&from=EN.

8 Art. 141 of Legislative Decree No. 206 of 2005.

9 Ministero della Giustizia, Dipartimento della Organizzazione Giudiziaria, del Personale e dei Servizi, Direzione Generale di Statistica 'Mediazione Civile Ex DL 28/2010 Statistiche Relative al Priodo Gennaio – Settembre 2014.

they are facing meritorious claims. Although courts can impose cost sanctions when a reasonable settlement has been refused, in practice they rarely do so, which disincentives parties to consider settlements.

5.2.2 ADR and Technology

Technology is increasingly being used by the lawyers involved in the mediation process. The main use of ODR technology comes from the ODR platform that is licensed by the National Association of Chambers of Commerce (Conciliacamera).[10] The license agreement has three modules with different fees. Module 1 is the back office used by 90 per cent of the chambers allowing them to filter data, generate statistics and organize a high volume of cases. Module 2, also used by the majority of chambers, includes an online conference mechanism. Module 3 allows users to send and receive mediation requests – this module is used especially by those lawyers who have a high number of cases.

More specifically in the consumer sector one of the most long-standing ODR entities in Italy is RisolviOnline,[11] which belongs to the Chamber of Arbitration of Milan. They offer online mediation services for commercial and consumer disputes. RisolviOnline started as a pilot project from the Chamber of Commerce in Milan in 2001. The experience with this ODR platform was used to develop Conciliacamera. RisolviOnline's rules are simpler than those used in Conciliacamera because the latter follows the requirements of mandatory mediation.[12] RisolviOnline currently receives a very small number of requests of mediation per year (around 20) with an average value of cases around €500. These requests for mediation often prompt an internal resolution of the dispute through the traders' in-house complaint system. Initially, the requests for mediation were free of cost, but applicants now have to pay €30 in order to discourage vexatious claims. The fee for mediation varies depending on the value of the dispute, and they start from €26.50 per party for disputes under €500 – of which two-thirds of the fee goes to the mediator.

The most common types of disputes are consumer problems related to hardware or software, problems with Internet connection, holiday packages and disputes arising from online auctions. The procedure commences when one party files a case in their website.[13] The case is sent

[10] www.conciliacamera.it. [11] www.risolvionline.com. [12] Decree 28/2010.
[13] See www.risolvionline.com.

by email to the other party, who is asked to accept and hence activate the online process within 15 days. If the other party does not respond within 60 days, then the case is dismissed. Conversely, if the other party is willing to participate in the dispute resolution process, then a mediator is appointed by the administrator of RisolviOnline on the basis of competence and other criteria. Parties are invited to express their views via chat or through a private discussion forum. The process finishes when either the parties or the mediator consider that an agreement is unlikely to be reached or when parties agree to a settlement that is drafted by the mediator. The settlement is signed by the parties and sent by fax or regular mail.

5.2.3 *The Regulation of the ADR in the Telecom Sector*

The sectorial regulation for electronic communications has established the participation in ADR as a prerequisite to the admissibility of a claim in court against a telecom service.[14] This regulation has passed the scrutiny of the Court of Justice of the European Union,[15] which held that the right to access to justice was not breached by a regulation that requires telecom users (consumers as well as businesses) who intend to sue a phone company, or a radio or tv broadcaster, to attempt the resolution of the dispute through ADR. Telecom users have three options when raising a complaint: (i) they can resolve the mediation or arbitration process provided by the chambers of commerce, which is normally used for high-value disputes;[16] (ii) they can use the ADR provided by the regulator and public enforcement body (Corecom) – this is the most popular option as it is free of cost and open to all users; or (iii) they can participate in the *conciliazione paritetica* offered by some consumer associations to their members.

The most popular ADR option is that provided through the regulator (*Autorità per le Garanzie nelle Comunicazioni* or AGCOM) which operates an ADR through its regional committees (Corecom).[17] Similar

[14] Authority for Telecommunications Supervision Regulation No. 173/07/CONS.

[15] *Rosalba Alassini and Others* v. *Telecom Italia* C-317/08.

[16] A. Bruni, 'The Use and Practise of Mediation in Italy' in F. Diedrich (ed.), *The Status Quo of Mediation in Europe and Overseas – Options for Countries in Transition* (Verlag Dr Kovac, Hamburg 2014) p. 2.

[17] See Act 249/97 and Regolamento in materia di procedure di risoluzione delle controversie tra operatori di comunicazioni elettroniche ed utenti, n. 173/07/CONS. Available at www.agcom.it. CORECOM stands for Comitati Regionali per le Comunicazioni. The

supervisory systems operate in other sectors, namely finance,[18] banking[19] and energy.[20] Corecom relies on public resources and officials to process around 75,000 complaints a year from telecom users.[21] However, complaints will only be processed when consumers have previously tried to resolve them directly with the trader. The telecoms have a statutory maximum of 45 days to resolve complaints; after this time consumers can go to Corecom, but in some cases the telecoms themselves have set a shorter limit of 30 days in their contracts with consumers. The regulation requires that Corecom should process complaints within a maximum period of 30 days, though in practice the average is around 60 days.

The participation of telecoms in the mediation is voluntary, but in practice telecoms participate and settle the majority of cases. The reason for the high level of participation is that if the telecom does not opt into the mediation process, the claim will move in most regions to an effective adjudication stage, where most decisions are decided in favour of the claimant. The average settlement in mediation is around €450 euros – an amount which is usually less than that claimed by the user.

Currently, Corecom is moving its process online, but this is proving challenging as it requires procedural changes. At the time of writing only some Corecom regional offices allow the electronic filing of complaints under €500. Yet, currently in only a very small percentage of Corecom mediations do parties communicate through a video-conference system offered by the regional Corecom.[22] With the aim of complying with the ADR Directive, the regulatory authority for telecoms is currently looking to establish a single ODR platform that can be used for all the regional Corecom offices.

distribution of competence between the regions and the State is contained in Art. 117 of the Italian Constitution. It should be noted that not all regions have achieved the same level of delegated powers, with some regions, such as Sardinian CORECOM, not having the competence to resolve consumer complaints.

18 Under the supervision of CONSOB.

19 Under the supervision of Banca d'Italia.

20 For instance, the conciliation offered in the energy sector is supervised by the Agenzia per l'Energia Elettrica ed il Gas (AEEG).

21 Interview to Enrico Maria Cotugno, Vice direttore AGCOM Autoritá per le Garanzie nelle Comunicazioni (13 February 2015). He stated that from May 2013 to May 2014 Corecom received around 75,000 complaints, while conciliazione paritetica manages around 13,000 complaints per year, and chambers of commerce around 1,000.

22 See, for example, the online mediation offered in Calabria. Available at http://corecom.consrc.it/hp2/default.asp?selez=AccessoL.

5.2.4 *Representative Negotiations* (Concilizione Paritetica)

The representative negotiations, by contrast to traditional mediation processes, are somewhat similar to the French *médiateurs* in the sense that one neutral third party works for the trader.[23] Yet, the Italian representative negotiations are different to the French counterpart with regards to the consumer not being present during the redress process. Instead, it is a negotiation carried out by a consumer representative (normally someone drafted from a consumer organization) and a business representative. These representative negotiations normally take place in the premises of the business and achieve a high level of settlements, which are often quite beneficial for the consumer. This is due to the high expertise of the representatives, the persuasive nature of the public independent consumer representative and the willingness to find a solution that would satisfy the consumer. The proposed settlement is then passed on to the consumer, who can either accept it or reject it, leaving the consumer with the possibility of pursuing the matter in court. However, in practice, the great majority of these proposed settlements are accepted by consumers. Interestingly, in most sectors, the use of the representative negotiation is voluntary.

Telecom Italia was the first company to use the representative negotiation process, which, like with the Corecom, can only be commenced once the consumer had already tried to resolve the complaint directly with the Telecom. If the consumer does not obtain an answer within 45 days, or is not satisfied with the answer given, then the consumer can contact online one of the consumer organizations that are signatory of a framework agreement. The consumer can also request a hearing but must outline the reasons why it is considered to be necessary, so the hearing is not automatically granted. If the consumer accepts the settlement proposal provided by the negotiators, then such settlement will become enforceable under Italian law.[24]

In 2012 there have been 17,000 consumer requests for representative negotiations, the majority of which were related to telecoms (72 per cent) and energy (16 per cent), where the average time for resolving these cases

[23] N. Scannicchio, 'L'Adeguamento dell' Ordinamento Italiano alla Nuova Disciplina Europea sulla Risolutzione Alternativea Delle Controversie di Consumo' in F. Esteban de la Rosa *La Resolución Alternativa De Litigios De Consumo En Los Estados Miembros De La UE: Impacto Del Nuevo Derecho Europeo* (Tirant, 2015).

[24] By virtue of Art. 1965 of the Italian Civil Code.

was around 70 days.[25] Currently the provision of representative negotiations is decentralized and it does not operate in all the sectors.

Like the ADR Directive embraces the French *médiateurs* subject to the compliance with a number of safeguards that guarantee their independence (e.g. separate budget), the Italian representative negotiation schemes can seek the certification as an ADR entity because they are not a direct negotiation between consumer and the trader, which are excluded from the scope of the Directive,[26] but negotiations between representatives of the trader and a representative acting on behalf of the consumer.

This ADR model has a number of strengths. First, it is of low cost; depending on the sector and who represents the consumer, it is either free of cost for the consumer or has a very low filing fee. Second, because of the high level of expertise of the parties' representatives, the process is highly effective in terms of successful resolutions (over 90 per cent). The training of the negotiators takes place periodically, and it is carried out jointly by the consumer organizations and the businesses that opted into the programme. There are however two recommendations that can be made in order to improve the present model of representative negotiations. First, using a national ODR platform would provide greater visibility and benefit from economies of scale. Second, examining best practices of the different procedures used in each region could lead to minimum standards, including improvements in the training of the parties' representatives.

5.2.5 *The Italian Financial Ombudsman*

In the financial sector the main ADR scheme is the ombudsman, but there are also conciliation and arbitration providers. The Banking and Financial Ombudsman (*Arbitrato Bancario Finanziario*) offers since 2009 an ombudsman process for settling disputes between consumers and banks, as well as with other intermediaries, such as brokers.[27] The participation of banks is mandatory, though consumers must first attempt to resolve the dispute directly with the financial institution,

[25] It has been reported that there have been around 200,000 cases since it started to operate in 2001. See Fonte, Consumers' Forum, 'Terzo Raporto Sulle Conciliazioni Paritetiche' (Rome, 2012).

[26] Art. 2(e) ADR Directive.

[27] Article 128-bis of the Consolidated Law on Banking, a provision introduced by Law 262/2005 (Investor Protection Law).

which must respond within 30 days.[28] The ombudsman can make recommendations up to €100,000, but these are not binding. However, if the financial body does not comply with the recommendation, then it is made public in a black list, so in practice the immense majority of the 11,000 annual recommendations are followed by the banks.[29]

Consumers can submit complaints in the ombudsman website.[30] The procedure is all in writing, where a case handler issues recommendations that are legally reasoned. A peculiarity of this scheme is that, unlike most ombudsman schemes elsewhere, consumers are required to pay a €20 filing fee, which is refundable if they succeed in their claim. In such a case, traders will be required to refund the consumer fee, plus pay an additional fee of €200.[31] In addition, banks and financial institutions must pay an annual fee depending on their size of business.

The financial ombudsman recognizes that their goals go beyond resolving individual cases. They seek to make the financial system more efficient and competitive with the publication of important outcomes, which are now in excess of 15,000.[32] This information in turn feeds, on one hand, financial institutions, whose internal complaints departments are required to take these recommendations into consideration when dealing with complaints in-house, and on the other hand, by the regulator (the Bank of Italy), who is legally required to consider these recommendations when carrying out its supervisory and regulatory activity.[33]

If the disputes do not concern banking or financial transactions, but rather investment products, they are dealt with by the Commission for Companies and Stock Exchange's[34] Conciliation and Arbitration Chamber and another ADR (e.g. *Giurì Bancario*). They cover disputes brought by investors against brokers concerning the violation of disclosure obligations, fairness and transparency.

All the aforementioned ADR schemes replace the procedural requirement to participate in a mediation information session prior to the submission of a claim in court.[35] In other words, when a claimant

[28] This is the most recent statistic available and it corresponds for the year of 2014. See Banca d'Italia Eurosistema, 'The Banking and Financial Ombudsman Annual Report' (January 2016) p. 8. Available at www.arbitrobancariofinanziario.it/pubblicazioni/relazioniAnnuali/en-relazione-ABF-2014.pdf.

[29] Ibid., p. 20. [30] www.arbitrobancariofinanziario.it. [31] Ibid., p. 9.

[32] Ibid., p. 17. [33] Ibid., p. 12. [34] Regulation n. 18275 of 18 July 2012.

[35] Art. 5 (1-*bis*) Legislative Decree 28/2010. E. Capobianco, 'Arbitrato e conciliazione. La risoluzione stragiudiziale delle controversie tra mediazione e procedura dinanzi all'Arbitro Bancario Finanziario' (2010) 8(9) *Obbl contr*, p. 571 ss.

has participated in one of these ADR schemes, it is no longer required to attempt the pre-action mediation.

5.2.6 *The Impact of the ADR Directive in the Italian Infrastructure for Consumer Redress*

The ADR Directive was implemented in Italy through the Legislative Decree 130 of 6 August 2015, which became effective from 3 September 2015.[36] The new statute was included within Part V of the Consumer Code, entitled 'Consumer Associations and Access to Justice'. However the development of some of the legal principles have been left to the secondary sectorial legislation. The Italian law has decided to certify only ADR entities that propose and not impose settlements. This approach is in line with the preference to promote its main consensual ADR processes for consumer matters: mediation and representative negotiations. Participation in these processes however can be mandatory for those who wish to lodge a claim in court, as was noted earlier with MIAMs for many civil claims and the mandatory conciliation for the telecoms sector.[37]

Italy has assigned the Ministry of Economic Development the role of the single contact point for the European Commission, and that of certifying representative negotiations providers when there is not another sectorial competent authority.[38] In addition, the Ministry of Justice has the role of certifying consumer mediation bodies.

Italy has not designated a single residual body; instead, it has allocated this role to its chambers of commerce. These are public bodies already operating with general competence for consumer matters, but in practice they do not deal with consumer matters of low value (saved from minor exceptions, such as ResolviOnline). Accordingly, it is not realistic to expect that the Italian chambers of commerce will improve the consumer redress landscape. A more effective approach would be to foster in the other consumer sectors the existing successful ADR schemes, such as the mediation offered by Corecom and representative negotiations.

[36] Art. 2(2) Legislative Decree 130/2015. See generally C. Pilia, P. Cortés and P. Vargiu, 'The Implementation of the Consumer ADR Directive in Italy' in P. Cortés (ed.), *The New Regulatory Framework for Consumer Dispute Resolution* (OUP, 2016).

[37] Consumer Code (Art. 141(5) and (6)).

[38] The other four authorities operating in their respective sectors are: the National Commission for Companies and Stock Exchange (CONSOB), the Authority for Electricity, Gas and Water (AEEGSI), the Communications Authority (AGCOM) and the Bank of Italy.

Furthermore, given that the existing courts in Italy are completely unsuited for low-value consumer matters, a key reform in Italy would be to make participation in consumer ADR schemes mandatory for most (if not for all) consumer cases. Mandatory consumer ADR schemes should depart from the current pre-action mediation in two fundamental ways. First, they should make it mandatory for traders to participate in the ADR process; second, they should not require consumers to have legal representation. A small refundable fee may be appropriate in some sectors in order to avoid vexatious or unmeritorious claims from consumers. Moreover, when the level of settlements is low, then the ADR entity should also integrate adjudication stage akin to that used by Corecom. Low-value decisions from this proposed scheme should allow parties to challenge it in court only in exceptional circumstances through a review process.

Overall the new legislation has not realized significant improvements to the consumer ADR landscape in Italy.[39] Currently the ADR coverage remains patchy and confusing for most consumers, which is not resolved due to the lack of coordination between the different consumer associations. Similar to the Spanish landscape, a number of Italian regions are pushing for de-centralization, so proposals to have a centralized ODR platform are facing political opposition. Yet, a national ODR platform or gateway would help to overcome this obstacle. The other main obstacle already noted is that the participation in ADR remains voluntary in most sectors. Thus, either it should become mandatory for traders, or they should have strong incentives to use it voluntarily.[40]

5.3 Consumer Redress in Spain

The Spanish ADR system for consumer disputes relies largely on the publicly regulated and managed arbitration boards, which operate as the residual ADR entity. In addition, there are local consumer associations that provide mediation services mostly using funds from local authorities.

There are also a small number of administrative bodies that operate as specialized ADR schemes, notably in the financial sector,[41] though these

[39] Pilia et al., n. 36. [40] Ibid.

[41] The three main ADR schemes in the financial sector are the Spanish Central Bank (Banco de España), the Directorate General of Insurance and Pensions Funds (Dirección General de Seguros y Fondos de Pensiones), and the Investors Office of the National Stock

are not effective because their procedures are not user-friendly for consumers, and they can only issue recommendations that are often not followed by the businesses.[42] It has been reported that financial institutions only follow one in four of the recommendations issued by the public ADR body – i.e. the Spanish Bank.[43] Furthermore, the financial sector has been reluctant to join the public and free arbitration system using as a justification that the technicality and complexity of their sector makes them unsuitable for a generic consumer arbitration scheme.[44] It is for this reason that there is an urgent need to set up a more efficient ADR system that deals with financial services disputes, such as the creation of a single ADR entity for the financial sector as originally envisaged in the draft ADR Bill.[45]

It must be noted that two ministries of the Spanish government, and the regional governments, have administrative competences to deliver ADR services in relation to disputes related to petrol, electricity and mail.[46] But, like in the financial sector, they are not used because they have very little publicity, they are slow, and their recommendations are frequently not followed by the businesses. A better option would be to have an ombudsman body whose decisions are binding on the trader.

In the telecommunications sector there is an ADR entity managed by the regulator which considers complaints within three months since the decision made by the trader's internal complaint system, and can require the trader to compensate the consumer. Under the present regulation, decisions must be resolved within six months and can be submitted in

Exchange Commission (Comisión de Nacional del Mercado de Valores). For an analysis of these schemes see Hodges et al., n. 3, pp. 219–224. The financial sector has recently had a significant ad hoc arbitration scheme to deal with claims related to the sale by major Spanish banks of preferred shares by fraudulent misrepresentation. See Ley September 2012.

42 ADICAE, Sistemas de Resolución Extrajudicial de Conflictos con los Consumidores (ADICAE, 2014). Available at http://laeconomiadelosconsumidores.adicae.net/catalogo.php?mode=hlist&pub=222&cat=27.

43 Asociación de Usuarios de Bancos, Cajas y Seguros ADICAE, 'Informe de ADICAE sobre el Anteproyecto de Ley de Resolución de Conflictos de Consumo' pp. 10–11 (on file with the author).

44 Ibid., p. 24.

45 Disposición Adicional Cuarta, Anteproyecto de Ley de Resolución Alternativa de Conflictos de Consumo 2015.

46 The relevant ministries are Ministerio de Industry, Turismo y Comercio and Ministerio de Fomento. See generally F. Esteban de la Rosa 'Challenges for the Implementation of the Consumer ADR Directive in Spain' in P. Cortés, *The New Regulatory Framework for Consumer Dispute Resolution* (OUP, 2016).

writing, online or by phone.[47] In 2015 it received over 100,000 enquiries and resolved around 30,000 cases, of which 60 per cent were in favour of the consumer and 40 per cent of the trader.[48]

Finally, there are two significant private, not-for-profit organizations that are interlinked, Autocontrol[49] and ConfianzaOnline,[50] which offer ADR services to consumers. Both are self-regulated schemes, but while the former deals with complaints related to advertisement, the latter relies on a trustmark of its members. Both ADR entities operate transparently and provide a good service to both consumers and traders.

The analysis of this section focuses on the legal framework of the consumer arbitration system, the new mediation law and the national law that implements the ADR Directive.

5.3.1 *The Regulation of Consumer Arbitration in Spain*

Consumer redress is enshrined in the Spanish Constitution, which requires the government to provide for effective procedures for the protection of consumers' rights.[51] The most important instrument to achieve this obligation is the Spanish public arbitration scheme, which is regulated under national law[52] and is supervised by the main public enforcement body in Spain: AECOSAN.[53]

Its procedure incorporates an optional mediation stage (i.e. med-arb), though the process is commonly referred to as consumer arbitration.[54] The Spanish regulation incorporates rules for an online procedure and it allows the regional arbitration bodies to develop their own platforms with the condition of complying with requirements of interoperability. The regulation deals with all the necessary aspects for the functioning of the online service, such as the determination of the competent arbitration board, the place of arbitration and the use of electronic signatures and electronic notifications.[55] Thus far, it is possible to submit the claim

[47] See Oficina de Atención al Usuario de Telecomunicaciones at www.usuariosteleco.es/Paginas/index.aspx.

[48] Ibid. [49] See www.autocontrol.es.

[50] See www.confianzaonline.es/conocenos/#quienessomos.

[51] Art. 51 Spanish Constitution 1978. [52] Royal Decree 231/2008.

[53] See www.aecosan.msssi.gob.es/AECOSAN/web/home/aecosan_inicio.htm.

[54] It is regulated under the Real Decreto 231/2008.

[55] See Arts. 51–55 and fourth final disposition RD 231/2008. See, for example, the Catalonian online arbitration platform at www.consum.cat and www.bcn.cat/juntaarbitral/es/formulari-de-reclamacions.html, which provides online case management tools for its users.

online using a certified email address or signing the application using the national ID card, which incorporates an electronic chip that enables its users to identify themselves online with a card reader. It is important to note that the set-up requirements are rather burdensome for low-value complaints as it requires users to take a number of technically complex steps.

The Spanish arbitration system offers a voluntary procedure that is characterized as being quicker than court litigation (though in practice it can take around six months to resolve), confidential, without economic limit and non-binding.[56] Although the process has competence for all types of consumer disputes, in practice it operates mostly as a sectorial redress scheme between consumers and large corporations that predominantly operate in the telecommunication sector, followed by utilities (i.e. gas, water and electricity) and to a lesser extent certain types of transport transactions and retail sales.[57]

In parallel to the consumer arbitration system, there is a compulsory arbitration scheme that operates in the transport sector, but only for road and rail transport. This ADR process is quick and free of cost for the parties.[58]Interestingly, the participation in this sector is compulsory for the parties by law for claims under €15,000, unless parties have opted out at the time of entering into the contract. Presumably, the pre-dispute restriction will disappear for the consumer with the implementation of the ADR Directive, which as of January 2016, has yet to occur due to political deadlock to form government during 2015.

Consumer arbitration cannot be used in those cases where there is intoxication, injury, death or reasons to believe that there is a crime involved in the dispute. The rationale behind this restriction probably lies on the preference from the legislator to ensure that parties in these cases will use a dispute resolution process with higher procedural standards (i.e. the judicial process). Yet, it is unclear why, if the arbitration system is free and more effective, it should not be the consumer who decides whether to use arbitration or the court forum to seek redress in these cases.

For more information see I. Barral Viñals, 'Consumers, Online Dispute Resolution and Small Claims' (2014) 10 *Revista Democracia Digital e Governo Electrônico* 394–415, 402–403.

[56] Art. 1 Real Decreto 231/2008 de 15 de febrero. [57] Barral, n. 55.

[58] See Arts. 37–38 of the Ley 16/1987 (BOE of 31 of July), amended by the Ley 29/2003 of 8 October and Arts. 6–12 of Real Decreto 1211/1990, (BOE of 8 October). For more information see http://tinyurl.com/jsm4y2v.

Arbitration disputes under €300 are decided by one arbitrator, while higher-value claims are decided by a panel of three arbitrators, the costs of which may arguably be difficult to justify for many low- or medium-value disputes. The arbitration is free for both consumers and businesses, which discourages the latter from investing in effective in-house complaints systems. This situation has recently prompted in the region of Catalonia an attempt to introduce a fee of €50 per case to all businesses that have over 100 complaints per year – at that time there were over 25 such businesses.[59]

Furthermore, a fine from the public enforcement body (i.e. AECOSAN) may be imposed to a business as a result of a high volume of complaints when the information on complaints triggers an investigation to assess whether a business is systematically infringing consumer protection laws. Although there are not data available on the number of cases, this is something that occurs on a regular basis through the information obtained in (supposedly confidential) arbitration schemes.

The Spanish consumer arbitration regulation only allows consumers to initiate the procedure[60] by submitting a claim that will be forwarded to the closest arbitration board to the consumer's domicile. Traders however can issue a counter-claim when submitting their response. For instance, if a consumer claims compensation for an undue bill on data used abroad against a mobile phone provider, the trader could issue a counter-claim if the consumer as a result of the higher bill has cancelled a contract without complying with the contractual period for acquiring the mobile phone. Given that the Spanish arbitration system is mainly paid by the public purse it does not seem justified that traders can benefit from this service free of cost, especially since traders do not have as many difficulties as the consumers to access the courts.[61]

The adherence of the business is optional and those businesses that opt in are registered in a public list, which, it must be highlighted, is not always easily available. Registered businesses can display the official logo or trustmark of the arbitration system in their premises and online, but

[59] The fee is applicable since April 2015. See 'Una Treintena de Empresas Pagarán por el Número de Quejas de Clientes' El País 23 Febrero 2015. Available at http://ccaa.elpais.com/ccaa/2015/02/22/catalunya/1424630680_615825.html.

[60] Arts. 33(1) and 34(1) RD 231/2008.

[61] F. J. Dávila González, 'La Tramitación de la Resolución de Conflictos Sometidos a las Juntas Arbitrales de Consumo Mediante Medios Electrónicos. Problemas Prácticos y Propuestas de Lege Ferenda' in E. Vázquez de Castro, *Estudios sobre la Justicia Online* (Comares, 2013) p. 59.

often it is either not displayed or not done in a prominent manner. Spanish businesses may restrict their adherence to the arbitration scheme by setting conditions, such as only accepting complaints in a number of local or regional arbitration boards, setting up a shorter time limit or establishing an economic threshold to compensations. The trustmark of these businesses states 'limited offer', which leads consumers to confusion as businesses do not disclose clearly these limitations when displaying the trustmark.[62]

The arbitration procedure starts when a consumer submits a claim, which is then forwarded to the business. If the business does not agree with the remedy proposed by the consumer, both parties will be invited to an optional mediation session.[63] Although the exact figure varies depending on the economic sector, the success of mediations appears to be on the rise.[64] However, it varies from region to region, with some commentators observing that mediation is under-used in most regions.[65] When parties go to mediation they reach agreements in over half of the cases.[66] If the mediation fails, a different neutral third party, the arbitrator, will listen to the parties at an oral hearing where parties present their evidence. Even though the arbitral process may be carried out without a hearing by submitting documents, often the preference is to hold one.

Arbitrators resolve the dispute based on equity, unless the parties agree to obtain an arbitral award based on law, which would be very rare. Arbitral awards are binding and enforceable but may be reviewed in the Provincial Court (*Audiencia Provincial*) on a number of narrow grounds, such as violation of due process rules. Overall, the consumer arbitration system is the most important redress model currently available in Spain, but its main weakness is that the adherence is voluntary for the trader. Consequently, most traders do not participate, and those who do frequently limit the scope of their participation.

Recommendations

There is a lot of room to improve the current consumer arbitration system. While maintaining its residual scope, it should develop sectorial

[62] Hodges et al., n. 3, p. 227. [63] Art. 38 RD 231/2008. [64] Barral, n. 55.

[65] M.J. Reyes López, 'La Reforma del TRLGDCU en Materia de Arbitraje' in G. Palao Moreno, *Los Nuevos Instrumentos Europeos en Materia de Conciliación, Mediación y Arbitraje de Consumo* (Tirant, 2016) p. 247.

[66] Endesa, one of the largest energy providers in Spain, stated in 2014 that around 77 per cent of claims are resolved in the mediation stage, while 23 per cent escalate to arbitration. See ADICAE, n. 42, p. 123.

expertise based on single panel arbitrators operating online. It should also develop a more user-friendly national ODR platform that allows for online access and resolves cases in less than 90 days as it currently takes much longer than that. Like in Portugal,[67] participation in ADR should be mandatory for businesses, at least in a number of regulated sectors such as banking and finance, and other universal services, such as telecoms, water, energy providers, transport, etc. In these sectors a better ADR model than arbitration would be the ombudsman system, especially one that is less formal than arbitration and offers sectorial expertise. If ADR remains optional for traders, then there must be an institutional effort to encourage the adhesion of traders. ADICAE, a Spanish consumer association, proposes a number of incentives to promote the use of the national consumer arbitration system in Spain.[68] But regardless of the DAR process, decisions should remain binding for the parties (at least for the traders), with a limited opportunity to review it in court. An ombudsman system with close ties with the enforcement body coupled with an exceptional court review mechanism would ensure greater consistency in decisions.

The present arbitration system is slow and inefficient.[69] This is due to its limited budget, which is entirely funded by the government. Although

[67] C. Marques Cebola, 'The Implementation of the Consumer ADR Directive in Portugal: The Necessary Reform or Missed Opportunity?' in P. Cortés (ed.), *The New Regulatory Framework for Consumer Dispute Resolution* (OUP, 2016).

[68] ADICAE, n. 42, pp. 8–9. Their main recommendations are the following:

i. Awareness campaigns to encourage the adhesion of businesses in those sectors where ADR is not widespread.
ii. Low-value disputes should be resolved by arbitration unless one of the parties expressly opts out.
iii. Reduce fines for an infringement of consumer laws when traders had processed claims through arbitration.
iv. Amend the powers of public enforcement bodies to allow them to require traders not only to pay a fine but also to compensate consumers.
v. All public procurement contracts should require the contracted party to be adhered to arbitration.
vi. Any business that benefits from public funds should also be adhered to the arbitration system.

[69] A. Cuenca García, 'Los Principios de Transparencia, Eficacia, Equidad, Libertad y Legalidad en la Directiva 2013/11/EU del Parlamento Europeo y del Consejo de 21 de Mayo de 2013, relativa a la Resolución Alternativa de Litigios en Materia de Consumo, y su Incidencia en el Sistema de Arbitraje de Consumo Español' in G. Palao Moreno (ed.), *Los Nuevos Instrumentos Europeos en Materia de Conciliación, Mediación y Arbitraje de Consumo* (Tirant, 2016) p. 77.

the number of cases has increased, the budget has not as it is subject to other policy priorities. The government should therefore either provide a higher budget for it, which is unlikely, or it should charge users: a nominal charge to the consumer and a higher fee for traders. Indeed, traders' obligation to pay a case fee would provide them with incentives to develop more effective in-house complaints systems. Moreover, the arbitration system should not accept consumer complaints which have not been considered previously by the trader's internal customer satisfaction service. Last, but not least, traders should clearly inform consumers about the arbitration or an ombudsman system, and the traders' discretion to restrict their liability through limited offers should be removed.[70]

5.3.2 *The Regulation of Mediation in Spain*

The Mediation Directive has been transposed in Spain through the Act 5/2012 on Mediation in Civil and Commercial Matters.[71] Interestingly, this Act excludes consumer disputes from its scope of application.[72] I submit that this exclusion is due to an opportunistic interpretation of the Mediation Directive, which in its Recital 11 states:

> This Directive should not apply to pre-contractual negotiations or to *processes of an adjudicatory nature such as certain judicial conciliation schemes, consumer complaint schemes*, arbitration and expert determination or to processes administered by persons or bodies issuing a formal recommendation, whether or not it be legally binding as to the resolution of the dispute. (emphasis added)

Although it is clear that the Mediation Directive would have intended to exclude processes with adjudicative elements, such as ombudsman schemes, it has not planned to exclude consumer mediation schemes from its scope of application, but only internal complaint schemes when the consumer submits its complaint directly to the trader. This is reinforced by the transposition of the Mediation Directive in the other Member States, which have not excluded consumer issues. Furthermore, the ADR Directive that is applicable exclusively in the consumer sector acknowledges the overlap of both Directives.[73] It is therefore compelling

70 Ibid., 78.

71 Ley 5/2012, de 6 de Julio, de mediación en asuntos civiles y mercantiles (Published in BOE num. 162, of 7 July 2012).

72 Art. 2(2)(d).

73 Whereas 19 ADR Directive 2013/11/EU. See Barral, n. 55.

that the Spanish exclusion of consumer mediation is inadequate, and likely due to the difficulty of implementing an area of law that had been devolved to the Spanish regional governments.

The Mediation Act does not only recognize the possibility of carrying out an online mediation, but also states that it is "preferable" for disputes not exceeding €600 to be mediated by electronic means, unless its use is not possible for one of the parties.[74] The Mediation Act states that online mediation must comply with two general requirements: (i) the process must guarantee the identity of the parties and (ii) the mediation principles (e.g. confidentiality) contained in the statute must be respected. The national law does not specify the way in which these principles must be complied with, leaving it to the parties to decide on how these requirements are met.[75]

The Mediation Act required the Spanish government to develop a simplified online mediation procedure for these low-value civil claims, many of which could also be classified as consumer claims. This fast track, unless agreed by the parties, should not last more than a month.[76] The Royal Decree 980/2013 implemented the Mediation Act recognizes two different procedures: a general procedure and a fast-track online procedure for disputes under €600.[77] The fast- track procedure can only be used if there is no dispute on a point of law, which in a way would be equivalent of fast-track processes employed for money claims. For these types of disputes, it might be suitable to complement the online mediation with an automated negotiation procedure, where the software compares parties' offers and counter-offers, and settles the claim when they overlap or reach a close pre-agreed range.[78] In fact this option was discussed and appeared in the Bill as automated negotiation ('*negociación automática*'), but it did not make it to the final text.[79] The final text however allowed parties to exchange offers and counter-offers, but it is

[74] Art. 24(2).

[75] A. Madrid Parra 'El Uso de Medios Electrónicos en la Mediación Patrimonial' (2013) 269 *Derecho de los Negocios* 2.

[76] Final Disposition 7.

[77] For the online mediation procedure see Arts. 30–35 of the Real Decreto 980/2013, de 13 de diciembre, por el que se desarrollan determinados aspectos de la Ley 5/2013, de 6 de Julio, de mediación en asuntos civiles y mercantiles (Published in BOE num. 310, of 27 December 2013).

[78] For more information on automated negotiation see P. Cortés, 'Online Dispute Resolution Services: A Selected Number of Case Studies' (2014) 20(6) *Comput Telecommun Law Rev* 172–178.

[79] Proyecto de Real Decreto de November 2012.

unclear whether the settlement has to be expressly accepted by both parties – i.e. whether the software can automatically identify the settlement through blind-bidding. Furthermore, at the time of writing it is unknown how the fast-track mediation operates in practice (if it is used at all), as the legislation does not require the government to provide an ODR platform, nor does it impose an obligation to mediators and mediation institutions to use it.

It is possible to criticize the exclusion in the Regulation of the fast-track online mediation for those cases where parties do not agree on the interpretation of a point of law.[80] This exclusion seems strange since there is no rule in either the primary or secondary legislation that excludes the use of online mediation, with the only exception of this fast-track process. Indeed, this approach contrasts with that taken in other jurisdictions, even in common law jurisdictions where case law is a source of law. In England and Wales, for example, the Court of Appeal, which normally only hears claims based on a point of law, automatically sends an invitation to the appellants to consider the suitability of mediation (which can be online) once the leave for appeal has been granted. It is therefore unclear why parties are required to go to face-to-face mediation when there is a disagreement on the legal interpretation of a substantive norm. One can think that the legislator thought of encouraging the use of the court as a forum for resolving the interpretation of legal issues. But if parties freely prefer to go to mediation, why would they be required to resolve their dispute in court? And if they prefer to communicate through electronic means, why would they be required to meet in person? Perhaps the legislator thought that these types of disputes are per se more complex, so a fast-track online process would not be suitable, regardless of the parties' preferences. Yet, this answer seems unsatisfactory.

Mediation in Spain is not mandatory, but a contractual agreement to mediate, if it is in writing, may be enforced by the courts, who will stay the proceedings while parties go to mediation.[81] The contractual clause will need to be explicit and clear, and it must determine the way to choose the mediator or the mediation institution.[82] The enforcement

[80] F. Martín Díz, 'Mediacion en Derecho Privado: Nuevas Perspectivas Prácticas' 33 (2014) *Revista General de Derecho Procesal* 1–38, 30.

[81] Arts. 6.2 and 10.2 Ley 5/2012.

[82] See F. Martín Díz, 'Mediacion en Derecho Privado: Nuevas Perspectivas Prácticas' 33 (2014) *Revista General de Derecho Procesal* 1–38, 6–8.

will require an attempt in good faith to settle the dispute through at least one mediation session. In the event of no compliance with this requirement, or a faulty compliance (acting in bad faith, unjustifiable delay, etc.), the innocent party could claim for damages in an eventual court process.

It however must be pointed out that consumer mediation outside the consumer arbitration boards is quite limited.[83] These mediations are carried out by local consumer associations that offer mediation services free of costs to the parties. These are the Municipal Offices for Consumer Information (*Oficinas Municipales de Información al Consumidor* or OMIC) and the Local Offices for Consumer Information (*Oficinas Comarcales de Información al Consumdior* or OCICS). The budget and the regulation of these bodies are controlled by the local authorities and the autonomous regions, so there is no national legal framework regulating these consumer mediations.

Another significant mediation procedure for consumers is called inter-mediation (*intermediación*). The procedure is similar to the Italian representative negotiations and it has been adopted in a number of Spanish regions, such as Catalonia and Valencia, and it is financed by the local and regional public authorities. It applies when consumers are unable to continue paying the mortgage of their main residence and the bank is about to request the repossession of their house. The inter-mediation is offered by members of the bar association who are qualified lawyers, have received training on mediation, and have expertise on mortgages and other financial products as well as consumer protection. They first offer legal advice to the consumer, and they act on behalf of the consumer negotiating a settlement with a representative of the bank. The success rate of these mediations is high, ranging from 60 to 70 per cent.[84] Settlements benefit from the fact that banks are not keen to repossess more houses so they are open to renegotiate mortgages while most consumers prefer to retain their homes.

[83] It has been observed that these mediations are largely marginal, amounting to 5 per cent of the total consumer mediations. See I. Barral-Viñals, 'Consumer Complaints and Alternative Dispute Resolution Methods: Harmonisation of the European ADR System' in J. Devenney and M. Kenny, *The Transformation of European Private Law* (CUP, 2013) p. 307.

[84] See Consejo General de la Abogacía Española 'Éxito Intermediación Hipotecaria en el CMICAV' (13 August 2015). Available at www.mediacion.icav.es/archivos/contenido/1176.pdf.

5.3.3 *Forthcoming Changes in the Redress Architecture*

As already mentioned in the previous chapter, Spain did not support the approval of the ADR Directive in the European Council (COREPER). The reason given for its decision to abstain in the vote was the information obligations contained in article 13, whereby those traders who are already adhered to an ADR entity have to notify their adherence twice: (i) pre-dispute, before entering into the contract the information must be contained in the website and in the T&C of the contract, and (ii) post-dispute, every time a complaint is not resolved by the trader in a manner satisfactorily to the consumer.[85] The Spanish official position was that the duplicated information requirements would discourage traders from joining ADR entities pre-dispute, as they can simply decide on an ad hoc basis with every dispute. Yet, it transpired that the opposition was strongly voiced by one of the main telecom providers in Spain (Telefónica, a previously public-owned business), which despite being a member of the arbitration scheme, disliked the new information obligations. Of course, this is precisely the moment when consumers are interested to know about ADR. The Spanish government reported at the time that all the telecommunication companies in Spain receive around 25 million complaints per year, so it is obvious that clear signposting to ADR would not only impact on the compensations these companies have to pay, but also on the huge cost to the public purse in running arbitration, which is free of cost to the parties. Therefore, it is unclear who was more against the information requirements, Telefonica or the Spanish government.

At the time of writing (January 2017) the Spanish government has not yet transposed the ADR Directive. There is only a draft Bill, which was published in 2015. The draft Bill sets AECOSAN as the point of contact and competent authority, while it also recognizes a number of competent sectorial authorities.[86] It would be preferable to separate the role of competent authorities with that of certified ADR. Yet, it is very likely that the same entity, AECOSAN, will certify and provide the main ADR entity: the consumer arbitration system.

[85] Statement by Spain on the 177795/11 CONSOM 196NI 616 JUSTCIV 339 CODEC 2242. Available at http://tinyurl.com/zlulx9z.

[86] The draft Bill only recognizes those that operate in the financial sector – namely Banco de España, la Comisión Nacional del Mercado de Valores and la Dirección General de Seguros y Fondos de Pensiones. See Art. 27(2).

According to the draft Bill the likely developments in the Spanish implementing law will be as follows: the inclusion of legal persons in the definition of consumers,[87] which follows the same approach contained in the existing arbitration boards; the establishment of a €30 cap to filing fees that ADR entities may require of consumers;[88] a set minimum of three days as a period of reflection for consumers to accept a mediated settlement;[89] ADR entities may reject claims under €50 and over €3,000;[90] when ADR entities issue binding decisions to consumers (i.e. arbitration processes) they will only obtain the certification if they are statutory bodies;[91] and neutral third parties must be covered by insurance, except when these services are delivered by public officials or civil servants.[92] In addition, an important and controversial element of the draft Bill is that it allows 'in exceptional circumstances' for the certification of ADR entities that are employed and financed by an individual trader as long as they operate in sectors where there is 'a high level of disputes and limited adherence to ADR'.[93] This provision grants wide discretion to the competent authorities.

In order to improve consumer redress in Spain, as noted earlier, the Spanish government will need to improve the residual ADR entity (i.e. the public arbitration system), it will need to make participation for traders mandatory in essential services and set effective incentives in other sectors, and it will need to invest in a user-friendlier national ODR platform. It should not require, as it currently does for arbitration, the use of a digital signature or a nationally certified email address. User name and password should be sufficient for the majority of cases, and it should complement the EU ODR platform processing cases outside its scope (notably non e-commerce transactions) following the example of equivalent platforms designed in other jurisdictions such as the Belgian platform.[94] The availability of an effective ODR platform could also be extended for the fast-track online mediations system regulated in the Mediation Act. Furthermore, as is being implemented in other jurisdictions,[95] such a national ODR platform could operate as a court-annexed ADR/ODR scheme, which could be offered to the parties prior to, or during, the civil procedure.

[87] Art. 1(2). [88] Art. 11. [89] Art. 13(2). [90] Art. 15(1)(e). [91] Art. 17(3).
[92] Art. 22(2). [93] Arts. 17(4) and 26.
[94] See Service de Médiation pour le Consommateur www.mediationconsommateur.be.
[95] See Lord Justice Briggs, *Civil Courts Structure Review* Interim Report (December 2015) and Final Report (July 2016).

5.4 Consumer Redress in the United Kingdom

The UK, as a common law jurisdiction based on the adversarial principle, has a strong culture of settlement within its court system where on average only 3 to 5 per cent of civil claims are determined by trial.[96] Although the majority of claims are settled (as many as 90 per cent),[97] many others are not defended and some are withdrawn.

The provision of consumer ADR in the UK has been growing organically over the last few decades. Traders' membership is compulsory in a number of economic sectors which can be characterized by a high level of regulation and consumer disputes, namely: energy, estate agents, financial services, higher education, gambling, green deal, legal services, pensions, postal services, property letting agents and telecommunications.[98] Currently, the more developed areas are the ombudsman schemes operating in financial, legal, telecom and energy sectors.

Consumer Focus estimated in 2012 that out of 6.4 million annual consumer complaints made to businesses, 2 million were unresolved.[99] This is the potential pool for ADR, but only a quarter of these escalate to an ADR scheme, mainly to the Financial Ombudsman Service (FOS).

The coverage is presently a bit patchy. Some well-established ADR entities operate in regulated sectors, which typically have a single statutory entity operating as an ombudsman, such as the FOS or the Legal Ombudsman, where adherence by traders is compulsory. In some regulated sectors the trader is obliged to be adhered to an ADR scheme but it may choose from several private ADR entities, such as the case of telecoms, where traders can choose from Ombudsman Services (OS) and the Communications and Internet Services Adjudication Scheme (CISAS) for telecommunications. In many other sectors ADR entities

[96] See, for instance, HMCTS, *Civil Justice Statistics Quarterly, England and Wales (Incorporating Privacy Injunctions Statistics January to June 2015)* at 10. Available at www.gov.uk/government/uploads/system/uploads/attachment_data/file/457979/civil-justice-statistics-april-june-2015.pdf.

[97] Briggs, Interim Report, n. 95.

[98] Department for Business Innovation & Skills (BIS), 'Alternative Dispute Resolution for Consumers: Government Response to the Consultation on implementing the Alternative Dispute Resolution Directive and the Online Dispute Resolution Regulation' (November 2014) p. 3.

[99] Consumer Futures (formerly Consumer Focus), an executive non-departmental public body of BIS, represented consumers across regulated markets. It was abolished on 1 April 2014, with all its functions transferred to other bodies (Citizens Advice, Citizens Advice Scotland and General Consumer Council for Northern Ireland) 4 'Consumer Detriment 2012', Consumer Focus (now disbanded) [not online].

operate as a requirement of businesses to join a trade association, such as travel agents or double glazing. Lastly, there are a small number of independent ADR providers who mostly deal with family and commercial matters.

ADR in the UK is largely free for consumers and it is privately funded by businesses paying on a 'polluter-basis' through a combination of an annual membership fee and case fees (though normally there is no requirement to pay a case fee for the first few cases). In some sectors the cost is covered by levies that traders pay to the regulator in order to obtain a license to operate.

The former Department for Business Innovation and Skills (which in July 2016 was replaced by Department for Business, Energy and Industrial Strategy) was in charge of the implementation of the ADR Directive. It must be noted that while consumer protection policy is a devolved power in Northern Ireland, the regional government has decided to adopt the English legislation that implements the ADR Directive. By contrast, despite that consumer protection is not a devolved power in Scotland and Wales, some of the provisions have impacted on policy areas that have already been devolved in Scotland, which already has a number of ADR entities that only operate there.[100] Moreover, there is an ongoing effort in Scotland to obtain competence in consumer matters, including consumer redress, possibly through the creation of a single ombudsman.[101]

In a consultation paper the UK government identified over 70 ADR schemes operating in the UK for resolving consumer disputes.[102] While it has been acknowledged that not all of these entities are expected to seek the certification as an ADR entity, there is an expectation that all statutory ADR entities (i.e. not only public but also private ADR entities that operate in a regulated sector) become certified ADR entities. By January 2016 there were 43 ADR entities listed in the EU ODR platform (though a small number of ADR entities have been listed more than once as they were approved by more than one competent authority). The risk of having too many ADR entities is that it leads to competition, which in

[100] Department for Business Innovation and Skills (BIS), Alternative Dispute Resolution for Consumers, Implementing the Alternative Dispute Resolution Directive and Online Dispute Resolution Regulation (March 2014) p. 12.

[101] Report of the Working Group on Consumer and Competition Policy for Scotland (October 2015).

[102] See BIS, n. 100, p. 33.

this sector inevitably promotes forum shopping where traders not only select but also pay for the ADR process.[103]

5.4.1 A Selected Number of Certified ADR Entities

Statutory ADR Entities

Financial Ombudsman Service FOS is the largest ombudsman scheme in the UK as well as in the EU and worldwide. FOS has already been discussed in Chapter 1. Thus, it suffices to say that it was established under the Financial Services and Markets Act 2000 to settle claims up to the value of £150,000. According to the annual review for 2014/15, FOS has over 3,000 staff (including more than 200 ombudsmen).[104] FOS receives nearly 1.8 million enquires a year (out of which around one in five become formal complaints with an unit cost in excess of £600) and provides information and responses in 50 different languages. Out of all the queries during that year, around 330,000 were turned into formal complaints, and only around 6 per cent of the claims reached the 'appeal stage' with the ombudsman. It must be highlighted that 63 per cent of complaints were related to personal protection insurance (PPI), while most of the remaining complaints were related by pay-day loans, credit card, current accounts and mortgages. At the time of writing there was a significant backlog of cases due to the high number of PPI cases, but this problem is expected to be resolved in the near future.

Ombudsman Services The next largest ADR in the UK is the Ombudsman Services (OS), whose 600 plus staff mostly deal with telecoms and energy enquiries and complaints – with over 200,000 enquiries a year received by telephone or in writing.[105] In 2014 it was reported that the unit cost in the telecoms and energy sector was around £350. OS is funded through a mix of case fees and annual subscription fees.

In 2016 OS reported to have received over 170,000 initial contacts from April to December 2015.[106] Most of the complaints were related to

[103] See Chapter 7.

[104] Financial Ombudsman Service Annual Review 2014/15. Available at www.financial-ombudsman.org.uk/publications/ar15/index.html#a2.

[105] OS Annual Report 2014/15. Available at www.ombudsman-services.org/downloads/OS_annualreport_2015.pdf. See also OS Annual Report 2015. Available at www.ombudsman-services.org/downloads/Ombudsman-Services-annual-report-2015.pdf.

[106] Ibid.

energy disputes. Outcomes from OS are reasoned, and OS endeavours to provide consistency in their decisions after complaints have gone through an independent evidence-based process. Their processes rely heavy on ICT (phone and email), and the limit of settlements in energy and telecoms is capped at £50,000, but the majority of settlements are much lower. Data from OS indicates that around 75 per cent of complaints are resolved in favour of the consumer complainant, though it must be noted that many of potential complaints do not escalate from the enquiry stage and consumers may not receive the compensation that they originally claimed.

In the energy sector the majority of decisions (more than 90 per cent) are resolved within six weeks from the submission of the complaint, and they must be implemented by the trader within 28 days. However, it must be noted that they do not receive as many complaints as they should. According to an Ofgem survey, only 5 per cent of those eligible take the complaint to OS.[107] Interestingly, OS is expected to monitor all complaints and to aggregate information in order to issue recommendations to businesses. The aim of this feedback is to improve the traders' policies and procedures to avoid future disputes, which in turn improves business practices and increases the levels of consumer satisfaction. Yet, in practice this does not occur as much as one would like to see, and partly this is because of the lack guidelines on how and when this task should take place.[108] Nonetheless, some interesting initiatives have taken place to provide transparency about disputes and incentivizing best practices. A notable initiative is the publication of the dispute data of the ten largest energy providers highlighting systematic problems in the energy sector.[109]

The Legal Ombudsman The Legal Ombudsman (LeO) has jurisdiction to process complaints from many legal activities, though legal services delivered by unregulated providers fall outside the LeO's scope.[110] LeO is an organization that has both a compulsory and a voluntary jurisdiction.

[107] Ombudsman Services, Response to the Competition Markets Authority Energy Market Investigation 'Issues Statement' (14 August 2014) p. 3.

[108] See *Review of Ombudsman Services: Energy. A Report for Ofgem* (London: Lucerna Partners, 2015).

[109] See OS Annual Report 2015 (n. 105) p. 7.

[110] Amongst the activities that are currently not necessarily covered by the LeO are will-writing, powers of attorney, online DIY products (e.g. tenancy agreements), and advice on matters such as employment disputes.

A report for the LeO has estimated that around 130,000 legal service providers in England and Wales operate outside the regulated domain.[111] However, for many of these services it would be nonsensical to require them to be linked to the LeO, especially if we take into account the unit cost of disputes, which is around £2,000 – nonetheless this figure is likely to drop given the fact that LeO is a relatively new ADR entity. The limit for settlements for legal services is capped at £50,000.

The LeO has assessors, investigators and ombudsmen, the process of which broadly falls within the normal structure of ombudsman schemes. The assessors are at the front line for all the communications that arrive by phone call, email and letter. Their main role is to assess whether a complaint falls within the jurisdiction of the LeO, so they check with whom is the complaint against, whether it falls within the timescale, whether the consumer has first raised the complaint to a lawyer, etc. Often complaints are premature, where the complainant has not yet tried to resolve the complaint directly with the legal service provider.[112] When the complaint falls outside the scope of the LeO, assessors may be able to point out if there is another relevant organization that may be able to assist in resolving the complaint.

The role of investigators is to gather information and evidence from both parties and, when possible, to assist them in reaching an amicable settlement. Investigators have an average of 17 live cases, which are normally treated in date order, unless a particular case can be resolved swiftly through a couple of phone calls.[113] LeO investigators are specialized. Although disputes are varied, they frequently fall within the areas of probate, divorce and conveyancing; the issue in dispute tends to be related to how much things cost, why things have taken longer than expected and why a certain course of action has been taken.[114]

When a settlement cannot be reached, they draft a report, which is distributed amongst the parties (some of which settle at this stage), and if parties do not settle at this stage, then it is submitted to the ombudsman who will issue a binding outcome for the legal service provider. The resolution of complaints is rarely clear-cut. The investigation is evidence based, but when there is not enough evidence, or it is inconclusive, then

[111] Legal Ombudsman, Annual Report 2013–14.

[112] See LeO News, View from Operations – Assessor. Issue 8 (2014). Available at www.legalombudsman.org.uk/leo-news/issue-8/view-assessor.html.

[113] Ibid. [114] Ibid.

the LeO's conclusions are based on the balance of probabilities. Cooperation by the parties is essential. According to the LeO,

> [the] easiest cases to resolve – even where the subject matter is complex – are the ones where both parties cooperate fully with LeO. For a lawyer, this means providing evidence within the timescale provided, and being available to answer questions and discuss possible resolutions.[115]

There are other non-ombudsman schemes operating in the UK. For instance, in Northern Ireland the main ADR scheme is the Consumer Council which is a non-departmental public body established through the General Consumer Council (Northern Ireland) Order 1984 to assists consumers' enquires and complaints in the areas of transport, natural gas, electricity, coal, water and postal services. The Consumer Council also provides a signposting service when consumers contact them in relation to other complaints. In 2013–2014 they reported to have handled around 3,500 enquires and complaints.

Overall, it must be noted that statutory ADR entities benefit from a quasi-monopoly – i.e. traders may agree with consumers to use a different ADR, but the consumer is entitled to insist in using the statutory ADR. These ADR entities operate more effectively than when there is competition between ADR entities. This is because this system benefits from economies of scale and the ability to aggregate data on disputes and quickly identify sectorial problems, which in turn allows the ADR to be more transparent (without the risk of losing out against competing ADR entities) and to design dispute resolution strategies with regulators and the industry. And they can do this by setting up an adequate budget that does not rely exclusively on case fees.

Non-Statutory ADR Entities Offered by Professional Associations

The British Vehicle Rental and Leasing Association (BVRLA) offers conciliation services to its members in accordance to their Code of Conduct, which is of mandatory observance for its members.[116] The procedure is similar to that of an ombudsman scheme. It commences with an informal conciliation where parties are required to submit the

[115] Ibid.

[116] British Vehicle Rental and Leasing Association (BVRLA), Response to the BIS Consultation Document on Implementing the ADR Directive and ODR Regulation (June 2014) p. 1. BVRLA Code of Conduct. Available at www.bvrla.co.uk/system/files/files/publication-order-forms/code_of_conduct_corporate_members.pdf.

relevant information with regards to the unresolved dispute between the car rental company and the consumer. The BVRLA will then offer a recommendation to both parties. If one of the parties is not satisfied with the recommendation, then a formal conciliation procedure can be invoked, in which case a Conciliation Committee will be appointed. The conciliation service will issue a decision that will be binding on the car rental company, but it will not restrict the consumer from taking legal action on the same matter in the courts. In 2014 the BVRLA reported to have approximately 550 complaints per annum.[117] It has received positive feedback from a number of European Consumer Centres on its published reports on car rentals.[118]

There is also a pan-European programme that assists in dealing with cross-border disputes related to car rentals called the European Car Rental Conciliation Service.[119] This service is available to customers who exhausted the internal complaints services of large rental companies, such as Alamo, Avis, Budget, Europacar, Hertz and Enterprise. This service investigates potential breaches of their Code for Best Practice, which includes the following areas: advertising, customer information, vehicle condition, pre- and post-rental inspections, and billing. Hence, it will not investigate matters which are criminal in nature or fall outside the scope of its Code for Best Practice. It is free of cost for consumers and it aims to resolve disputes within 30 days of submitting the complete complaint file.[120]

Another significant private ADR entity is the ADR process used by the members of the Association of British Travel Agents (ABTA Ltd.), which, like many other associations such as the British Retail Consortium, offers informal mediation services to their members, as well as an outsourced ADR entity for unresolved complaints. ABTA requires its members to participate in a med-arb process offered by the Centre for Effective Dispute Resolution (CEDR).

5.4.2 The ADR Regulations

The UK government has transposed the core provisions of the ADR Directive through the Alternative Dispute Resolution for Consumer

[117] Ibid., p. 3.

[118] European Consumer Centre - Ireland, Car Rental Contracts Business Practices, Contract Terms and Consumer Protection (2008) Available at www.eccireland.ie/wp-content/uploads/2013/07/ECC_Car_Rental_Contracts_Report_2008.pdf.

[119] See www.ecrcs.eu.

[120] See ECRCS, Q&A at www.ecrcs.eu/questions-answers.aspx.

Disputes (Competent Authorities and Information) Regulations 2015 and the (Amendment) Regulations 2015.[121] The Regulations, which apply to the whole of the UK,[122] designate the Secretary of State as the contact point and as a competent authority, together with a number of regulators as the competent authorities in their sectors.[123] The scope of the Regulations includes public providers of higher education and adjudicative schemes such as arbitration bodies, but excludes 'in-house' ADR schemes provided or funded directly by the trader. The exclusion of these in-house schemes was based on the concern that in the event of not reaching a settlement through the in-house mediation, the consumer will find it difficult to find another certified ADR entity willing to consider that dispute.[124] Furthermore, in-house ADR would not be perceived by the consumer as offering the same level of impartiality and independence to external ADR schemes, and it may confuse consumers undermining their confidence in the whole ADR system.

Although the Regulations do not include any additional procedural standards for ADR schemes that apply for the certification, they do recognize that the designated competent authorities have the power to increase these minimum standards. Competent authorities could for instance require ADR entities operating in one sector to issue binding decisions on traders.

With regard to the Directive's requirement to set up 'effective, proportionate and dissuasive penalties' when traders do not comply with the information obligations, the Regulations simply refer to the Enterprise Act, which allows an enforcer to apply for an enforcement order from the court, which may lead to an unlimited fine and up to two years of imprisonment.[125]

The UK government has contracted the Chartered Trading Standards Institute (CTSI) to act as the UK's competent authority covering ADR

[121] Explanatory Memorandum to the ADR Regulations 2015, para. 9.

[122] It should be noted that the Directive could have been implemented by Northern Ireland as consumer policy is one of its competences, but it was agreed to have the transposition on a UK basis.

[123] Trading Standards Institute (TSI) will act on behalf of the Secretary of State as the competent authority covering ADR schemes in non-regulated sectors. The sector specific competent authorities are: The Financial Conduct Authority, the Legal Services Board, the Civil Aviation Authority, Gambling Commission, the Gas and Electricity Markets Authority, Office of Communications, and the lead enforcement authority for the purposes of the Estate Agents Act 1979(a). See Reg. 17 and Sch. 1.

[124] See BIS, n. 100, p. 6.

[125] See Part 8 of the Enterprise Act 2002 and Regulation 19 of the ADR Regulations 2015.

entities in non-regulated sectors, while the sector regulators remain as the competent authorities for their own sectors. The government has appointed the following competent authorities: the Civil Aviation Authority (for the aviation sector), Ofgem (for the energy sector), Powys Council (for estate agents), the Financial Conduct Authority (for financial services), the Gambling Commission (for the gambling sector), the Department for Work and Pensions (for pensions), Ofcom (for the telecoms and post) and the Legal Service Board (for regulated legal services in England and Wales).

The competent authorities charge a fee to those ADR entities who seek the accreditation. It is an annual fee that is based on the size of the ADR entity. The various competent authorities produce the anomaly of ADR schemes required to apply and pay for different sectorial certifications.

CTSI operates as the single contact point, which creates an opportunity, if adequate funding were allocated, to develop a holistic and strategic review of ADR in the UK. The collected intelligence could then be applied across the whole economy to examine the gaps in provision of consumer ADR and identify the best way to rationalize the national redress system.

5.4.3 *The Helpdesk*

The UK government decided to launch a helpdesk that is run by the Citizens Advice Bureau.[126] Its primary aim is to help consumers navigate through the ADR landscape. The helpdesk is accessible by telephone, assisting consumers who seek information on how to resolve their dispute and where to go, and if necessary also assisting them in filing a dispute and giving advice on how to include the supporting information that would be necessary for an ADR entity to consider a complaint. But, the actual assessment of the circumstances surrounding the complaint is left to the ADR entity and its case handlers. The government intended to automate this service as far as possible, including a searchable database with information on all the certified ADR entities and all the traders adhering to an ADR entity or with a legal obligation to adhere. This development has not happened yet.

The helpdesk focuses on domestic disputes, so its role is complementary to that of the ODR contact point and its two ODR advisers who have

[126] See www.citizensadvice.org.uk/scotland/consumer/alternative-dispute-resolution/settling-out-of-court-s1/using-alternative-dispute-resolution-to-solve-your-consumer-problem-s/.

been recruited from the European Consumer Centre UK to assist consumers with e-commerce, and especially cross-border, disputes. This division of labour intends to avoid the risk of duplicating activities and ensuring that the ODR contact point has enough resources to cover cross-border complaints. Although the ODR contact point may be able to help (if it so chooses) consumers with domestic complaints, it does not consider complaints submitted by businesses. Hence, in theory, consumers with e-commerce disputes will be able to find information about certified ADR entities in the EU ODR platform, while consumers with 'off-line' domestic disputes could obtain this information through the national helpdesk, and for cross-border disputes will continue to use the European Consumer Centres. In practice, however, all these organizations are expected to signpost consumers to the relevant ADR.

The role of the helpdesk may in time become less necessary if traders comply with their obligations to point consumers towards ADR entities, or if the ADR landscape becomes simplified. The UK government has considered to look beyond the requirements of the Directive in order to rationalize the confusing provision of ADR providers. It is unclear whether something will happen anytime soon in the UK, though Scotland seems more determined to set up a single ombudsman where consumers could submit all their complaints.[127] The rest of the UK should also consider to rationalize the provision of ADR, at least setting up an umbrella organization that provides a single online access point or gateway, which could then allocate each consumer complaint to the appropriate ADR entity.

5.4.4 Gaps in the Provision of ADR and Residual ADR Entities

The UK government initially considered to fund the setting up costs of a residual ADR entity that would operate an ombudsman process capturing all the consumer complaints which are not already covered by the existing sectorial ADR schemes.[128] But the government decided to withdraw its procurement call as soon after its publication emerged

[127] Report of the Working Group on Consumer and Competition Policy for Scotland (October 2015).

[128] See the prior information notice with the call for tender to choose the residual ADR entity at http://ted.europa.eu/udl?uri=TED:NOTICE:394225-2014:TEXT:EN:HTML&src=0. The government suggested that the residual ADR entity will focus during its first year of operation on the following sectorial gaps identified: home maintenance, improvements or installation services, retail, second hand cars and car repair and

numerous private ADR suppliers offering to fill the gaps; thus it was noted that the legal requirement could be filled by the open market, without the need to allocate public funds to ensure compliance with the ADR Directive. However, it pointed out that it might reconsider this call again if gaps in the provision of ADR were to remain in the future.

The use of ADR is not widespread in areas such as homebuilding, property management and care homes for older people.[129] Other sectors which are currently not well catered are mobile phones, television, second hand cars, car repair and servicing, and generally low-value retail.[130] Although the higher-value retail, such as sellers of furniture and bathrooms, may belong to an ADR scheme, the basic low-value transactions are not. Some commentators have argued that there was no need for ADR schemes in this sector since retailers already have a high level of consumer satisfaction as its business model depends on keeping customers happy.[131]

5.4.5 *Simplification of the ADR Infrastructure and Its Mandatory Nature*

The UK government is looking beyond the requirements of the Directive and has considered whether future reforms are necessary in order to rationalize the disperse structure of ADR schemes in order to improve the provision of consumer redress.[132] The government deems first necessary to assess the cost and benefits of such rationalization, and it is considering various options: (i) creating a single umbrella for all ADR entities; (ii) reducing the number of existing ADR entities and (iii) upgrading the helpdesk, so that it would operate as a full ODR platform. A public consultation noted that primary legislation may be needed as well as an adequate budget. Furthermore, the government is pondering whether it should retain the mixed approach making it compulsory for traders operating in certain regulated sectors to be

servicing. These sectors have been based on the following consumer detriment surveys: Consumer Detriment 2012 – prepared for Consumer Focus by TNS BNRB.

[129] See Competition & Markets Authority, 'Alternative Dispute Resolution for Consumers, Response to the Consultation on Implementing the Alternative Dispute Resolution Directive and the Online Dispute Resolution Regulation' (3 June 2014) paras. 2–4.

[130] BIS Response, n. 98, pp. 15 and 27. [131] Ibid. [132] Ibid, pp. 33–34.

adhered to an ADR body, or to extend this obligation to all businesses in order to make it easier for consumers to know that all unresolved complaints could be addressed through an ADR entity.[133]

The government's initial consultation found that there was very little support for having a single consumer ombudsman body as it may lose the expertise in the delivery of services by sectorial ADR schemes. The government found that most respondents preferred an umbrella model:

> Most favoured an umbrella model, providing clear access to consumers and helping to raise levels of awareness and uptake. Sector specific bodies with their particular expertise could continue to co-exist under the umbrella system, but there are still significant questions to be considered, such as whether ADR should be compulsory for all sectors, whether the number of ADR bodies operating in each sector should be limited and how far to harmonise the type of ADR on offer to consumers.[134]

Although as already noted ADR is already mandatory in a number of regulated sectors, the majority of businesses in unregulated sectors still retain the choice of whether or not to use ADR. As will be discussed in Chapter 7, a full mandatory coverage is likely occur in due course, but some jurisdictions, such as the UK, may opt instead for developing a user-friendly court that is accessible online and that incorporates ADR/ODR techniques.[135]

The responses to the public consultation on extending the mandatory ADR were evenly split. The arguments against included: high costs for business; greater bureaucracy in processing complaints; a drive towards adjudicative processes, since unless both parties agree to participate in mediation decisions need to be binding; and the preference for other incentives to increase the use of mediation, such as transparency and cost penalties from courts.[136] Conversely, the arguments in favour of a mandatory ADR noted that this approach would further simplify the landscape, removing consumer confusion about the availability of ADR; it would be less detrimental to those sectors where ADR is already compulsory; and ADR would be more cost-effective as it would benefit from economies of scale.[137]

[133] Ibid., p. 34. [134] Ibid., p. 24.

[135] P. Cortés, 'The Online Court: Filling the Gaps of the Civil Justice System?' (2017) 36(1) *Civil Justice Q* 54–71.

[136] Ibid., p. 47. [137] Ibid.

In any event the mandatory coverage of ADR is likely to continue to increase in a piecemeal manner, expanding in other regulated sectors, such as in public transport[138] and in the sharing economy. Additional factors impacting the coverage may depend on the political will of the government of the time and in the level of acceptance – thus, if the majority of traders opt in voluntarily, it will be easier for the government to make it mandatory for the rest (the minority) to join an ADR entity. Doyle observes that mandatory ADR is unlikely to happen in the short term, particularly under a conservative government which is reluctant to impose 'constraints on market freedom'.[139] While she acknowledges that reputable businesses will opt into ADR entities there will be many businesses '– and not just the rogues, but the tiny, the tired and the overstretched – [that] are all likely to say "no thanks" to a consumer asking for independent redress. So ADR will be available, but it won't necessarily be used.'[140]

5.5 Conclusion

This chapter has evaluated how the main consumer ADR infrastructure in Italy, Spain and the UK should develop; it suggested that observing the minimum criteria set in the ADR Directive will be a missed opportunity. If businesses comply with their information obligations and understand the value of ADR, this could create momentum, increasing the take up of ADR while installing greater trust in consumer transactions. By contrast, if businesses are reluctant to go to ADR, which seems to be the trend in most sectors, then the legislator should consider whether to make adherence compulsory.

The previous chapter noted that one of the main barriers to the development of ADR is the lack of awareness. This chapter showed how the national fragmentation of ADR entities that operate in individual sectors does not contribute to the knowledge and accessibility of these

138 See for instance the recent motion to bring a new statutory Rail Ombudsman as a result of the strikes in the sector. See Rail Ombudsman, Motion for Leave to Bring in a Bill (Standing Order No. 23) House of Commons Hansard (20 December 2016) vol. 618, columns 1324–1327. Available at hansard.parliament.uk/commons/2016-12-20/debates/E835E520-A495-4794-AF8C-1157AF512F82/RailOmbudsman.

139 M Doyle, 'Gazing at the ADR landscape – Is the EU Directive just a mirage?' (9 October 2013). Available at http://domarmediation.co.uk/2013/10/09/gazing-at-the-adr-landscape-is-the-eu-directive-just-a-mirage/.

140 Ibid.

processes, coverage of which remains patchy and confusing.[141] Thus, in addition to the EU ODR platform there is a need for interoperable national ODR platforms. This is particularly urgent in those Member States where there are many certified ADR entities that operate in different sectors, notably in the UK, and where the ADR systems is de-centralized in regional centres, such as in Italy and Spain; moreover, in these Member States the regions are pushing for a de-centralization so proposals to have a centralized ODR platform are facing political opposition. Yet, only a national ODR platform would help to overcome the lack of awareness and confusion. The national platform should become a single online access point for all nationally certified ADR entities. The national (as well as the EU) ODR platform should provide a list with the participating traders as well as their contact details, including their email addresses. This information should be supplied by the ADR entities, which should also be required to publicize it on their own websites.

There should only be one ADR entity per sector in order to avoid consumer confusion and forum shopping. This will enable greater efficiencies through economies of scale and facilitate the collection of information delivering useful feedback to the industry and regulators. This chapter noted that when this happens, there is more collaboration between some ADR entities and enforcement bodies. The financial ombudsman in Italy, the arbitration boards in Spain and FOS in the UK have a close collaboration with the regulators. The common feature of these ADR entities is that they are either public bodies, or are private ADR bodies that have a monopoly in their sectors through a procurement contract, so they are able to aggregate information and publish the problems in their sectors without concerns from competitors.

Another important barrier to consumer redress is that in many sectors traders can, and do, refuse to participate in an ADR process – this attitude is particularly notorious in a number of sectors, such as traditional retail and air travel for most countries. This refusal undermines the whole ADR system in so far as traders inform, but do not participate in ADR/ODR. Consequently, the participation in an ADR entity should be mandatory for traders operating in regulated sectors, especially in essential services (e.g. water, energy, telecoms, banking, etc.) as is the case

[141] It must be noted there are a number of EU Member States such as Sweden and Belgium that have a residual ADR entity which processes complaints against traders even when they have not opted into the ADR process. However their decisions are not binding. For more information see Chapter 1.

in the UK. In addition, trade associations, which normally have a code of conduct incorporating best practices, should require its members to be adhered to one ADR entity chosen by the trade association. In those sectors where adherence is voluntary, as will be further discussed in Chapter 7, traders should have economic incentives to participate in an ADR entity.

This chapter has provided a number of country-specific recommendations. The chapter observed that Italian courts are ill fitted to provide consumer redress. The requirement of mandatory mediation has been a first step towards a cultural change to incorporate ADR as part of the resolution of civil disputes. But there should be greater incentives for traders to provide consumer redress. Accordingly, it is recommended that mandatory consumer ADR should be extended, especially through mandatory schemes mirroring those offered by regulators and the extension of *conciliazione paritetica* schemes. However, consumer ADR should depart from the current pre-action mediation in two fundamental aspects: first, it should be mandatory only for traders to participate in the ADR process; second, it should not require consumers to have legal representation. A small fee and a prerequisite to use the trader's internal complaint system may be appropriate in order to avoid vexatious or unmeritorious claims from consumers. Competent authorities should monitor their performance, and when the settlement rate falls below an unacceptable level, then a binding adjudicative process should complement the consensual processes. The adjudicative step could be one akin to that used by Corecom, but its decisions should only be challenged in court through a review process.

With regards to Spain, this chapter argued that the public arbitration system should not allow traders to restrict the scope of their participation as they currently do with the option of 'limited offers'. It proposed to extend the use of panels with single arbitrators in order to ensure a more proportionate dispute resolution process, and either restrict or eliminate the ability of traders to make counter-claims (especially when it remains to be free of cost for traders). It also recommended the mandatory adherence to ADR in all regulated sectors, but consumers should be required first to elevate a complaint through the traders' internal complaint system. When it is not mandatory, then there must be an easily available list with the name and address of those traders who have voluntarily opted into the ADR system. These traders should display a trustmark that must be in the landing page or up to two clicks away from the landing page. Lastly, it was observed that ADR in Spain is starved of funding. If public investment is not an option, then parties, especially traders, should pay for it, though public investment would be highly recommended to develop a more user-friendly ODR platform for arbitration and other ADR processes. The use of this platform could be extended for court-annexed online mediation processes.

Finally, with regards to the UK it was noted that, like in Italy and in Spain, there are still important gaps in the provision of consumer redress. Moreover, in the UK the provision of ADR is confusing for consumers given its sectorial approach with a high number of entities, even within the same sector. Furthermore, competition in the supply of ADR leads to forum shopping with ADR entities of questionable independence as these are selected (and paid) for by traders. Moreover, this chapter observed that in those sectors where there is only one ADR certified and the participation for traders is mandatory (such as with FOS, OS-Energy and LeO, which won competitive tenders) the ADR provides a better service that incorporates dispute prevention strategies which also benefit non-complainants. In non-regulated sectors, trade associations should require their members to join a certified ADR entity. In order to help consumers to identify the relevant ADR, the UK has assigned Citizens Advice the operation of a helpdesk, but currently they only provide consumers with a phone number to assist in finding an ADR entity. A better option would be to set up an effective national ODR platform that facilitates the consumers' pathway to resolving disputes. Although sectorial ADR coverage is improving in a piecemeal manner, as with the other jurisdictions, the UK urgently needs to set up an effective residual ADR entity, which should not only fill the gaps but also incentivize traders to join specialized ADR entities. As will be discussed in Chapter 7, the online court may take on this role in the UK.

6

Pursuing Global Consensus on Consumer Redress

The UNCITRAL Technical Notes for Online Dispute Resolution

6.1 Introduction

The purpose of this chapter is to confine the discussion of consumer redress to international disputes, especially those arising out of e-commerce, which are often of low value and more complex than their off-line counterparts as they involve additional issues, such as the applicable law and forum, the language of the dispute and the need for translation, the distance between the parties and different cultural expectations.[1] Judicial processes for cross-border disputes, especially if are of low value, are too slow and too expensive.[2] Indeed, only the cost of determining the applicable law will be disproportionate to the value of these disputes.[3] The traditional approach in private international law, which is the application of the law of the country and jurisdiction in which the consumer is resident,[4] is insufficient to provide the consumer redress in a globalized e-commerce. The unsuitability of judicial enforcement as the

[1] An early version of some of the paragraphs discussed appeared in P. Cortés and F. Esteban, 'Building a Global Redress System for Low-Value Cross-Border Disputes' (2013) 62(2) *Int Comp Law Q* 407–440 and P. Cortés, 'A New Regulatory Framework for Extra-Judicial Consumer Redress: Where We Are and How to Move Forward' (2015) 35(1) *Legal Stud* 114–141.

[2] See generally Organisation of American States, Draft [Model Law/Cooperative Framework] for Electronic Resolution of Cross-Border E-Commerce Consumer Disputes (2010). Cf. D. Fernández Arroyo, 'Current Approaches towards Harmonisation of Consumer Private International Law in the Americas' (2009) 58(2) *Int Comp Law Q* 420.

[3] Ibid. at 421; M. Dennis 'Diseño de una Agencia Práctica para la Protección de los Consumidores en las Américas' in D. Fernández Arroyo and J. Moreno Rodríguez (eds.) *Trabajos de la CIDIP VII* (Asunción, 2007) 219; and E. O'Brian 'The Hague Convention on Jurisdiction and Judgments: The Way Forward' (2003) 66(4) *Mod Law Rev* 491.

[4] See Art. 16 of the Regulation 44/2001 of 22 December on Jurisdiction and the Recognition and Enforcement of Judgements in Civil and Commercial Matters, (Brussels I) O.J. (L. 12) and Article 6 of the Regulation 593/2008 of the Parliament and the Council of 17 June 2008 on the Law Applicable to Contractual Obligations (Rome I), [2008] OJ L177/6.

default channel through which to deal with these low-value disputes has therefore become apparent.[5]

Chapter 4 already advanced that not only the EU but also the UN has brought forward regulatory initiatives to promote the use of Online Dispute Resolution (ODR). This chapter is circumscribed to the analysis of the Technical Notes on ODR that are being drafted after an agreement has been reached in 2016 by all the country delegations of the Working Group III of the United Nations Commission for International Trade Law (UNCITRAL).[6] Working Group III was established in 2010 'to undertake work in the field of online dispute resolution (ODR) relating to cross-border electronic commerce transactions, including business-to-business (B2B) and business-to-consumer (B2C) transactions'.[7] Accordingly, their mandate acknowledged that traditional judicial avenues are inadequate for settling these disputes, and set the goal of improving access to redress by drafting guidelines that support the development of ODR. National delegations met twice a year at the UN from 2010 to 2016 and discussed the drafting of what initially were going to be ODR rules; at the time of writing the Secretariat is finalizing the drafting of the final version of the Technical Notes (hereinafter the Notes).[8]

These Notes are guidelines that would need to be supplemented with Rules. The inspiration for this form of legal document was taken from the UNCITRAL Notes on Organizing Arbitral Proceedings. The Notes are non-binding instruments that provide guidance and give the UN's stamp of approval and endorsement to ODR. The Notes propose a tiered procedure that commences with negotiation and escalates to the appointment of a neutral third party that acts as conciliator/facilitator;

[5] Report of UNCITRAL Working Group III (Online Dispute Resolution) on the Work of Its Twenty-Second Session (Vienna, 13–17 December 2010) A/CN.9/716, para. 16. Cf. C. Hodges, I. Benohr, N. Creutzfeldt-Banda, *Consumer ADR in Europe* (Civil Justice Systems) (Beck/Hart, 2012). See also Cf. R. Bordone, 'Electronic Online Dispute Resolution: A System Approach – Potential, Problems, and a Proposal' (1998) 3 *Harv Negot Law Rev* 175.

[6] UNCITRAL Working Group III (Online Dispute Resolution) Thirty-Third Session (New York, 29 February–4 March 2016). Note by the Secretariat 'Draft Outcome Document Reflecting Elements and Principles of an ODR Process'. Available at https://documents-dds-ny.un.org/doc/UNDOC/LTD/V15/089/59/PDF/V1508959.pdf?OpenElement.

[7] See UNCITRAL Report on the Work of Its Twenty-Third Session (New York, 21 June–9 July 2010).

[8] The work which has taken place in the various different sessions may be found at www.uncitral.org/uncitral/en/commission/working_groups/3Online_Dispute_Resolution.html.

unresolved disputes may be adjudicated through either binding arbitration (Track I) or through adjudication or recommendation when parties choose a second track (Track II). This ODR procedure will be activated when both parties agree to it.

It must be noted from the outset that ODR rules for these types of disputes require balancing minimum due process requirements with the economic constrains of resolving low-value disputes. Ensuring due process for these disputes creates tension between efficiency and fairness, particularly in binding processes such as arbitration. It can be argued that, on the one hand, due process requirements should be reduced because increasing legal formalities has a knock-on effect on the cost and time of the dispute resolution process; on the other hand, due process standards should be even more stringent in asymmetric relationships as they can counteract the advantages enjoyed by the stronger party. Some commentators have highlighted this crucial concern.[9] For instance, Hörnle correctly argues that commercial arbitration is not suitable for resolving Internet disputes because there is often an important imbalance of power between the parties, with the stronger party easily able to take advantage of the dispute resolution process.[10] Hence, it is necessary to consider whether an ODR process takes imbalances of power into account, or whether an independent monitoring mechanism exits. It is also important to consider whether higher standards of due process result in a more costly process. It seems obvious that the level of due process requirements in say consumer online arbitration cannot be as high as that in high-value traditional commercial arbitration. In this regard Schultz observes that

> the very *raison d'être* of online arbitration is the parties' pursuit of a radically faster and cheaper form of disputes resolution ... For such disputes, arbitration is no longer the truth-seeking process that it is for commercial, investment or interstate disputes, ... but a process to avoid crass disrespect of the contract or basic legal obligations in a consumer transaction.[11]

[9] See, for example, C. Rule, *Online Dispute Resolution for Businesses. B2B, E-Commerce, Consumer, Employment, Insurance, and Other Commercial Conflicts* (Jossey Bass, 2002). Cf. P. Cortés book review of J. Hörnle, *Cross-Border Internet Dispute Resolution*, (Cambridge University Press, 2009) (2010) 73(1) MLR 171; F. Esteban de la Rosa, 'Principios De Protección Del Consumidor Para Una Iniciativa Europea En El Ámbito De La Resolución Electrónica De Diferencias (ODR) De Consumo Transfronterizas (2011) 25 *Revista General de Derecho Europeo* 1.

[10] J. Hörnle, *Cross-Border Internet Dispute Resolution* (Cambridge University Press, 2009).

[11] T. Schultz, 'Internet Disputes, Fairness in Arbitration and Transnationalism: A Reply to Julia Hörnle' (2011) 19(2) *Int J Law Inform Technol* 156–157.

Thus, ODR in the e-commerce context is aimed at settling niche disputes, which, given their small value and the location of the parties, cannot be resolved in any other way. Accordingly, the Notes aim to assist in the resolution of high-volume, low-value cross-border disputes through ODR mechanisms. However, the negotiations failed in the sense that they did not deliver their intended outcome. The Working Group had originally a much more ambitious project, which included the preparation of the following documents in addition to the procedural ODR rules: (i) rules dealing with the accreditation of ODR providers and third-party neutrals, (ii) cross-border enforcement protocol and (iii) substantive legal principles for resolving disputes.[12]

This chapter analyses the discussions carried out in UNCITRAL Working Group III, including the preparatory draft rules, and contrasts them with the EU initiatives in the field of consumer ODR. This chapter also examines the issues which could not have been included in the agreed Notes – namely, the accreditation system, the enforcement protocol and the substantive principles. The analysis notes that the arbitration process will not bring many advantages, as the legally binding nature of arbitral awards will not necessarily ensure that they will be enforced as these low-value outcomes should be primarily enforced outside the courts. Furthermore, it is argued that consumer laws in the EU require arbitral procedures to apply burdensome consumer protection policies related to due process and mandatory national laws. Consequently, it is argued that, even if arbitration can comply with the requirements contained in national consumer laws, the cost of compliance would not be proportionate to the cost of international low-value consumer disputes.

6.2 An Analysis of UNCITRAL's Technical Notes

6.2.1 Scope of Application of the Technical Notes

The Notes are designed for the resolution of low-value, high-volume cross-border transactions conducted in whole or in part by the use of electronic means of communication, including mobile phones.[13] These Notes are thus intended to apply to disputes that arise from e-commerce,

[12] Art. 2 of the draft procedural Rules of the Twenty-Third Session (New York, 23–27 May 2011) A/CN.9/WG.III/WP.109.

[13] Draft Preamble. Although UNCITRAL has a mandate to develop procedural rules to assist in the resolution of cross-border electronic transactions, not domestic ones, there is no reason why national legislators cannot use these Rules, since in practice it may be

and in particular from online transactions for the sale of goods and provision of services, including both consumer and commercial transactions.

The Notes do not distinguish between businesses and consumers; they simply refer to parties. This new taxonomy underscores how online vendors are often not aware whether they are trading with consumers or businesses. Buyers (both consumers and business) in e-commerce share a number of characteristics: they cannot normally negotiate the terms of the contract; they pay the vendors in advance, before receiving the goods or services; they often have less experience in entering into that particular transaction, etc. The Notes underpin a dispute resolution system that seeks to ensure that the buyer, who is most likely to be the claimant, is afforded adequate protection. Thus, the Notes allow for the option of having 'consumer-defendants', which in turn raises further concerns and challenges for the design of the ODR procedure that need to take account of the imbalance of power between the parties, especially since consumer-defendants may be less likely to defend a case than are business-defendants.

Although there was discussion on some restrictions to the scope of application (e.g. tort issues, family law disputes, taxation and intellectual property, just to name a few),[14] the definition of 'low-value claims' was not agreed upon. UNCITRAL has only indicated that it will embrace disputes related to subject matters that are capable of being settled by arbitration. However there is an underlying assumption that the grounds for a claim may be in practice limited to specific headings, such as those employed by eBay and major credit card providers – i.e. 'goods not delivered', 'goods delivered but not as described in the transaction' or 'unpaid delivered goods'. The advantage of reducing the number and grounds for claims would simplify the standardized treatment of disputes, thus streamlining the ODR process and increasing the availability of redress through automated means or with minimal neutral third-party intervention.

difficult for sellers to know whether they are entering into a contract with foreign or local buyers.

[14] This limitation on its scope has also been inserted in Article 1(2) of Electronic Consumer Dispute Resolution (ECODIR) Rules and in Article 2 of Online Dispute Resolution Proposal – United States Submission at the Organisation of American States 2010. Cf. L. Del Duca, C. Rule and V. Rogers, 'Designing a Global Consumer Online Dispute Resolution (ODR) System for Cross-Border Small Value – High Volume Claims – OAS Developments' (2010) 42(3) *Uniform Commercial Code Law J* 221.

6.2.2 *The Tiered ODR Procedure*

The draft rules that preceded the Notes proposed a tiered procedure starting with a consensual stage in which parties first participate in an automated negotiation process; if the dispute remains unresolved, parties are invited to participate in an optional facilitated negotiation; and if that fails, the dispute may escalate to an adjudicative stage. In its 26th session the Working Group proposed that the draft ODR rules should offer two discrete sets of rules: one ending in binding arbitration (Track I) and another one (Track II) with two possible final outcomes: (i) an outcome terminating in facilitated settlement stage, where a final settlement cannot be guaranteed or (ii) when a voluntary settlement has not been reached, a non-binding decision by a third neutral, enforceable via private mechanisms, such as a trustmark scheme or a chargeback. A dispute resolution clause would specify whether disputes would be resolved under Track I or II of the Notes.

The Track specified in the dispute resolution clause would apply irrespectively of the nature of the purchaser (i.e. a business or a consumer). The two Tracks are the result of dealing with jurisdictions where pre-dispute arbitration agreements are not considered binding on consumers. In these jurisdictions an arbitral award against a consumer, who participated via a pre-dispute arbitration clause, would not be binding on the consumer. Therefore, consumers from countries where pre-dispute arbitration is banned (e.g. EU Member States) must either agree to use Track I after the dispute arises or they must be only offered to participate in Track II. In order to identify consumers from these jurisdictions, traders must consider two elements: the shipping or billing address of the consumer-buyer and whether the purchase was for private or professional purposes. The basic features of each stage of the ODR procedure will now be looked at.

The Negotiation Stage and Negotiated Settlements

According to the procedure envisaged in the Notes, the ODR process commences when a claimant submits the online claim explaining the reasons for the complaint and outlining the proposed settlement. It is expected that this stage of the ODR process will become highly automated. In online negotiation the parties use the framework provided by the software, which is often referred to as assisted or facilitated negotiation, as the software helps the parties to reach a settlement. One key element of computer-facilitated negotiation is the use of standard forms provided by the normally web-based ODR platform, which parties will use to negotiate with each other.[15] The ODR platform can facilitate communication by, for example, contacting the other party, identifying and clarifying important information, etc.

The Notes establish a short period of time for parties to reach a negotiated agreement – the discussions in UNCITRAL initially suggested a period of 10 days.[16] Given the low value of the dispute and the need for an expeditious ODR process,[17] setting a short deadline may be justified. Clearly, time limits can act as incentives to settle the dispute, particularly when claims are resolved by negotiation on the basis of the available factual evidence rather than by exploring other legal dimensions.[18] Time limits bolster the principle of effectiveness in out-of-court proceedings.[19] Nevertheless, ODR systems should take into consideration that the time limit of the negotiation phase should be sufficient to allow the respondent to accept the solution or to be able to propose an alternative, which the claimant will then also need time to consider: parties should have the time necessary to ascertain their legal entitlements. Indeed, it would undermine the principle of fairness if consumers have insufficient time to negotiate or to accept a proposed settlement under time pressure.[20]

If the respondent admits the claim, the Notes provide for the conclusion of the negotiation and the ODR proceedings. If one of the parties requests it, or if the respondent does not reply to the notice,[21] the Notes presume that the opportunity to negotiate has been declined and the parties are automatically invited to participate in a facilitated settlement.

[15] Draft Rules Art. 2 states that '"ODR platform" means one or more than one online dispute resolution platform which is a system for generating, sending, receiving, storing, exchanging or otherwise processing electronic communications used in ODR'.

[16] Draft Rules Arts. 5(3) and 5(4).

[17] Research carried out by the online payment system PayPal found that parties often prefer an expeditious ODR process than a lengthier and more accurate process. A. Lodder and J. Zeleznikow, Enhanced Dispute Resolution Through the Use of Information Technology (Cambridge University Press, 2010) p. 21.

[18] See, e.g., R. Mnookin and L. Kornhauser, 'Bargaining in the Shadow of the Law: The Case of Divorce' (1979) 88 *Yale Law J* 950 and R. Cooter et al., 'Bargaining in the Shadow of the Law: A Testable Model of Strategic Behavior' (1982) 11 *Legal Stud* 225.

[19] We thank the reviewers for raising this point.

[20] Cf. the ADR Directive where consumers are allowed a reasonable period of time to reflect before expressing their consent to a suggested solution or amicable agreement.

[21] Draft Rules Art. 5.2.

The Appointment of Neutral Third Parties and the Optional Facilitated Settlement Stage

When parties cannot reach a negotiated agreement stage, the ODR provider will select a neutral third party (i.e. the neutral).[22] Once the neutral has assessed all the information submitted, the Notes provide that the neutral will invite the parties to a conciliation session, i.e. the facilitated settlement stage.[23] At this point the neutral, or the ODR platform automatically, may propose a settlement to the parties. If the parties agree to a settlement, the dispute will be resolved. However, there are a number of issues related to the choice of language and new procedural paradigms that need to be considered further.

The discussions first suggested that the language of the proceedings could be the same as the language of the transaction, as it is assumed that this will be the mutual language of the parties.[24] However, depending on their respective locations, the language used by the seller and buyer when making the transaction might be different.[25] The Notes state that an ODR agreement or ODR rules agreed by the parties may specify the language, but that an ODR system may allow parties to express the language preference that the ODR platform may accept. The next few paragraphs briefly examine four procedural peculiarities of the third-party neutrals that result from ODR processes, especially when dealing with low-value consumer issues.

First, the simple nature of a claim may mean that it is not necessary for the neutral to be a qualified lawyer. The Notes, similar to the ADR Directive, consider it sufficient that neutrals have obtained some relevant skills in legal dispute resolution. Nevertheless, the training of neutrals should not be a matter of self-regulation as they are involved in determining legal entitlements; hence they should be able to make decisions that respect the law, especially when issuing arbitral awards, since such awards ought to be compatible with the 1958 Convention on the Recognition and Enforcement of Foreign Arbitral Awards (i.e. the

[22] At the 22nd session of the Working Group, there was general agreement that, in the absence of agreement by the parties, there should be a sole neutral (see in this chapter n. 5, para. 62).

[23] Draft Rules Art. 7.

[24] See A/CN.9/WG.III/WP.112/Add.1, paras. 20–25.

[25] Draft Art. 12 UNCITRAL Report of Working Group III (Online Dispute Resolution) on the Work of Its Twenty-Seventh Session (New York, 20–24 May 2013). Available at www.uncitral.org/uncitral/commission/working_groups/3Online_Dispute_Resolution.html.

New York Convention). The monitoring of neutrals by independent accreditation agencies is considered later.

Second, the Notes depart from the criterion adopted in the Model Law on International Commercial Conciliation[26] in that they allow the same neutral to be involved in the facilitated settlement stage and in arbitration.[27] In order to ensure that arbitration is impartial, the normal practice in commercial, and sometimes in consumer, arbitration is for the arbitrator to be different from the mediator or conciliator.[28] Yet, employing two neutrals would increase costs and time, as two different professionals would have to examine the same dispute. This is indeed the approach taken by case handlers in most ombudsman schemes. Moreover, since this is an online process for the resolution of low-value disputes, it can be argued that, in the interests of speed and simplicity, the ODR should depart from the traditional approach found in off-line processes. A more flexible position, however, could be to allow parties to request a different neutral for arbitration, but since this would increase the cost of the procedure, the request should be subject to the requirement of a payment of an additional fee by the applicant.

Third, the Notes require neutrals to be independent and impartial,[29] and to disclose any circumstance that may raise doubts about their own impartiality.[30] Once appointed, the parties will be given a short period of time within which to disqualify the neutral, with each party being able to reject up to a maximum of three neutrals without providing grounds for doing so.[31] The UNCITRAL Arbitration Rules recommend that when appointing an independent neutral, the arbitration provider should take into account the advisability of appointing a national of a State other than that of the parties.[32] A concern would be if the same neutral were frequently allocated to disputes concerning the same businesses. Procedural disclosures, transparency and diligent

[26] Draft Rules Art. 12 of UNCITRAL Model Law on International Commercial Conciliation (2002) states that 'unless otherwise agreed by the parties the conciliator should not be [the arbitrator]'.

[27] The Model Law allows this only if the parties' agree (Art. 12). The Model Law is accessible at www.uncitral.org/uncitral/en/uncitral_texts/arbitration/2002Model_conciliation.html.

[28] See for instance the Spanish consumer arbitration system, Art. 22.1 Royal Decree 231/2008. There is also traditionally a preference for separate ethics codes for mediators and arbitrators. See C. Menkel-Meadow, 'Are there Systematic Ethic Issues in Dispute System Design? and What We Should [Not] Do About It: Lessons from International and Domestic Fronts' (Winter 2009) 14 *Harv Negot Law Rev* 202.

[29] Draft Rules Art. 8.1. [30] Draft Rules Art. 6. [31] Draft Rules Art. 6.3.

[32] UNCITRAL Arbitration Rules Art. 6.7 (as revised in December of 2010).

accreditation mechanisms should be put in place to minimize potential forum shopping and conflict of interests.

Fourth, the level of access by the neutral to the information exchanged between the parties during the negotiations has not yet been decided. There was not consensus on this point. One possibility is for neutrals to have full access to the records of negotiation stage,[33] while another would be to allow one of the parties to limit access in order to respect the confidentiality of the negotiations. This latter approach reflects traditional judicial and arbitral systems, which grant complete confidentiality to the negotiations.[34] Maintaining the confidentiality of the negotiations is intended to ensure that parties are not discouraged from disclosing evidence or settlement proposals by a concern that they might be used against them during a subsequent adjudicative process. It also ensures that the adjudicators are not coloured by parties' prior discussions and admissions of liability. Given that ODR seeks to ensure an expeditious and efficient resolution of low-value disputes, the confidentiality of the negotiations should be limited; but if ODR providers adopt such an approach, then parties should be notified of the level of confidentiality of the negotiations.

The Arbitration Stage in Track I and the Adjudicative Stage in Track II

At the time of the transaction, and thus before a dispute arises, parties can agree to use Track I, which concludes in arbitration. Alternatively, after the dispute arises parties can agree to use Track I concluding in arbitration. This option would be the only legally acceptable model for those jurisdictions where pre-dispute arbitration agreements are invalid in consumer contracts. The final arbitral award will be final and binding.[35] This means that the claimant will not be able to make a claim before the national court in relation to a situation which has already been dealt with at the arbitration stage of the ODR process.

The other option for the parties is to agree to Track II, the last procedural stage of which is non-legally-binding adjudication. In practice this last stage is very likely to resemble that of arbitration, but with the

[33] This Rule is in the rules for ODR providers funded by the European Commission: ECODIR. See www.ecodir.org.

[34] Anonymous authors, 'Mandatory Mediation and Summary Jury Trial: Guidelines for Ensuring Fair and Effective Processes' (1990) 103 *Harv Law Rev* 1086.

[35] Draft Rules Art. 9.2.

main difference of having a final outcome which, while it is not be enforceable in the courts, may well be enforceable by the market place. For example, a payment provider or escrow may shift the money in dispute from one party to the other; yet, the loser could potentially challenge that decision *de novo* in a court of law. Although this option is not feasible for most low-value cross-border disputes, there could be the possibility of bringing a class or collective action if a substantial number of claims can be aggregated.

Irrespective of which track is used, the neutral should resolve the claim within days. The draft rules proposed seven calendar days counting from the moment the parties submitted all the required documents. It also provided for a period of five days during which parties may request the correction of an 'error in computation, any clerical or typographical error, or any error or omission of a similar nature'.[36] This safeguard reflects the reality that because decisions are expected to be issued expeditiously, errors are more likely to occur. Although challenges to arbitral awards of low-value cross-border claims would be extremely rare, the appellant could only challenge the enforceability of the award on the grounds set out in Article V of the New York Convention.

6.3 Achieving Convergence between the UNCITRAL Notes and the European Approach to Consumer Protection

6.3.1 A Common Goal of Increasing Cross-Border Trade

The policy behind the EU legislation is to build consumers' confidence in the Internal Market by coordinating and making ADR services more accessible through the EU ODR platform and providing consumers with greater assurance in relation to traders' compliance with consumer protection laws. Similarly, UNCITRAL provides guidelines for an ODR procedure in order to facilitate the efficient resolution of low-value cross-border disputes.[37] UNCITRAL Notes can be adopted by ODR providers in order to complement their own procedures.

Although UNCITRAL stated that it is mindful not to displace consumer protection legislation, its approach to redress may inevitably

[36] Draft Rules Art. 9.4.

[37] C. Rule and L. Del Duca, 'From Lex Mercatoria to Online Dispute Resolution: Lessons From History in Building Cross-Border Redress Systems' (2011) 43(3) *Uniform Commercial Code Law J* 1–15, 13. See also A/CN9/WG III/WP112 UNCITRAL Working Group III (Online Dispute Resolution) Note by the Secretariat 28 February 2012.

limit the application of national and regional consumer laws. This approach contrasts with that of the EU, where there is a substantial body of harmonized (or partly harmonized) consumer protection law,[38] and where the principle of legality is enshrined in its regulatory framework. Furthermore, with the goal of making consumer rights more accessible in the EU, consumer law is going through a process of unification and clarification, which is also permeating down to the national level.[39]

6.3.2 *Different Scope of Application*

The mandate of UNCITRAL Working Group III applies to 'disputes arising from the many low-value transactions, both B2B and B2C (and also C2C), which were occurring in very high volumes worldwide and required a dispute resolution response which was rapid, effective and low-cost'.[40] By contrast, the ADR Directive only requires the establishment of ADR entities where consumers are the complainants,[41] regardless of the value of the dispute, concerning contractual obligations stemming from sales contracts or service contracts.[42] Moreover, while UNCITRAL proposes a multi-step process that moves from automated negotiation to adjudication, the European ODR initiative is open to different ODR processes that range from adjudicative to consensual extrajudicial processes. The EU approach reflects the various traditions

[38] See for instance the Directive on Consumer Rights 2011/83/EU and the proposal for a Regulation on a Common European Sales Law SEC(2011) 1165 final. See a critical analysis on the limitations of the consumer acquis at H. Micklitz and N. Reich, 'Crónica de una Muerte Anunciada: The Commission Proposal for a Directive on Consumer Rights' (2009) 46(2) *Common Mark Law Rev* 471; H. Eidenmuller, F. Faust, H.C. Grigoleit, N. Jansen, G. Wagner and R. Zimmerman 'Towards a Revision of the Consumer Acquis' (2011) 48 *CML Rev* 1077–1123; S. Weatherill 'The Consumer Rights Directive: How and Why a Quest for "Coherence" Has (Largely) Failed' (2012) 49 *Common Mark Law Rev* 1279–1318.

[39] See for instance in the UK the implementation of the Consumer Rights Directive 2011/83/EU went through a process of harmonizing and clarifying UK national consumer law. See the Department for Business and Innovation Skills (BIS) Report on 'Consolidation and Simplification of UK Consumer Law' (November 2010) and the Consumer Rights Bill 2013.

[40] A/CN.9/716, January 17, 2011.

[41] It must be remembered that the ODR Regulation allows for B2C complaints in the EU ODR platform when the national law permits this option. However, the principle of liberty ensures that consumers cannot be dragged to an adjudicative process pre-dispute.

[42] Art. 2 of the ADR Directive.

and models of consumer redress currently found in the EU and leaves the establishment of specific procedures to the individual ODR schemes themselves.

This raises the question of whether the approach followed by UNCITRAL is the most suitable one, as one procedural model cannot cover all the diversity and complexity of e-commerce disputes.[43] In his publications on legal processes, Lon Fuller foresaw that the type of factors involved in a dispute should determine the most suitable procedure for its resolution.[44] Thus, the adequate level of due process should vary according to the value and complexity of the dispute. However, the difficulty of developing a set of standards for a variety of legal processes is well attested.[45] While procedural standards need to be broad enough to encompass various processes, they also need to be sufficiently narrow to guarantee an acceptable level of due process. This is why in the European context it has been argued that it would be preferable for legislation to distinguish clearly between binding (or adjudicative) and non-binding (or consensual) processes.[46]

6.3.3 *The Use of Arbitration*

The major bone of contention in the development of the Notes, and the reason why they were watered down so much, was the entrenched approaches between the EU and the USA on the use of arbitration for consumer disputes. The proposal for the two-tracks distinction displayed an effort to reconcile the different approaches held in various jurisdictions, where according to many national laws pre-dispute arbitration clauses are allowed (particularly in the USA to protect businesses from consumer class actions);[47] whereas the national laws in most of the other jurisdictions (including the EU Member States, Japan,

[43] V. Rogers, Institute of International Commercial Law (Pace Law School) Note on the Resolution Process Designated by the Draft ODR Rules Vienna, 14–18 November 2011.

[44] L. Fuller 'The Forms and Limits of Adjudication' (1978) 92 *Harv Law Rev* 353; L. Fuller 'Mediation – Its Forms and Functions' (1971) 44 *Calif Law Rev* 305; K. Winston, 'Introduction to the Revised Edition' in K. Winston, *The Principles of Social Order: Selected Essays of Lon L. Fuller* (Hart, 2001).

[45] Menkel-Meadow, n. 28, pp. 195, 201.

[46] J. Hörnle 'Encouraging Online Dispute Resolution in the EU and Beyond- Keeping Costs Low or Standards High?' Queen Mary School of Law Legal Studies Research Paper No. 122/2012, section 7.

[47] The USA has largely upheld the validity of pre-dispute arbitration agreements unless they are 'unconscionable' for the consumer. The US Supreme Court has given a very restrictive

Canada and a number of Latin American and African States) invalidate these clauses in consumer contracts.[48]

The arguments on the validity of pre-dispute consumer arbitration clauses remain split. On the one hand, the main argument in favour of having a binding arbitration provided for from the outset is that it ensures finality by encouraging parties to participate in a process that issues a decision that is final and binding. On the other hand, there is a vast literature dealing with the counter-arguments,[49] which generally revolve around the idea that consumers, as the weaker parties, should be able to rely on mandatory laws and national courts when they have been unable to secure redress through extrajudicial means of dispute resolution. In order to protect this right, the principle of liberty (now contained in the ADR Directive) does not permit consumers to limit themselves to arbitration before the dispute arises.

The application of the national mandatory law in consumer contracts would be a key element at the time to determine the application of the New York Convention in the enforcement of arbitral awards. According

interpretation to these exceptions and has also restricted the use of state law in limiting the application of the Federal Arbitration Act (FAA). See *Carnival Cruise Lines, Inc.* v. *Shute*, 499 S.Ct. 585 (1991). The US Supreme Court has also upheld that state law cannot invalidate arbitration clauses that restrict consumers to join in class actions. See *AT&T Mobility* v. *Concepcion* 131 S.Ct. 1740 (2011) giving force to the Federal Arbitration Act. US courts are however more likely to strike down mandatory arbitration clauses in online contracts when the consumer could not have found an alternative supplier. See *Bragg* v. *Linden Research, Inc.*, 487 F. Supp. 2d 593 (E. D. Penn. 2007).

48 See Proposal by the European Union Observer Delegation of the Twenty-Seventh Session of UNCITRAL Working Group III (New York, May 2013) Online Dispute Resolution for Cross-Border Electronic Commerce Transactions: Draft Procedural Rules. A/CN.9/WG.-III/WP.121.

49 A. Schmitz, 'Legislating in the Light: Considering Empirical Data in Crafting Arbitration Reforms' (2010) 15 *Harv Negot Law Rev* 194 and '"Drive-Thru" Arbitration in the Digital Age: Empowering Consumers through Regulated ODR' (2010) 62 *Baylor Law Rev* 178–244; J. W. Hamilton, 'Pre-Dispute Consumer Arbitration Clauses: Denying Access to Justice?' (2006) 51 *McGill Law J* 693; J. M. Matthews, 'Consumer Arbitration: Is it Working Now and Will it Work in the Future?' (2005) 79 *Fl Bar J* 1; J. Sternlight and E. Jensen, 'Using Economic Arbitration to Eliminate Consumer Class Actions: Efficient Business Practice or Unconscionable Abuse?' (2004) 67 *Law Contemp Prob* 75; J. Sternlight, 'Is Alternative Dispute Resolution Consistent With the Rule of Law' (2006) 56 *DePaul Law Rev* 569; J. Sternlight, 'In Defense of Mandatory Arbitration (If Imposed on the Company)' (2007) 8 *Nevada Law J* 82; K. Stewart and J. Matthews 'Online Arbitration of Cross-Border, Business to Consumer Disputes' (2002) 56 *Univ Miami Law Rev* 1119; T. Stipanowich 'The Arbitration Penumbra: Arbitration Law and the Rapidly Changing Landscape of Dispute Resolution' (2007) 8 *Nevada Law J* 427.

to Art. II(1) of the Convention, pre-dispute arbitration agreements are valid and signatory States must give them legal validity; yet, Art. V contemplates the refusal of recognition and enforcement of arbitral award where such recognition or enforcement would be contrary to public policy of the country where the enforcement is sought, thus opening the question as to whether consumer protection legislation would be part of such public policy.

The Court of Justice of the EU has indicated in *Asturcom Telecomunicaciones* and *Mostaza Claro* that consumer protection laws rank as public policy.[50] This approach extends to the arbitrator's obligation to raise the jurisdictional point of his own motion.[51] A difficult issue is to determine to which extent the arbitrator may investigate of his own motion. It seems sensible that when dealing with consumers without legal representation, some degree of research may be necessary in order to avoid the other party leading to an award in error. In many jurisdictions, such as the UK, an arbitrator is not entitled to reach a conclusion on a point not put forward by a party,[52] but in consumer arbitrations it is expected that the arbitrator will draw the parties' attention to points that have not been raised by either of them and ask that they be addressed.[53] Furthermore, as noted in Chapter 4, the ADR Directive states that certified ADR entities cannot use pre-dispute arbitration clauses in consumer contracts. In some jurisdictions, such as in Germany, the national law implementing the ADR Directive has excluded completely arbitration from its accreditation services. However, arbitration can still be used by non-certified ADR bodies.

Indeed, EU Member States presently allow for pre-dispute consumer arbitration under very limited circumstances. Those who are not

[50] C-40/08 *Asturcom Telecomunicaciones* and C-168/05 *Mostaza Claro*. It must be also noted that the CJEU has distinguished pre-dispute mediation clauses from arbitration clauses. The former are valid provided that they meet the conditions set out by the Court. See C-317/08 *Rosalba Alassini* at 67. In *Mostaza Claro* the Court of Justice of the EU held that 'a national court seized of an action for annulment of an arbitration award must determine whether the arbitration agreement is void and annul that award where that agreement contains an unfair term, even though the consumer has not pleaded that invalidity in the course of the arbitration proceedings, but only in that of the action for annulment'.

[51] Chartered Institute of Arbitrators, Practice Guidelines 17: Guidelines for Arbitrators Dealing with Cases Involving Consumers and Parties with Significant Differences of Resources (2012). Available at www.ciarb.org/information-and-resources/Practice%20Guideline%2017.pdf.

[52] *Fox* v. *Wellfair Ltd* [1981] 1 Lloyd's Rep 514.

[53] Chartered Institute of Arbitrators, n. 51.

accredited will be subject to the Unfair Contract Terms Directive, which restricts the validity of pre-dispute agreements but is subject to the national law implementing the Directive. In some cases, the reason for allowing pre-dispute clauses is the high value of the dispute. The UK permits pre-dispute arbitration provisions when claims are above £5,000.[54] In France too, pre-dispute consumer arbitration agreements are also valid in some situations concerning high-value and international disputes.[55] In other jurisdictions, such as Germany and Austria, the law requires there to be clear and adequate notice of arbitration in consumer transactions. In order to be valid, a pre-dispute arbitration agreement must be contained in a separate document in order to ensure that the consumer has made an informed choice.[56] In the e-commerce context, the separate document is normally a click-wrap agreement which the consumer enters into by ticking an 'OK-box'. This measure aims to protect consumers against hidden clauses that subject their claims to arbitration.

6.3.4 Different Views on the Functions of the ODR Platform

The ODR Regulation established a single pan-European ODR platform that links parties with e-commerce disputes to nationally certified ADR entities. In contrast, UNCITRAL does not foresee such a centralized ODR platform. Moreover, while the ODR Regulation states that complaints submitted to the platform will be forwarded to national ADR entities, UNCITRAL envisages a first stage of the ODR process (the negotiation) to be carried out within the ODR platform. As discussed

[54] See Arts. 89–91 of the Arbitration Act 1996.

[55] Article 2061 of the French Civil Code only allows arbitration clauses in contracts concerning professional activities, i.e. not in consumers' contracts, but this article does not apply to international arbitration. A case on the legality of an international arbitration clause was discussed by the French courts in the Jaguar case [*Sté V 2000 and Sté XJ 220 Ltd c M Meglio and M Renault* Rev. Arb. 1997, p. 537 and *Cass Civ Ire* (21 May 1997)] where the first instance court held the clause to be illegal, but the Court of Appeal reversed that decision and the Supreme Court confirmed that the dispute, in the circumstances (it was a transaction of high value and the consumer was not in a weaker position), was subject to arbitration.

[56] These clauses would require vendors to take reasonable steps to ensure buyers are sufficiently well informed of the dispute resolution process at the time of entering into transactions. See N. Horn, 'Arbitraje de Consumo en el Derecho Alemán y Europeo', in F. Esteban de la Rosa and G. Orozco Pardo, *Mediación y Arbitraje de Consumo, una Perspectiva Española, Europea y Comparada* (Tirant lo Blanch, 2010) pp. 221–233.

in Chapter 3, the EU ODR platform might be connected to, or complemented by, a referral system to a court procedure, such as the European Small Claims Procedure, particularly once e-justice technology is implemented in the national courts.[57] However, such an option will not be available in the near future at a global level. In a similar vein, whereas the (off-line) judicial enforcement of low-value decisions is not currently a feasible option for cross-border disputes (at the European as well as at the international level),[58] the EU has enacted legislation to streamline this process within the Internal Market.[59] Conversely, judicial enforcement outside the EU would be more cumbersome, with the possible exception of the enforcement of significant-value arbitral awards.

6.4 Outstanding Issues

Before the agreement on the Technical Notes, UNCITRAL Working Group III had previously identified four pillars of the UNCITRAL ODR initiative: (i) procedural rules (which basically formed the Notes), (ii) rules dealing with the accreditation of ODR providers and neutrals, (iii) an enforcement protocol and (iv) legal principles for resolving disputes. The difficulty in reaching an agreement on the procedural rules led to a discard of further discussions to develop the other three pillars. This final section makes an approximation of some of the key issues that should have been included in the remaining three pillars.

6.4.1 The Accreditation of ODR Providers and Neutrals

The role of an accreditation system is to ensure that ODR processes comply with certain standards, which may be included in a code of

57 See European Parliament Resolution of 25 October 2011 on Alternative Dispute Resolution in Civil, Commercial and Family Matters (2011/2117(INI)). Cf. Cortés 'Does the Proposed European Procedure Enhance the Resolution of Small Claims?' (2008) 27(1) *Civil Justice Q* 83–97. See Recital 53 of the E-Commerce Directive 2000/31/EC encouraging access to justice by employing appropriate electronic means in the judicial process.

58 Research in the EU has suggested that parties would not consider to go to court for less than €500. See J. Stuyck, E. Terryn, V. Colaert, T. Van Dyck, N. Peretz, N. Hoekx and P. Tereszkiewicz, 'Study on Alternative Means of Consumer Redress other than Redress through Ordinary Judicial Proceedings' (Catholic University of Leuven, 17 January 2007). The economic threshold is even higher (€786) for cross-border claims. See Special Eurobarometer (2013) p. 8.

59 E.g. Rome I Regulation (O.J. 2008, L 177/6); Brussels I Regulation (O.J. 2001, L 012); and the Mediation Directive (O.J. 2008, L 136/3).

conduct or other norms. The aim of accreditation is thus to provide uniform standards that ensure a minimum level of quality.

The EU has established these minimum principles in the ADR Directive, and required competent authorities to certify those ADR entities that meet the criteria as implemented by national law. Yet, there is nothing equivalent at the global level. This is the reason why UNCITRAL considered the preparation of accreditation standards. Initially, it had been proposed for these standards to be included as an annex to the procedural rules,[60] but since the Working Group on ODR has been discontinued, the discussion has never taken place. Yet, it is a question of time before the discussion at a global level takes place. At that point, the first issue for consideration would be whether accreditation should be awarded to neutrals or to ADR/ODR providers who then, in turn, would accredit their own neutrals. The latter option seems the most common one. Indeed, it is the approach taken in the EU with the appointment of competent authorities, as well as the approach adopted by ICANN, which approve ODR providers of domain names.[61]

Such a system should contain a list of minimum requirements regarding the training and skills of neutrals. Although legal training may not be necessary, some legal knowledge and dispute resolution skills ought to be required. Forum shopping between ODR providers and between neutrals will be an important issue to consider, as will be the decision on who selects the neutrals. In this regard, lessons should be learned from the ODR process established for the resolution of domain name disputes, which, even though it had been proposed as a model for resolving consumer disputes,[62] faced criticisms for inherited bias.[63]

Accreditation agencies must act as independent evaluators. Regular follow-up and monitoring should take place to ensure that ODR

[60] Preamble, para. 2.

[61] Cf. P. Cortés, 'The UDRP Reviewed: The Need for a 'Uniform' Policy' (2008) 14(6) *Comput Telecommun Law Rev* 133–139 and 'An Analysis of the UDRP Experience: Is It Time for Reform?' (2008) 24(4) *Comput Law Secur Rep* 349–359.

[62] S. Donahey 'The UDRP Model Applied to Online Consumer Transactions' (2003) 20(5) *J Int Arb* 475.

[63] A. Froomkin, 'ICANN Uniform Dispute Resolution Policy, Causes and (Practical) Cures' (2002) 67 *Brooklyn Law Rev* 690; M. Geist, 'Fair.com? An Examination of the Allegations of Systematic Unfairness in the ICANN UDRP' (2002) 27 *Brooklyn J Int Law* 903; M. Mueller, 'Rough Justice: An Analysis of ICANN's Uniform Dispute Resolution Policy' (2000) Syracuse University Convergence Centre http://dcc.syr.edu/PDF/roughjustice.pdf.

providers are acting in accordance with the established standards. Compliance should not only be reliant on the self-assessment of the ODR providers themselves or on the consideration of reports submitted by them to accreditation agencies: accreditation entities should themselves have the duty to actively check compliance with quality standards. Furthermore, consideration needs to be given to establishing a complaints system, should ODR providers and neutrals not follow the rules. Such complaints could be submitted directly to the accreditation agencies.

To be effective an accreditation system would require ODR providers to be adequately and constantly monitored. An accreditation or certificating entity must have a body that monitors compliance with the minimum requirements and issues the necessary certifications to those providers that meet them.[64] In the EU, this is presently carried out by the national 'competent authorities' appointed by each Member State. Outside the EU these entities may be either public or private. For example, in the USA, the American Bar Association has created a task force to provide guidelines for the development of ethical ODR systems.[65] The Association for Conflict Management has prepared a proposal for guidelines on ODR,[66] and the International Mediation Institute, based in The Hague, has also developed standards for international mediation competency and provides certification for mediators.[67] Similar private certification programmes also exist for arbitrators.[68] Careful consideration should be given to the question of who should carry out accreditation. This could be carried out at the national, regional or global level, but efficiently tackling e-commerce disputes requires that accreditation agencies be properly coordinated. If there is not adequate supervision by competent national authorities then this accreditation system runs the risk of misleading ODR users into

64 M. Conley Tyler and J. Bornstein, 'Accreditation of On-line Dispute Resolution Practitioners' (2006) 23(3) *Confl Resol Q* 383.

65 See www.americanbar.org/groups/dispute_resolution/policy_standards.html.

66 The National Alternative Dispute Resolution Advisory Council (NADRAC) in the Australian Department of Justice commissioned a study on the accreditation of ODR in 2002. See Conley Tyler, '115 and Counting: The State of ODR 2004', in M. Conley Tyler, E. Katsh and D. Choi (eds.) Proceedings of the Third Annual Forum on Online Dispute Resolution. International Conflict Resolution Centre in collaboration with the United Nations Economic and Social Commission for Asia and the Pacific (UNESCAP).

67 See Qualifying Assessment Program at www.imimediation.org.

68 See the Chartered Institute of Arbitrators at www.arbitrators.ogr.

trusting neutrals and ODR providers who, though claiming otherwise, may not in fact, be compliant.[69]

6.4.2 *The Enforcement Protocol*

Currently court enforcement is not cost-efficient for low-value disputes – let alone for cross-border disputes, such as those arising often from e-commerce. Consequently, private enforcement mechanisms are a better option, since inefficient and costly court enforcement would make the whole ODR process futile. In order to guarantee prompt enforcement it would be beneficial if accredited ODR providers could rely on out-of-court enforcement through for instance payment channels or escrows. Although, it may be preferable to collaborate with existing payment providers (e.g. Visa, Mastercard or PayPal) than to create new intermediaries, such as escrows, as these could increase costs and hinder the payment flow for sellers; online currencies, such as Bitcoin, can also ensure the enforcement of outcomes.[70]

By outsourcing disputes to accredited ODR providers, payment providers would maintain their position of neutrality as both the medium for payment and the enforcement of settlements. It must be noted that such an enforcement system would only be effective if the payment intermediaries have access to the accounts of the parties. In addition, as discussed in Chapter 8, there are a number of incentives that may be used to encourage voluntary compliance with a settlement: these include the publication of negative reviews, black-lists, trustmark logos that may be withdrawn once the vendor fails to comply with a final outcome, and communication of the outcome to the relevant public authority in the respondent's State.

The settlements and adjudicated decisions issued by accredited ODR providers would be expected to be final for most cases, possibly subject to a very limited number of exceptions (for instance when consumers might take a class action in their national courts or when mandatory laws had not been respected in the ODR process). Yet, the monitoring of relevant standards in each case cannot be carried out effectively by the national courts or the accreditation agencies, and so has to be

[69] P. Cortés, *Online Dispute Resolution for Consumers in the European Union* (Routledge 2010) ch. 5.

[70] P. Ortolani, 'Self-Enforcing Online Dispute Resolution: Lessons from Bitcoin' (2016) 36(3) *Oxf J Legal Stud* 595–629.

achieved by having independent neutrals and transparent ODR processes that for instance publish decisions.

6.4.3 Legal Principles for Resolving Disputes

It is possible to identify three approaches to the selection of the substantive norms for resolving consumer disputes: national laws, regional laws and international principles. This section considers the suitability and limitations of these three approaches.

National Laws

It has been traditionally argued that the consumers' national law should be followed when resolving consumer disputes, in order to protect them from the traders' choice of laws and forum shopping.[71] Under EU law both courts and arbitral bodies, when resolving cross-border consumer disputes, must comply with the mandatory consumer law of the consumer's country of residence if the trader had directed its activity to the consumer's jurisdiction.[72] The drawbacks of this approach for the international trader are the higher costs and the less predictability of the outcomes, which may vary depending on the jurisdiction of the consumer. In addition, the mere determination of national law generates complexity and costs, which is why it is argued that this is not the best approach when resolving international e-commerce disputes.

As a result, EU consumer law is increasingly based in maximum harmonization principles such as the unfair business to consumer commercial practices.[73] Moreover there are appearing examples where the plication of consumer national law is being relaxed for the purposes of low-value cross-border dispute resolution – for instance, the Consumer Rights Directive allows Member States its application to low-value cases (transactions below the value of €50 or lower value if the national law so states).[74] Paradoxically, the EU is still in favour of upholding the principle of legality in the context of out-of-court redress for consumers but, importantly, this is not because it believes that ADR processes

[71] This has been the approach taken by the EU. See Regulation 44/2001 of 22 December on Jurisdiction and the Recognition and Enforcement of Judgements in Civil and Commercial Matters, (Brussels I) O.J. (L. 12) and Regulation 593/2008 of the Parliament and the Council of 17 June 2008 on the Law Applicable to Contractual Obligations (Rome I), O.J. (L. 177).

[72] Art. 6 of Rome I Regulation, see n. 4 in this chapter.

[73] Directive 2005/29/EC.

[74] Art. 3.4 of the Directive on Consumer Rights 2011/83/EU.

should strictly follow national substantive laws, but because it sees ADR and ODR as complementing the courts, which should remain the ultimate guarantors of the rule of law when applying consumer protection law.

EU Consumer Aquis

In the EU an important pillar of consumer protection is the restriction on unfair practices,[75] which considers a commercial practice unfair if it is misleading, aggressive or blacklisted by the Directive.[76] In addition, the European Commission has issued two proposals in December 2015 that fully harmonize the rules covering the supply of digital content and the online sale of goods.[77] The proposals set out rules that would enable traders to sell digital content and goods online throughout the EU, applying the same set of contract rules. The proposed rules try to react to the newest developments in the digital society while updating existing European legislation. Their aim is to facilitate cross-border e-commerce by enhancing legal certainty and avoiding unnecessary costs for traders. Both proposals set remedies for consumers in the event of breach of contract. Under the proposals consumers are entitled to choose between the repair or the replacement of the goods, a price reduction, or the termination of the contract when the lack of conformity cannot be remedied with the repair or replacement. Thus, these rules go hand in hand with redress mechanisms.[78]

[75] Unfair Commercial Practice Directive 2005/29/EC, [2005] OJ L149/22; S. Weatherill and U. Bernitz (eds.), *The Regulation of Unfair Commercial Practices under Directive 2005/29: New Rules and New Techniques* (Hart, 2007); B. De Groote and K. De Vulder, 'European Framework for unfair commercial practices: analysis of Directive 2005/29 (2007) *J Bus Law* 16–42; G. Anagnostaras, 'The Unfair Commercial Practices Directive in Context: From Legal Disparity to Legal Complexity?' (2010) 47 *Common Mark L Rev* 147.

[76] See the 31 unfair commercial practices contained in Annex I of the Directive. It must be also noted that the Directive is implemented in the Consumer Protection from Unfair Trading Regulations 2008 (CPRs) and works alongside the Advertising Standard Authority code of practice. C. Riefa, *Consumer Protection and Online Auction Platforms* (Ashgate, 2015) p. 262. See also Guidance on the Application of the Unfair Commercial Practices Directive SWD(2016) 136.

[77] Proposal for a Directive on Certain Aspects Concerning Contracts for the Supply of Digital Content COM(2015) 634 and Proposal for a Directive on Certain Aspects Concerning Contracts for the Online and Other Distance Sales of Goods COM(2015) 635.

[78] Commissioner Reding had initially planned to publish the ODR Regulation together with the now defunct Common European Sales Law, but after the difficulties faced in passing it a decision was made to link the ODR Regulation with the ADR Directive instead. See H. Micklitz and G. Sartor, 'Assessing the Scope of the European Online Dispute

Presently, however, full harmonization of consumer and contract laws exists in the EU only in some areas. It is thus relevant to examine briefly three key consumer rights that apply in distance selling (i.e. in online, mail and telephone sales) – namely, the right of withdrawal, the right to reject and the two-years guarantee.

According to the Directive on Consumer Rights, all European consumers have a right to withdraw from an online contract within 14 calendar days (i.e. the cooling-off period) of receiving the goods or concluding a contract for the provision of services without any reason or penalty. The consumer would only have to carry the shipping costs of returning the purchased goods, while the trader will normally carry the reimbursement for the delivery costs, unless the delivery at the consumer's request was expressed.[79] Crucially, if the trader does not inform the consumer about the right of withdrawal, the 14 calendar days will turn into a year. When the consumer exercises the right, the trader is obliged to reimburse the consumer's payment within 14 days from receiving notice of the consumer's withdrawal from the contract, but the trader may withhold the refund until he receives the goods. It must be noted that goods sold to the consumers' specifications (e.g. an altered dress) or certain intellectual property items (e.g. music or games) are excluded from the right of withdrawal.[80]

In addition to the cooling-off period, consumers have the right to reject when they receive faulty goods within 30 days – but the time stops when the consumer brings this to the attention of the seller. All consumer goods must be of merchantable quality (taking into account what they are meant to do, durability and price), must be fit for their purpose (they must do that they were reasonably expected to do), and must be as described (consumers should not be misled in the description of the goods).

Resolution Platform' (2012) www.europarl.europa.eu/document/activities/cont/201204/20120417ATT43146/20120417ATT43146EN.pdf.

[79] CJEU, 15 April 2010, Case C-511/08 (Heinrich Heine), ECLI:EU:C:2010:189. Art. 14(2) Directive 2011/83/EU of 25 October 2011 on consumer rights, [2011] OJ L304/64 and CJEU C-489/07 *Messner*, ECLI:EU:C:2009:502. See generally J. Luzak, 'Online Consumer Contracts' (2014) 15(3) *ERA Forum* 381–392. Exceptionally, the consumer may also have to compensate the trader for the diminished value of the goods if the consumer has used the goods during the withdrawal period and diminished their value as a result of the use – this compensation would only apply if the trader has notified the consumer about the right of withdrawal.

[80] Art. 16 Consumer Rights Directive.

The last key right is a two-year guarantee recognized in the Directive 1999/44/EC for faulty or misdescribed goods.[81] Although all goods purchased in the EU will have a minimum of two-years guarantee, the onus of proving that the goods were faulty at the time of the sale move from the trader to the consumer after six months. When the onus is on the consumer for electrical goods, the cost of producing the evidence from an expert witness can be disproportionate, discouraging most consumers from seeking redress.[82] This limitation recognizes that leaving the onus on the trader for long periods of time may be unreasonable for small traders. In order for consumers to benefit from this right they must notify the trader within two months after the fault appeared and they have to show that they did not damage the goods (i.e. the goods must not show signs of misuse or damage through the consumers' actions). It must be noted that in practice many traders, including the largest corporations, such as Apple, have offered consumers a one-year guarantee. Public enforcement bodies, as well as ADR/ODR bodies, that identify that the trader's warranty is below the legal guarantee set under the mandatory consumer law should require the traders in question to change their guarantee.[83]

International Norms

Unlike with national laws, it is clear that if supranational laws are the basis for decisions of cross-border cases (as was once the case of *lex mercatoria* and now may be the case with the UNIDROIT principles or the Convention on Contracts for the International Sale of Goods), these disputes will be resolved on the basis of the same principles regardless of where the parties are located. It can be argued that this approach brings more consistency to dispute resolution, and therefore more certainty and

[81] This right is also reinforced by the information obligation on commercial guarantees contained in the Art. (1)(e) of the Consumer Rights Directive. English law (Sale of Goods Act 1979) already allows consumers to make a claim for up to six years from the date the consumer bought the goods and for up to five years in Scotland. Yet, most Member States have only stipulated a period of two years e.g. in Spain Art. 123.1 of the Ley General para la Defensa de Consumidores y Usuarios 1/2007.

[82] F. J. Dávila González, 'La Tramitación de la Resolución de Conflictos Sometidos a las Juntas Arbitrales de Consumo Mediante Medios Electrónicos. Problemas Prácticos y Propuestas de *Lege Ferenda*' in E. Vázquez de Castro (ed.), *Estudios sobre la Justicia Online* (Comares, 2013) p. 54.

[83] See Chapter 8 in this book.

legitimacy to the process.[84] The advantage of using international uniform rules is that it allows for the resolution of cross-border consumer disputes without having to determine the national applicable law.[85]

A different, and perhaps even more important, question is whether these low-value disputes should be resolved by neutrals according to a legalistic set of principles, or whether they should be dealt with following the more basic international principles. The latter approach, which was initially favoured by UNCITRAL, would require the development of a simple list of principles that would need to be agreed upon by all the jurisdictions. It appears probable that a starting point for drafting these basic substantive law principles might be the rules used by credit card providers for issuing chargebacks.[86]

UNCITRAL contemplated limiting the type of remedies available to claimants that might be restricted to: discounts in the cost of the transaction, full refunds, replacement of the goods and return of the goods.[87] An element that could have been considered by ODR providers is the grounds for defence for respondents; such provisions could constitute an effective way for providing legal certainty and uniformity in the resolution of these claims while at the same time promoting early settlement without the intervention of neutrals.[88] A good model to follow could again be the ODR services for domain names, which contain a list of examples of typical defences for respondents while stating which party has the burden of proof.[89]

When relying on International norms it must be clearly acknowledged that these cannot overrule the mandatory laws stemming from national consumer protection laws.[90] It is important to emphasize that although a global ODR system should adjudicate disputes, ODR providers should

[84] T. Schultz, 'Private Legal Systems: What Cyberspace Might Teach Legal Theorists' (2007) 10 *Yale J Law Tech* 159.

[85] H. Schulte-Nölke, 'EC Law on the Formation of – from Common Frame of Reference to the "Blue Button"' (2007) 3 *Eur Rev Cont L* 332.

[86] Cf. R. Brand, 'Analysis and Proposal for Incorporation of Substantive Principles for ODR Claims and Relief into Article 4 of the Draft Procedural Rules' Note submitted by the Center for International Legal Education to UNCITRAL Working Group III Twenty-Fifth Session, New York, 21–25 May 2012.

[87] UNCITRAL, n. 7, para. 33.

[88] On the requirements of the principle of legal certainty, see A.E. Pérez Luño, *La Seguridad Juridical* (Ariel, 1994).

[89] Uniform Domain-Name Dispute-Resolution Policy (UDRP) para. 4(b).

[90] UNCITRAL Working Group III (Online Dispute Resolution) Twenty-Sixth Session (Vienna, 5–9 November 2012). A/CN.9/WG.III/WP.117, para. 5.

not be able to issue binding arbitral awards in consumer disputes, unless those awards respect minimum due process principles and national consumer laws or equivalent instruments. It is therefore recognized that the Track II system is more desirable since resolving disputes on the basis of national law will be more costly, thus hindering consumers' access to redress without providing the benefit of court enforcement. However, non-binding decisions or recommendations should rely on self-enforceable options.[91]

6.5 Conclusion

The expansion of e-commerce is limited by having the courts as the default channel for resolving problems, as this forum is clearly unsuited to deal with cross-border disputes, especially given the high-volume of low-value disputes arising from the online market. Regardless of how consumer protection laws are developed, there is a need for effective redress mechanisms that can offer swift remedies to consumers. Against this backdrop, UNCITRAL and the EU have developed rules to stimulate the use of ODR for resolving these disputes. In doing so they acknowledge that ODR can contribute towards increasing parties' trust in cross-border transactions. The benefits of ODR will be particularly felt amongst consumers and SMEs, which would benefit from greater trust in transnational trade. In turn, it is hoped that greater consumer confidence in reliable traders will help turn e-commerce into a more competitive market.

This chapter has focused on the UNCITRAL Notes and has observed that pre-dispute arbitration has represented an insurmountable hurdle in the design of global norms for ODR. After six years of negotiations, UNCITRAL Working Group III has only managed to develop watered-down Technical Notes that illustrate elements of an ODR procedure that can be contractually chosen by the parties. This chapter has noted that arbitration may not be the most adequate method for resolving low-value cross-border consumer disputes as it may allow market abuses to go undetected. In order to prevent these abuses, transparency ought to be promoted through the publication of awards and monitoring carried out by the appropriate accreditation agencies. This chapter argued that the binding nature of the award does not provide any advantages in terms of

[91] See Chapter 8 in this book.

ensuring out-of-court enforcement. Although arbitration supposes the maximum of certainty for the parties, this certainty would be illusory in international consumer disputes, as having an award will not ensure its enforceability, which needs to take place quickly and inexpensively out of court. Moreover, when the use of mandatory consumer law is not guaranteed in arbitration, the outcome may be incompatible with national laws. Accordingly, these decisions should not be legally binding, thus allowing domestic judicial processes to remain the guarantor and interpreter of national consumer law, and more generally, the rule of law itself. While it is recognized that in nearly all low-value claims this option may not be feasible, there may be opportunities for collective actions or government intervention, which cannot be restricted by the *res judicata* effect. Even when arbitration could theoretically be adapted to comply with the special requirements of consumer laws, in the majority of e-commerce disputes the complexity, formality and costs of these procedures would not justify having recourse to arbitration.

UNCITRAL and the EU have adopted different models for promoting the use of ODR. It is only a question of time before ODR changes the way we engage in e-commerce and widens the road of cross-border trade. The turn of the new century is already starting to see a shift in international consumer law, which is changing the priorities of policy makers. Their focus is no longer on guaranteeing the protection of consumers by means of national courts and laws, but on promoting ADR and ODR techniques that provide real and tangible redress for consumers.

The next two chapters address a key element that is missing from UNCITRAL Notes and from the European ODR Regulation, but which is crucial to the success of these out-of-court schemes: the development of incentives to ensure parties' participation in these extrajudicial process, to settle disputes early and to ensure out-of-court enforcement of outcomes.

7

Voluntariness as the Achilles' Heel of ADR

The Case for Incentives and Mandatory Redress Schemes

7.1 Introduction

ADR and ODR first emerged as an alternative redress forum, but it is increasingly seen as the most appropriate dispute resolution forum for many civil disputes, where minimal government intervention is preferred to the judicial forum.[1] This approach does not only apply to consumer matters, but to all types of private disputes.[2] There are two driving forces behind this shift of policy: first, it is the realization that the 'means and cost of resolving disputes should be proportionate to the importance and nature of the disputes at stake';[3] and second, liberal governments see ADR and ODR as a way to empower citizens to find effective redress, which has a knock-on effect in increasing competition and economic growth.[4]

The previous chapter discussed UNCITRAL Notes on ODR, the rational behind of which is the promotion of international trade, especially e-commerce. These consumer redress techniques are particularly suitable for cases where the application of the law is fairly clear and where only basic facts need to be determined in order to allocate rights

[1] L. McGregor, 'Alternative Dispute Resolution and Human Rights: Developing a Rights-Based Approach through the ECHR' (2015) 26(3) *Eur J Int Law* 607–634.

[2] For instance, with regards to family disputes the UK government wants 'to foster a cultural change to enable people to solve their own disputes in a less acrimonious way and not look to government to do it for them'. See Ministry of Justice 'Caroline Dinenage responds to the launch of 'Breaking up Is Hard to Do' report' (17 December 2015) www.gov.uk/government/speeches/caroline-dinenage-responds-to-the-launch-of-breaking-up-is-hard-to-do-report.

[3] M. Elliott and R. Thomas, 'Tribunal Justice and Proportionate Dispute Resolution' (2012) 71(2) *Camb Law J* 279, 299. See also F. Sander and S. Goldberg, 'Fitting the Forum to the Fuss: A User-Friendly Guide to Selecting and ADR Procedure' (1994) 10 *Negot Law J* 49.

[4] Department for Business Innovation and Skills, 'Civil Enforcement Remedies: Consultation on Extending the Range of Remedies Available to Public Enforcers of Consumer Law' (November 2012) para. 1.3.

and obligations, which is often in the case of disputes related to the sale of goods and services. Indeed, the UNCITRAL Notes presuppose that online buyers and sellers will be interested in using ODR for settling their disputes. However, this may not always be the case for all traders because either they may not be aware of what ODR has to offer or they may not be convinced that the cost of funding the process would provide immediate economic returns. Although marketplaces such as eBay and Amazon quickly understood that resolving satisfactorily consumer disputes is essential to get repeat as well as new customers, the approach to consumer redress varies significantly. For instance, while eBay provides a largely automated dispute resolution centre often using PayPal as its enforcement arm, Amazon offers a generous compensation policy as a way to deal with the vast majority of buyers' complaints.

Hodges observes that the adherence by traders to an ADR/ODR scheme comes either from a top-down imposition under national law or from a voluntary bottom-up movement by a business or trade association.[5] He notes that traders will join ADR schemes if they can see it 'in their commercial advantage (usually in terms of maintaining reputation, and an element of erecting a barrier to entry to the market sector)'.[6]

Whereas in some economic sectors it is compulsory for traders to participate in an ADR scheme, in most sectors traders are free to decide whether they opt in. Traders may see consumer redress as part of a marketing opportunity. For instance, adherence to an ADR entity may be part of a membership in a code of conduct, which may be a requirement for obtaining a trustmark system or for belonging in a trade association, or even for participating in an online marketplace such as eBay. Conversely, in other sectors traders have been reluctant to embrace it. For example, many airlines have been notoriously reluctant about settling any complaint out of court. This situation has led in some cases to the approval of sectorial laws requiring the traders' participation in certified ADR entities (as Germany did to all its airlines).[7]

[5] C. Hodges, 'Consumer Ombudsmen: Better Regulation and Dispute Resolution' (2015) *ERA Forum* 2–3.

[6] Ibid., p. 3.

[7] The German law, the Settlement in the Aviation Sector Act 2013 (Gesetz zur Schlichtung im Luftverkehr) creates SOP. This German ADR entity can reject claims that they consider being unmeritorious and they can refer a case to the court if there is a need for a test case on a point of law – all the costs of these cases in first instance will be carried out by the airline.

The lack of awareness of ADR and ODR mechanisms and the lack of incentives for their use are considered the most important hindrances to their growth[8] – the Achilles' heel. The ADR Directive attempts to mitigate this by requiring traders to inform consumers about which ADR entities are competent to resolve consumers' complaints, and the ODR Regulation requires online traders to provide a link to the ODR platform. Yet, when a trader refuses to participate in an ADR process, the consumer will be basically left with two undesirable options, either to take the trader to court or not to pursue the complaint any further; in nearly all cases consumers opt for the latter.

This chapter examines when and why traders participate in ADR and notes that the availability and diversity of ADR providers create confusion amongst consumers and lead to forum shopping. This chapter examines the procedural grounds set in the Directive upon which ADR entities can rely when refusing to deal with a consumer complaint. In addition, this chapter argues that while other incentives, such as data on customer loyalty and a pan-European trustmark, could encourage traders' participation, the most effective incentive would be a mandatory ADR entity with residual or complementary jurisdiction that respects the consumer's right of access to justice.

7.2 The Limited Availability of ADR

7.2.1 Sectorial Coverage: A Confusing Picture

There are EU laws as well as national laws requiring the setting up of consumer redress systems. Although the legal obligations vary significantly, they can be broadly divided in three distinguishable prongs: public enforcement bodies, certified ADR entities and traders' in-house complaints handling schemes. These redress schemes range from public and independent bodies to private internal consumer satisfaction systems. Hence, their focus goes from the seeking of public interest to the provision of private individual redress.

[8] Communication on Alternative Dispute Resolution for Consumer Disputes in the Single Market COM(2011) 791; Directive 2013/11/EU of the European Parliament and of the Council of 21 May 2013 on alternative dispute resolution for consumer disputes and amending Regulation (EC) No 2006/2004 and Directive 2009/22/EC, [2013] OJ L165/63; and Regulation (EU) No 524/2013 of the European Parliament and of the Council of 21 May 2013 on online dispute resolution for consumer disputes and amending Regulation (EC) No 2006/2004 and Directive 2009/22/EC, [2013] OJ L165/1.

It is often in the interest of individual consumers and traders to settle complaints quickly using the traders' in-house consumer satisfaction architecture. In terms of the availability of internal customer satisfaction systems, there are a number of sectors where traders have very good customer services (e.g. typically large supermarkets or stores) whereas other sectors are notorious for their poor internal complaints procedures (e.g. many airlines). Only when a satisfactory resolution cannot be found directly with the trader may disputes escalate to an ADR/ODR entity. If traders have breached systematically consumer laws, then regulators and public enforcement bodies should require regulatory compliance (through information communications, fines and even court action).

The availability of redress options varies a lot depending on the economic sectors and the jurisdictions at hand. This situation has led to the approval of EU-wide regulations that require traders' adherence to certified ADR schemes for essential services where there is a high number of consumer disputes, such as in energy, telecommunications and financial matters. Yet, the present coverage at national and European levels is far from logical or uniform, with legal requirements that vary significantly from sector to sector. Indeed, the decision over which markets provide consumers with access to ADR, and exactly what type of scheme they are able to access, has been determined by history and political opportunity rather than rational design. The following brief analysis of the sectorial approach to consumer redress, especially in essential services, demonstrates these disparities.

The regulation in the energy sector requiring traders to offer an ADR scheme to consumers varies depending on whether consumers use electricity or gas. Member States have an obligation to ensure that electricity providers have incorporated in their business an efficient in-house process and, more importantly, that they are linked to an independent ADR scheme, and that they inform consumers about it.[9] The effectiveness of these ADR schemes varies from country to country, and regulators often provide them.[10]

By contrast, in terms of gas, European law does not contain a specific obligation related to the setting up of an independent ADR mechanism;

[9] Art. 3(13) Directive 2009/72/EC concerning common rules for the internal market in electricity.

[10] For an analysis of individual countries see P. Cortés (ed.), *The New Regulatory Framework for Consumer Alternative Dispute Resolution* (OUP, 2016).

an in-house system would suffice.[11] The same situation applies in the insurance sector where there is a mandate to establish an in-house complaints procedure, but it simply encourages the adherence to independent ADR schemes.[12]

With regards to telecommunications services, the EU sectorial law requires Member States to ensure the provision of effective ADR processes, but the law does not specifically require the participation of the service providers, nor does it require that they must be independent.[13] In a similar vein, in postal services the EU sectorial regulation imposes an obligation to provide for a complaints procedure, but the adherence to an ADR scheme does not need to be independent from the postal service.[14] In other sectors, such as timeshare and e-commerce, the regulation simply encourages the creation of complaints and redress procedures.[15]

Similarly, in the financial services there are a number of Directives, such as those on credit agreements and distant marketing, which promote the use of ADR (including traders' in-house schemes), but do not establish an obligation to join independent ADR entities.[16] Conversely, other European instruments, such as the regulations on payments, require Member States to designate independent ADR bodies to deal with complaints in this sector.[17]

The regulation in the transport sector is quite mixed. While in rail transport there is a regulation that requires rail companies to provide

[11] Annex I (1)(f) Directive 2009/73/EC concerning common rules for the internal market in natural gas.

[12] Arts. 11–12(1) (e) Directive 2002/92/EC on insurance mediation.

[13] Art. 34(1) Directive 2002/22/EC on universal service and users' rights relating to electronic communications networks and services, and Art. 26(c)(1) Directive 98/10/EC on the application of open network provision (ONP) to voice telephony and on universal service for telecommunications in a competitive environment.

[14] Art. 19 Directive 2008/6/EC with regard to the full accomplishment of the Internal Market of Community postal services.

[15] Art. 14 Directive 2008/122/EC on the protection of consumers in respect of certain aspects of timeshare, long-term holiday product, resale and exchange contracts; Art. 17 Directive 2000/31/EC on e-commerce.

[16] For financial services see Arts. 80 and 83 of the Directive 2007/64/EC on payment services. Art. 10(2) (t) and Art. 24 Directive 2008/48/EC on credit agreements for consumers; Art. 14 Directive 2002/65/EC on distance marketing of financial services; Art. 10 of the Directive 97/5/EC on cross-border credit transfers.

[17] Arts. 10–12 of the Regulation 924/2009/EC; Art. 42 of the Directive 2009/110/EC and Directive 2007/64/EC on payment services; art. 100 Directive 2009/65/EC on the coordination of laws, regulations and administrative provisions relating to undertakings for collective investment in transferable securities (UCITS). There is an obligation to provide ADR schemes in this sector (Recital 51 and Art. 42 (7)).

in-house complaints mechanisms,[18] in maritime transport the law obliges not only the provision of in-house complaints mechanisms by businesses, but also the establishment of a national enforcement body, which may be an ADR entity, as long as it deals with passengers' individual complaints.[19]

7.2.2 *A Case Study: The Airlines Sector*

Aviation is an interesting sector because it is characterized for having a high level of complaints (mostly due to delays and flight cancelations) and it has traditionally refused to engage with ADR schemes. Indeed, some airlines do not even provide an effective complaints process. Moreover, consumers do not have the choice of airlines for many destinations. This situation has led Germany to bring sectorial legislation making it compulsory for airlines to participate in ADR.[20] Across the EU, the information obligations imposed by the ADR Directive and the ODR Regulation are putting additional pressure on airlines to consider joining an ADR entity.[21]

The two ADR models that this sector is looking at are the ombudsman model, which is predominant in the EU, and the arbitration model. While the industry seems to favour the latter because it is cheaper to run, consumers normally pay a small fee for its use and outcomes bind consumers; regulators and consumers, by contrast, prefer the former, as ombudsman schemes tend to be more transparent, free for consumers and can have closer links with regulators.[22]

The EU Regulation dealing with air passenger rights – in the event of denied boarding, cancellation or long delay of flights – requires Member States to set up a national enforcement body (NEB) which must allow for consumers to submit complaints, but it does not require this body to process individual complaints.[23] A proposed amendment by the

[18] Art. 27 Regulation 1371/2007/EC on rail passengers' rights and obligations.

[19] Art. 25 Regulation 1177/2010/EC concerning the rights of passengers when travelling by sea and inland waterway.

[20] See, for example, the German Conciliation Body for Public Transport at https://soep-online.de/welcome.html.

[21] Centre for Consumer and Essential Services, University of Leicester 'Complaint Handling by Airlines: Development of Best Practices' Research Report for the Civil Aviation Authority (July 2014) p. 33.

[22] Ibid., p. 34.

[23] Art. 16 Regulation 261/2004/EC and Art. 14 of the Regulation 1107/2006/EC.

European Commission will make it mandatory for airlines to be part of an ADR entity and to inform passengers in their bookings about it.[24] Under the proposed law, consumers have three months to bring a complaint to the airline; the complaint must be acknowledged within seven days; once it is decided, or if the airline does not resolve it after two months (which is a rather long time), then the consumer can escalate the complaint to the ADR, which will have three months to resolve it. The initial complaint and the final decision, which does not need to be binding, would need to be communicated to the NEB. The proposal is being examined by the European Parliament and Council, and at this point it is not clear which changes will occur, but it seems that most of the sticky points relate to substantive issues, such as what are extraordinary circumstances, the length of the delay and compensation rates.[25]

In the UK, the NEB is the Civil Aviation Authority (CAA), whose complaint service arm (the Passenger Advice and Complaints Team or PACT) used to handle around 20,000 airline passenger complaints a year.[26] Interestingly, the policy of the CAA (as well as that of many other regulators and enforcement bodies) is to outsource the ADR scheme.[27] The rationale behind this policy is that the enforcement function should not overlap with the ADR function, removing concerns about independence – for instance in taking enforcement action against an airline that is involved in ADR. Moreover, if regulators certify themselves as ADR entities, then the certification process lacks independence.

Experience demonstrates that airlines need strong incentives to resolve complaints effectively and fairly in-house. This can be promoted with an accessible ADR system provided by the regulator, especially if airlines have to pay for it. This is exactly what the CAA is doing. Currently

24 Art. 16(a) 2013 EC proposal amending the Reg 261/2004 COM/2013/0130 final. The proposal requires the provision of mandatory nationally certified complaint handling processes (i.e. one or various ADRs) separate from the NEB.

25 Presently the national law is still relevant at the time of interpreting what are extraordinary circumstances and technical fault. Some of these issues have already been clarified by the Court of Justice of the EU, whose rulings are set to inform the amendments to the Regulation. In the meantime the present situation is still raising some issues that requires statutory interpretation. See, for example, *Jet2.com* v. *Huzar* [2014] EWCA Civ 791.

26 Around 80 per cent of complaints are derived from the Regulation (EC) 261/2004 complaints related to denied boarding, delays and cancellations. Other complaints would include damage to baggage or problems faced by disable people.

27 Civil Aviation Authority, 'Consumer Complaints Handling and ADR' CAP 1286 (15 April 2015).

airlines in the UK have the option of joining a certified ADR entity[28] or the complaints are processed by PACT. For every complaint that PACT accepts, the airline is required to pay a £150 fee (which is higher than the fee that private ADR entities charge for processing a single complaint). In addition, PACT does not charge complainants, but certified ADR entities may be allowed to charge them with a nominal fee.[29] In fact, two out of the three approved ADR entities charge a fee that ranges from £25 to £10 per case. Another important difference between the PACT and certified ADR entities is that the decisions stemming from PACT are not binding on the airlines, while decisions issued by ADR entities need to be followed by the airlines. However, if airlines refuse to offer any type of redress to consumers and do not follow the recommendations issued by PACT, they may be subject to enforcement action by the CAA when there are indications of infringements on the sectorial law.

7.2.3 *The Risks of Competition and Forum Shopping*

A difficult question which policy makers have been grappling with is whether competition between ADR schemes can be a positive thing. The main argument in favour of competition is that it can lead to more competitive prices and innovation. Lower prices in ADR services could benefit traders, who at the end of the day foot the bill, and consumers, since traders' savings could trickle down as cost savings may be passed onto consumers through cheaper goods and services. Interestingly the ADR Directive encourages ADR entities to seek private forms of funding.[30] This is partly because private ADR schemes can increase the efficiency in the delivery of ADR services by being more flexible than public schemes. They also have economic motivations to be faster, offer their services at a lower cost and can operate more consistently in different jurisdictions.

By contrast, there are a number of important disadvantages since competition leads to forum shopping and can have an impact on the independence of ADR entities. On one hand, private ADR entities have a business model that requires them to charge clients while judging their business behaviour. On the other hand, businesses have an incentive to

[28] The CAA has so far certified CEDR and the Retail Ombudsman.
[29] Department for Transport – CAA, Changes to the CAA's Policy on Consumer Complaint Handling and ADR (3 March 2016).
[30] Recital 46.

choose ADR entities based on costs as well as to factor the likelihood of the ADR deciding in their favour. Accordingly, there is the inevitable risk of ADR entities trying to attract businesses (who after all are their clients) by being trader-friendly (and thus potentially biased), which in turn can affect the trust that consumers place on these ADR entities. The issue of quality as well as the need for critical mass has been raised by Hodges who noted that

> too much diversity in provision of advice and services (say between different court, small claims, arbitration or ombudsmen schemes) will not maximise consumer action nor maximise the ability to aggregate market data. There is also a risk that price competition between CDR providers would undermine quality, and hence public trust in the mechanism.[31]

Similarly, this risk has been noted by the Competition and Market Authority in the UK who observed that 'multiple schemes could lead to businesses basing their decision to join solely on costs and therefore leading to lower quality provision within [ADR] schemes as they compete for business'.[32] In fact, the experience in the financial sector in the UK shows how competition between ADR schemes is not beneficial and it is preferable to have a single certified ADR entity operating in a given sector.[33] As already noted in Chapter 4, this is why in some sectors (such as finance, legal services and energy in the UK) the solution found was to have a single ADR scheme that is publicly run or monitored and where traders' membership is compulsory. This is a good practice that should be extended to other sectors.

Furthermore, the availability of multiple ADR entities may limit user awareness,[34] and make ADR more difficult to monitor. Although the undesirable effect of competition might be restricted by ensuring proper monitoring by competent authorities and consumer advocates (or by using more creative measures, such as allowing consumers to select the ADR entity out of those certified), a much more effective system would

[31] Hodges, n. 5, p. 6.

[32] See Competition & Markets Authority, 'Alternative Dispute Resolution for Consumers, Response to the Consultation on Implementing the Alternative Dispute Resolution Directive and the Online Dispute Resolution Regulation' (3 June 2014) para. 22.

[33] For an analysis on the evolution of out-of-court redress in the financial services see A. Samuel, 'Consumer Financial Services in Britain: New Approaches to Dispute Resolution and Avoidance' (2002) 3(3) *Eur Bus Organ Law Rev* 649–694.

[34] S. Yuthayotin, *Access to Justice in Transnational B2C E-Commerce* (Springer, 2015) p. 255.

be to limit the number of certified ADR entities. Allowing for one (or a small number of ADR entities) per sector would ensure better public monitoring and allow for economies of scale.

Another important issue that needs to be examined are the circumstances under which ADR entities are allowed to refuse processing consumer complaints.[35] If traders can choose amongst different ADR entities, they may well prefer those that restrict the claims they accept. The next section examines these procedural restrictions since they determine the scope of ADR entities and thus the availability of redress to consumers.

7.3 Procedural Restrictions for Processing Consumer Complaints by Certified ADR Entities

This section examines from a normative and doctrinal approach the grounds contained in the ADR Directive upon which, according to the national law that implements it, a certified ADR entity may refuse to process a consumer complaint.[36] According to Article 5(4) of the ADR Directive, the refusal must be reasoned and communicated to the complainant within three weeks of receiving the complete complaint file. This legal provision states that national law may permit certified ADR entities to decline processing a complaint based on six procedural rules. It should be noted that these six grounds are exhaustive, so new grounds cannot be added. The only two possible exceptions are complaints outside the scope of the ADR entity and complaints that do not deal with the nature of the dispute but with the behaviour of the parties – for example, when they have settled the dispute, when parties have missed deadlines[37] or fabricated evidence or being abusive.[38] It is very important that national competent authorities monitor closely these procedural restrictions, otherwise, if these restrictions are too wide, they pose the risk of undermining consumer trust in the whole ADR system. The limitations of these six procedural grounds are discussed later in the chapter.

[35] Art. 5(4) ADR Directive.

[36] An early version of this section appeared in P. Cortés, 'The Impact of EU Law in the ADR Landscape in Italy, Spain and the UK: Time for Change or Missed Opportunity?' (2015) 16(2) *ERA Forum* 125–147.

[37] For instance, OS:C rules state that if a consumer does not reply to the ombudsman within 28 days, then the case will be automatically withdrawn.

[38] BIS, Guidance on Specific Points of Checklist for Attributes of ADR Entities (April 2014) pp. 2–3. Document on file with author.

7.3.1 *When the Consumer Has Not Attempted to Resolve the Complaint Directly with the Trader*

This is by far the most significant restriction. Its objective is to favour an early resolution of complaints. Yet, this can only occur if traders have provided consumers with the contact details of a person or department in charge for handling complaints. It would be important for online traders to offer distance means of communication, such as simple online forms that can be submitted through the traders' website or via email, and not to establish the fax as the only means of communication as a notorious Irish airline used to do. Telephone support should be accepted as a valid means of distance communications as long as the helpline does not charge more than the 'basic rate' for its use.[39]

Consumers should be allowed to go to the ADR entity in the event that the trader's internal complaints process is offered in a language that the consumer cannot understand, which as a minimum should be in the language of the consumer transaction that led to the complaint.

But most importantly, there must be a short deadline for the trader to acknowledge a complaint as well as to provide a reply to complaints. If a complaint is not acknowledged within a few days (e.g. one week), then consumers should be allowed to submit their complaint through the ADR entity. If a complaint is acknowledged, then traders will need more time to resolve it in-house, but traders should have incentives to resolve it quickly.

One of the largest ADR schemes in the UK, Ombudsman Service – Energy, reported that the main reason for accepting complaints against telecoms and energy suppliers was that businesses did not resolve a consumer complaint within the time frame of eight weeks – which seems to be the standard period used in most sectors.[40] According to a recent report, only a very small proportion of consumers (5 per cent) escalate their complaints to the ombudsman after receiving the so-called deadlock letter from energy suppliers, which states that their complaints could not be resolved in the eight-weeks time frame in favour of the consumer.[41] The report found that this was partly due to the lack of awareness and

[39] Art. 21 Directive 2011/83/EU. [40] OS:C annual report 2011/12, p. 12.

[41] The reasons for not complaining varied, but often weighed the lack of awareness about the ombudsman scheme and the perception that escalating the complaint will be additional hassle and more stress. GFK, Complaints to Ombudsman Services: Energy, Report for Ofgem Exploring Why Few Consumers Refer Their Complaint to Ombudsman Services: Energy (2013).

understanding of what is Ombudsman Service – Energy, and how to access it. A more worrying interpretation of this finding is that energy suppliers have an economic incentive to use up the eight weeks because they know that after this period the majority of complaints will not be pursued.

While some consumer sectors, such as pensions or even energy, may need time to resolve complaints due to their complexity, or because for instance they may require an onsite inspector to do a meter reading or run some tests, it is vital that traders have incentives to process complaints internally within a reasonable period of time. Swift resolution of complaints also benefits traders. Empirical research has demonstrated that consumer satisfaction will only be maintained when these deadlines are kept short, especially if complaints arise from e-commerce.[42] With the increase of technology communications, the eight-week period is too long, especially when consumer complaints are factual and relatively straightforward. It is therefore proposed that the competent authorities in charge of monitoring certified ADR entities should provide rules (or at least guidelines) on the time frame that businesses have to investigate complaints. For most cases one to four weeks should be sufficient – the most adequate time limit would depend on the average time that it takes for complaints to be resolved in-house in each sector.

7.3.2 Complaints That Are Frivolous or Vexatious

The ADR Directive distinguishes between frivolous and vexatious complaints. In general terms a frivolous complaint is considered one that is not adequately evidenced or justified, while a vexatious complaint is normally referred to as a meritless claim brought forward with the sole purpose of aggravating the respondent. This should be distinguished from complaints that fall outside the scope or when the complainant does not qualify (e.g. he may not be the account holder of the services he is complaining about). In fact, this filtering process can take a lot of resources, especially of ombudsman schemes, which normally have a

[42] A study on eBay found that the resolution of disputes between sellers and buyers increased their trade regardless of whether they win or lose their case, but as long as the dispute was resolved fast, within a matter of days. See C. Rule, 'Quantifying the Economic Benefits of Effective Redress: Large E-Commerce Data Sets and the Cost-Benefit Case for Investing in Dispute Resolution' 34 (2012) *Univ Ark Little Rock Law Rev* 767–777. See also the discussion in the next section.

front desk dedicated to this role as often only one in five or six contacts proceed to the formal complaint process.[43]

The rationale behind this ground of refusal is to restrict the misuse of ADR entities by complainants. But the ability to refuse complaints that are considered to be frivolous or vexatious is a discretionary power that can be easily abused if it is not properly monitored by the national competent authorities. A key issue would be to determine what can be considered a frivolous or vexatious complaint. It could be a complaint of very low value or one that on its face does not have any merit.

A way to discourage these types of claims may be to introduce a fee for complainants. Although court fees are used in court litigation partly to discourage these claims, ombudsman schemes have reported not to experience them often.[44] In some sectors, such as in aviation, businesses have expressed concerns that free access to redress would incentivize spurious or meritless complaints seeking to obtain financial compensation.[45] But, if fees were considered necessary for this purpose, they should be nominal and refundable upon complainants succeeding in their claims. Indeed, in the short experience in this sector in the UK it is showing that in most cases consumer complainants get some recognition of their claim and are consequently refunded their filing fee.[46]

7.3.3 Disputes That Have Been Considered by Another ADR Entity or by a Court

Consumer complaints may be rejected by another certified entity on the basis that such complaints have already been considered by another ADR entity or by a court. Similarly, according to English law a court can dismiss or dispose summarily a claim which has already been resolved by an ADR scheme.[47] An exception may be included when new evidence

[43] M. Doyle, V. Bondy and C. Hirst, 'The Use of Informal Resolution Approaches by Ombudsmen in the UK and Ireland: A Mapping Study' (October 2014). Available at www.ombudsresearch.org.uk.

[44] C. Hodges, n. 5, p. 3 and C. Hodges, N. Creutzfeldt and S. Macleod, 'Reforming the EU Consumer ADR Landscape: Implementation and Its Issues' Third Oxford Consumer Conference Report (30–31 October 2014) p. 2.

[45] Civil Aviation Authority, 'Consumer Complaints Handling and ADR' CAP 1286 (15 April 2015) para. 72.

[46] Westminster Business Forum Keynote Seminar: The Future of Consumer Law and ADR in the UK' (London, 14 September 2016) Conference Proceedings.

[47] *Binns* v. *Firstplus Financial Group LPC* [2013] EWHC 2436 (QB) 24 July 2013. In this case the English High Court struck out a claim for being unreasonable because the

appears. In these cases, the court or the same ADR entity should be able to reconsider a complaint.

When a claim is being considered by a court, litigants can request the court to stay proceedings so they can attempt to resolve a dispute via ADR. In this case the complaint is not being considered by the court at the same time, so in such an event this ground for refusal should not be applied.

Policy makers and competent authorities must take into account whether the previous ADR entity had the power to adjudicate the complaint or whether it only offered a consensual method of dispute resolution, especially so if parties have used a mediation service which was offered in-house by the trader. Actually, the certification of in-house mediators as ADR entities is not ideal, as these bodies are not entirely independent and cannot assure a final resolution of complaints, which could potentially undermine consumer trust in the redress process.

Lastly, it is necessary to consider the possibility of a consumer raising a complaint against the services provided by an ADR entity. In this situation it is first essential to ascertain whether the contractual relationship between the consumer and the ADR entity qualifies as a consumer contract. This is more likely to be the case if the consumer has had to pay to participate in the process. In any event, the second ADR could only reject a claim if it is based on the disagreement the consumer had with the outcome of the case, but not if it was based, for instance, on the poor customer services provided by the first ADR entity if for instance it took an unreasonable period of time to resolve the complaint.

7.3.4 *The Value of the Claim Falls Below or Above a Pre-Specified Monetary Threshold*

This restriction revolves around the need to balance consumer access to ADR while avoiding disproportionate costs. The majority of the Member States implemented this provision rather literally, allowing each ADR entity to decide whether to set caps; however such caps must be appropriate since the Directive states that a threshold cannot 'significantly impair the consumers' access to' ADR.[48]

claimant had already obtained a remedy under an ADR scheme. Furthermore, the claimant was not entitled to request the court for an award in his favour of legal costs for bringing the claim through ADR.

[48] Art. 5(5).

As noted earlier, a small minimum fee may help in stopping vexatious claims, but there must be proportionality in setting up these economic thresholds. The view taken by most competent authorities is that the fee should not be higher than that charged by the courts in small claims procedures, though a slightly higher fee may be allowed for claims of high value.

Economic limits must take into consideration the economic sector and the value of the average transactions. For example, Spain initially proposed a threshold of €30. Although this limit would be unreasonably high for low-value digital sales of music and games, it would not be for disputes related to car sales.

7.3.5 Complaints Submitted to the Trader More Than One Year Ago

ADR entities may be allowed to reject a complaint that was submitted to the trader over a year ago. Hence, the minimum time limit of one year does not start counting from the moment of the transaction, but from the moment when the consumer submitted the complaint to the trader. It could thus catch many disputes dealing with consumer guarantees, which under EU law sellers must guarantee the conformity of the goods with the contract for a period of two years after delivery.[49]

While a one-year time limit seems appropriate, this timeline should not run if the trader has not notified the consumer about the possibility of elevating the complaint to an ADR entity, particularly if the trader is under mandatory jurisdiction.[50] The stop to the prescription period should encourage traders to comply with their information obligations.

In any event, this ground of refusal, like the others aforementioned, is discretionary, so an ADR entity, especially a statutory one, could accept a complaint which arose more than a year ago. Indeed, some ADR entities, such as the Legal Ombudsman in England and Wales, state that in exceptional circumstances they may investigate complaints that arose over a year ago.

49 Arts. 3 and 5 of the Consumer Sales and Guarantee Directive 99/44/EC.

50 According to the Financial Conduct Authority, which determines the jurisdiction of FOS, only 5–10 per cent of claims are referred to FOS. There are some concerns that part of the low take-up may be due to financial firms not informing consumers about the scope of FOS. See Financial Conduct Authority, Consultation Paper, Improving Complaints Handling (December 2014) p. 13.

7.3.6 *Complaints That Would Seriously Impair the Effective Operation of the ADR Scheme*

The exclusion of complaints that may seriously impair the effective operation of the ADR entity could potentially be interpreted too widely. The UK government stated that 'it should be included only if the provision – and the basis on which a dispute could be rejected under it – are fully explained and the risk of it operating unfairly against consumers is mitigated'.[51] Furthermore, a very complex dispute may be excluded by the certified ADR entity if there are valid reasons to believe that the dispute should be better resolved by the courts.[52] This would be the case where the complaint raises an important point of law that would be better addressed in court, so subsequent cases could be resolved in the same fashion.

According to the Financial Conduct Authority in the UK, examples of this exception may include where there are multiple complainants to one complaint, so that appropriate consent is obtained before the investigation.[53]

Lastly, it must be remembered that the Directive requires ADR entities to publish in their websites annual activity reports. These reports must include information on the percentage of disputes that ADR schemes have refused to deal with based of each of the grounds discussed earlier.[54] This safeguard seeks to provide an extra layer of transparency, which no doubt will be monitored by users and competent authorities.

7.4 The Trader's Information Obligation

Chapter 4 observed that the stated aim of the ADR Directive is to stimulate trade by increasing consumer trust, especially in cross-border trader and digital transactions. For that reason it imposes information obligations on traders about ADR entities and the ODR platform. But if traders, especially online sellers, do not participate in any ADR process, the information obligation could run counter to the rationale of the new legislation, misleading consumers into believing that they might obtain redress where none is offered.

[51] Ibid., p. 33.

[52] Department for Business, Innovation & Skills (UK) Checklist of Requirements for Providers of Alternative Dispute Resolution Services Who Wish to Become Certified 'ADR Entities' for the Purposes of the ADR Directive (April 2014). Document on file with author.

[53] Financial Conduct Authority, n. 50, p. 31.

[54] Art. 7(2)(c).

The ADR Directive only requires Member States to ensure the availability of certified ADR entities and for traders to inform about them in their sectors, but it does not impose an obligation on traders to participate in ADR or ODR processes. As discussed in Chapter 4, the ADR Directive sets two types of information requirements. First, it requires only certain traders – those obliged by their national sectorial laws to be affiliated with an ADR entity and those which have voluntarily opted by contract to do so – to inform consumers on their websites and in their general terms and conditions of sale about their links to specific ADR entities.[55] The rationale behind this information obligation is to influence the consumer choice of trader, so it should be provided at an early stage of the dealings before entering into the contract in order to allow consumers to make informed transactional decisions.[56] Yet, this would only happen if consumers recognized this adherence, for instance, through the use of a trustmark.

The second information requirement, which is more important, applies to all traders, regardless of whether or not they belong to an ADR entity. It requires the trader to inform consumers about certified ADR entities operating in their sectors – the information obligation kicks in once the dispute has not been resolved in-house to the satisfaction of the consumer. In order words, what is mandatory for traders is to inform about ADR entities, not to participate in their processes. This approach often leads to compliant traders to inform about the availability of ADR while stating that they are not going to participate in these processes. Consequently, this information confuses consumers and deprives them from obtaining accessible ADR redress. Furthermore, it is difficult to monitor compliance as this is not published information, but rather it is ad hoc information which is required to be sent to individual consumers once the traders' in-house complaint system has finished and the consumers have not succeeded with their complaints.

Similarly, the ODR Regulation requires all online traders to inform consumers about the ODR Platform through the provision of a link in their websites.[57] This information requirement applies regardless of

[55] Art. 13(1) of the ADR Directive. In an effort to assist traders in reducing the legal costs in complying with the information requirements, the UK government is considering providing a template or a standard wording that traders could use. See Department for Business and Innovation Skills (BIS) Government Response to the Call for Evidence, EU Proposals on Alternative Dispute Resolution (May 2012) p. 21.

[56] CMA, n. 65, para. 34. See also Consumer Protection from Unfair Trading Regulations 2008.

[57] Art. 14(1) of the ODR Regulation.

whether the trader is committed or not to participate in any nationally approved ADR process. Since only a small proportion of these traders are legally required to participate in an ADR process, this requirement creates 'false expectations' for consumers, who remain unable to resolve their grievances online when traders refuse to cooperate. In addition, online traders (i.e. those engaging in e-commerce only) have the legal obligation to provide consumers with an email address where to address their complaints, which is often a different email address than that used to confirm the transaction. Hence, as noted in Chapter 4, the ODR platform should incorporate a database with the adhered traders email addresses, which should be supplied by the certified ADR entities. The national contact points and the ADR entities should gather this information.

Yet again, in most cases traders do not have a legal obligation to respond to consumer complaints – let alone to participate in a process offered by an ADR entity. In sum, a consumer complaint will not be processed by the ODR platform if one of the following occurs: first, the consumer was unable to obtain the trader's email address; second, the trader does not respond to the consumer complaint sent by the ODR platform; and third, the trader responds stating that it will not participate in a process offered by an ADR entity.[58] In other words, consumers will submit their complaint in the online *dispute resolution* platform, but they will not *resolve their disputes* if a trader refuses to engage in the redress process.

Furthermore, what is more worrisome is that if the trader opts for one of the three options above, then the complaint will not be processed further by the ODR platform, even when the trader has a legal or contractual obligation to participate in an ADR entity. That is, if the trader does not cooperate, then the ODR platform will not forward the dispute to an ADR entity, even when the latter had statutory jurisdictions to process the complaints. At this point, the only assistance that a consumer may get is from the contact point, which has the task to inform consumers about other means of redress when the dispute cannot be resolved through the ODR platform.[59] Therefore, one of the two advisors forming the ODR contact point for each Member State can inform consumers about the options to purse their claim either by a mandatory ADR scheme, if one exists, or, more likely, to use a domestic small claims procedure for a domestic process, or the European Small Claims

[58] Art. 9 ODR Regulation. [59] Art. 7(2)(a)(v) ODR Regulation.

Procedure for a cross-border matter. One can expect that the great majority of consumer complaints, which are of low value, will be dropped at that point.

The consequences of not complying with an information requirement are similar to those contained in other EU legislation, such as the e-Commerce Directive and the Consumer Rights Directive.[60] The breach of the obligation would thus be treated similarly to other breaches of the obligation to inform, allowing Member States to issue proportionate sanctions to ensure compliance.[61] In practice, regulators and enforcement bodies (e.g. Trading Standards in the UK) will inform traders about their breach and they will give them a few weeks to comply. If they refuse, then a court order can be sought – and if the court order is not complied with then there could be a fine, and even a jail sentence.[62] However, since in most sectors the information does not require the participation of traders in the ADR process, then they will simply notify (and confuse) consumers about the availability of ADR.

It is also worth considering the contractual standing of the parties in the event that the trader states that it is committed to participate in an ADR process, but refuses to do so when a consumer institutes the process. The consequences in such an event would vary depending on the type of ADR process. In arbitration, the existence of the contractual agreement gives power to the arbitrator to resolve the case, even when the trader does not recognize the competence of the arbitral tribunal.[63] A similar scenario would occur when a trader falls within the scope of an institutional ombudsman. With regards to mediation, normally only a

[60] Directive 2000/31/EC on Electronic Commerce and Directive 2011/83/EU on Consumer Rights. In the event that a trader adhered to an ADR scheme continuously refuses to participate it could be considered to be an unfair commercial practice under the Directive 2005/29/EC on Unfair Commercial Practices.

[61] E.g. in the UK the Enterprise Act 2002 confers enforcement powers to the Office of Fair Trading, the Local Authority Trading Standards Services and other enforcement bodies that have powers to consider complaints and seek court orders for compliance when there is a blatant breach of these information obligations.

[62] In the UK maximum penalty is an unlimited fine and two years' imprisonment. Ibid.

[63] For instance, under the Spanish Arbitration System, in cases where there exists a public offer of arbitration, the arbitral agreement will be valid once the consumer files the complaint and this is covered in the scope of application of the public offer. See Art. 24.2 Spanish Royal Decree 231/2008. Cf. E. Vilalta, 'ODR and E-Commerce' in M. Wahab, E. Katsh and D. Rainey, *Online Dispute Resolution: Theory and Practice* (Eleven International Publishing, 2012) p. 42.

court can enforce a contractual agreement to mediate.[64] However, it should be underscored that in most low-value claims consumers may not be able, or may not want, to pursue the claim through the courts.

Overall, it is expected that those traders that are legally required to participate in ADR processes by sectorial legislation, or by their industry or trade association, will inform consumers and participate in an ADR process; however, it is argued here that other traders need added incentives for agreeing to participate in (and often finance) ADR processes.

7.5 Incentives for Traders to Participate in Out-of-Court Processes

7.5.1 The Business Case for Customer Loyalty

The cost of redress, which in many jurisdictions is carried out mostly by traders, means that traders would only opt in voluntarily if they are confident that there is a good business case for outsourcing part of their complaint handling system.[65] The cost of participating in ADR is often shared with the cost of building an effective internal complaint system, which appears to be often undervalued and misunderstood by traders.[66] There are various studies that show that improving in-house redress schemes can in turn improve customer retention and acquisition, as well as providing efficiency improvements.[67] This is because complaint

[64] Art. 5(1) of the Mediation Directive empowers national courts to recommend the use of mediation (but not other ADR processes) when they consider appropriate to do so. Under English law this is possible according to *Cable and Wireless* [2002] 2 All ER (Comm) 1041. See generally Hopt and Steffek, *Mediation: Principles and Regulation in Comparative Perspective* (OUP, 2012).

[65] J. Hörnle, 'Encouraging Online Dispute Resolution in the EU and Beyond- Keeping Costs Low or Standards High?' Queen Mary School of Law Legal Studies Research Paper No. 122/2012, at section 7. See Competition & Markets Authority, 'Alternative Dispute Resolution for Consumers, Response to the Consultation on Implementing the Alternative Dispute Resolution Directive and the Online Dispute Resolution Regulation' (3 June 2014) p. 4. Consumer Council of Northern Ireland, 'Back to Business: Are Businesses Getting Consumers' Rights Wrong?' (December 2013) p. 18–19.

[66] Goodman observed that 'Every organisation's success depends on its keeping customers satisfied with goods and services that it offers, yet most executives tend to view the customer service function of their business as little more than a necessary nuisance.' J. Goodman, *Strategic Customer Service: Managing the Customer Experience to Increase Positive Word of Mouth, Build Loyalty, and Maximize Profits* (Amacon, 2009) p. 1.

[67] Economic Insight, 'The Business Case for Good Complaints Handling in Legal Services' Report for the Legal Ombudsman (November 2013). Available at www.legalombudsman.org.uk/downloads/documents/research/Business-Case-for-Good-

handling as well as ADR/ODR not only resolve individual complaints but, if properly designed, also generate information that can help to improve quality of service and avoid future disputes.[68]

An advantage of a well-designed dispute resolution scheme, especially one that is supported by adequate ODR technology, is that it can provide useful feedback to companies, helping them understand where customer relationship could be strengthened. This role is particularly common in ombudsman schemes, which often identify commonly encountered topics and provide information on how businesses should deal with them in their internal complaints mechanism and even improve business practices. This is also what is expected by consumers. Indeed, research has shown that the most cited reason why consumers bring a complaint, even before compensation, is that they want the business to change in how a service is provided.[69]

Although it may vary depending on the economic sector, there is existing research that shows that it is often cheaper to retain a customer than to attract a new one.[70] According to a study dissatisfied consumers are over three times more likely to talk about their negative experiences to other consumers than those who are satisfied.[71] Positive word of mouth can significantly reduce the cost of marketing since customers do the selling for themselves.[72] On the contrary, negative word of mouth can be very damaging to the reputation of a business. Over a quarter or dissatisfied consumers posted their grievance in at least one website. When disgruntled buyers vent their frustration in social and review networks, such as Yelp or TripAdvisor, the damage to the economic

Complaints-Handling-Final-for-publication-20-11-13.pdf. See also A. O. Hirschman, 'Exit, Voice, and Loyalty: Responses to Decline in Firms, Organizations, and States' (1970, Harvard University Press) and L. Goetzinger, J.K. Park and R. Widdows, 'E-Customers' Third Party Complaining and Complementing Behavior (2006) 17(2) *Int J Serv Ind Manag* 193–206.

68 Centre for Consumer and Essential Services, University of Leicester 'Complaint Handling by Airlines: Development of Best Practices' Research Report for the Civil Aviation Authority (July 2014) p. 11.

69 Consumer Focus and DJS Research, 'Dealing with Dissatisfaction: Complaint Handling in Energy, Water, Telecoms, Financial and Legal Services and Royal Mail' (2012). Available at www.consumerfutures.org.uk/wpfb-file/dealing-with-dissatisfaction-pdf.

70 T. Speer 'They Complain Because They Care' (1996) 18 *Am Demogr* 13 and L. Webb, 'Brainstorming Meets Online Dispute Resolution' (2004) 15 *Am Rev Int Arb* 337, 357–358.

71 See Consumer Care Alliance Study (2011) at www.customercarealliance.com/index.php. Study is in file with the author.

72 Goodman, n. 66, p. 4.

business could be significantly higher. These types of reviews can cause significant economic damage to businesses.[73] By contrast, appeased consumers are more loyal and more likely to recommend a business.[74] It took four years for eBay to note that providing ODR mechanisms would help to develop its business model.[75] Katsh and Rabinovich-Einy observed that:

> Over time, eBay and others learned something that Sharing Economy companies will also need to understand. This is that disputes can actually be beneficial to a company. There are several reasons for this. The most obvious one is that dispute resolution represents a promise to users that if something goes wrong, it will be fixed. It helps to build trust and reduce risk, thus influencing a user's willingness to try the system. In addition, and perhaps more importantly from the company's point of view, dispute resolution is important in identifying bad experiences.[76]

Empirical studies have shown that well-designed ODR platforms give parties a sense of justice and fairness in the marketplace, which, in turn, increases the loyalty and trust of those who benefit from the redress system.[77] eBay and PayPal have found that the users that encountered disputes and resolved them efficiently have subsequently increased their commercial activity through eBay more than those who have not encountered any disputes during the same period of time; this is because users' confidence in the fairness of the marketplace is enhanced.[78] Indeed, previous studies had also found that effective resolution of consumer complaints increases repurchase intentions more than if the consumer

[73] P. Blackwell, Satisfied Customers Tell Three Friends, Angry Customers Tell 3,000 (Tantor Media, 2008). It must be acknowledged that in the last few years review sites are cropping up and not all of them intend to offer an impartial review of businesses. For this reason it is important that there is greater transparency on how these sites are funded and whether they are set in the best interest of consumers.

[74] Rule, n. 42, p. 767. A. Schmitz, 'Introducing the "New Handshake" to Expand Remedies and Revive Responsibility in eCommerce' (2014) 26 *St. Thomas Law Rev* 522. GFK, Complaints to Ombudsman Services: Energy, Report for Ofgem Exploring Why Few Consumers Refer their Complaint to Ombudsman Services: Energy (2013).

[75] E. Katsh, J. Rifkin and A. Gaitenby, 'E-Commerce, E-Disputes, and E-Dispute Resolution: In the Shadow of "eBay Law"' 15 (2000) *Ohio St J Disp Resol* 705.

[76] E. Katsh and O. Rabinovich-Einy 'Dispute Resolution in the Sharing Economy' *Internet Monitor* 2014. Available at https://thenetmonitor.org/research/2014/.

[77] N. Rogers, R. Bordone, F. Sander and C. McEwen, *Designing Systems and Processes for Managing Disputes* (Kluwer, 2013) pp. 24 and 25.

[78] C. Rule, CEO at MODRIA (and former ODR Director for eBay and PayPal), Presentation on eBay ODR Experience at the 10th International ODR Forum, Chennai, India. 9 February 2011.

was satisfied and did not complain.[79] These startling findings prove that effective redress can successfully install confidence in trusted traders.

According to eBay, out of its 60 million disputes a year around 80 per cent are resolved through its ODR software without the intervention of a neutral third party.[80] This high amount of cases gives eBay a useful database upon which to find out their users' behaviour and reaction to disputes. Interestingly, empirical research done at eBay found out that these types of settlements increase parties' loyalty in the marketplace.[81] This finding was observed by Colin Rule, the former ODR director for eBay and PayPal, who carried out a quantitative study on the economic activity of eBay buyers during they three months after they have entered into a dispute and used eBay's ODR model. This group of buyers was contrasted with a sample of buyers who had not encountered a dispute during the previous month. The study showed that 'on average, users who reported a transaction problem and went through the online dispute resolution process increased their usage of the marketplace, regardless of outcome'.[82]

The increase was around 10 per cent but it varied depending on the procedure used and the time taken for resolving the dispute. Interestingly, this increase included not only the group of people who had succeeded in the dispute, but those who lost their cases also had greater activity in eBay than those who never filed a dispute, with the exception of the one group whose claims took over six weeks to be resolved.[83] This finding suggests that buyers prefer to lose a case quickly within a few days, than to win a case that takes weeks or months in being resolved. Another interesting finding was that the group most active in eBay (i.e. the group who spent the most amount of money) was the group of buyers who resolved their disputes with the sellers amicably, with only the assistance of eBay's ODR software – this group increased their purchasing activity during the following three months by 9 per cent more than those who had not filed a dispute. Rule observed that

> the explanation for this phenomenon is that trust in your fellow users to do the right thing in good faith is more powerful than the belief that a

[79] D. Halstead and T. Page, 'The Effects of Satisfaction and Complaining Behavior on Consumers Repurchase Behavior 5 (1992) *J Satisf Dissatisf Complaining Behav*, 1–11.

[80] US Department of Health and Human Services, 'Policy Issues Related to Patient Reported Data' (8 June 2012) p. 8, available at http://tinyurl.com/jsc42oz.

[81] Rule, n. 42, pp. 767–777. [82] Ibid., p. 772. [83] Ibid., p. 773.

> marketplace administrator will intervene and use their power to decide disputes between users who disagree.[84]

The study demonstrated empirically that trust is the keystone of increasing usage in online services. But trust is not gained when an online purchase goes well, as this is what is expected by the buyer, but at how the buyer is treated once a dispute arises. Rule argues that when a dispute arises it 'is when the marketplace is presented with an opportunity to step up, do the right thing, and make a lasting, positive impression on that customer'.[85]

It is debatable whether the effect of an expeditious ODR scheme in increasing trust in a marketplace such as eBay can be transferred to online traders. That is, Rule's findings suggest that offering buyers an effective redress scheme results in those buyers entering in a greater number of transactions on eBay – but not necessarily with the same sellers. This begs the question whether effective redress mechanisms would have the same effect when buyers deal directly from the seller's website. Only empirical research could answer that question, but it seems obvious that an expeditious, effective and independent redress scheme can only have a positive impact on buyers' perception of an online trader.

7.5.2 *The Launch of a Pan-European Trustmark*

A big global brand with a good customer service, like Apple, may not need an independent ODR system because it already has a good reputation and a very effective in-house customer care offering a sophisticated and user-friendly complaints handling system. Although some larger businesses see the value of trusting in an independent third party for dispute resolutions, the main target for ODR/ADR schemes are online businesses that potential customers may not trust. Consumers need reassurance from the businesses they buy from, and if they do not get this reassurance, then they go elsewhere.

A trustmark can assist consumers in recognizing reliable traders, and it can encourage the latter to join an independent redress scheme. A trustmark can be described as an electronic label displayed in the traders' website signifying that they pledge to comply with a code of

[84] Ibid., p. 776. [85] Ibid.

conduct and the relevant law, and that disputes will be addressed by an independent redress scheme.[86] Thus, the goal of a trustmark is to steer consumers' purchasing decisions towards traders with trustmarks.

A pan-European trustmark could operate as an online label for ADR entities, as well as being included in the traders' websites, linking traders to the ADR entity and the ODR platform. However the European Commission and the Council have been reluctant in sponsoring the creation of a pan-European trustmark due to, inter alia, the aversion of the Member States in being held liable for the performance of private ADR entities and traders. Although the European Economic Social Committee and the European Parliament recommended the creation of a trustmark for certified ADR entities that comply with the quality criteria set out in the ADR Directive, regrettably the final text did not include it.[87] Hörnle observed that:

> [The ODR Regulation] does impose an obligation on businesses to link to an ODR platform and once the consumer has a complaint to tell the consumer about any ODR options available. The idea here is to put pressure on businesses to use ODR, but arguable it would be better if businesses informed consumers at the outset of a transaction whether they agree to use ODR (through a logo - putting it in the terms & conditions is a waste of time, given that no-one reads them). In the long run consumers will be smart enough to look for this logo.[88]

It should be acknowledged that currently there is insufficient evidence to show how effective trustmarks are. In the field of dispute resolution trustmarks have been used for well over a decade, but there has been largely a lack of success.[89] This is partly due to the existing high number of trustmarks that confuse consumers, who in turn may not pay attention to them.[90] Accordingly, the key factor for the success of trustmarks is

[86] Cf. P. Balboni, *Trustmarks in E-Commerce* (CUP, 2009) 35–37.

[87] EESC, Alternative Dispute Resolution for Consumer Disputes, Rapporteur: Pegado Liz (CESE 803/2012 – INT/609) para. 3.3. European Parliament, Committee on the Internal Market and Consumer Protection, Draft Report of 18 April 2012, 2011/0373(COD) Rapporteur L. Grech, p. 65. It is unclear to this author the reason for deciding its exclusion, but a plausible motivation might be the interest of the Commission in making a general consumer trustmark.

[88] J. Hörnle, 'Dispute Resolution: Digital Alternative' *Law Gazette* (14 June 2014).

[89] J. Hörnle, *Cross-Border Internet Dispute Resolution* (Cambridge University Press, 2009), pp. 262–263.

[90] P. Cortés *Online Dispute Resolution for Consumers in the European Union* (Routledge, 2011), pp. 62–64.

awareness, which can only be achieved by reaching a critical mass and credibility. The ODR platform would be a suitable instrument to sponsor an effective trustmark that is jointly managed by the European Commission or a designated public institution, such as the ECC-Net, and the national competent authorities that certify ADR entities. The idea of a public trustmark is not new and it has already achieved some success at a national level.[91]

A trustmark should not be awarded to traders for the mere participation in consensual ADR processes, especially if they have a high rate of unresolved complaints. Traders should only be allowed to display a trustmark when they are linked to a redress scheme that operates in the language of the transaction where the trader displays the trustmark. In turn, as will be further discussed in the next chapter, compliance with final decisions could also contractually allow traders to require the removal of negative reviews posted by consumers, or at least to add a note in a review website stating that a complaint has been independently considered and subsequently resolved.

7.5.3 Feedback in Review Websites

Reviews have an increasing role in influencing consumers' decision on whether or not to buy goods or services from a business. The role of reviews can be much more influential than that of trustmarks, and for that reason it is important to examine whether reviews could do more than informing consumers about reliable traders, helping them to obtain redress. Reviews are becoming increasingly common in e-commerce, and it is especially popular in the hotel sector. These involve websites, often held by intermediaries, which record users' experience. Sometimes they operate through an opt-in system for traders (e.g. eBay or Booking.com); sometimes they allow consumers to leave reviews for any type of business (e.g. Yell, Trust Pilot and Review Centre),[92] while others relate to a specific sector (e.g. Trip Advisor for travel reviews). Also becoming increasingly common is the use of rate sites for services provided by

[91] For example, the Spanish government has created a trustmark (Confianza en Linea) that is controlled by the national consumer association and which provides assurance that its traders will participate in the institutional consumer arbitration scheme. See *Real Decreto* (Regulation) 292/2004 20 February 2004, which establishes a public trustmark for the services of the information society and the electronic commerce.

[92] See www.yell.com, www.trustpilot.com and www.reviewcentre.com.

different professionals, including lawyers.[93] The UK government noted the importance of reviews observing that:

> If used in advance of a purchase, feedback and review sites can help consumers to judge the trustworthiness of a trader and the likely quality of goods and services. Such sites are becoming increasingly popular with consumers: an [Office of Fair Trade] OFT survey (2009) found that 36 per cent consumers always used consumer reviews before making an online purchasing decision; 48 per cent sometimes used such reviews and just 16 per cent never used these reviews.[94]

Yet, for these reviews to be successful they must reflect the genuine opinions of consumers and ensure that appropriate safeguards are built into the review site in order to ensure the filtering of fraudulent content, which may include fake positive or negative reviews posted on behalf of the traders or competitors.[95] These fake reviews are becoming more common and they can be hard to detect,[96] but technology can help to weed them out. For instance, while TripAdvisor allows for the posting of reviews without any verification, it has invested heavily on technological tools that avoid fake reviews. It must be noted that these sites incorporate the aggregated number of reviews, so consumers should use their own judgement when pondering the value of these reviews, giving greater weight to those goods that have a higher number of reviews.

Negative feedback can be very damaging – in fact, the effect of negative feedback is much greater than that of positive feedback.[97] Remarkably, feedback within eBay has become a very useful mechanism for incentivizing parties to participate in the dispute resolution process. If eBay sellers would like to request the removal of negative comments, which will affect their competitive position in the online market, they will have to either reach a settlement or agree to have them adjudicated by a neutral third party.

Similar incentives could in time be incorporated in ODR platforms and consumer review sites, so that when settlements are reached, traders

[93] E.g. http://vouchedfor.co.uk started initially as a rating site for financial advisers and in 2014 expanded to include the rate solicitors who opted into the system. See J. Hyde, 'Ratings Website Moves into Law' *Law Society Gazette* (4 August 2014).

[94] Department for Business Innovation and Skills, n. 4, para. 3.26.

[95] 'Amazon to Sue Over 1,000 Fake Reviews' *Digital J* 18 October 2015 and 'Buyers Beware as Fake Online Review Business Booms' *The Irish Times* (25 June 2015).

[96] J. Malbon, 'Taking Fake Online Consumer Reviews Seriously' (2013) 35 *J Consum Policy* 4.

[97] D. Lucking-Reiley, D. Bryan, Naghi Prasad and D. Reeves, 'Pennies from eBay: The Determinants of Price in Online Auctions' (2007) *J Ind Econ* 224, 229.

can request their incorporation in the review sites. This notification could automatically remove the negative post, or be included as a note to the consumer's review stating that the complaint was considered by an independent body, and when applicable, scrutinized by a neutral third party. If the participation in the redress process is voluntary, then the removal of the post should be done when a settlement or a decision is reached (regardless of whether it is or not in favour of the consumer). In order to avoid the consumer blackmailing traders, it will be necessary to include some tools, such as cease-and-desist letters, to ensure the filtering of vexatious reviews.[98] Moreover, a trader should be able to invite the consumer to initiate a claim in an ODR platform. If the consumer refuses to do so within an adequate period of time, then the negative posting should be automatically deleted or followed by a post that records the consumer's refusal to participate in the dispute resolution process.

The Internet opens up new possibilities to use technology as leverage both to reward good traders and to penalize those who dismiss consumer complaints. Currently, when Google Shopping displays online sellers in its browser it includes third-party reviews.[99] Google's algorithms aggregate the reviews (as well as extracts from such reviews) found from a search of the sellers' domain name. Similarly, the EU ODR platform and review sites could cooperate with the search engines to rank down traders who have a high number of unresolved complaints or that have not complied with final outcomes. Although search engines are committed to neutrality, and so they would be reluctant to change their own settings, search engines could incorporate filters with this option, allowing users to decide whether to refine their browsers. Indeed, European regulations could require them to do so.

7.5.4 Other Economic Incentives

There are other incentives that may be taken into account by traders when deciding whether they participate in an independent redress scheme. An important incentive for traders is the fact that their

[98] It should be noted that Art. 14 of the E-Commerce Directive 2000/31/EC establishes a safe haven regime for hosting providers as long as they are not informed of its illegal character, and that they act promptly when informed of it. By contrast in the USA, s. 230 of the Communications Decency Act 1996 provides greater protection for website publishers. See *Zeran* v. *AOL*, 129 F.3d 327 (4th Cir. 1997).

[99] See www.google.com/ads/shopping/ and www.google.com/wallet/.

participation will limit their exposure to chargebacks. When a consumer initiates a chargeback process, the trader is required to pay a fee.[100] In addition, the credit score of that trader is affected; hence, the number of chargebacks issued affects the interest rates that the trader pays per transaction.

Courts could also play a role in providing economic incentives for participating in a more cost-efficient dispute resolution process. For example, they could employ cost sanctions[101] when one party has unreasonably refused to participate in an out-of-court process. Although national courts are not currently adequate avenues for resolving low-value e-commerce disputes, as previously mentioned, small claims courts may become over time more accessible with the launch of online courts and tribunals and recourse to collective redress.[102] It has been pointed out that the Netherlands is considering increasing the court fees of traders who have lost a claim and are not members of an ADR process.[103] However, it must be noted that while these systems provide traders with incentives to participate in ADR as a more cost-effective redress option, they do not necessarily ensure that ADR is available to consumers.

Outside the UK and the EU there are examples of ADR and ODR bodies which penalize traders who do not participate in their processes. For instance, PROFECO in Mexico requires traders to participate in the public conciliation scheme when consumers submit their complaints, and fines are imposed on traders who refuse to participate in the process without a justification.[104] Similarly, in Argentina there is a free-of-cost conciliation service which is mandatory for traders to participate in, and if they do not appear at the conciliation session, then a fine is levied

[100] D. E. Sorkin, 'Payment Methods for Consumer-to-Consumer Online Transactions' (2001) 35(1) *Akron Law Rev* 9–10.

[101] This incentive would go hand in hand with the Art. 5.1 of the Mediation Directive, which allows national courts to recommend the use of mediation. Established case law in the UK states that cost penalties for unreasonably refusing to participate in ADR comply with Art. 6 ECHR and Art. 47 of the CFREU. See *Halsey* v. *Milton* EWCA Civ 576 (2005), and Pt. 36 of the Civil Procedure Rules 1998 (England and Wales).

[102] See European Parliament Resolution of 2 February 2012, 'Towards a Coherent European Approach to Collective Redress' (2011/2089(INI)).

[103] Hodges et al., n. 44, p. 163.

[104] In Mexico a trader can be fined between 15USD and 1,500USD, depending on the value of the complaint, and a new session is scheduled. If the trader misses the second hearing, then a new fine will be issued and the consumer complaint will be considered proven. See Arts. 112 and 123 Federal Consumer Act 2004. See also A. Arley, 'ODR on Consumer Protection in Mexico: Cultural, Legal and Political perspective' (on file with author) forthcoming.

against them. Interestingly, under Argentinian law, one-third of the fine is allocated to compensate the consumer claimant.[105]

Positive economic incentives can be used to increase traders' participation in out-of-court processes. Government procurement contracts should only be offered to businesses that participate in ADR. Lastly, fiscal incentives can also provide an effective economic incentive, and could encourage traders to expand their commitment to independent redress schemes.

7.6 The Need for New Default Redress Options

In some sectors it will be more difficult to convince traders to opt into an ADR entity, especially in sectors where competition amongst traders is not high; as BEUC observed 'the lack of competition may remove the incentives for high standards of commercial relationships, including participation in ADR'.[106] This has led a number of Member States, such as the UK or Germany, to pass sectorial legislation making it compulsory for traders join an ADR scheme in areas where there is a high number of consumer disputes. Other jurisdictions, notably Scandinavian countries, rely on complaint boards that do not require the traders' express agreement to participate in the process.

This section argues that the most effective incentive to ensure traders' participation in ADR/ODR would be to provide consumers with an effective residual redress forum.[107] Such a default redress option could take the shape of either a tribunal or court as is currently being designed for England and Wales, or a residual ADR/ODR entity with mandatory jurisdiction.

7.6.1 The Online Court for England and Wales

The option of an online tribunal or court, as noted in Chapter 2, is not a completely novel idea and it is one that is gaining traction in a number of

[105] See Servicio de Conciliación Previa en las Relaciones de Consumo in Act 2014 (S.I. 26993).

[106] The European Consumer Organisation (BEUC), 'Alternative Dispute Resolution (ADR) & Online Dispute Resolution (ODR) of Consumer Disputes', BEUC Position Paper X/2012/010 (14 February 2012) p. 7.

[107] An earlier version of this section appeared in P. Cortés, 'Conclusion' in P. Cortés (ed.), *The New Regulatory Framework for Consumer Alternative Dispute Resolution* (OUP, 2016).

jurisdictions, including the Civil Resolution Tribunal in Canada and the (very similar) proposal to establish an Online Court in England and Wales.[108] These initiatives follow the idea of the multi-door courthouse, which was first posed by Professor Sander in the 1970s at the Pound Conference in the USA.[109] The rationale behind the multi-door system is to assist litigants to find the most appropriate dispute resolution method for their disputes. Interestingly, these updated initiatives to the multi-door courthouse are based on lessons and techniques from modern ODR and ADR which are resolving 'huge numbers of relatively low value or low stakes cases . . . simply, quickly and cheaply by avoiding hearings all together'.[110]

As already noted in Chapter 2, an Online Court for self-represented litigants is being implemented in England and Wales following two landmark reports on the Civil Courts Structure Review by Lord Justice Briggs, whose main recommendation was the introduction of Online Courts.[111] The Online Court will depart from the traditional adversarial process, operating instead an online tiered procedure following rules designed for litigants in person (i.e. those without legal representation). The procedure will have three main stages: (i) it will consist of a fully automated triage process, where parties fill in the claim and are offered simple commoditized online advice; (ii) the unresolved claims will pass to a case officer who will offer a mix of ADR/ODR techniques and case management – this stage hopes to settle the majority of claims; (iii) the remaining of the claims will be sent to a judge for final determination on the documents (and when necessary via telephone,

[108] An earlier version of this section appeared in P. Cortés, 'The Digitalisation of the Judicial System: Online Tribunals and Courts' (2016) 22(6) *Comput Telecommun L Rev* 141–143 and 'The Online Court: Filling the Gaps of the Civil Justice System?' (2017) 36(1) *Civil Justice Q* 54–71. See also the e-Courts initiative in China at China.org.cn 'E-courts promise online justice for Chinese shoppers' (11 December 2015). Available at http://tinyurl.com/j9yxwkz.

[109] F. Sander, 'Varieties of Dispute Resolution' National Conference on the Causes of Popular Dissatisfaction with the Administration of Justice 7–9 April 1976 Pound Conference (1976) 79 FRD 111.

[110] N. Ceeney, 'Modernising Courts and Tribunals' HM Courts and Tribunals Service (23 September 2015). Available at www.gov.uk/government/speeches/modernising-the-courts-and-tribunals.

[111] Lord Justice Briggs, *Civil Courts Structure Review* Interim Report (December 2015) and Final Report (July 2016). Hereinafter, Briggs Interim Report and Final Report respectively.

video or face to face hearings). A final fourth stage might be incorporated in time to streamline the enforcement of judgments.

The procedure will use its own rules and rely on standard forms and written procedures for monetary claims. Thus the European Small Claims Procedure (the financial limit of which has recently been increased to €5,000) discussed in Chapter 3 would also be a good fit for the Online Court, especially when there are no language barriers. It will however exclude cases that are complex or follow a separate procedure, or even those that use a digital platform such as that for repossession cases and personal injury matters. The Online Court will be able to transfer cases to the county court, which although will digitalize in the next few years all the documents, will continue using the procedure following the Civil Procedure Rules and will maintain face-to-face hearings.

There are a number of design options that need to be taken into account. First, it will be necessary to provide adequate tools for court users without IT skills. The online portal for the Online Court should provide links to supporting networks, such as Citizens Advice centres. These centres will need additional resources to train their staff and provide clinics where one-to-one support can be obtained in order to avoid the exclusion of these citizens from the Online Court.[112]

Another important design element will be to incentivize settlements, both pre-action and during the court process. However, as currently envisaged, the pre-action stage may lose relevance. Briggs argues that pre-action protocols[113] are not suitable for litigants in person, who for most parties should be required to exchange written correspondence in advance of lodging a claim in court. Instead the pre-action protocols are expected to be replaced by stage one of the procedure.

English courts normally rely on costs-shifting rules to encourage settlements. Accordingly, there should be cost consequences when a judge considers that one litigant has behaved unreasonably in refusing to participate in settlement discussions or in accepting a reasonable offer

112 JUSTICE, 'What Is a Court' (May 2016). Available at https://2bquk8cdew6192tsu41lay8t-wpengine.netdna-ssl.com/wp-content/uploads/2016/05/JUSTICE-What-is-a-Court-Report-2016.pdf.

113 Pre-action protocols are the steps that parties are expected to take before lodging a civil claim in court. These steps are annexed to the procedural rules and include notifying in writing the other party and considering the use of ADR.

to settle.[114] Cost consequences and cost sanctions should, however, be proportionate, affecting mostly the shifting court fees, and imposed only in exceptional cases on consumers acting as litigants in person when facing businesses with legal representation. Conversely, economic sanctions may be justified when a party has been unreasonable in refusing to participate in ADR (especially when provided for free or at a low cost by certified ADR entities) and when a party has an unreasonable behaviour during stages one and two of the Online Court. In order to encourage early settlements the fee structure should be a 'pay-as-you-go' system, subject to court fees for each of the court stages.

Overall, the cost regime is expected to follow the small claims track system, which restricts the recoverability to court fees and a very small amount for legal representation.[115] In addition it may allow parties to recover the cost of pre-action legal advice on the merits of the claim.[116] This is expected to encourage the unbundling of the package of legal services and sharing this between the consumers and the lawyers. Although the unbundling will bring greater proportionality to the cost of litigation, parties will inevitably incur higher costs than when using ADR.

The Online Court should draw lessons from ADR/ODR bodies, such as successful ombudsman schemes like the Financial Ombudsman Service and the eBay Resolution Centre as well as the Small Claims Mediation.[117] Nonetheless, it must be noted that the incentives in the dispute system design of these systems is very important for its success and may not be easily replicated. For instance, as already noted, the strength of Financial Ombudsman Service is that it is staffed by well-trained case handlers that provide advice to the parties and push towards and are backed up by an authoritative ombudsman that can impose a decision. At this point it is unclear how much advice, if any, a legal or case officer may be able to provide the parties with. In the case of eBay, as discussed before, which famously claims to resolve around 60 million disputes a year, most of which without the intervention of humans – this is possible because all disputes in eBay (and in other marketplaces such as

[114] Part 36 Civil Procedure Rules 1998. See P. Cortés, 'A Comparative Review of Offers to Settle – Would an Emerging Settlement Culture Pave the Way for their Adoption in Continental Europe?' (2013) 32(1) *Civil Justice Q* 42–67.

[115] Rule 27.14 Civil Procedure Rules. [116] Final Report, 111, para. 6.74.

[117] These websites are available at www.financial-ombudsman.org.uk and http://resolutioncentre.ebay.co.uk.

Amazon) can be categorized into a few groups (i.e. non-delivery, delays, non-payment or goods not matching description), so the solutions are also limited (refund, partial refund, return of goods, etc.), and, importantly, parties have strong incentives to settle because the buyer wants compensation and the seller needs positive feedback to keep selling goods in the competitive market. Similarly, the Small Claims Mediation scheme in England incorporates incentives that may not be easily replicated in the Online Court. When parties opt into the telephone mediation, they know that if they do not settle over the telephone they will have to attend an oral hearing (and take time off work to do so).

As currently envisaged, the Online Court does not incorporate the existing out-of-court ODR/ADR infrastructure, bar the possibility of a case officer recommending parties to attempt ADR/ODR. This is partly because the Online Court and ADR are emerging in an organic way from different governmental departments to meet specific sectorial needs. For instance, while the Financial Ombudsman was created to address lack of redress in the UK banking system, the rationale behind the launch of the Online Court is inter alia to tackle the collapse of legal aid and an expensive court system. Thus, there is an urgent need to build pathways that align these schemes that often operate in parallel. Accordingly, the Online Court should have pathways to lead users to the most appropriate redress option. The goal should be to avoid duplication and to encourage consumers and traders to use pre-action ADR entities and to consider reasonable offers to settle through cost incentives.[118]

7.6.2 Residual ADR Entity

In most countries judicial processes are too formal, slow, inefficient and nearly always offline. Thus, if there is not a truly accessible court (or tribunal, like the Canadian Civil Resolution Tribunal), then consumers will not have a redress avenue for their complaints. One option of course is to follow the English example and develop an online court that has ADR techniques built into the process. However, another less cumbersome option, and one that would work better for low-value consumer matters, would be to set up a residual ADR/ODR body with mandatory jurisdiction for those consumer complaints that cannot be processed by any other certified ADR entity. A truly accessible residual ADR entity will

[118] Cortés, n. 108, p. 71.

be an incentive for traders to opt into a specialized certified ADR entity, and it will guarantee that consumers will have an accessible redress option while reducing confusion and enhancing trust in the national ADR infrastructure. The residual ADR scheme could follow the complaint boards' model, which is popular in Scandinavian countries, whereby an independent entity would examine the complaint and issue a recommendation or resolution. These processes do not require the traders' agreement to participate and recommendations are often followed, especially when traders have incentives to comply.[119]

Mandatory adherence to ADR is already occurring in an incremental and piecemeal manner in regulated sectors. For instance, as noted in Chapter 5, in the UK traders' participation in ADR is already mandatory in many regulated sectors, including finance, insurance, gas, electricity, telecoms, gambling, legal services, public higher education and estate agents. Depending on the political appetite, this list may expand in other jurisdictions and into other regulated sectors, such as public transport and then move to other sectors where there is a high demand for ADR, such as second-hand car sales and accommodation. Also, trade associations and regulators could require businesses' adherence to ADR schemes. As already happens in jurisdictions such as the Netherlands, membership of a trade association can require the traders to participate in an ADR entity with sectorial expertise. Furthermore, regulators can require adherence to an ADR scheme (normally a statutory body) as a prerequisite to obtaining a license. Yet, sectorial adherence is insufficient and confuses consumers. Therefore, a residual body, especially one that it is known to the consumer, would help to bridge these huge gaps in consumer redress.

It has already been noted that all traders regardless of whether they are part of an ADR entity (which in most Member States are the minority) have the legal obligation to inform consumers about certified ADR entities and about the EU ODR platform. However most traders are not required to participate in their processes, which as a result confuses consumers, and because of the nonsensical nature of the requirement (i.e. informing about a redress option that is not available to the consumer) they rarely inform about it. Thus, it is submitted that the information obligation should be amended in order to require traders to inform

[119] For instance the Swedish ADR scheme publishes blacklists in a consumer magazine with the names of those traders that did not comply with their recommendations. See ARN National Board for Consumer Disputes. Available at www.arn.se.

consumers about the ADR entity operating in their sector if they have opted into their process, or, if they are not adhered, then the obligation should be to inform about the residual ADR entity.

This residual ADR entity should have discretion to consider whether to accept consumer complaints that have not been settled by mediation or other consensual ADR processes, especially one that is run by the trader like an in-house mediator. But, it should not accept claims when an ombudsman process (or other processes such as early neutral evaluation) was used by consumers and which ended with recommendations that become binding upon their acceptance. In addition, pursuant to Article 5(4) of the ADR Directive, the residual ADR entity should be allowed to reject consumer complaints that have not previously been through the trader's internal complaint handling system –the trader should resolve complaints internally in less than four weeks, unless there is a justifiable reason to grant an extension.

While decisions from any ADR entity should be subject to court review when procedures were not followed, these appeals should be discouraged when one party wants to challenge the interpretation of the facts, especially when cases are of low value and they do not have public relevance.

7.6.3 *The Right to Access to Justice*

There is mostly an academic debate on whether out-of-court redress can offer greater access to justice or whether it is simply a mechanism to resolve disputes, without necessarily giving parties their legal entitlements, which, some argue, can only be offered by the courts.[120] By contrast, as it has been argued throughout this book, ADR/ODR can offer consumers better redress than the courts, which in turn helps them

[120] O. Fiss, 'Against Settlement' 93 (1984) *Yale Law Review* 1073 and R. Abel 'The Contradictions of Informal Justice' in R. Abel (ed.), *The Politics of Informal Justice*, vol. 1 (Academic Press, 1982) p. 287, making a radical attack on ADR methods and referring to these as 'poor justice to the poor'. See also H. Genn, *The Hamlyn Lectures 2008: Judging Civil Justice* (Cambridge University Press, 2010) p. 117 and H. Genn 'What Is Civil Justice for? Reform, ADR, and Access to Justice' (2012) 24(1) *Yale J L Humanit* 397–417, 411. Cf. C. Irvine, 'Mind the Gap: Mediation and Justice' Kluwer Mediation Blog (12 May 2014) distinguishing between substantive justice enforced by the courts and procedural justice that allows parties to craft their own just outcome. Available at http://kluwermediationblog.com/2014/05/12/mind-the-gap-mediation-and-justice/.

to obtain a better compliance with their legal entitlements. Consumer ADR increases access to justice especially when there are assurances that the mandatory law is respected.[121] Cappelletti's view of ADR processes can be extended to today's digital economy and the need for online access to these processes:

> We have to be aware of our responsibility; our duty is to contribute to making law and legal remedies reflect the actual needs, problems and aspirations of civil society. Among these needs are surely those of developing alternatives to the traditional processes and remedies any time such remedies are too expensive, slow and inaccessible to the people; hence, the duty to find alternatives capable of better accommodating the urgent demands of a time of societal transformations at an unprecedently accelerated pace.[122]

Furthermore, the Mediation Directive sees ADR as a route to increase access to justice stating that '[t]he objective of securing better access to justice ... should encompass access to judicial as well as extrajudicial dispute resolution methods'.[123] Accordingly, it is not surprising that increasingly courts processes in many jurisdictions require that parties with civil disputes first consider or attempt to resolve their disputes privately. It is therefore pertinent to empower consumers to resolve disputes extrajudicially, and to provide a wider concept of access to justice than that restricted to the courts.[124]

Yet, when an out-of-court body provides a decision that is final and binding for one or both parties, such process must comply with the right of fair trial, which in Europe is contained within Article 6 of the European Convention of Human Rights (ECHR) and Article 47 of the Fundamental Charter of Fundamental Rights (ECFR). The right to a fair trial must be considered in conjunction to the right to an effective remedy (Art. 13 ECHR). Such a process, whether an arbitration

121 F. Martín Díz, 'Mediacion en Derecho Privado: Nuevas Perspectivas Prácticas' 33 (2014) *Revista General de Derecho Procesal* 1–38, 4.

122 M. Cappelletti, 'Alternative Dispute Resolution Processes within the Framework of World-Wide Access-to-Justice Movement' 56 (1993) *Mod Law Rev* 282–296, 296.

123 Recital 5.

124 This view is shared by the Council of Europe. See Council of Europe Committee on Equality and Non-Discrimination 'Equality and Non-Discrimination in the Access to Justice' Report Doc 13740, Rapporteur: V. Riceard Badea (31 March 2015) para. 10 and Council of Europe Committee on Legal Affairs and Human Rights 'Access to Justice through Online Instruments' Draft Report, Rapporteur: J. Xucla, (2 November 2015) para. 13.

procedure or an ombudsman system, must, inter alia, offer the parties a public hearing (saved to justifiable exceptions). Unsurprisingly, in the consumer sector parties do not normally want to exercise the right to a public hearing, especially if this is conducted face to face because this is costly, inconvenient and time consuming.[125] Moreover, technology enables greater transparency and open justice than the face-to-face process counterpart.[126]

In arbitration, awards can only be reviewed under a very limited number of grounds related to a gross disregard of procedural rights or the validity of consent in agreeing to go to arbitration. As already discussed in this book, in most cases in the EU, a consumer must agree to go to arbitration once the dispute arises, and this is always the case when the arbitration is provided by a certified ADR entity. But once an award is issued, then it can only be reviewed by a court under very exceptional circumstances when there has been a serious procedural breach. In some jurisdictions, parties can very exceptionally also appeal an award if there is a novel point of law, especially when a dispute brings issues of wider importance than to only the parties.[127] This is because consumer law is based on general principles rather than on detailed provisions, which if there were no restrictions, could easily lead to abundant litigation on points of law, creating high costs for business, which would then raise prices for consumers.

Article 6 ECHR therefore allows for restrictions in court access if these restrictions are considered to be legitimate and proportionate as was found in favour of decisions made by administrative authorities.[128] Its only requirement is the subsequent control by a judicial body.[129] The judicial review should cover the facts, the substantive law and the

[125] A. Samuel, 'Consumer Financial Services in Britain: New Approaches to Dispute Resolution and Avoidance' (2002) 3(3) *Eur Bus Organ Law Rev* 649–694, 670.

[126] Briggs Final Report, n. 111, para. 6.85.

[127] See, for example, s. 69 UK Arbitration Act 1996. See also Sir Brian Leveson, 'Security and Justice' 13th Annual Isaiah Berlin Lecture (12 November 2015) para. 40. Available at www.judiciary.gov.uk/wp-content/uploads/2015/11/berlin-lecture-nov-2015.pdf.

[128] ECtHR, *Le Compte, Van Leuven and De Meyere* v. *Belgium* Appl. no. 6878/75 and 7238/75, Judgment of 23 June 1981, para. 51. See also the view of the Court of Justice of the EU in the joined Cases C-317/08 to C-320/08, *Rosalba Alassini and Others* v. *Telecom Italia SpA and Others* (18 March 2010).

[129] ECtHR, *Zumtobel* v. *Austria*, Appl. no. 12235/86, Judgment of 21 September 1993, paras. 29–32.

minimum standards of due process employed in reaching the decision.[130] Moreover, the rights to access to court under Article 6 can be waived by the parties, provided that the waiver is unequivocal, there is no constraint, and it is 'attended by minimum safeguards commensurate to its importance', including impartiality of the neutral third party.[131]

Mandatory ADR processes established by statute are typically subject to judicial review. For instance, decisions from UK Financial Ombudsman cannot be appealed in court, but they can be reviewed. In the review process courts examine whether due process was followed and whether the decision was reasoned, rational, legal and based on valid evidence. For instance, the European Court of Human Rights found that the UK Financial Ombudsman offered a fair procedure that complied with Article 6 of the ECHR and Article 47 ECFR, even though they can decide cases on equitable principles (i.e. considering what is fair and reasonable taking into account the law, but not necessarily following it strictly).[132] Courts can play a role in ensuring that ADR apply the consumer law correctly and maintain adequate procedural standards. However, as the experience of the Irish Financial Ombudsman demonstrates, an easy appeal process can take a significant part of the budget of the ADR body.[133] Interestingly, in order to avoid the high number of appeals in Ireland, the ombudsman has recently decided to employ more mediation techniques in its dispute resolution process.

While making it too easy to appeal decisions in court may not be in the best interest of consumers, it would be desirable that mandatory ADR systems allow for the referral of the interpretation of the most important legal issues to regulators and the courts, as a ruling on the statutory interpretation would provide legal certainty. An interesting model is that used by the UK Pensions Ombudsman, which can refer legal questions to

[130] L. McGregor, 'Alternative Dispute Resolution and Human Rights: Developing a Rights-Based Approach through the ECHR' (2015) 26(3) *Eur J Int Law* 607–634.

[131] Ibid., pp. 617–618. ECtHR, *Osmo Suovaniemi and others* v. *Finland*, Appl. no. 31737/96, Judgment of 23 February 1999 and ECtHR, *Pfeifer and Plankl* v. *Autria*, Appl. no. 10802/84, Judgment of 25 February 1992.

[132] *Heather Moor & Edgecomb Ltd* v. *the United Kingdom* 1550/09 [2011] ECHR 1019.

[133] The Irish Financial Ombudsman allows for any party to appeal a decision in the High Court. Defending the appeals have reportedly cost the ombudsman one-fifth of its annual budget. See J. Williams and C. Gill, 'A Dispute System Design Perspective on the Future Development of Consumer Dispute Resolution' in P. Cortés, *The European Framework for Consumer Dispute Resolution* (OUP, 2016).

the High Court.[134] Regulators could also escalate the query on statutory interpretation to a national court. The aim of the referral is not to change the outcome of a specific case, but to provide guidelines and greater certainty for future cases.

7.7 Conclusion

A key function of our legal system is to provide adequate mechanisms to ensure compliance with the rule of law. This function does not necessarily mean that every justiciable dispute, no matter how small, should be resolved in a court of law. For example, it is nonsensical that low-value and cross-border disputes, particularly those arising online, should be resolved in the courts. Indeed, this field is an example where ensuring the provision of extrajudicial processes should be mainstream. That is why, as discussed in the previous chapter, UNCITRAL promoted ODR for these categories of cases.

This chapter has noted that an effective consumer redress system that meets the policy aims of the European legislation (i.e. improving competition and invigorating the Internal Market) as well as UNCITRAL's goals (i.e. stimulating cross-border e-commerce) will only be met if traders participate in ADR/ODR processes. In reality, the participation of traders is often determined by a legal obligation, a requirement imposed by their trade association or as a voluntary choice based on their expectation to obtain a competitive advantage. This chapter argued that when traders can choose and pay amongst different ADR providers, this situation promotes forum shopping, benefiting those entities that are cheaper and decide more often in favour of the trader. In order to avoid this undesirable effect, competent authorities should only allow one (or a small number) of ADR entities per sector. This market restriction would facilitate better public monitoring by enforcement authorities, and it would provide economies of scale to benefit certified ADR entities. Conversely, if open competition amongst ADR entities is promoted, then competent authorities must be particularly watchful inter alia on how ADR entities restrict the number of consumer complaints. Accordingly, this chapter has examined critically how these procedural restrictions should be adopted by certified ADR entities.

[134] Pension Schemes Act 1993, s. 150(7).

The ADR Directive only assures the availability of ADR entities, but it does not ensure that traders participate in these processes. Voluntary adherence only occurs when traders see a business case to join in or when incentives are incorporated into the system. As a result, currently in most countries there is only a sectorial coverage, mostly in regulated sectors, which often confuses consumers and undermines their trust in the ADR system. This chapter has observed that the information requirement per se is insufficient to encourage traders to opt into ADR, so it submitted that it will be necessary to couple it with additional incentives, such as an institutional pan-European trustmark, evidence on the market impact of ADR and other economic incentives such as cost sanctions. Furthermore, this chapter has argued that the most successful incentive would be to have an effective redress forum, which may either be an online court that incorporates ADR techniques, or a national ADR entity with residual jurisdiction which issues recommendations coupled with incentives that ensure their compliance. Lastly, this chapter has argued that ADR processes advance access to justice in the consumer field, though the courts should retain their role in providing statutory interpretation on key issues in consumer law.

8

Dispute System Design Features of Effective Consumer Redress Models

8.1 Introduction

Dispute system design (DSD) is a distinct and important discipline within the civil justice system[1] that encompasses the planning of dispute resolution schemes, including civil procedure, Alternative Dispute Resolution (ADR), Online Dispute Resolution (ODR), internal complaints mechanisms, as well as international strategies that seek to bring peace and reconciliation.

The design of consumer redress models is challenging and it often faces competing issues such as effectiveness (i.e. low cost) and fairness (i.e. justice and addressing systematic issues).[2] Goals and priorities vary depending on who are the most influential stakeholders. For instance, policy makers may want to increase efficiency in public budgets and reduce pressure on courts, while businesses will want to avoid litigation as well as to limit reputational damage in order to boost trust in their business model and increase their competitive advantage.[3] This in turn contrasts with the priorities of consumer organizations who prefer to prioritize 'transparency, widening access and addressing systematic and collective issues'.[4] Despite that, Gill et al. note that the DSD of consumer redress processes have a number of shared goals such as

> improving efficiency in dispute resolution, increasing access to justice, ensuring disreputable traders do not flourish at the expense of legitimate

[1] A. Le Sueur, 'Designing Redress: Who Does It, How and Why? (2012) 20 *Asia Pacific Law Review* 17.

[2] C. Gill, J. Williams, C. Brennan and C. Hirst 'Designing Consumer Redress: A Dispute System Design (DSD) Model for Consumer-to-Business Disputes' (2016) 36(3) *Legal Studies* 438–463.

[3] Ibid., p. 452.

[4] Ibid. See also T. Schultz, 'Does Online Dispute Resolution Need Governmental Intervention? The Case for Architectures of Control and Trust' (2004) 6 *N C J Law Technol* 71.

> traders, and ensuring appropriate procedural and quality safeguards are in place to secure consumer and business trust.[5]

To find equilibrium amongst these goals is not an easy task, especially for private redress providers. This is because, as discussed in the previous chapter, while they are trying to maintain an acceptable level of independence, they are incentivized to offer processes that appeal to traders, who are after all their clients. In order to minimize the risk of forum shopping and a race to the bottom in terms of standards (including independence and impartiality), the previous chapters advocated for a restriction in the number of ADR entities allowed to operate in each sector as well as robust monitoring from the certifying bodies.

Technology also impacts significantly in the design of consumer redress processes. The move from an off-line to an online procedure can deliver disruptive changes in the procedure challenging traditional redress processes.[6] For instance, online processes such as the ODR system for resolving disputes between domain names and trademark owners do not require the courts to enforce outcomes because they can self-enforce their own decisions – i.e. they have access to the registry and can therefore transfer or cancel domain names. As a result, instead of using arbitration they use an adjudicative model, the decisions of which are public and enforceable, but that can be reviewed *de novo* in court. A similar example is Israel's Benoam online arbitration system, which is used to resolve disputes between insurance companies. Arbitral awards stemming from this scheme are not confidential so that a system of precedent and information sharing can be put in place.[7] These two examples are relevant for the consumer field because typically low-value claims cannot be enforced in courts in a cost-effective manner, and greater transparency with outcomes leading to predictability is necessary in processes where the types of disputes are likely to be similar and there is an asymmetry of power between the parties (i.e. traders participating as repeat players while consumers are one-time users in the dispute resolution process).

This chapter focuses on two key DSD features that are essential for a successful consumer redress process: a high level of settlements and out-of-court compliance with final outcomes. This chapter examines the main consensual redress models and how they incentivize settlement, and it

5 Gill et al., n. 2, p. 455.

6 O. Rabinovich and E. Katsh, 'Technology and the Future of Dispute System Design' (2012) 17 *Harv Negot Law Rev* 175.

7 Ibid.

notes that the online forum offers the possibility of designing multi-tiered procedures that promote early settlements and facilitate out-of-court compliance with outcomes. This chapter concludes arguing that since consumer redress models are providing a public service, they must incorporate adequate governance and corporate social responsibility policies that favour settlement as well as dispute avoidance strategies. This is indeed a feature of some statutory redress schemes that collaborate with enforcement bodies (such as statutory ombudsman schemes), which, in addition to offering dispute resolution services, provide consumers with advice, and the industry and the enforcers with intelligence data to prevent future disputes. If these DSD features are spread into other consumer redress processes, they will deliver greater benefits for the society at large, thus realizing the often overstated policy aims of consumer redress, which is not simply achieving compensation for entitled consumers, but also the provision of consumer protection, the widening of access to justice, and the boost of consumer trust in e-commerce.

8.2 The Preference for Consensual Outcomes in Consumer Redress

A recurrent feature of most successful redress processes is that they empower parties to settle disputes with the assistance of a neutral third party who often has some degree of authority and public recognition. However, the exact procedure applied varies depending on the sector and the country. Its design is frequently chosen by regulators who take into account their own national and sectorial redress cultures. These choices receive limited influence from other national models,[8] with the exception perhaps of neighbouring countries where it may be possible to see confluence in the DSD choices.

Chapter 5 examined in some detail the consumer redress models in Italy, Spain and the UK. But similar redress models exist in neighbouring countries. For example, Italy and France rely on consensual-based or mediation schemes, which have strong links to regulators and large

[8] The Leuven study found the multitude of ADR methods for consumer disputes operating in the EU are deeply rooted in 'historic, legal, political, socio-economic, educational or cultural factors'. See J. Stuyck, E. Terryn, V. Colaert, T. Van Dyck, N. Peretz, N. Hoekx and P. Tereszkiewicz, *Study on Alternative Means of Consumer Redress Other Than Redress through the Ordinary Judicial Proceedings* (Catholic University of Lueven, 14 January 2007) p. 38.

industries which offer these services in-house.[9] In Spain, and also in Portugal, by contrast, the most important consumer redress scheme is a publicly regulated consumer arbitration system with an optional mediation stage.[10] The UK and Ireland rely mostly on sectorial ombudsman schemes, notably in the financial sector. In addition, another consumer redress model which is predominant in Scandinavian countries, such as Sweden, Norway and Denmark, are the complaints boards.[11]

Therefore, in general terms it is possible to distinguish the following consumer redress procedures: mediation, arbitration, complaint boards and ombudsman schemes. This section discusses how these procedures have the common denominator of seeking first informal and consensual settlements.

8.2.1 Mediation and Consensual-Based Redress Processes

The majority of consumer redress procedures incorporate mediation techniques that rely on a neutral third party who assists consumers and traders to negotiate a settlement. The preference for this model is based on the higher satisfaction levels of the parties since they experience a better perception of fairness in the procedure and the outcome.[12]

However, traditional facilitative mediation is not suitable for the consumer environment where there is a vast difference of power between the parties, and thus purely negotiated settlements cannot achieve consumer protection. The role of the mediator in the facilitative model is limited to assisting parties to settle their disputes without advising them about their merits. This model of mediation is more common in commercial disputes, and sometimes, in med-arb schemes, but less so in the consumer cases where the asymmetry of power can lead consumers to settle for much less than what they are entitled to.[13]

[9] P. Cortés (ed.), *The New Regulatory Framework for Consumer Alternative Dispute Resolution* (OUP, 2016).

[10] Ibid.

[11] C. Hodges, I. Benohr and N. Creutzfeldt-Banda, *Consumer ADR in Europe (Civil Justice Systems)* (Beck/Hart, 2012).

[12] N. Creutzfeldt-Banda, 'How Important Is Procedural Justice for Consumer Dispute Resolution? A Case Study of an Ombudsman Model for European Consumers', (2014) 37(4) *J Consum Policy* 527–546.

[13] A. Samuel, 'Consumer Financial Services in Britain: New Approaches to Dispute Resolution and Avoidance' (2002) 3(3) *Eur Bus Organ Law Rev* 649–694, 656.

By contrast, evaluative mediation or conciliation models, such as those used by ombudsman schemes, are proving to be more useful in persuading businesses to compensate consumers, and complainants to withdraw a claim if the conciliator considers the complaint to be ill-founded. Some ombudsman schemes have even given instructions to their case handlers so that they will not pass on to consumers inadequate offers to settle.[14] This is in effect a form of directed mediation.[15] The advantage of this model is that consumers benefit from the advice of technical experts that act as neutral third parties. A similar approach is adopted in other countries, such as in Italy when consumers participate in joint conciliations, or in Spain when they go to *intermediación* for house repossessions from banks.[16]

8.2.2 Settlements in Arbitration and Adjudicative Processes

Arbitration schemes for consumer matters are normally (and increasingly so) preceded by mediation stages. This is not just the case in institutionalized schemes, such as the aforementioned examples of Portugal and Spain, but also when private schemes are used, such as the Association for British Travel Agents (ABTA) dispute resolution scheme offered in the UK for travel agents and consumers.

In addition to arbitration, there are adjudicative schemes, the decisions of which are contractually binding. An example of that is Nominet, which resolves disputes between trademark owners and '.uk' domain name holders. Its procedure offer parties a mediation stage prior to the adjudication.

Even the courts of England and Wales offer free-of-cost telephone mediation for civil claims under £10,000; as already discussed in the previous chapter, they are now in the process of setting up an online court with hopes to settle online the majority of disputes before these escalate to judicial adjudication. The preference for settlement reflects the common law tradition where civil claims that reach the courts, and are defended, rarely end up in trial because they are settled beforehand – this is due to the adversarial nature of the procedure and the risks of having to bear high (and even disproportionate) costs in the event of not succeeding.

In these tiered processes, the adjudicative stage only takes place as a last resort for those complaints where mediation techniques have not

[14] Ibid., 657. [15] Ibid. [16] See Chapter 5.

succeeded in reaching settlements. Common features of these adjudicative schemes are that they tend to adopt an inquisitorial role (though not as pronounced as the investigatory role employed by ombudsman schemes), decisions are often based on principles of fairness rather than law, and they do not have a prescribed system for the standard of proof. This flexibility allows these schemes to achieve fair resolutions in markets where consumers have gaps of information and lack bargaining power.

8.2.3 *Complaints Boards and Ombudsman Schemes*

Complaints boards vary from country to country, but the common feature is that consumer disputes are decided by a panel of experts who represent the consumer and the sector where the trader operates. In Sweden, the administrator of the board deals with straightforward cases (i.e. those where there is a clear precedent or where the trader has not responded to the complaint) without the involvement of the board.[17] A peculiar feature of the Swedish model is that the outcomes are not binding recommendations. Yet, these recommendations are often followed because the boards have a good public reputation, and they use a blacklist – i.e. they publish online the names of traders who do not comply with their recommendations as well as twice a year in a consumer magazine. Similar to other consumer redress procedures, especially ombudsman models, complaints go first through an advice stage provided by an expert who filters most cases.[18]

Like complaints boards, ombudsman schemes only process complaints that are not manifestly unfounded or trivial. In doing so ombudsman models provide consumers with free legal advice,[19] which helps consumers to better understand the weaknesses and strengths of their claims, assisting them to manage expectations and providing a better sense of justice. This information process promotes settlements at an early stage, especially when similar cases have been resolved before by the ombudsman scheme. The ombudsman procedure adopts an inquisitorial approach, it puts the onus of the proof on the traders, and it provides a high level of technical competence.[20] Typically case handlers will attempt

[17] Hodges et al., n. 11, p. 242. [18] Ibid., p. 251.
[19] C. Hodges, 'Consumer Ombudsmen: Better Regulation and Dispute Resolution' (2015) *ERA Forum* 5.
[20] C. Gill, J. Williams, C. Brennan and N. O'Brien, 'The Future of Ombudsman Schemes: Drivers for Change and Strategic Responses' (15 July 2013) p. 4.

first to find an acceptable settlement for the parties, and when this cannot be found, then they issue a decision that becomes legally binding on the trader if accepted by the consumer.

Thus, most ADR procedures, but especially ombudsman schemes, try to facilitate settlements before they adjudicate decisions. According to Ombudsman Services in the UK, less than half of the complaints related to telecoms and energy are resolved by some kind of formal determination.[21] When decisions are determined in various levels, senior ombudsmen can make a final decision when a recommendation is not accepted by a case officer. The Financial Ombudsman Service in the UK reported that their ombudsmen deal with around 6 per cent of the total caseload.[22] Parties frequently agree to the recommendations because they follow the established approach of previous cases. Accordingly, the cases that are most likely to be escalated to an ombudsman are those that are new – i.e. where similar cases have not been dealt with before or where there are different material facts of the case, which means that the established approach may not be right for that particular case.

The early settlement of complaints is therefore a key feature in the DSD for consumer redress processes, but in order to operate effectively parties need incentives to settle their disputes. These incentives are examined in the next section.

8.3 Incentives to Settle Complaints

Successful processes are those that manage effectively communication flows and provide incentives that encourage settlements before cases escalate to more costly and acrimonious adjudicative processes. This section examines various tools that can be incorporated into the DSD of consumer redress processes in order to achieve the goal of promoting early settlements. In doing so, this section examines how automated negotiation tools assist in early settlements without the intervention of neutral third parties; it then suggests that funding models and costs penalties can have an impact on early settlements; and lastly, it identifies multi-tiered processes and the publication of final decisions as best practices leading to more transparent and early resolutions.

[21] According to Ombudsman Services Annual Report 2013–14, only 44 per cent of energy complaints were resolved by determination, while the figure was 48 per cent for the telecom sector.

[22] See www.financial-ombudsman.org.uk/publications/.

8.3.1 An Effective Automated Negotiation Tool

The previous section noted that most consumer redress schemes, especially ombudsman schemes, use a filtering process that discards unfounded complaints. Typically, the first step of an ADR scheme is to provide an initial diagnosis of the strength of the complaint and inform complainants about their rights.[23] As noted in Chapter 6 when examining the UNCITRAL system, which to some degree mirrors the eBay dispute resolution mechanism, effective consumer redress schemes should adopt a pyramid shape, where most disputes are resolved in its base, after parties have exchanged all the necessary information, and only a small proportion of complaints progress to the next stage, where a neutral third party intervenes to facilitate negotiations. An even smaller number of disputes reach the adjudicative stage where a decision is imposed by a neutral third party.[24]

The first stage, which can be called triage or diagnosis stage, is increasingly being carried out with the assistance of ODR technology, with no, or limited, support from humans. Yet, it is important to be careful when using ODR tools since over-automating processes in the name of efficiency could overshadow fairness of the process for those consumers who do not feel comfortable or understand the automated process.[25] For that reason, it is vital to provide some human support, either by phone or chat, in order to assist those that find barriers with the ODR technology.

ODR platforms can assist in the communication between the parties. Indeed, the most successful ODR platforms are those where the majority of disputes are settled without the intervention of neutral third parties. eBay represents an interesting model as it wants to minimize conflicts and it knows that the less clicks an user has to make to lodge a dispute, the more disputes will be filed. Furthermore, it knows that disputes are a source of information to obtain a clear picture of what sort of problems arise within its marketplace. eBay relies on trust between its users, so it

[23] On this point, see also Hodges et al., n. 11, pp. 90–94, 121, 289–290, 358; S. Roberts and M. Palmer, *Dispute Processes: ADR and the Primary Forms of Decision Making*, 2nd edn (CUP, 2005) 346–357.

[24] See J. Hörnle, 'Encouraging Online Dispute Resolution in the EU and Beyond- Keeping Costs Low or Standards High?' Queen Mary School of Law Legal Studies Research Paper No. 122/2012, section 4a, and C. Hodges, I. Benohr and N. Creutzfeldt-Banda, 'Consumer-to-Business Dispute Resolution: The Power of CADR' (2012) 13 *ERA Forum* 214.

[25] Scott J. Shackelford and Anjanette H. Raymond, 'Building the Virtual Courthouse: Ethical Considerations for Design, Implementation, and Regulation in the World of ODR' (2014) *Wis. Law Rev.* 616, 640–645.

encourages claimants not to submit disputes directly to the marketplace without a prior attempt to resolve them directly with the other party. eBay assists complainants providing them with accessible guides and resources that help them to make corrections with the purpose of clarifying misunderstood information as well as settling disputes as early as possible.

eBay demonstrated that a good ODR platform that deals with a high number of consumer complaints can benefit from automating the diagnosis stage. As already discussed this is possible to do when there are many similar types of disputes – for instance, the most recurring disputes in e-commerce are the non-delivery of purchased goods, a late delivery or non-conformity of delivered goods. Likewise, as proposed in Chapter 4, the EU ODR platform should incorporate an effective automated negotiation tool, which would manage the communication between the parties using the parties' complaint and response forms.[26] The negotiation stage will be more effective when parties are aware of their rights and what would be the likely outcome if the case goes on to adjudication. Thus, for instance, it will be essential to incorporate clear guidance guidelines on legal guarantees that represent around half of the claims in the retail sector, as well as information on key procedural factors. In a similar vein, information on who has the burden of proof of the item delivered, if the complaint progresses to an adjudicative process, is essential to meet the expectations of the parties while helping them to settle their disputes. Indeed, the more predictable an outcome is, the quicker that parties will be willing to reach a settlement.

8.3.2 Economic Incentives

The fee structure also impacts on the parties' willingness to settle a case. As already mentioned, this is self-evident in common law courts, especially those that operate a 'pay-as-you-go' system, and where typically less than 5 per cent of civil claims (excluding family matters) reach the trial stage.

In the context of consumer redress, the most common approach to join an ADR entity is a blended one, where traders pay a case fee and an

[26] See also P. Cortés and A. Lodder, 'Consumer Dispute Resolution Goes Online: Reflections of the Evolution of European Law for Out of Court Redress' (2014) 12 *Maastricht J* 37; and D. Doktori, E. Karlik and L. Perkins, 'Stakeholder Analysis and Design Recommendations for an EU-Wide Online Dispute Resolution System' Harvard Negotiation & Mediation Clinical Program (2 May 2012).

annual fee for the membership, which includes the enquiries and a number of cases for which the traders do not pay a case fee. The purpose of this approach is as follows. First, it provides ADR entities with the necessary revenue stability to fund its staff and operations, and second, it puts some pressure on traders to deal with these complaints internally and to consider meritorious settlements. Third, it ensures that those traders that generate more complaints are not subsidized by the traders that have fewer complaints. Although case fees may not cover the whole cost of the process, they install some sense of proportionality to the redress system, particularly if a fee reduction applies when parties settle disputes early. Some entities do not charge (or charge less) before the appointment of the neutral third party. The reason for this is to encourage traders to settle meritorious complaints before they progress to procedures where a third party is appointed and case fees are requested.[27] Other entities do not request fees until parties have exchanged information or just before the documents are sent to the adjudicator.[28]

A drawback of this fee system is that it may pressurize traders to settle unmeritorious claims where the costs of settlement is similar or under the cost of the case fee. A way around this risk is to require consumer complainants to file a small case fee, although certified ADR entities can only require a nominal fee to consumers.[29] The fee can be refunded in the event of succeeding wholly or partially in the complaint. This is the approach employed by the ADR entity of the package holiday sector (ABTA) that deals with complaints from consumers against travel agents and tour operators.[30] This scheme requires consumers to pay a small fee that is refundable in the event of settling or getting a complaint upheld. However, it must be noted that filling fees can deter consumers from bringing claims and indeed the British and Irish Ombudsman Association states that its members cannot require fees of claimants.

Cost sanctions can also be used for encouraging parties to settle their disputes, instead of employing more costly adjudicative models. For instance, English courts use cost sanctions when parties disregard the

27 Hodges et al., n. 24, p. 212. 28 Ibid.

29 Art. 8(c) ADR Directive. See the previous chapter for a discussion on what is a nominal fee. See also Chapter 7.

30 CEDR Solve Consumer Arbitration Scheme. See www.cedr.com/solve/schemes/#abta_dispute_resolution.

participation in an ADR scheme before starting a legal action,[31] or when an offer to settle is not beat in court.[32] Although most consumer disputes do not reach the courts, these cost incentives could be transposed to the ADR entity. Accordingly, it may be worth examining whether parties who do not achieve a more favourable outcome in adjudication than what was offered in the negotiation should be required to carry an additional cost to use the adjudicative process, and whether unreasonable refusals should carry an economic penalty. ABTA also provides an example of this economic incentive in ADR. The procedural rules state that when the consumer-complainant is awarded less than what was previously offered by the trader, the consumer will be ordered to pay an amount that is equal to the registration fee.[33]

8.3.3 *Multi-Tiered Dispute Resolution Processes and the Publication of Adjudicated Decisions*

It has already been discussed that DSD processes for consumer redress schemes frequently employ processes that deal with disputes in various stages. The first stage is a consensual process, and, only if this fails, can parties move to an adjudicative process where a neutral third party recommends or imposes the solution. While it is clear that not everything is negotiable, and there are circumstances in which an extrajudicial process is not suitable,[34] a multi-tiered ODR process can be used for the majority of consumer disputes. In fact, as already mentioned, it is the ADR model employed by many ombudsmen and med-arb schemes, and the approach recommended by UNICTRAL for the resolution of e-commerce disputes.

In ombudsman schemes, parties normally receive a preliminary decision or recommendation before the final decision is made – this technique is very similar to early neutral evaluation, which is employed for civil and commercial matters, where an adjudicator (sometimes even a trained judge) provides a non-binding assessment of a dispute after a

[31] *Binns* v. *Firstplus Financial Group Plc* [2013] EWHC 2436 (QB). The High Court struck out a claim where the claimant received an award in an ADR process (FOS) giving him full compensation for the losses incurred but no legal costs.

[32] Pt. 36 CPR. Cf. P. Cortés, 'A Comparative Review of Offers to Settle – Would an Emerging Settlement Culture Pave the Way for their Adoption in Continental Europe?' (2013) 32(1) *Civil Justice Q* 42–67.

[33] See www.abta.com/consumer-services/travel_problems/arbitration.

[34] O. Fiss, 'Against Settlement' (1984) 93 *Yale Law J.* 1073.

preliminary analysis. The rationale behind this step is to provide parties with an opportunity to respond to the arguments given by the adjudicator. This stage often prompts settlements between the parties. The effectiveness of settlement in a tiered process depends on the parties' being realistic about their claims, particularly for consumers who may be inexperienced in reaching settlements. As a result, facilitating consumers' access to information on their rights may contribute towards speedy and amicable agreements. This information is particularly persuasive when it comes from a party who has expertise in the area of conflict, and hence is seen as a recognized independent authority.

Regulators and enforcement bodies also use economic incentives to reach early settlements in collective redress. For instance, the energy business in the UK (Ofgem), when investigating a breach, offers three tiers of discounts to energy companies found in breach – the earlier the settlement, the greater is the discount, which goes from 30 to 10 per cent of the penal element of the overall financial liability imposed on the business.[35]

Consumer redress models that rely on informal methods of dispute resolution face a number of risks related to accountability, transparency and consistency of decision making.[36] Although disputes settled through negotiation are not required to follow national substantive laws, it is evident that negotiation generally takes place against the backdrop of the parties' rights, as defined by the relevant legal structures.[37] However, the design of an effective redress system should include a binding stage whereby a dispute can be resolved regardless of how reasonable the parties are. Furthermore, it has been argued that the right-based approach is a model preferable for the consumer sector because of the imbalance of power between the parties.[38] This is especially because of

[35] See Ofgem, 'Enforcement Guidelines' (2014) at 5.26. Available at www.ofgem.gov.uk/ofgempublications/89753/enforcementguidelines12september2014publishedversion.pdf. For an overview of this system see M. Canto-Lopez, 'Ofgem's Recent Trends in Enforcement: Settlements, Redress and the Consumer's Interest' (2016) 21(2) *Utilities Law Rev* 65–70.

[36] M. Doyle, V. Bondy and C. Hirst 'The Use of Informal Resolution Approaches by Ombudsmen in the UK and Ireland: A Mapping Study' (October 2014). Available at www.ombudsresearch.org.uk.

[37] M. Eisenberg, 'Private Ordering through Negotiation' (1976) 89 *Harv Law Rev* 637; R. Mnookin and L. Korn Hauser, 'Bargaining in the Shadow of the Law: The Case of Divorce' (1979) 88 *Yale Law J* 950.

[38] H. Eidenmullery and M. Engel, 'Against False Settlement: Designing Efficient Consumer Rights Enforcement Systems in Europe' (2014) 29 *Ohio St J Disp Resol* 261; G. Wagner,

the risks associated with consumers being one-time users while traders act as repeat players; traders learn how to game the system and use it to their advantage, and they develop a relationship with the provider and the neutral third parties.[39]

In order to minimize these risks that may affect the impartiality and independence of ADR entities, it is important to develop mechanisms, such as the publication of decisions that safeguard the impartiality of these schemes and neutral third parties. This is why the Financial Ombudsman in the UK decided in 2014 to publish all their decisions.[40] The public record of complaints can operate as an important incentive for settling meritorious claims and adopting regulatory responses to market problems. The Financial Conduct Authority has introduced rules whereby if businesses resolve complaints within three days through its internal complaint handling mechanisms, they will not need to provide a formal written response or to record the complaint for reporting purposes.[41] Although neither the UNCITRAL rules nor the ADR Directive require the publication of adjudicated decisions, the publication of decisions is an important safeguard for consumer redress schemes. Outcomes from adjudicative processes, as opposed to consensual agreements, should not remain confidential in order to enhance transparency. Indeed, an adequate level of transparency is essential in asymmetric relationships where traders decide on the terms and conditions and require consumers to pay in advance of providing goods or services.

It is therefore submitted that the publication of decisions would have at least three important roles: first, it brings transparency to a process where parties do not contest on an equal footing and where traders are repeat players while consumers are inexperienced users of the redress process; second, it helps to establish a body of model cases, facilitating legal certainty and the predictability of outcomes;[42] and third, it acts as

'Private Law Enforcement Through ADR: Wonder Drug or Snake Oil?' (2014) 51(1) *Common Mark Law Rev* 165–194.

39 Cf. C. Menkel-Meadow, 'Do the "Haves" Come out Ahead in Alternative Judicial Systems? Repeat Players in ADR' (1999) 15 *Ohio St J on Disp Resol* 19–61.

40 See www.ombudsman-decisions.org.uk/Default.aspx.

41 Financial Conduct Authority, Consultation Paper, Improving Complaints Handling (December 2014) p. 9.

42 H. Micklitz and G. Sartor, 'Assessing the Scope of the Online Dispute Resolution Platform' European Parliament (March 2012). Available at www.europarl.europa.eu/document/activities/cont/201204/20120417ATT43146/20120417ATT43146EN.pdf and H. Jacquemin, 'Optimal Integration European Dispute Resolution Platform' European Parliament (13 April 2012) p. 12 Available at www.europarl.europa.eu/document/

an incentive for traders to settle reasonable complaints. Whereas personal data may be restricted and not made available in the publications,[43] the name of a business should not have the same protection and for that reason it should be published.

8.4 Incentives for Out-Of-Court Compliance of Outcomes

When parties cannot reach a settlement it is up to the redress scheme to provide the parties with a solution to their dispute, which should be complied with in a cost-effective manner, that is, outside the court, particularly when dealing with low-value and cross-border disputes. This section explores what techniques (particularly technological ones) can be used in the design of a redress body in order to encourage voluntary compliance of resolutions without the need for judicial enforcement.

8.4.1 'Name and Shame' Techniques and Blacklists

The 'name and shame' techniques and blacklists can be used to list recalcitrant businesses that refuse to comply with the outcomes of ADR entities (which may be also those who refused to participate in the ADR process). However, if the information contained in the blacklist is false, the publication could give rise to civil liability for defamation, and even to criminal prosecution in those jurisdictions where defamation is a crime and shamed traders are able to bring a legal claim for reputational damage. Nevertheless, even in these jurisdictions the publication of this data may be justified when there is a public interest.

Indeed, a number of ADR and ODR schemes already use 'naming and shaming' as an incentive for compliance and to warn consumers.[44] For instance, the main ADR entity in Sweden (the ARN) cannot force traders to participate in its redress scheme, but they publish online and twice a

activities/cont/201204/20120413ATT42990/20120413ATT42990EN.pdf arguing for the publication of decisions in binding and non-binding processes, but maintaining the anonymity of the parties when they so request.

43 See Data Protection Directive 95/46/EC.

44 For example, the Internet Ombudsman in Austria publishes a Watch-list of traders that have generated multiple consumer complaints www.ombudsmann.at/schlichtung.php/cat/5/aid/17/title/Watchlist; and the Swedish National Board for Consumer Disputes makes available to the public its decisions for 'naming and shaming' traders for non-compliance. See European Parliament Study Cross-Border Alternative Dispute Resolution in the EU (2011) p. 40.

year in their consumer magazine the names of businesses that did not comply with their recommendations.[45]

Blacklists can also be used to incentivize traders to participate in redress, especially in those industries where the majority have opted in or where there is not a very high number of businesses. In the UK, the Civil Aviation Authority suggested the possibility of creating a blacklist to include those airlines that are not adhered to a certified ADR entity.[46]

Another option that would speed up compliance would be to use a public registry to include the name of those traders that refuse to comply with the outcomes. An example of this model would be the Registry Trust Ltd, which is a private company that has been contracted by the Ministry of Justice in the UK to keep a registry of defendants who have not complied with judgments from court or tribunals.[47] This information is publicly available and it is accessed by commercial organizations, such as credit reference agencies, credit grantors and others seeking information regarding an individual's financial standing.[48]

Outside the EU, an important scheme is carried out by the Better Business Bureau (BBB), which rates traders in Canada and the USA.[49] The BBB lists all traders, including those that have been accredited by them through their trustmark scheme and those who are not accredited, though having the BBB accreditation improves the traders' rating. It must be noted that while consumers perceive it as a useful mechanism, many traders do not like it because they cannot opt out. Hence, consumers can search online for businesses and submit complaints, even when the trader does not participate in the redress scheme.[50] The BBB offers disputants an ADR which is non-binding. But traders often agree because their participation and compliance with the final outcome affect

45 See magazine *Råd & Rön* and online database at www.radron.se/svarta-listan/.

46 Civil Aviation Authority, Reforming Complaints Handling – Consultation on the CAA's Draft Policy CAP 1257 (December 2014) para. 39.

47 See www.trustonline.org.uk/understand-judgments-fines/entries-on-the-england-and-wales-register/tribunal-awards-and-the-register.

48 Chapter 7 expands on other incentives that facilitate extrajudicial compliance with ADR outcomes.

49 It should be first noted that the BBB is not a government or law enforcement agency but a long-standing not-for-profit network hub for businesses operating in the USA and in Canada. See www.bbb.org.

50 L. Webb, 'International BBB Ratings a la eBay: A Proposal for an Improved Online Better Business Bureau to Facilitate International Business Transactions' (2004) 35 *Calif W Int Law J* 127.

the traders' BBB rating.[51] The BBB scheme is the largest scheme of its kind in the USA, receiving every year over 800,000 complaints, out of which more than 70 per cent are settled amicably by the parties.[52]

8.4.2 *Online Intermediaries*

Online intermediaries may be effective in encouraging compliance with final outcomes.[53] Such intermediaries can be those who hold the money related to the transaction, such as escrow services that determine who keeps the transaction money when there is a dispute between the buyer and seller.[54] Payment providers, such as credit card companies (i.e. Visa, Mastercard and American Express) and other online payment intermediaries (i.e. PayPal or Bitcoin) can reverse payments in compliance with outcomes, moving sums in dispute from the seller's account to the buyer's. Thus, an enforcement option could mimic the chargeback mechanism provided by credit card companies through an escrow service, providing the reversal of a payment to the buyer when the complaint is upheld. In 2015 the US and Columbian delegations proposed the use of chargebacks as the main route of enforcement of decisions emanating from the UNCITRAL draft ODR rules. Yet, at this point, it remains unclear whether payment channels would be interested in collaborating with an outsourced ADR process.

An interesting model is that offered by online currencies, such as Bitcoin, which offer an escrow service that hold the payment until both parties are satisfied with a transaction or until a decision is adjudicated by the dispute resolution process. An interesting example is Bitrated, which uses trusted agents that hold a public reputation system who decide who keeps a Bitcoin payment made in a disputed transaction.[55] The system works through the use of encrypted payments (i.e. using multi-signatures) which use three keys (one held by the buyer, one by the seller

51 S. Gott, 'BBB Offers Tips on When and How to File a Complaint' Better Business Bureau. (24 April 2013) Available at www.bbb.org/blog/2013/04/bbb-offers-tips-on-when-and-how-to-file-a-complaint/.

52 Better Business Bureau, '2014 Statistics: Sorted by Complaints' www.bbb.org/globalassets/local-bbbs/council-113/media/complaint-stats/2014/2014us-sorted-by-complaint.pdf.

53 Hodges et al., n. 11, p. 216.

54 See, for example, www.escrow.com. The Payment Services Directive 2007/64/EC (O.J. 2007, L 319) allowed the introduction of low-cost escrows in the EU that are properly licensed and regulated by the public authorities.

55 See www.bitrated.com.

and one by the trusted agent). The money can only be released when two keys are used, so if the buyer and seller are not in agreement, the trusted agent adjudicates for a fee who keeps the money and gives the key to that party.[56] Interestingly, Bitrated has set a reputation system for buyers and sellers, as well as for trusted agents. These trusted agents can compete in the so-called arbitration marketplace where anyone can offer their domain expertise as adjudicators, build their reputation and earn fees through an open and competitive environment. The reputation system limits the risk of a dishonest buyer or seller colluding with the trusted agent.

Furthermore, in extreme cases, online regulators such as ICANN could potentially play a key role in blocking traders that engage in criminal activities through the cancellation of their domain names when required by public enforcement bodies. These intermediaries can therefore play useful roles in blocking rogue traders without the need of judicial intervention.

8.4.3 *Assistance from Courts and Regulators*

This book has already advocated for greater collaboration between different redress bodies, and especially amongst ADR entities, courts and public enforcement bodies.[57] There are instances where traders do not comply in time with the determination or settlement reached through ADR processes. This is more likely to occur with SMEs and under mandatory ADR schemes, especially when the trader is undergoing financial difficulties or disagrees with the third party's decision. In these scenarios courts and other enforcement intermediaries should carry out an important role in speeding up compliance with final outcomes, without the need to start *de novo* a case in court. Hodges et al. recommend a fast-track enforcement procedure arguing that

> If a party to a CADR case wishes to enforce a non-binding CADR determination, there should be a fast track court procedure, so as to save

[56] See G. Prisco, 'Bitrated Unveils Reputation System and Multisig Escrow' (24 February 2015) https://bitcoinmagazine.com/articles/bitrated-unveils-reputation-system-multisig-escrow-1424750534. See also R. Koulu, 'Blockchains and Online Dispute Resolution: Smart Contracts as an Alternative to Enforcement' (2016) 13(1) *Scripted* 41–69, and P. Ortolani, 'Self-Enforcing Online Dispute Resolution: Lessons from Bitcoin' (2015) *Oxf J Legal Stud* (advance publication pp. 1–35).

[57] See in particular Chapters 1 and 3.

> costs. The procedure should not require the need to re-examine all the evidence afresh (the case file would be transferred to the court by the CADR), and give a reasonable opportunity for either side to introduce fresh evidence (but subject to a possible cost penalty if the court's time is wasted). The court should be free to make its own determination on the evidence: there should not be a presumption of liability.[58]

As already discussed in the context of the EU ODR platform, an automatic referral to the court or to a public enforcement body could speed up voluntary compliance.[59] ADR entities could be required to automatically refer a decision to the court or public enforcer when there is no compliance within 30 days. Although this option is likely to be more cumbersome than the other incentives (and so it should be only used as a last resort), its mere existence will foster voluntary and expeditious compliance by the trader.

8.5 Consumer Redress Schemes Should Offer More Than a Dispute Resolution Tool

8.5.1 The Need for Adequate Governance and Social Corporate Responsibility for Private ADR Entities

Consumer redress, whether it is delivered by public or private schemes, provides a public service. Currently, ADR entities complement, and sometimes replace, the role of courts. Accordingly, it is essential that private providers of consumer redress, especially publicly certified ADR entities, have an adequate governance that ensure the performance of a number of public functions that benefit not only the individual parties, but more generally the industry and its consumers – in other words, the society at large in akin to corporate social responsibility (CSR) policies, which must be strengthened via a proper structure of adequate governance.

In the context of consumer redress adequate governance involves the application of procedural standards and the continuous monitoring by the organization's governing body.[60] Accordingly, it would require the creation and implementation of policies and rules to ensure that redress procedures are just, leading to the professionalization and legitimization

[58] Hodges et al., n. 11, p. 452. [59] See Chapter 4.

[60] *Black's Law Dictionary* (Thomson West, 2016) as cited in N. Ebner and J. Zeleznikow, 'No Sheriff in Town: Governance for Online Dispute Resolution' (2016) 32(4) *Negotiation Journal* 297–323, 300.

of the field of consumer redress.[61] Unlike commercial ADR, consumer ADR is now a regulated activity in the EU. Moreover, given the disparity of power between consumers and traders, and the nature of legal services provided by ADR entities, regulation in this field of consumer redress will continue to grow at the national and international level.

By contrast, lack of adequate governance will tarnish the reputation and growth of the field of consumer redress. In the ODR context, Ebner and Zeleznikow observe that 'A lack of governance reduces users' trust, sense of security, and confidence that the dispute resolution process is fair, which are all the key factors in their decisions to use' it.[62] Further, they note that 'governance endows service providers with evidence of legitimacy ... [while lack of governance brings ethical risks such as] trying to curry favor with a repeat client at the expense of a one-time participant'.[63]

As consumer ADR in the EU is gaining greater legitimacy through the existing regulation that ensures minimum compliance with due process and public monitoring, these ADR entities should incrementally be moving from the provision of private individual redress to putting greater emphasis on delivering justice, that is, ensuring better compliance with consumer law and transforming collective learning from dispute resolution to inform dispute prevention strategies. Indeed, effective consumer redress models should influence traders' behaviour towards consumers, encouraging appropriate behaviour and compliance with outcomes.[64]

Alberstein noted that the function of law in resolving conflicts is 'considered a by-product of its authoritative role of determining rights and assessing them'.[65] Equally, since the use of out-of-court schemes is becoming the primary form of consumer redress, these procedures should pursue similar objectives to those sought in court litigation. Thus, the functions of all consumer ADR bodies (especially publicly certified ones), like those of courts, should not be restricted to resolving disputes;

[61] Ibid.

[62] Ibid., and N. Ebner and J. Zeleznikow, 'Fairness, Trust and Security in Online Dispute Resolution' (2015) 36(2) *Hamline Univ Sch Law J Pub Law Policy* 143–160.

[63] Ibid., 303.

[64] P. Resnick, R. Zeckhauser, J. Swanson and K. Lockwood, 'The Value of Reputation on eBay: A Controlled Experiment' (2006) 9 *Exp Econ* 79–101, 80.

[65] M. Alberstein, 'Judicial Conflict Resolution (JCR): A New Jurisprudence for an Emerging Judicial Practice' (2015) 16 *Cardozo Law J Conflict Resol* 886.

they should contribute to other functions, including preventing future disputes, informing parties about their rights and obligations, improving businesses standards and providing greater trust in economic transactions.

Stone stated in the 1960s that arbitration did not involve the adjudication of rights, but their actual creation because without arbitration in certain economic sectors, parties could not rely on the rights conferred in their contract.[66] Similarly, today consumer ADR schemes offer compensation to consumers who, in most cases, would be unable to obtain it through any other avenue. Therefore, these consumer redress bodies should carry out a public function that goes beyond dispute resolution. Consequently, it is possible to contend that the CSR approach fits in with the view that private ADR entities must offer a greater economic value to society than the mere resolution of individual disputes. Arguably, this view of consumer redress falls in line with the European model and contrasts with the approach adopted by private ADR models, especially when they are for-profit organizations. The latter category includes private arbitration and commercial ADR schemes, which are more predominant in certain jurisdictions such as the USA.

Thus, publicly certified ADR entities must be proactive and for instance tell traders to compensate all those consumers affected, and not just those who make a complaint. Yet, while compliance must remain as the primary function of regulators and public enforcement bodies, certified ADR entities should inform regulators about systemic problems. It must be remembered that under the ADR Directive, certified entities are required to cooperate with public enforcement bodies.[67] The exchange of information must include the types of consumer disputes lodged repeatedly. ADR entities can also request information from consumer protection agencies and enforcers when they consider that additional information is necessary to resolve individual disputes. Furthermore, ADR entities are encouraged to participate in European networks and they are required to collaborate with other European entities vis-à-vis cross-border and domestic disputes.[68] Although it is unclear how much of this is happening, in practice there is more cooperation when an ADR entity operates in a regulated sector in which there

[66] He was referring to compulsory arbitration in the US insurance industry. See M. Stone, 'A Paradox in the Theory of Commercial Arbitration' (1966) 21(3) *Arbitration J* 156–163.

[67] Art. 17(2) of the ADR Directive.

[68] Art. 16 of the ADR Directive.

are restrictions in the number of ADR providers, especially when there is only one ADR entity.

Therefore, publicly certified ADR entities should be progressively expected to prioritize dispute avoidance strategies in their activities. In doing so, consumer ADR entities should be required to advise consumers, address imbalances of power between traders and consumers, and feedback intelligence to traders and enforcers in order to ensure better compliance with the law.[69] However, these functions can only be performed if ADR entities are not competing against others (i.e. they have a monopoly in their sectors), if they are not for profit, and if their functions are clearly defined by the regulators. Thus, the design of consumer redress should be expected to carry out the following functions:

- Advising consumers
- Accounting and providing additional support for vulnerable parties
- Ensuring that consumers are compensated for economic losses
- Providing dispute resolution quickly and at a proportionate cost
- Collaborating with public enforcement bodies
- Ensuring compliance with consumer law
- Feeding information to traders and regulators with the aim of avoiding future disputes

8.5.2 Sharing of Learning in the Ombudsman Model

The ombudsman model may be the best suited redress process to carry out these CSR functions as in addition to dispute resolution, they can provide advice and help to raise standards in the industry.[70] Typically, the ombudsman model departs from the principle that ADR is a tool for individual consumers to obtain redress, but it also provides consumers with expert advice, offers a user-friendly dispute resolution process that is inquisitorial, prioritizes settlement over adjudication, and provides a point of information for consumers, traders and regulators. Indeed, ombudsman schemes often incorporate dispute prevention in their strategy. However, as discussed in the previous section, in order to achieve the goals of dispute prevention it is important to design a funding model that encourages dispute prevention over dispute resolution, finding the right

[69] Síndic de Greuges de Catalunya, 'The Catalan Ombudsman and General Interest Companies' (February 2014) p. 8.

[70] C. Gill et al., n. 2.

balance between case fees and membership fees. For instance, in the UK, Ombudsman Services changed the proportion of their annual fee from 10 per cent of the total (i.e. the rest being case fees) to 60 per cent, in order to rebalance the funding model.[71]

Hodges has advocated for the migration of arbitration schemes to a restrictive number of publicly monitored ombudsman models.[72] He foresees two stages in the evolution of consumer redress:

> first, a migration of existing arbitration-based ADR schemes to an ombudsman model and, second, a coalescing of the existing sectoral ombudsman landscape towards a small number of ombudsmen who have strong inter-operability and consistency in modes of operation.[73]

According to him, ombudsman schemes are better for the economy as they are well placed to provide widespread advice and aggregate data of cases creating useful feedback for traders, market regulators and enforcement bodies.[74] Indeed, aggregating and analysing data from off-line processes that are not standardized in their data collection is a more complicated and costly exercise. In this regard Sela notes that ODR technology can be instrumental:

> identifying usage patterns can help to expose bottlenecks, delays, inefficiencies or inaccuracies; inform betterment strategies and optimization of resource-allocation or restructuring of typical or redundant aspects of the process in iterative cycles.[75]

Learning from disputes is instrumental for correcting market abuses and avoiding future disputes through regulatory responses and identifying appropriate enforcement strategies. For instance, the Financial Ombudsman Service in the UK noticed that one in six payday lending complaints were related to fraud, which led to these cases to be dealt with by the enforcement authorities.[76] Improvements have also taken place through

[71] *Review of Ombudsman Services: Energy. A report for Ofgem* (London, Lucerna Partners, 2015).

[72] C. Hodges, N. Creutzfeldt and S. Macleod, 'Reforming the EU Consumer ADR Landscape: Implementation and Its Issues' Third Oxford Consumer Conference Report (30–31 October 2014) p. 7.

[73] Ibid., 10. [74] Ibid.

[75] A. Sela, 'The Effect of Online Technologies on Online Dispute Resolution System Design: Antecedents, Current Trends and Future Directions' (2017) 21(3) *Lewis Clark Law Rev* forthcoming 1–48, 45.

[76] Payday Lending: Pieces of the Picture. Financial Ombudsman Service Insight Report, August 2014.

the sharing of learning between ADR entities with the industry in other regulated sectors, such as the telecoms,[77] leading to improvements in traders' in-house complaint systems as well as in the services delivered by the businesses.[78] Interestingly, those who understand the operation of ombudsman schemes see this potential for consumer redress too. Kirkham observes that consumer ADR should be more than an expeditious dispute resolution system; it should ensure a good standard of fairness while enabling 'the complaints process to become part of the solution in terms of facilitating organisational learning'.[79]

Yet, currently the ADR entities' role in sharing intelligence is far below its full potential in many economic sectors; this is partly due to the underdevelopment of ADR on the one hand, and the private and competitive nature of ADR schemes in countries like the UK on the other hand. Research carried out to identify future changes in ombudsman schemes in the UK has recommended the delivery of 'greater sharing of learning'.[80] Although the role of ADR entities should not overstep the competences of sectorial supervisors, regulators and consumer protection authorities,[81] ADR entities could and should cooperate more with them as well as with the traders through the exchange of information. To this end ADR entities should not only identify problematic areas, but also recommend solutions to recurring problems, and discuss these solutions with the different stakeholders. In other words, they should identify best practices and share these with enforcers and traders. While regulators can incorporate these as minimum standards in the sectorial regulations, businesses can improve their codes of conduct leading to better internal complaints systems and CSR strategies.[82] Thus, regulators could then change the law to eradicate causes of complaints where the law is unclear or operates inefficiently, while business can set up mechanisms to deal with claims more efficiently

[77] Hodges et al., n. 24, p. 252 (referring to the Swedish complaints boards system).

[78] M. Doyle, 'Gazing at the ADR landscape – Is the EU Directive Just a Mirage?' (9 October 2013). Available at http://domarmediation.co.uk/2013/10/09/gazing-at-the-adr-landscape-is-the-eu-directive-just-a-mirage/.

[79] R. Kirkham, 'Analysis: Richard Kirkham on the Government's Plans for Consumer ADR: Innovation or More of the Same' (26 November 2014). Available at http://ukaji.org/2014/11/26/analysis-kirkham-the-governments-plans-for-consumer-adr-innovation-or-more-of-the-same/.

[80] C. Gill, J. Williams, C. Brennan and N. O'Brien, 'The Future of Ombudsman Schemes: Drivers for Change and Strategic Responses' (15 July 2013) pp. 2–3.

[81] Hodges, n. 19. [82] Ibid., p. 9.

through their internal consumer satisfaction offices or by stopping complaints from arising by changing their own practices.

One of the main promises of ODR tools in consumer redress schemes is how technology and big (as well as small) data opens up the opportunity to explore statistics and trends in similar categories of cases. If the information compiled is adequately analysed it could provide important information on dispute patterns, as we have seen with eBay. Similarly, Goodman observes that many businesses put themselves in a competitive disadvantage by focusing on telephone communications for processing complaints,[83] while those businesses that harness the advantages of web-based applications can improve their business practices by quickly reacting to the collective feedback.[84]

8.6 Conclusion

Consumer ADR entities are increasingly replacing the courts as the main means of consumer redress, especially since now they can be certified by public competent authorities. Paradoxically, these emerging ADR entities were not originally designed to replace the courts, but rather to complement them by offering a more proportional, informal and accessible means of redress to consumers. Effective consumer redress should meet the goals of providing access to justice (including via ADR where courts are not as accessible and convenient)[85] and enhance consumer trust in the market. This chapter has highlighted two DSD features that are important to achieve an effective ADR structure that achieve these goals: processes that promote early settlements and that incorporate out-of-court enforcement mechanisms.

Accordingly, in order to achieve proportionality in a dispute resolution process that mostly deals with low-value claims, it must promote informal and early settlements when possible. The main tools to achieve a high level of settlements are automated negotiation tools when complaints patterns can be identified; the use of funding models, case fees

83 J. Goodman, *Strategic Customer Service: Managing the Customer Experience to Increase Positive Word of Mouth, Build Loyalty, and Maximize Profits* (Amacon, 2009) p. 8.

84 See also A.O. Hirschman, *Exit, Voice, and Loyalty: Responses to Decline in Firms, Organizations, and States* (Harvard University Press, 1970) and L. Goetzinger, J.K. Park and R. Widdows, 'E-Customers' Third Party Complaining and Complementing Behavior' (2006) 17(2) *Int J Serv Ind Manag* 193–206.

85 M. Cappelletti, 'A World Survey' in M. Cappelletti and B. Garth (eds.) *Access to Justice* vol. 1 (Sijthoff and Noordhoff, 1978) 6–9.

and cost penalties to discourage escalation of disputes; and the incorporation of multi-tiered procedures that start with consensual techniques and move up to binding determination of published decisions, which also provide greater transparency and predictability of outcomes as well as promote the evolution of a jurisprudential case law for consumer matters.

Furthermore, this chapter has argued that consumer redress models cannot rely exclusively on the courts to ensure compliance with final outcomes. It has examined how the online forum offers the possibility to incorporate innovative tools that can be used as leverage to persuade parties to comply voluntarily with final outcomes – namely blacklists and name-and-shame techniques, and the use of payment providers and other intermediaries.

Lastly, this chapter has noted that consumer redress models provide a public service, and as such their design should incorporate adequate governance that pursues CSR policies, whereby processes are designed to learn from disputes and feedback businesses and regulators, so that dispute prevention policies can be put in place to reduce consumer disputes.

Conclusion

The Need for Greater Collaboration in the Provision of Consumer Redress in the Digital Market

Disputes between consumers and traders are growing,[1] and they do so exponentially in those economic sectors, such as the Digital Market, where the number of transactions increases and where traditional redress options, especially the courts, are less efficient.[2] At the same time consumer substantive rights are also growing,[3] in particular for digital consumers, who paradoxically have greater protection than those who enter into off-line transactions. For instance, when consumers buy something online they have more information rights than when they buy it in their local stores – yet, these rights are not more than wet paper if consumers do not have effective means to ensure their compliance. In other words, consumer rights are as effective as their route to ensure their enforceability.[4] Furthermore, many consumer grievances occurring in the market place are simply due to honest mistakes, errors, misunderstandings and poor customer service. All these disputes need to be resolved in an effective and fair manner, and lessons should be learnt so that they will not occur again.

[1] R. Fisher, W. Ury and B. Patton, *Getting to Yes, Negotiating an Agreement without Giving In*, 2nd edn (Random House, 1999) p. xiii.

[2] M. Cappelletti 'Alternative Dispute Resolution Processes within the Framework of World-Wide Access-to-Justice Movement' 56 (1993) *Mod Law Rev* 282–296, 284.

[3] Recent examples are the Commission (EC), 'Proposal for a Regulation of the European Parliament and of the Council on addressing geo-blocking and other forms of discrimination based on customers' nationality, place of residence or place of establishment within the internal market' COM(2016) 289 final, 25 May 2016; Commission (EC), 'Proposal for a Regulation of the European Parliament and of the Council on cross-border parcel delivery services' COM(2016) 285 final, 25 May 2016; and Commission (EC), 'Proposal for a Regulation of the European Parliament and of the Council on cooperation between national authorities responsible for the enforcement of consumer protection laws' COM (2016) 283 final, 25 May 2016.

[4] G. Howells and S. Weatherill, *Consumer Protection Law*, 2nd edn (Ashgate, 2005) 660.

This book has explored how the law and best practices in dispute resolution should be applied to provide consumers with more effective redress options, including public enforcement (i.e. the role of regulators), private enforcement mechanisms (i.e. courts and Alternative Dispute Resolution or ADR schemes) and market options, such as public reviews, chargebacks and escrow systems, as well as traders' in-house complaints handling schemes. These various levels of consumer redress move from public and independent bodies to private internal consumer satisfaction systems. Accordingly, their focus shifts from redress mechanisms that seek the public interest to the provision of private individual redress. The focus of this book however has been on publicly certified ADR entities, which in the EU are currently undergoing an institutionalization and professionalization process. This book has argued that many consumer redress systems, and in particular publicly certified ADR entities, are more than a mere dispute resolution mechanism as they provide a public service for consumers that complements, and often replaces, the role of the courts, as the former provide a more accessible and cost-efficient redress option. In examining the current regulations and best practices this book has called for greater integration amongst the various redress options and for a more efficient rationalization of certified ADR entities which should be better coordinated and accessible through technological means. These consumer redress schemes, norms and best practices in dispute resolution and dispute prevention are collectively referred to in this book as the *Law of Consumer Redress*.

Chapters 1 to 3 noted the variety of consumer redress options, which are increasingly complemented by information technology, and it called for greater collaboration between public enforcement bodies, courts (especially collective actions and small claims procedures) and Alternative Dispute Resolution bodies, whose roles are increasingly complementing that of courts and public enforcement bodies.

Chapter 1 noted that public enforcement bodies have the function of ensuring compliance with consumer law, which encompasses a role not only in chasing rouges traders but also, through their soft powers, informing and notifying (often unaware) non-compliant traders. Their functions are more effectively deployed when complemented by private enforcement initiatives (i.e. through certified ADR entities) and when they collaborate through pan-European networks like the Consumer Protection Cooperation and the European Consumer Centres. It was observed that the latter operates *de facto* as an ADR entity for cross-border disputes in the EU. Moreover, this chapter discussed the variety of techniques and procedures used by ADR providers (i.e. arbitration, mediation, ombudsman and complaint boards) and highlighted some of its common features. Lastly, it called for greater collaboration between enforcement bodies and ADR entities in order to guarantee consumers greater access to individual redress. To that end, this chapter recommended that regulators provide a back-up residual ADR scheme (as is already done in certain sectors by national enforcement bodies) funded by the industry, and for ADR entities to exchange periodical information with enforcement bodies.

Chapter 2 discussed the transformative impact of technology, which not only changes the paradigm of dispute resolution, altering the role and perception of the parties, but also offers new range of redress processes. These Online Dispute Resolution (ODR) processes may be more accessible, easier, faster and less expensive than their face-to-face counterparts. ODR technology as a fourth party in the dispute resolution process, like third-party neutrals, can shape the way parties interact. This chapter has examined the processes of private ODR providers (namely, the eBay Dispute Resolution Centre, Modria, Youstice, Resolver, Rechtwijzer and the dispute resolution process for domain names) as well as how ODR technology is being adopted by tribunals and courts (in particular, the processes employed by the English Traffic Penalty Tribunal, the Canadian Civil Resolution Tribunal and the forthcoming Online Court in England and Wales). Although informal and accessible ODR processes seem the most suitable avenues for enhancing consumer redress, they face a number of obstacles in their expansion given the lack of awareness, the costs of technology and the lack of incentives for traders to participate in these processes.

Chapter 3 argued that technology should permeate into the judicial process in order to achieve efficiencies and to increase access to justice. Greater use of technology would bring more benefits to those judicial processes, which have been originally designed as tools of consumer redress: namely, in collective redress processes and in small claims procedures, and especially when dealing with cross-border disputes of low value. This chapter suggested that technology opens the possibility of building greater cooperation between judicial and out-of-court processes, referring litigants to the most suitable redress option. This chapter examined the Commission Recommendation on Collective Redress and the recent amendments on the European Small Claims Procedure Regulation. The chapter noted that in order for a judicial process on small claims to become a more effective redress tool, it needs to be more user-friendly and integrate processes that facilitate the enforcement of judgments in a Member State different to where the consumer is residing. In addition, it argued that judicial processes would benefit from greater collaboration with ADR processes and ODR techniques that promote settlements when possible. In particular, it submitted that first, procedural laws should require parties to consider pre-action ADR; second, parties should be offered court-annexed ADR schemes when available, including for cross-border issues with support from European networks; third, litigants should face cost consequences for unreasonable refusals to participate in ADR; and fourth, ADR schemes should be able to refer certain complaints to the courts (i.e. those where there is manifest evidence of certain criminal offences or other public policy concern, when a point of law needs to be clarified, when there is a need to enforce an outcome, and when an appeal or a review is allowed).

The Law of Consumer Redress: Upgrading from Alternative to Online Dispute Resolution

Although the application of ODR is not limited to disputes arising out of online transactions, it seems to be particularly apt for these disputes, since it is normally preferable to use the same digital medium (the internet) for the resolution of e-commerce disputes. For that reason there have been institutional efforts, notably from the EU and the UN, to enhance the use of ODR for resolving these types of disputes. These regulatory efforts, which have permeated into national laws and ADR procedures, are embedding firmly these redress avenues within the civil justice system,[5] forming the backbone of what this book terms as the Law of Consumer Redress. In so doing the new regulatory framework has identified best practices in consumer redress that guarantee, inter alia, the independence and effectiveness of the process, and it has elevated them to minimum regulatory standards. Thus, at the core of consumer redress is the emerging legal framework for ADR and ODR which regulates what is becoming the primary route of redress for the majority of consumers. The legal framework was examined in Chapters 4, 5 and 6 of this book.

[5] P. Cortés, 'Online Dispute Resolution for Businesses – Embedding Online Dispute Resolution in the Civil Justice System of the EU' in C. Adamson *Online Dispute Resolution: An International Business Approach to Solving Consumer Complaints* (NetNeutrals, 2015) 36–46.

Accordingly, Chapter 4 discussed the new European regulatory framework on consumer dispute resolution and it evaluated the EU ODR platform. This chapter welcomed the regulatory developments but argued that the three goals set in the Commission Communication[6] have yet to be met. First, the ADR Directive has not closed the gaps in the provision of ADR services as it mostly remains voluntary for traders to use it – hence in many sectors consumers still do not have access to an ADR option. Second, although the accreditation process for ADR entities ensures compliance with minimum due process standards, there is a risk of forum shopping since traders can often choose (and frequently are required to fund) the ADR entities. Consequently, if the model of multiple ADR entities is used, then it is paramount to ensure that national competent authorities restrict competition (especially when there is evidence of forum shopping) and monitor compliance with the quality criteria set in the Directive. Third, in most cases the information obligations are not complied with by traders, especially by those that have not joined an ADR scheme and by the many who remain largely unaware of their information obligations. Moreover, those who are aware either do not comply or bury the information within the T&C, and often do not provide a contact email address to be contacted by the consumer through the ODR platform. Furthermore, most national authorities do not seem keen in enforcing information obligations given the lack of resources and given that such information will mislead consumers when traders have opted not to participate in the ADR process.

This chapter also argued that using the ODR platform as a mere referral website is not enough to enhance consumer redress in the EU, so it proposed the following additional functions: a problem diagnosis tool designed to inform consumers about their rights (i.e. preventing the escalation of complaints), an online negotiation function, a customizable case management tool for ADR entities, a referral function to forward cases to courts and regulators, and a monitoring function.

Moreover, the legal framework by itself does not ensure greater consumer redress if the national law does not properly apply it and adequate resources are not allocated to ensure its proper functioning. Chapter 5 explored the consumer redress landscape in three radically different jurisdictions: Italy, Spain and the UK. Each country faces its own specific challenges, so this chapter provided some suggestions on how to

[6] Communication on Alternative Dispute Resolution for Consumer Disputes in the Single Market COM(2011) 791.

overcome them. In Italy it was noted that the court system is particularly ill-fitted to provide consumer redress. The chapter advocated the promotion of *conciliazione paritetica* schemes and the extension of mandatory ADR schemes for traders operating in regulated sectors following the ADR model for telecommunication providers. The Spanish public arbitration system needs to undergo transformative changes by receiving greater investment (preferably from traders who use it on a 'polluter-basis'), restricting the ability of traders to limit their liability, increasing the economic threshold for single arbitrations and ensuring that traders clearly inform consumers when they are adhered to arbitration by displaying the national trustmark. Lastly, the UK sectorial landscape needs to be simplified by moving from multiple providers to a single ADR entity per sector (all accessible through a national platform). An effective residual redress body, whose role may fall on the forthcoming Online Court, must complement the existing partial sectorial ADR coverage.

Moreover, there are some obstacles in consumer redress that are shared in the three jurisdictions. Namely, there is a high level of fragmentation and a low level of compliance with the information requirements, and as a result most consumers continue without knowing where to go to obtain redress. This chapter recommended the launch of national ODR platforms or gateways to help to rationalize the fragmented (and often de-centralized) redress options, thus facilitating the consumer pathway to redress. It called for greater compliance with the information obligations and it recommended that national law should make it mandatory for traders operating in regulated sectors (and especially those offering essential services) to be part of an ADR entity. However, it suggested that consumers should be required first to elevate a complaint to the traders' internal complaint system. Lastly, it argued that in order to assure trust and quality in the ADR system it is essential that competent authorities monitor that ADR entities are not engaged in a forum shopping that affects their independence and impartiality. The best way to control this risk is by restricting the number of ADR entities operating in each sector. If only one ADR entity is allowed to operate per sector via a renewable public tender, then consumer confusion will be avoided and the concerns on charging fees while determining the traders' behaviour will not affect the independence of ADR entities.

The EU emerging regulatory framework has been prompted by the development of a Digital Market that challenges traditional means of redress. Naturally, e-commerce transcends national and European borders. Chapter 6 examined the ODR Technical Notes elaborated by

UNCITRAL Working Group III. These Notes illustrate a number of best practices of an ODR procedure that can be contractually chosen by the parties. Yet, these Notes did not meet the original objectives of the Working Group. This was due to the unsurmountable challenge in reconciling the US approach, which promotes arbitration as its main dispute resolution procedure, and the European approach, which largely bans pre-dispute arbitration. This chapter observed that arbitration is likely to decline as there are more user-friendly and less formalistic procedures and since the main advantage of having enforceable arbitral awards does not ensure their compliance without the need of going to court. Moreover, its confidential nature does not meet the goals of consumer redress, which go beyond dispute resolution. Accordingly, this chapter argued that arbitration may not be the best procedure for resolving cross-border consumer disputes as it may allow market abuses to go undetected. Thus, in order to prevent potential abuses, the chapter submitted that transparency ought to be promoted through the publication of resolutions and adequate monitoring by the accreditation agencies.

It has been argued that the main motivation behind the institutional regulatory push from the EU and the UN may not have been rooted in a desire to improve consumer access to justice, but rather in an economic preference to increase trust in reliable businesses, especially with a view to invigorate cross-border trade of digital users. However, this book notes that in so far as ADR/ODR provides an avenue for redress for consumers where there was none before, it increases access to justice. Some commentators have noted that the promotion of ADR processes that rely on mediation techniques does not ensure compliance with consumer protection laws and undermines the constitutional role of the courts.[7] By contrast, it has been argued that effective ADR can provide better regulatory control than judicial private enforcement.[8] Similarly, this book posed that out-of-court redress can and should increase access to justice, and extend the benefits to non-complainants by providing feedback to traders, enforcement bodies and regulators. This book suggested that

[7] See, for example, H. Eidenmiller and M. Engle, 'Against False Settlement: Designing Efficient Consumer Rights Enforcement System in Europe' 29(2014) *Ohio St J Disp. Resol* 261; G. Wagner, 'Private Law Enforcement through ADR: Wonder Drug or Snake Oil?' (2014) 51(1) *Common Mark Law Rev* 165–194; and J. M. Glover, 'Disappearing Claims and the Erosion of Substantive Law' (2015) 125 *Yale Law J* 3.

[8] C. Hodges, 'The Consumer as Regulator' in D. Leczykiewicz and S. Weatherill, *The Images of the Consumer in EU Law* (Hart, 2015) pp. 245–256.

courts, like regulators and enforcement mechanisms (both public and private, including for instance chargeback schemes), have different roles to play in the consumer redress. What policy makers should stride to provide is to sync them better, guiding consumers towards the most effective redress option at any given time.

Dispute System Design Recommendations for Effective Consumer Redress

Consumer redress processes should assist parties to settle genuine disputes between businesses and consumers. Although normally a trader will be willing to rectify and deal with a consumer complaint in order to maintain its reputation, there will always be cases where facts are disputed between the parties, or when the business is reluctant to resolve the matter to the satisfaction of the consumer. But it is unacceptable that for these cases the only means of redress for consumers is the courts, especially since by in large these are not accessible to consumers with low-value disputes. While a modest refundable fee from consumers may be justifiable, traders should be required, or at least incentivized, to participate and fund the majority of the cost of the redress process. This book has submitted that in regulated sectors, especially in essential services where there is often an oligopoly (i.e. energy, water, telecommunications and financial services), traders' adherence to accessible redress mechanisms must be mandatory. In addition, trade associations should require their members to participate and fund ADR since traders' participation raises quality standards. For other sectors it should be optional for traders, but they should have strong economic incentives to opt in. Therefore, national governments and the EU should gradually require traders to participate in certified ADR/ODR processes as this is the main (and often the only proportionate) redress option available to consumers.

Chapter 7 observed that the participation of traders in ADR is often determined by a legal obligation, a requirement imposed by their trade association or as a voluntary choice based on their expectation to obtain a competitive advantage. The present situation leaves many gaps in the provision of consumer redress. Accordingly, this chapter called for an effective redress forum for consumers, and proposed a mandatory residual ADR entity as the best strategy to realize such an objective. Indeed, it is irrational that low-value consumer disputes, especially those arising online, can only be resolved in the courts. For these disputes consumers should be able to access an ODR process, and the trader should be required, or highly incentivized, to participate in it. Voluntary adherence of traders will only occur when they see a business case to join in or when incentives are incorporated into the system. This chapter argued that the information requirements are insufficient to encourage traders to opt into ADR, so it will be necessary to couple it with additional incentives, such as a pan-European trustmark, blacklists, procurement restrictions and fiscal benefits. Furthermore, it submitted that the most effective incentive would be to either have an online court or tribunal which incorporates ADR and ODR techniques in its procedure, or a mandatory ADR/ODR entity with residual competence that is closely monitored by the regulator, and thus underpinned by national law.

Finally, Chapter 8 noted that as ADR entities are increasingly replacing the courts as the default fora for consumers, ADR should meet its dual goals of increasing access to justice and enhancing trust in the market. This chapter examined best practices from the dispute system design field and it advanced that two key features for a successful ADR procedure are tiered processes that deliver a high level of settlements and incentives that guarantee traders' out-of-court compliance with final outcomes. ODR technology can assist to achieve this through a platform that as part of a tiered procedure promotes early settlements through, inter alia, a triage function, costs incentives and public outcomes. Although a one-size procedure may not be suitable to resolve all types of consumer matters, it is possible to identify best practices for a consumer dispute resolution procedure that incorporate these features. Such a procedure must offer pyramidal procedural stages that filter complaints through the provision of advice to consumers that, on one hand, manages their expectations, and, on the other hand, promotes informal settlements over adjudication. This chapter noted that the online forum widens the options for voluntary out-of-court enforcement of outcomes (especially through the use of online reviews, blacklists and payment intermediaries). Lastly, this chapter argued that since ADR entities provide a public service, as such they should contribute in the design of dispute prevention strategies for the sectors where they operate. However, this can only be properly achieved if there is not more than one certified ADR entity per sector, and if such an entity cooperates with courts and feedbacks businesses and regulators, thus ensuring better compliance with the consumer law and hence improving trading standards.

Therefore, all publicly certified consumer redress entities, whether courts or ADR entities, should go beyond the provision of individual dispute resolution. They should not only work for a few, but for all consumers, unlocking the policy goals of increasing access to justice as well as consumer trust in the market by boosting competition, especially on its digital side.

BIBLIOGRAPHY

Legislative Texts

EU Legislation

Charter of Fundamental Rights of the European Union COM(2010) 573

Commission, Guidance on the Application of the Unfair Commercial Practices Directive SWD(2016) 136

Commission, Impact Assessment of the Proposal for a Regulation of the European Small Claims Procedure SWD(2013) 460

Commission, Report on the Application of Regulation (EC) 861/2007 of the European Parliament and the Council Establishing a European Small Claims Procedure COM(2013) 795 final

Commission, Report on the Functioning of Regulation (EC) 2006/2004 on Cooperation between National Authorities Responsible for the Enforcement of Consumer Protection Laws (CPC Regulation) COM(2014) 439 final

Commission Communication, 'Towards a Coherent European Approach to Collective Redress' COM(2013) 401

Commission Recommendation 2001/310/EC of 4 April 2001 on the Principles for the Out-of-Court Bodies Involved in the Consensual Resolution of Consumer Disputes (OJ 2001, L109/56)

Commission Recommendation 98/257/EC of 30 March 1998 on the Principles Applicable to the Bodies Responsible for Out-of-Court Settlement of Consumer Disputes (OJ 1998, L115)

Commission Recommendation on Common Principles for Injunctive and Compensatory Collective Redress Mechanisms in the Member States Concerning Violations of Rights Granted Under Union Law (OJ 2013, L201)

Commission Staff Working Paper, Impact Assessment Accompanying the Document of the Proposal for a Directive on Alternative Dispute Resolution for Consumer Disputes and the Proposal for a Regulation on Online Dispute Resolution for Consumer Disputes SEC(2011) 1408 final

Communication from the Commission to the European Parliament, the Council, the Economic and Social Committee and the Committee of the Regions,

'A European Consumer Agenda – Boosting Confidence and Growth' COM (2012) 225
Communication on Alternative Dispute Resolution for Consumer Disputes in the Single Market COM(2011) 791
Decision 2007/76/EC Setting out the Details on the Cooperation (OJ L32/192)
Directive 84/450/EEC on Misleading Advertising (OJ L250)
Directive 93/13/EEC on Unfair Terms (OJ L95/29)
Directive 95/46/EC on Data Protection (OJ L281)
Directive 97/5/EC On Cross-Border Credit Transfers (OJ L43)
Directive 98/10/EC on the Application of Open Network Provision (ONP) to Voice Telephony and on Universal Service for Telecommunications in a Competitive Environment (OJ L101)
Directive 99/44/EC on Consumer Sales and Guarantee (OJ L171)
Directive 2000/31/EC on Electronic Commerce (OJ L178/1)
Directive 2002/65/EC on Distance Marketing of Financial Services (OJ L271)
Directive 2002/8/EC to Improve Access to Justice in Cross-Border Disputes by Establishing Minimum Common Rules Relating to Legal Aid for Such Disputes (OJ L26)
Directive 2002/92/EC on Insurance Mediation (OJ L009)
Directive 2005/29/EC Unfair Commercial Practice (OJ L149/22)
Directive 2006/114/EC Concerning Misleading and Comparative Advertising (OJ L376/21)
Directive 2007/64/EC on Payment Services in the Internal Market (OJ L319)
Directive 2008/6/EC with Regard to the Full Accomplishment of the Internal Market of Community Postal Services (OJ L52/3)
Directive 2008/48/EC on Credit Agreements For Consumers (OJ L133/66)
Directive 2008/52/EC on Civil and Commercial Mediation (OJ L136/3)
Directive 2008/122/EC on the Protection of Consumers in Respect of Certain Aspects of Timeshare (OJ L33/10)
Directive 2009/110/EC on Electronic Money (OJ L267/7)
Directive 2009/22 on Injunctions for the Protection of Consumers' Interests (OJ L110/30)
Directive 2009/65/EC on Undertakings for Collective Investment in Transferable Securities (OJ L257/186)
Directive 2009/72/EC Concerning Common Rules for the Internal Market in Electricity (OJ L211/55)
Directive 2009/73/EC Concerning Common Rules for the Internal Market in Natural Gas (OJ L211/94)
Directive 2011/83/EU on Consumer Rights (OJ L304/64)
Directive 2013/11/EU on Alternative Dispute Resolution for Consumer Disputes (OJ L165/63)
Directive 2014/104/EU on Antitrust Damages Actions (OJ L349/1)

Parliament Resolution on Alternative Dispute Resolution in Civil, Commercial and Family Matters (2011/2117(INI))

Parliament Resolution 'Strategy for Strengthening the Rights of Vulnerable Consumers' (2011/2272(INI))

Parliament Resolution 'Towards A Coherent European Approach to Collective Redress' (2011/2089(INI))

Proposal Amending the Regulation 261/2004 COM/2013/0130

Proposal for a Directive on Alternative Dispute Resolution for Consumer Disputes (Directive on Consumer ADR) COM(2011) 793

Proposal for a Directive on Certain Aspects Concerning Contracts for the Online and Other Distance Sales of Goods COM(2015) 635

Proposal for a Directive on Certain Aspects Concerning Contracts for the Supply of Digital Content COM(2015) 634

Proposal for a Regulation on a Common European Sales Law SEC(2011) 1165

Proposal for a Regulation on Addressing Geo-Blocking and Other Forms of Discrimination Based on Customers' Nationality, Place of Residence or Place of Establishment Within the Internal Market COM(2016) 289

Proposal for a Regulation on Cooperation Between National Authorities Responsible for the Enforcement of Consumer Protection Laws COM(2016) 283

Proposal for a Regulation on Cross-Border Parcel Delivery Services COM(2016) 285

Proposal for a Regulation on Online Dispute Resolution for Consumer Disputes (Regulation on Consumer ODR) COM(2011) 794

Regulation (EC) 44/2001 on Jurisdiction and the Recognition and Enforcement of Judgments in Civil and Commercial Matters (OJ L12)

Regulation (EC) 261/2004 Complaints Related to Denied-Boarding, Delays and Cancellations (OJ L46)

Regulation (EC) 2006/2004 on Cooperation between National Authorities Responsible for the Enforcement of Consumer Protection Laws (OJ L364)

Regulation (EC) 1107/2006 Concerning the Rights of Disabled Persons and Persons with Reduced Mobility when Travelling by Air (OJ L204/1)

Regulation (EC) 861/2007 of the European Parliament and of the Council of 11 July 2007 Establishing a European Small Claims Procedure (OJ L1999/1)

Regulation (EC) 1393/2007 on the Service in the Member States of Judicial and Non-Judicial Documents in Civil or Commercial Matters (OJ L324/79)

Regulation (EC) 1371/2007 on Rail Passengers' Rights and Obligations (OJ L315/14)

Regulation (EC) 593/2008 on the Law Applicable to Contractual Obligations (OJ L177)

Regulation (EC) 1177/2010 Concerning the Rights of Passengers When Travelling by Sea and Inland Waterway (OJ L334/1)

Regulation (EU) 1215/2012 on Jurisdiction and the Recognition and Enforcement of Judgments in Civil and Commercial Matters (OJ L351/1)

Regulation (EU) 524/2013 on Online Dispute Resolution for Consumer Disputes (OJ L165/1)
Regulation (EU) 2015/2421 Creating a European Order For Payment Procedure (OJ 341/1)

Canada

(British Columbia) Civil Dispute Resolution Tribunal Act 44-2012

France

Consumer Act (*Loi Hamon* 423–17) of 13 February 2014

Germany

Aviation Sector Act 2013 (Gesetz zur Schlichtung im Luftverkehr)

International Law

European Convention of Human Rights 1950

Italy

Banking Act 262/2005
Investor Protection Act 262/2005
Regulation 206/2005
Regulation 28/2010
Regulation 130/2015
Regulation on the Procedure for Resolving Disputes between Communication Providers and Consumers 173/07/CONS

Mexico

Mexico Servicio de Conciliación Previa en las Relaciones de Consumo in Act 2014

Spain

Civil and Commercial Mediation Act 5/2012
Civil Procedure Act 1/2000
Draft Bill on Alternative Dispute Resolution for Consumers 2015
General Defence of Consumers and Users Act 1/2007
Reforming the Financial System Act 44/2002

Regulation 292/2004 Establishing a Public Trustmark for the Services of the Information Society and the Electronic Commerce
Regulation 231/2008 on Consumer Arbitration
Regulation 980/2013 on Civil and Commercial Mediation
Spanish Constitution 1978

UK

ADR Regulations 2015
Arbitration Act 1996
Business Names (Sensitive Words and Expressions) Regulations 2014
Civil Procedure Rules 1999
Companies Act 2006
Consumer Credit Act 1974
Consumer Protection from Unfair Trading Regulations 2008
Consumer Rights Act 2015
Cross-Border Mediation Regulations 2011/1133
Enterprise Act 2002
Estate Agents Act 1979
Regulatory Enforcement and Sanctions Act 2008
Sale of Goods Act 1979
Unfair Arbitration Agreements (Specified Amounts) Order 1999
Unfair Terms in Consumer Contracts Regulations 1995 and 2000

UN

UNCITRAL Conciliation Rules 1980
UNCITRAL Model Law on International Commercial Conciliation 2002
UNCITRAL Working Group III (Online Dispute Resolution) Report on the Work of Its Twenty-Second Session (Vienna, 13–17 December 2010)
UNCITRAL Working Group III (Online Dispute Resolution) Report on the Work of Its Twenty-Third Session (New York, 21 June–9 July 2010)
UNCITRAL Working Group III (Online Dispute Resolution) Report on the Work of Its Twenty-Fifth Session, 'Online Dispute Resolution for Cross-Border Electronic Commerce Transactions: Draft Procedural Rules' (New York, 21–15 May 2012)
UNCITRAL Working Group III (Online Dispute Resolution) Report on the Work of Its Twenty-Sixth Session (Vienna, 5–9 November 2012)
UNCITRAL Working Group III (Online Dispute Resolution) Report on the Work of Its Twenty-Seventh Session (New York, 20–24 May 2013)
UNCITRAL Working Group III (Online Dispute Resolution) Note by the Secretariat 'Draft Outcome Document Reflecting Elements and Principles of an ODR Process' (New York, 29 February–4 March 2016)

USA

Federal Arbitration Act 1970
Communications Decency Act 1996
Federal Consumer Act 2004
Code of Federal Regulations 2015

Case Law

Arbitration

Sté v. 2000 and Sté XJ 220 Ltd c M Meglio and M Renault Rev. Arb. 1997

ECtHR

Heather Moor & Edgecomb Ltd v. *the United Kingdom* Appl. no. 1550/09, Judgment of 14 June 2011
Le Compte, Van Leuven and De Meyere v. *Belgium* Appl. 6878/75 and 7238/75, Judgment of 23 June 1981
Osmo Suovaniemi and others v. *Finland*, Appl. no. 31737/96, Judgment of 23 February 1999
Pfeifer and Plankl v. *Autria*, Appl. no. 10802/84, Judgment of 25 February 1992
Zumtobel v. *Austria*, Appl. no. 12235/86, Judgment of 21 September 1993

CJEU

C-186/95 *Landgericht Krefeld*
C-168/05 *Claro* v. *Centro Movil Milenium*
C-489/07 *Messner*
C-511/08 *Heinrich Heine*
C-585/08 *Peter Pammer*
C-317/08 *Rosalba Alassini and Others*
C-40/08 *Asturcom Telecomunicaciones*
C-299/12 *Green Swann*
C-75/16 *Livio Menini and Maria Antonia Rampanelli*

Ireland

Ulster Bank Investment Funds Ltd v. *FSO* [2006] IEHC 323
Molloy v. *FSO* [2010] IEHC 182

Italy

Constitutional Court Decision 272/2012

UK

Allen Wilson v. *Buckingham* [2005] EWHC 1165 (TCC)
Binns v. *Firstplus Financial Group Plc* [2013] EWHC 2436 (QB)
Cable and Wireless [2002] 2 All ER (Comm) 1041
Fox v. *Wellfair Ltd* [1981] 1 Lloyd's Rep 514
Halsey v. *Milton* EWCA Civ 576 (2004)
Heifer International v. *Christiansen* [2007] EWHC 3015
Jet2.com v. *Huzar* [2014] EWCA Civ 791
Mylcrist Builders Ltd v. *Mrs G Buck* [2008] EWHC 2172
Office of Fair Trade v. *Abbey National plc & Others* [2009] UKSC 6
ParkingEye Ltd (Respondent) v. *Beavis (Appellant)* [2015] UKSC 67
Picardi v. *Cuniberti* [2002] EWHC 2923
Westminster Building Company v. *Beckingham* [2004] BLR 508

USA

AT&T Mobility v. *Concepcion*, 563 U.S. 321 (2011)
Bragg v. *Linden Research, Inc.*, 487 F. Supp. 2d 593 (E. D. Penn. 2007)
Carnival Cruise Lines, Inc. v. *Shute*, 499 S.Ct. 585 (1991)
In Re Facebook Privacy Litigation 791 F. Supp. 2d 705 (2011)
Zeran v. *AOL*, 129 F.3d 327 (4th Cir. 1997)

Literature

'Amazon to Sue Over 1,000 Fake Reviews' *Digital Journal* (18 October 2015). Available at www.digitaljournal.com/internet/amazon-to-sue-over-1-000-fake-reviewers/article/446891

Abel, R., 'The Contradictions of Informal Justice' in R. Abel (ed.), *The Politics of Informal Justice*, vol. 1 (Academic Press, 1892)

Abernethy, S., 'Building Large-Scale Online Dispute Resolution and Trustmark Systems' in E. Katsh & D. Choi (eds.), *Online Dispute Resolution: Technology as the 'Fourth Party'* (International Conflict Resolution Centre, University of Melbourne, 2003)

ADICAE, *Informe de ADICAE sobre el Anteproyecto de Ley de Resolución de Conflictos de Consumo* (ADICAE, 2014)

Sistemas de Resolución Extrajudicial de Conflictos con los Consumidores (ADICAE, 2014)

Alberstein, M., 'Judicial Conflict Resolution (JCR): A New Jurisprudence for an Emerging Judicial Practice' (2015) 16 *Cardozo Law J Confl Resol* 886

Alleweldt, F. et al., 'Cross-Border Alternative Dispute Resolution in the European Union' IMCO (June 2011) IP/A/IMCO/ST/2010-15

Anagnostaras, G., 'The Unfair Commercial Practices Directive in Context: From Legal Disparity to Legal Complexity?' (2010) 47 *CMLR* 147

Anonymous authors, 'Mandatory Mediation and Summary Jury Trial: Guidelines for Ensuring Fair and Effective Processes' (1990) 103 *Harv Law Rev* 1086

Armstrong, M., 'Interactions between Competition and Consumer Policy' (2008) 4(1) *Competition Policy Int* 97–147

Balboni, P., *Trustmarks in E-Commerce* (Cambridge University Press, 2009)

Balwin, J., 'The Small Claims Procedure and the Consumer' (London: Office of Fair Trading, 1995)

Banca d'Italia Eurosistema, 'The Banking and Financial Ombudsman Annual Report' (January 2016)

Barral-Viñals, I., 'Consumer Complaints and Alternative Dispute Resolution Methods: Harmonisation of the European ADR System' in J. Devenney and M. Kenny (eds.), *The Transformation of European Private Law* (Cambridge University Press, 2013)

Barral Viñals, I., 'Consumers, Online Dispute Resolution and Small Claims' (2014) 10 *Revista Democracia Digital e Governo Electrônico* 394

Barton, B. H., 'The Lawyer's Monopoly – What Goes and What Stays' (2014) 82 *Fordham Law Rev* 3067

Better Business Bureau, '2014 Statistics: Sorted by Complaints'. Available at www.bbb.org/globalassets/local-bbbs/council-113/media/complaint-stats/2014/2014us-sorted-by-complaint.pdf

BIS, Guidance on Specific Points of Checklist for Attributes of ADR Entities (April 2014)

Blackwell, P., *Satisfied Customers Tell Three Friends, Angry Customers Tell 3,000* (Tantor Media, 2008)

Black's Law Dictionary (Thomson West, 2016)

Bordone, R., 'Electronic Online Dispute Resolution: A System Approach – Potential, Problems, and a Proposal' (1998) 3 *Harv Negot Law Rev* 175

Bradney, A. and Cownie, F., 'Access to Justice?: The European Small Claims Procedure in the United Kingdom' in N. Neuwahl and S. Hammamoun (eds.), *The European Small Claims Procedure and the Philosophy of Small Change* (Les Éditions Thémis, 2014) p. 118

Brand, R., 'Analysis and Proposal for Incorporation of Substantive Principles for ODR Claims and Relief into Article 4 of the Draft Procedural Rules' Note submitted by the Center for International Legal Education to UNCITRAL Working Group III Twenty-Fifth Session (New York, 21–25 May 2012)

British Vehicle Rental and Leasing Association, Code of Conduct. Available at www.bvrla.co.uk/system/files/files/publication-order-forms/code_of_conduct_corporate_members.pdf

Response to the BIS Consultation Document on Implementing the ADR Directive and ODR Regulation (June 2014)

Bruni, A., 'The Use and Practise of Mediation in Italy' in F. Diedrich (ed.), *The Status Quo of Mediation in Europe and Overseas – Options for Countries in Transition* (Verlag Dr Kovac, 2014)

Bucilla II, J., 'The Online Crossroads of Website Terms of Service Agreements and Consumer Protection: An Empirical Study of Arbitration Clauses in the Terms of Service Agreements for the Top 100 Websites Viewed in the United States' (2014) 15 *Wake Forest Law Rev* 102

'Buyers Beware as Fake Online Review Business Booms' *The Irish Times* (25 June 2015)

Calliess, G-P., 'Online Dispute Resolution: Consumer Redress in a Global Market Place' (2006) 7(8) *German Law J* 647

Canto-Lopez, M., 'Ofgem's Recent Trends in Enforcement: Settlements, Redress and the Consumer's Interest' (2016) 21(2) *Utilities Law Rev* 65–70

Capobianco, E., 'Arbitrato e conciliazione. La risoluzione stragiudiziale delle controversie tra mediazione e procedura dinanzi all'Arbitro Bancario Finanziario' (2010) 8(9) *Obbl contr* 571

Cappelletti, M., 'Alternative Dispute Resolution Processes within the Framework of World-Wide Access-to-Justice Movement' (1993) 56 *Mod Law Rev* 282

'A World Survey' in M. Cappelletti and B. Garth (eds.), *Access to Justice* vol. 1 (Sijthoff and Noordhoff, 1978)

Ceeney, N., 'Modernising Courts and Tribunals' *HM Courts and Tribunals Service* (23 September 2015). Available at www.gov.uk/government/speeches/modernising-the-courts-and-tribunals

Centre for Consumer and Essential Services, University of Leicester 'Complaint Handling by Airlines: Development of Best Practices' Research Report for the Civil Aviation Authority (July 2014)

Centre for Retail Research, 'Online Retailing: Britain, Europe and the US 2014'. Available at www.retailresearch.org/onlineretailing.php

Chartered Institute of Arbitrators, Practice Guidelines 17: Guidelines for Arbitrators Dealing with Cases Involving Consumers and Parties with Significant Differences of Resources (2012)

Civic Consulting, European Parliament Study Cross-border Alternative Dispute Resolution in the EU (2011)

Civic Consulting Study for DG SANCO, 'Study on the Use of Alternative Dispute Resolution in the EU' (2009)

Civil Aviation Authority, 'Consumer Complaints Handling and ADR' CAP 1286 (15 April 2015)

Reforming Complaints Handling – Consultation on the CAA's Draft Policy CAP 1257 (December 2014)

Civil Justice Council Advisory Group 'Online Dispute Resolution for Low Value Civil Claims' (February 2015)

Competition and Markets Authority, 'Alternative Dispute Resolution for Consumers, Response to the Consultation on Implementing the Alternative Dispute Resolution Directive and the Online Dispute Resolution Regulation' (3 June 2014)

UK Presidency of ICPEN Report (30 June 2016)

Conley Tyler, M., '115 and Counting: The State of ODR 2004', in M. Conley Tyler, E. Katsh and D. Choi (eds.), *Proceedings of the Third Annual Forum on Online Dispute Resolution*. International Conflict Resolution Centre in collaboration with the United Nations Economic and Social Commission for Asia and the Pacific (UNESCAP)

Conley Tyler, M. and Bornstein, J., 'Accreditation of On-line Dispute Resolution Practitioners' (2006) 23(3) *Confl Resol Q* 383

Consejo General de la Abogacía Española,'Éxito Intermediación Hipotecaria en el CMICAV' (13/08/2015)

Consumer Council of Northern Ireland, 'Back to Business: Are Businesses Getting Consumers' Rights Wrong?' (December 2013)

Consumer Focus and DJS Research, 'Dealing with Dissatisfaction: Complaint Handling in Energy, Water, Telecoms, Financial and Legal Services and Royal Mail' (2012). Available at www.consumerfutures.org.uk/wpfb-file/dealing-with-dissatisfaction-pdf

Cooter, R. et al., 'Bargaining in the Shadow of the Law: A Testable Model of Strategic Behavior' (1982) 11 *Legal Stud* 225

Cortés, P., 'An Analysis of the UDRP Experience: Is It Time for Reform?' (2008) 24(4) *Comput Law Secur Rep* 349

'A Comparative Review of Offers to Settle – Would an Emerging Settlement Culture Pave the Way for Their Adoption in Continental Europe? (2013) 32(1) *Civil Justice Q* 42–67

'The Digitalisation of the Judicial System: Online Tribunals and Courts' (2016) 22(6) *Comput Telecommun Law Rev* 141

'Directive 2013/11/EU on Alternative Dispute Resolution for Consumers and Regulation (EC) 524/2013 on Online Dispute Resolution' in A. Lodder, A. Murray and T. Wisman (eds.), *Commentary on the EU Regulation of Electronic Commerce and Information*, 2nd edn (Edward Elgar, 2017)

'Does the Proposed European Procedure Enhance the Resolution of Small Claims?' (2008) 27(1) *Civil Justice Q* 83–97

'Enforcing EU Consumer Policy More Effectively: A Three-Pronged Approach' in S. Drake and M. Smith (eds.), *Effective Enforcement of EU Law and Policy* (Edward Elgar, 2016)

'A European Legal Perspective on Consumer ODR' (2009) 15(4) *Comput Telecommun Law Rev* 92

Cortes, P., 'European Small Claims Procedure and the Commission Proposal of 19 November 2013' *Report for the European Parliament* (JURI, 2015)

pp. 249–279. Available at www.europarl.europa.eu/RegData/etudes/STUD/2015/510003/IPOL_STUper cent282015per cent29510003_EN.pdf

'The Impact of EU Law in the ADR Landscape in Italy, Spain and the UK: Time for Change or Missed Opportunity?' (2015) 16(2) *ERA Forum* 125

'Improving the EU's Proposals for Extra-Judicial Consumer Redress' (2012) 23(2) *Comput Law* 27

'The Need for Synergies in Judicial Cooperation and Dispute Resolution: Changes in the European Small Claims Procedure' in X. Kramer and B. Hess (eds.), *From Common Rules to Best Practices in European Civil Procedure* (Hart, 2017) forthcoming

(ed.), *The New Regulatory Framework for Consumer Dispute Resolution* (Oxford University Press, 2016)

'A New Regulatory Framework for Extra-Judicial Consumer Redress: Where We Are and How to Move Forward' (2015) 35(1) *Legal Stud*, 114

'Online Dispute Resolution for Businesses – Embedding Online Dispute Resolution in the Civil Justice System of the EU' in C. Adamson (ed.), *Online Dispute Resolution: An International Business Approach to Solving Consumer Complaints* (NetNeutrals, 2015) pp. 36–46

Online Dispute Resolution for Consumers in the European Union (Routledge, 2010)

'Online Dispute Resolution Services: A Selected Number of Case Studies' (2014) 20(6) *Comput Telecommun Law Rev* 172–178

'Small Claims in Ireland and the EU: The Need for Synergy between National Courts and Extrajudicial Redress' in N. Neuwahl and S. Hammamoun (eds.), *The European Small Claims Procedure and the Philosophy of Small Change* (Les Éditions Thémis, 2014) pp. 125–146

'The UDRP Reviewed: The Need for a "Uniform" Policy' (2008) 14(6) *Comput Telecommun Law Rev* 133

Cortés, P. and Esteban de la Rosa, F., 'Building a Global Redress System for Low-Value Cross-Border Disputes' (2013) 62(2) *Int Comp Law Q* 407

Cortés, P. and Lodder, A., 'Consumer Dispute Resolution Goes Online: Reflections on the Evolution of European Law for Out-of-Court Redress' (2014) 21(1) *Maastricht J* 14

Council of Europe Committee on Equality and Non-Discrimination, 'Equality and Non-Discrimination in the Access to Justice' Report Doc 13740, Rapporteur: Mr V. Riceard Badea (31 March 2015)

Council of Europe Committee on Legal Affairs and Human Rights, 'Access to Justice through Online Instruments' Draft Report, Rapporteur: Mr J. Xucla (2 November 2015)

'Access to Justice through Online Instruments' Introductory Memorandum, Rapporteur: Mr J. Xucla (23 September 2014)

Cownie, F. Bradney, A. and Burton, M., *English Legal System in Context*, 5th edn (Oxford University Press, 2010)

Creutzfeldt, N., 'Ombudsman Schemes - Energy Sector in Germany, France and the UK' in P. Cortés (ed.), *The New Regulatory Framework for Consumer Dispute Resolution* (Oxford University Press, 2016)

Creutzfeldt-Banda, N., 'How Important Is Procedural Justice for Consumer Dispute Resolution? A Case Study of an Ombudsman Model for European Consumers' (2014) 37(4) *J Consumer Policy* 527–546

Cuenca García, A., 'Los Principios de Transparencia, Eficacia, Equidad, Libertad y Legalidad en la Directiva 2013/11/EU del Parlamento Europeo y del Consejo de 21 de Mayo de 2013, relativa a la Resolución Alternativa de Litigios en Materia de Consumo, y su Incidencia en el Sistema de Arbitraje de Consumo Español' in G. Palao Moreno (ed.), *Los Nuevos Instrumentos Europeos en Materia de Conciliación, Mediación y Arbitraje de Consumo* (Tirant, 2016) pp. 37–80

Cunningham, A., 'Caveat Consumer? Consumer Protection and Cloud Computing - Part I' Queen Mary School of Law Legal Studies Research Paper, n. 130, pp. 1–29 (January 2013)

Davies, J., 'ADR/ODR: Too Much Optimism in the Promotion of Cross-Border Trade?' in B. Hess, M. Bergstrom and E. Storskrubb (eds.), *EU Civil Justice: Current Issues and Future Outlook* (Hart, 2016) pp. 35–56

Dávila González, F.J., 'La Tramitación de la Resolución de Conflictos Sometidos a las Juntas Arbitrales de Consumo Mediante Medios Electrónicos. Problemas Prácticos y Propuestas de *Lege Ferenda*' in E. Vázquez de Castro (ed.), *Estudios sobre la Justicia Online* (Comares, 2013) pp. 43–60

De Groote, B. and De Vulder, K., 'European Framework for Unfair Commercial Practices: Analysis of Directive 2005/29' (2007) *JBL* 16–42

Del Duca, L., Rule, C. and Loebl, Z., 'Facilitating Expansion of Cross-Border E-Commerce-Developing a Global Online Dispute Resolution System' (2012) 1(1) *Penn St J Law Int Aff* 59

Del Duca, L., Rule, C. and Rimpfel, K., 'eBay de Facto Low Value High Volume Resolution Process: Lessons and Best Practices for ODR Systems' (2015) 4 *Penn St J Law Int Aff* 242

Del Duca, L., Rule, C. and Rogers, V., 'Designing a Global Consumer Online Dispute Resolution (ODR) System for Cross-Border Small Value - High Volume Claims - OAS Developments' (2010) 42(3) *Uniform Commercial Code Law J* 221

Deloitte, 'An Assessment of the Socio-Economic Impacts of the Policy Options for the Future of the European Small Claims Regulation' Final Report (19 July 2013)

Dennis, M., 'Diseño de una Agencia Práctica para la Protección de los Consumidores en las Américas' in D. Fernández Arroyo and J. Moreno Rodríguez (eds.) *Trabajos de la CIDIP VII* (Asunción, 2007) p. 219

Department for Business Innovation and Skills (BIS), 'Alternative Dispute Resolution for Consumers: Government Response to the Consultation on Implementing the Alternative Dispute Resolution Directive and the Online Dispute Resolution Regulation' (November 2014)

'Alternative Dispute Resolution for Consumers, Implementing the Alternative Dispute Resolution Directive and Online Dispute Resolution Regulation' (March 2014)

'Checklist of Requirements for Providers of Alternative Dispute Resolution Services Who Wish to Become Certified "ADR Entities" for the Purposes of the ADR Directive' (April 2014)

'Civil Enforcement Remedies: Consultation on Extending the Range of Remedies Available to Public Enforcers of Consumer Law' (November 2012)

Government Response to the Call for Evidence, EU Proposals on Alternative Dispute Resolution (May 2012)

'Guidance on Specific Points of Checklist for Attributes of ADR Entities' (April 2014)

Report on 'Consolidation and Simplification of UK Consumer Law' (November 2010) and the Consumer Rights Bill 2013

Department for Transport – CAA, Changes to the CAA's Policy on Consumer Complaint Handling and ADR (3 March 2016)

DG Justice and Consumers, European Commission, Consumer Conditions Scoreboard (2015)

DJS Report, 'Understanding consumer experiences of complaints and redress' Citizens Advice, (June 2016)

Doherty, M. and Leighton, P., 'Research in Law: Who Funds It and What Is Funded? A Preliminary Investigation' (2004) 38(2) *Law Teach* 182

Doktori, D. Karlik, E. and Perkins, L., 'Stakeholder Analysis and Design Recommendations for an EU-Wide Online Dispute Resolution System' Harvard Negotiation & Mediation Clinical Program (2 May 2012)

Donahey, S., 'The UDRP Model Applied to Online Consumer Transactions' (2003) 20(5) *J Int Arb* 475

Doyle, M., 'Gazing at the ADR landscape – Is the EU Directive just a Mirage?' (9 October 2013). Available at http://domarmediation.co.uk/2013/10/09/gazing-at-the-adr-landscape-is-the-eu-directive-just-a-mirage/

Doyle, M., Bondy, V. and Hirst, C., 'The Use of Informal Resolution Approaches by Ombudsmen in the UK and Ireland: A Mapping Study' (October 2014). Available at www.ombudsresearch.org.uk

Drahozal, C., 'New Experiences of International Arbitration in the United States' (2006) 54 *Am J Comp Law* 233

Duch-Brown, N. and Martens, B., 'Barriers to Firms' Cross-Border E-Commerce in the EU Digital Single Market', JRC/IPTS Digital Economy Working Paper, 2015

eBay Business Equipment Protection. Available at http://pages.ebay.com/help/buy/business-protection.html

eBay Motors Vehicle Purchase Protection. Available at http://pages.motors.ebay.com/buy/purchase-protection/

Ebner, N. and Zeleznikow, J., 'Fairness, Trust and Security in Online Dispute Resolution' (2015) 36(2) *Hamline Univ Sch Law J Pub Law Policy* 143

'No Sheriff in Town: Governance for Online Dispute Resolution' (2016) 32(4) *Negot J* 297

ECC Ireland, The Development of Alternative Dispute Resolution in Ireland – An Analysis of Complaints, Best Practices and Future Recommendations, 2008

ECC-Net, 'Chargeback in the EU/EEA' (2014)

'Cross-Border Dispute Resolution Mechanisms in Europe-Practical Reflections on the Need and Availability' (2009)

European Small Claims Procedure Report (September 2012). Available at http://ec.europa.eu/consumers/ecc/docs/small_claims_210992012_en.pdf

Economic Insight, 'The Business Case for Good Complaints Handling in Legal Services' Report for the Legal Ombudsman (November 2013).

Edwards, H., 'Alternative Dispute Resolution: Panacea or Anathema?' (1985) 99 *Harv Law Rev* 668

Edwards, L. and Theunissen, A., 'Creating Trust and Satisfaction Online: How Important Is ADR? The eBay Experience' (2007) 5 *Web J Curr Legal Issues*

EESC, Alternative Dispute Resolution for Consumer Disputes, Rapporteur: Pegado Liz (CESE 803/2012 – INT/609)

Eidenmiller, H. and Engle, M., 'Against False Settlement: Designing Efficient Consumer Rights Enforcement System in Europe' 29(2014) *Ohio St J Disp Resol* 261

Eidenmuller, H., Faust, F., Grigoleit, H.C., Jansen, N., Wagner, G. and Zimmerman, R., 'Towards a Revision of the Consumer Acquis' (2011) 48 *Common Mark Law Rev* 1077–1123

Eidenmullery, M. and Engel, H., 'Against False Settlement: Designing Efficient Consumer Rights Enforcement Systems in Europe' (2014) 29 *Ohio St J Disp Resol* 261

Eisenberg, M., 'Private Ordering through Negotiation' (1976) 89 *Harv. Law Rev* 637

El País, 'Una Treintena de Empresas Pagarán por el Número de Quejas de Clientes' (23 Febrero 2015)

Elliott, M. and Thomas, R., 'Tribunal Justice and Proportionate Dispute Resolution' (2012) 71(2) *Camb Law J* 279

Esteban de la Rosa, F., 'Challenges for the Implementation of the Consumer ADR Directive in Spain' in P. Cortés (ed.), *The New Regulatory Framework for Consumer Dispute Resolution* (OUP 2016) pp. 275–296

La protección del consumidor en dos espacios de integración: Europa y América (Tirant lo Blanch, 2015)

'Principios De Protección Del Consumidor Para Una Iniciativa Europea En El Ámbito De La Resolución Electrónica De Diferencias (ODR) De Consumo Transfronterizas (2011) 25 *Revista General de Derecho Europeo* 1

EU Code of Conduct for Mediators 2014

European Commission, 'Consumer Attitudes towards Cross-Border Trade and Consumer Protection. An Analytical Report' Flash Eurobarometer 299 (March 2011)

'The Consumer Conditions Scoreboard – Consumers at Home in the Single Market' 9th edn (July 2013)

EU Consumer Policy Strategy 2007–2013, COM(2007) 99 final

'The Online Dispute Resolution Platform' *Expert Group Meeting* (Brussels, 12 December 2014)

European Consumer Centre – Ireland, Car Rental Contracts Business Practices, Contract Terms and Consumer Protection (2008). Available at www.eccireland.ie/wp-content/uploads/2013/07/ECC_Car_Rental_Contracts_Report_2008.pdf

European Consumer Centres Network, '10 Years Serving Europe's Consumers Anniversary Report 2005–2015'. Available at http://tinyurl.com/zuxz4ch

European Consumer Organisation (BEUC), 'Alternative Dispute Resolution (ADR) & Online Dispute Resolution (ODR) of Consumer Disputes', BEUC Position Paper X/2012/010 (14 February 2012)

'Improving Enforcement Cooperation – BEU Response to the Consultation on the Review of Consumer Protection Cooperation (CPC) Regulation' BEUC-X-2014-005 (3 February 2014)

European Parliament, Committee on the Internal Market and Consumer Protection, Draft Report of 18 April 2012, 2011/0373(COD) Rapporteur L. Grech

Cross-Border ADR Final Report (2011) IP/A/IMCO/ST/2010-15

Study Cross-Border Alternative Dispute Resolution in the EU (2011)

Federal Reserve Bank of St. Louis, 'Personal Consumption Expenditures (PCE)/Gross Domestic Product (GDP)' (2013). Available at https://fred.stlouisfed.org/graph/?g=hh3

Fernández Arroyo, D., 'Current Approaches Towards Harmonisation of Consumer Private International Law in the Americas' (2009) 58(2) *ICLQ* 420

Financial Conduct Authority, Consultation Paper, Improving Complaints Handling (December 2014)

Financial Ombudsman Service Annual Review 2014/15. Available at www.financial-ombudsman.org.uk/publications/ar15/index.html#a2

Fisher, W. and Ury, M., *Getting to Yes: Negotiating Agreement Without Giving In* (Penguin, 1981)

Fisher, R., Ury, W. and Patton, B., *Getting to Yes, Negotiating an Agreement without Giving In*, 2nd edn (Random House, 1999)

Fiss, O., 'Against Settlement' 93 (1984) *Yale Law Rev* 1073

Flash Eurobarometer Report Cross-Border and Consumer Protection (March 2011)

Fowlie, F., 'Online Dispute Resolution and Ombudsmanship' in M. Wahab, E. Katsh and D. Rainey (eds.), *Online Dispute Resolution: Theory and Practice* (Eleven International Publishing, 2012) pp. 313–328

Froomkin, A., 'ICANN Uniform Dispute Resolution Policy, Causes and (Practical) Cures' (2002) 67 *Brooklyn Law Rev* 690

Fuller, L., 'The Forms and Limits of Adjudication' (1978) 92 *Harv Law Rev* 353

'Mediation – Its Forms and Functions' (1971) 44 *Calif Law Rev* 305

Gabuthy, Y., 'Online Dispute Resolution and Bargaining' (2004) 17(3) *Eur J Law Econ* 353

Gascón Inchausti, F., 'Algunas Reflexiones Acerca de la Oralidad y la Prueba en el Proceso de Escasa Cuantía' (2006) VI *Anuario Español de Derecho Internacional Privado* 285–308

Geist, M., 'Fair.com? An Examination of the Allegations of Systematic Unfairness in the ICANN UDRP' (2002) 27 *Brooklyn J Int Law* 903

Genn, H., 'Civil Mediation: A Measured Approach?' (2010) 32(2) *J Soc Welf Fam Law* 195

The Hamlyn Lectures 2008: Judging Civil Justice (Cambridge University Press, 2010)

'What Is Civil Justice for? Reform, ADR, and Access to Justice' (2012) 24(1) *Yale J Law Humanit* 397–417

GFK, Complaints to Ombudsman Services: Energy, Report for Ofgem Exploring Why Few Consumers Refer Their Complaint to Ombudsman Services: Energy (2013)

Gill, C. Williams, J. Brennan, C. and Hirst, C., 'Designing Consumer Redress: A Dispute System Design (DSD) Model for Consumer-to-Business Disputes' (2016) 36(3) *Legal Stud* 438

Gill, C. Williams, J. Brennan, C. and O'Brien, N., 'The Future of Ombudsman Schemes: Drivers for Change and Strategic Responses' (15 July 2013)

Glover, J. M., 'Disappearing Claims and the Erosion of Substantive Law' (2015) 125 *Yale Law J* 3

Goetzinger, L., Park, J.K. and Widdows, R., 'E-Customers' Third Party Complaining and Complementing Behavior (2006) 17(2) *Int J Serv Ind Manag* 193

Goodman, J., *Strategic Customer Service: Managing the Customer Experience to Increase Positive Word of Mouth, Build Loyalty, and Maximize Profits* (Amacon, 2009)

Gott, S., 'BBB Offers Tips on When and How to File a Complaint' Better Business Bureau (24 April 2013). Available at www.bbb.org/blog/2013/04/bbb-offers-tips-on-when-and-how-to-file-a-complaint/

Graham, C., 'Collective Consumer Redress' in P. Cortés (ed.), *The New Regulatory Framework for Consumer Dispute Resolution* (OUP, 2016)

Grundmann, S., 'Targeted Consumer Protection' in D. Leczykiewicz and S. Weatherill (eds.), *The Images of the Consumer in EU Law* (Hart, 2015) pp. 223–244

Halstead, D. and Page, T., 'The Effects of Satisfaction and Complaining Behavior on Consumers Repurchase Behavior' (1992) 5 *J Satisf Dissatisf Complaining Behav* 1

Hamilton, J. W., 'Pre-Dispute Consumer Arbitration Clauses: Denying Access to Justice?' (2006) 51 *McGill Law J* 693

Henry, R., 'Med-Arb: An Alternative to Interest Arbitration in the Resolution of Contract Negotiation Disputes' (1988) 3(2) *Ohio St J Disp Resol* 385

Hirschman, A., *'Exit, Voice, and Loyalty: Responses to Decline in Firms, Organizations, and States'* (Harvard University Press, 1970)

HMCTS, Civil Justice Statistics Quarterly, England and Wales (Incorporating Privacy Injunctions Statistics January to June 2015)

Hodges, C., 'Collective Redress: A Breakthrough or a Damp Squib?' (2014) 37 *J Consum Policy* 67

'Collective Redress in Europe: The New Model' (2010) 29(3) *Civil Justice Q* 373

'Consumer Ombudsmen: Better Regulation and Dispute Resolution' (2015) 16 *ERA Forum* 1

'The Consumer as Regulator' in D. Leczykiewicz and S. Weatherill (eds.), *The Images of the Consumer in EU Law* (Hart, 2015) pp. 245–256

'Ethical Business Regulation: Understanding the Evidence' Better Regulation Delivery Office, *Department for Business Innovation & Skills* (February 2016)

'The Need for a Holistic Review of the Dispute Resolution Landscape in England and Wales' (2017) forthcoming

'The Way Forward: Policy Principles on the Role of Law and Interests in ADR' at the Fourth Annual Oxford Consumer ADR Conference (18–20 April 2016)

Hodges, C., Benohr, I. and Creutzfeldt-Banda, N., 'Consumer-to-Business Dispute Resolution: The Power of CADR' (2012) 13 *ERA Forum* 199–225

Consumer ADR in Europe (Civil Justice Systems) (Beck/Hart, 2012)

Hodges, C. Creutzfeldt, N. and Macleod, S., *'Reforming the EU Consumer ADR Landscape: Implementation and Its Issues' Third Oxford Consumer Conference Report* (30–31 October 2014)

Hodges, C. and Stadler, A., *Resolving Mass Disputes – ADR and Settlement of Mass Claims* (Edward Elgar, 2013)

Hoofnagle, C. and Whittington, J., 'Free: Accounting for the Costs of the Internet's Most Popular Price' (2014) 61 *UCLA Law Rev* 606

Hopt, K. and Steffek, F., *Mediation: Principles and Regulation in Comparative Perspective* (Oxford University Press, 2012)

Horn, N., 'Arbitraje de Consumo en el Derecho Alemán y Europeo', in F. Esteban de la Rosa and G. Orozco Pardo (eds.), *Mediación y Arbitraje de Consumo, una Perspectiva Española, Europea y Comparada* (Tirant lo Blanch, 2010) pp. 221–233

Hörnle, J., *Cross-Border Internet Dispute Resolution* (Cambridge University Press, 2009)

'*Dispute Resolution: Digital Alternative*' *Law Gazette* (14 June 2014)

'Encouraging Online Dispute Resolution in the EU and Beyond-Keeping Costs Low or Standards High?' Queen Mary School of Law Legal Studies Research Paper No. 122/2012

Hörnle, J. and Cortés, P., 'Draft Report for the ODR Advisory Group, Working Paper on Legal Issues in Online Dispute Resolution' (July 2014)

Howells, G. and Weatherill, S., *Consumer Protection Law*, 2nd edn (Ashgate, 2005)

Hyde, J., 'Ratings Website Moves into Law' *Law Society Gazette* (4 August 2014)

Irvine, C., 'Mind the Gap: Mediation and Justice' *Kluwer Mediation Blog* (12 May 2014)

Jacquemin H., 'Optimal Integration European Dispute Resolution Platform' European Parliament (13 April 2012). Available at www.europarl.europa.eu/document/activities/cont/201204/20120413ATT42990/20120413ATT42990EN.pdf

JUSTICE, 'What Is a Court' (May 2016). Available at https://2bquk8cdew6192tsu41lay8t-wpengine.netdna-ssl.com/wp-content/uploads/2016/05/JUSTICE-What-is-a-Court-Report-2016.pdf

Katsh, E. and Rabinovich-Einy, O., 'Dispute Resolution in the Sharing Economy' *Internet Monitor* 2014. Available at https://thenetmonitor.org/research/2014/

Katsh, E. and Rifkin, J., *Online Dispute Resolution: Resolving Conflicts in Cyberspace* (Jossey-Bass, 2001)

Katsh, E., Rifkin, J. and Gaitenby, A., 'Ecommerce, E-disputes, and E-dispute Resolution: In the Shadow of "eBay Law"' (2000) 15(3) *Ohio St J Disp Resol* 705

Kaufmann-Kohler, G. and Schultz, T., *Online Dispute Resolution* (Kluwer Law International, 2004)

Kirkham, R., 'Analysis: Richard Kirkham on the Government's plans for consumer ADR: Innovation or more of the same' (26 November 2014). Available at http://ukaji.org/2014/11/26/analysis-kirkham-the-governments-plans-for-consumer-adr-innovation-or-more-of-the-same/

'Regulating ADR: Lessons from the UK' in P. Cortés (ed.), *The New Regulatory Framework for Consumer Dispute Resolution* (Oxford University Press, 2016)

Koulu, R., 'Blockchains and Online Dispute Resolution: Smart Contracts as an Alternative to Enforcement' (2016) 13(1) *Scripted* 41

Larson, D., 'Technology Mediated Dispute Resolution (TMDR): A New Paradigm for ADR' (2006) 21(3) Ohio *St J Disp Resol* 629

Le Sueur, A., 'Designing Redress: Who Does It, How and Why? (2012) 20 *Asia Pac Law Rev* 17

Leczykiewicz, D. and Weatherill, S., 'Images of the Consumer in EU Law' in D. Leczykiewicz and S. Weatherill (eds.), *The Images of the Consumer in EU Law* (Hart, 2015)

Legal Ombudsman, Annual Report 2013–14

Legal Ombudsman News, View from Operations – Assessor. Issue 8 (2014). Available at www.legalombudsman.org.uk/leo-news/issue-8/view-assessor.html

Leggatt, Sir Andrew, *Tribunals for Users: One System, One Service*, Report of the Review of Tribunals (2011)

Leveson, B., 'Security and Justice' 13th Annual Isaiah Berlin Lecture (12 November 2015) Available at www.judiciary.gov.uk/wp-content/uploads/2015/11/berlin-lecture-nov-2015.pdf

Lincoln Law School, 'Representative Actions and Restorative Justice' (2008). Available at www.bis.gov.uk/files/file51559.pdf

Lodder, A. and Zeleznikow, J., *Enhanced Dispute Resolution through the Use of Information Technology* (Cambridge University Press, 2010)

Loos, M., 'Consumer ADR After the Implementation of the ADR Directive: Enforcing European Consumer Rights at the Detriment of European Consumer Law' Amsterdam Law School Legal Studies Research Paper No. 2015–42

'Individual Private Enforcement of Consumer Rights in Civil Courts in Europe' Centre for the Study of European Contract Law Working Paper Series No. 2010/01

Lord Justice Briggs, *Civil Courts Structure Review* Final Report (July 2016)

Civil Courts Structure Review, Interim Report (December 2015)

Lucerna Partners, *Review of Ombudsman Services: Energy. A Report for Ofgem* (London: Lucerna Partners, 2015)

Lucking-Reiley, D., Bryan, D., Prasad, N., Reeves, D., 'Pennies from eBay: the Determinants of Price in Online Auctions' (2007) *J Ind Econ* 224

Luzak, J., 'Online Consumer Contracts' (2014) 15(3) *ERA Forum* 381

MacFarlane, J., 'ADR and the Courts: Renewing our Commitment to Innovation' (2012) 95(3) *Marquette Law Rev* 927

Madrid Parra, A., 'El Uso de Medios Electrónicos en la Mediación Patrimonial' (2013) 269 *Derecho de los Negocios* 2

Malbon, J., 'Taking Fake Online Consumer Reviews Seriously' (2013) 35 *J Consum Policy* 4

Manko, R., 'European Small Claims Procedure: Commission Proposal to Remedy Weaknesses in the Current System', *EPRS In-depth analysis*, PE 542.137 (November 2014)

'Europeanisation of Civil Procedure: Towards Common Minimum Standards?' *European Parlaimentary Research Service In-depth Analysis*, PE 559.499 (June 2015)

Marchal Escalona, N., 'La Protección del Consumidor en los Litigios Transfronterizos de Escasa Cuantía en la Unión Europea y en América Latina' in F. Esteban de la Rosa (ed.), *La Resolución Alternativa de Litigios de Consumo en los Estados Miembros de la UE: Impacto del Nuevo Derecho Europeo* (Tirant, 2015) pp. 1015–1054

Marques Cebola, C., 'The Implementation of the Consumer ADR Directive in Portugal: The Necessary Reform or Missed Opportunity?' in P. Cortés (ed.), *The New Regulatory Framework for Consumer Dispute Resolution* (Oxford University Press, 2016) pp. 251–274

Martic, D., 'Redress for Free Internet Services Under the Scope of the EU and UNCITRAL's ODR Regulations' (2014) 10 *Revista Democracia Digital e Governo Electrônico* 360

Martín Díz, F., 'Mediacion en Derecho Privado: Nuevas Perspectivas Prácticas' 33 (2014) *Revista General de Derecho Procesal* 1–38

Matthews, J. M., 'Consumer Arbitration: Is It Working Now and Will It Work in the Future?' (2005) 79 *Fl Bar J* 1

Mayer-Schonberger, V. and Cukier, K., *Big Data, a Revolution That Will Transform How We Live, Work, and Think* (Houghton Mifflin Harcourt, 2013)

McGill, S., 'Consumer Arbitration after Seidel v TELUS' (2011) 51 *Can Bus Law J* 187

McGregor, L., 'Alternative Dispute Resolution and Human Rights: Developing a Rights-Based Approach through the ECHR' (2015) 26(3) *Eur J Int Law* 607–634

Menkel-Meadow, C., 'Are There Systematic Ethic Issues in Dispute System Design? And What We Should [Not] Do About It: Lessons from International and Domestic Fronts' (Winter 2009) 14 *Harv Negot Law Rev* 202

'Do the "Haves" Come out Ahead in Alternative Judicial Systems? Repeat Players in ADR' (1999) 15 *Ohio St J Disp Resol* 19

Menkel-Meadow, C., Love, L., Schneider, A. and Sternlight, J., *Dispute Resolution: Beyond the Adversarial Model* , 2nd edn (Aspen, 2011)

Micklitz, H.W., The Future of Consumer Law – Plea for a Movable System (2013) 2(1) *J Eur Consum Mark Law* 5

Micklitz, H. and Reich, N., 'Crónica de una Muerte Anunciada: The Commission Proposal for a Directive on Consumer Rights' (2009) 46(2) *Common Mark Law Rev* 471

Micklitz, H. and Sartor, G., 'Assessing the Scope of the Online Dispute Resolution Platform' European Parliament (March 2012). Available at www.europarl.europa.eu/document/activities/cont/201204/20120417ATT43146/20120417ATT43146EN.pdf

Mimica, N., *EU Commissioner for Consumer Policy, 'EU Consumer Summit 2014: Ensuring that Consumers Reap the Benefits of the Digital Economy' Press Release IP/14/353* (1 April 2014)

Ministero della Giustizia, Dipartimento della Organizzazione Giudiziaria, del Personale e dei Servizi, Direzione Generale di Statistica 'Mediazione Civile Ex DL 28/2010 Statistiche Relative al Priodo Gennaio – Settembre 2014'

Ministry of Justice, 'Caroline Dinenage responds to the launch of 'Breaking up is Hard to Do' report' (17 December 2015). Available at www.gov.uk/government/speeches/caroline-dinenage-responds-to-the-launch-of-breaking-up-is-hard-to-do-report

Miquel Sala, R., *El Proceso Europeo de Escasa Cuantía* (Aranzadi, 2009) pp. 81–85

Mnookin, R. and Korn Hauser, L., 'Bargaining in the Shadow of the Law: The Case of Divorce' (1979) 88 *Yale Law J* 950

Moffitt, M., 'Three Things to Be against ("Settlement Not Included")' (2009) 78 *Ford Law Rev* 1203

Morek, R., 'The Regulatory Framework for Online Dispute Resolution: A Critical View' (2006) 38 *Univ Tol Law Rev* 163

Mueller, M., 'Rough Justice: An Analysis of ICANN's Uniform Dispute Resolution Policy' (2000) Syracuse University Convergence Centre http://dcc.syr.edu/PDF/roughjustice.pdf

Mullenix, L., 'Ending Class Actions As We Know Them: Rethinking the American Class Action' (2014) 64 *Emory Law J* 399

Nielsen, P.A., 'The New Brussels I Regulation' (2013) 50 *Common Mark Law Rev* 503–528

Nordic Council of Ministers, 'A Study on Alternative Dispute Resolution and Cross-border Complaints in Europe' (TemaNord, 2002)

O'Brian, E., 'The Hague Convention on Jurisdiction and Judgments: The Way Forward' (2003) 66(4) *Mod Law Rev* 491

OECD, *Conference on Empowering E-consumers Strengthening Consumer Protection in the Internet Economy, Background Report DSTI/CP(2009)20/FINAL*, Washington DC, (8–10 December 2009)

Economics Department Policy Notes 'What Makes Civil Justice Effective' (18 June 2013)

Ofgem, 'Enforcement Guidelines' (2014). Available at www.ofgem.gov.uk/ofgempublications/89753/enforcementguidelines12september2014publishedversion.pdf

Ombudsman Services, *Response to the Competition Markets Authority Energy Market Investigation 'Issues Statement'* (14 August 2014)

Online Retail Monitor, British Retail Consortium (2016). Available at www.brc.org.uk/bis/default.asp?main_id=7

Organisation of American States, Draft [Model Law/Cooperative Framework] for Electronic Resolution of Cross-Border E-Commerce Consumer Disputes (2010)

Ortiz, J.C., 'La Aplicación en España de los Procesos Europeos Monitorio y de Escasa Cuantía: La Reforma de la Legislación Española en Virtud de la Ley 4/2011, de 24 d Marzo' (2011) 24 *Revista General de Derecho Procesal* 2

Ortolani, P., 'Self-Enforcing Online Dispute Resolution: Lessons from Bitcoin' (2016) 36(3) *Oxf J Legal Stud* 595–629

OS Annual Report 2015. Available at www.ombudsman-services.org/downloads/Ombudsman-Services-annual-report-2015.pdf

Peretz, N., 'The Single Euro Payment Area: A New Opportunity for Consumer Alternative Dispute Resolution in the European Union' (2008) 16 *Mich St J Int Law* 573

Pérez Luño, A.E., *La Seguridad Juridical* (Ariel, 1994)

Petrucci, C., 'Collective Redress and Competition Law' in S. Drake and M. Smith (eds.), *Effective Enforcement of EU Law and Policy* (Edward Elgar, 2016)

Pilia, C., Cortés, P. and Vargiu, P., 'The Implementation of the Consumer ADR Directive in Italy' in P. Cortés (ed.), *The New Regulatory Framework for Consumer Dispute Resolution* (Oxford University Press, 2016) pp. 209–228

Ponte, L. and Cavenagh, T., *Cyberjustice, Online Dispute Resolution for E-Commerce* (Parson Prentice Hall, 2005)

Posner, R., 'Conventionalism: The Key to Law as an Autonomous Discipline' (1988) 38 *Univ Tor Law J* 333

Prince, S., 'Mediating Small Claims: Are We on the Right Track?' (2007) 26(2) *Civil Justice Q* 328–340

Prisco, G., 'Bitrated Unveils Reputation System and Multisig Escrow' (24 February 2015). Available at https://bitcoinmagazine.com/articles/bitrated-unveils-reputation-system-multisig-escrow-1424750534

Rabinovich-Einy, O., 'Technology's Impact: The Quest for a New Paradigm for Accountability in Mediation' (2006) 11 *Harv Negot Law Rev* 253

Rabinovich-Einy, O. and Katsh, E., 'Lessons from Online Dispute Resolution for Dispute System Design' in M. Wahab, E. Katsh and D. Rainey (eds.), *Online Dispute Resolution: Theory and Practice* (Eleven International Publishing, 2012) pp. 39–60

'Technology and the Future of Dispute System Design' (2012) 17 *Harv Negot Law Rev* 175

Ramsay, I., *Consumer Law and Policy*, 3rd edn (Hart, 2012)

Reding, V., Vice-President of the European Commission and EU Commissioner for Justice 'Towards a More Coherent Enforcement of EU Consumer Rules' (19 March 2013). Available at http://europa.eu/rapid/press-release_SPEECH-13-237_en.htm

Reich, N., 'Party Autonomy and Consumer Arbitration in Conflict: A "Trojan Horse" in the Access to Justice in the EU ADR Directive 2013/11?' (2015) 4(1) *Penn St J Law Int Aff* 290

'A "Trojan Horse" in Access to Justice – Party Autonomy and Consumer Arbitration in Conflict in the ADR-Directive 2013/11/EU' (2014) 10(2) *Eur Rev Contract Law* 258

Report of the Working Group on Consumer and Competition Policy for Scotland (October 2015)

Resnick, P., Zeckhauser, R., Swanson, J. and Lockwood, K., 'The Value of Reputation on eBay: a Controlled Experiment' (2006) 9 *Exp Econ* 79

Reyes López, M.J., 'La Reforma del TRLGDCU en Materia de Arbitraje' in G. Palao Moreno (ed.), *Los Nuevos Instrumentos Europeos en Materia de Conciliación, Mediación y Arbitraje de Consumo* (Tirant, 2016) pp. 231–248

Riefa, C., *Consumer Protection and Online Auction Platforms* (Ashgate, 2015)

Roberts, S. and Palmer, M., *Dispute Processes: ADR and the Primary Forms of Decision Making, 2nd ed* (Cambridge University Press, 2005)

Rogers, N. Bordone, R. Sander, F. and McEwen, C., *Designing Systems and Processes for Managing Disputes* (Kluwer, 2013)

Rogers, V., Institute of International Commercial Law (Pace Law School) Note on the Resolution Process Designated by the Draft ODR Rules Vienna, 14–18 November 2011

'Managing Disputes in the Online Global Marketplace: Reviewing the Progress of UNCITRAL's Working Group III on ODR' (2013) 19 *Disp Resol Mag* 21

Ross, G., 'The Possible Unintended Consequences of the European Directive on Alternative Dispute Resolution and the Regulation on Online Dispute Resolution' (2014) 10 *Revista Democracia Digital e Governo Electrônico* 206–221

Rühl, G., 'Alternative and Online Dispute Resolution for (Cross-Border) Consumer Contracts: A Critical Evaluation of the European Legislature's Recent Efforts to Promote Competitiveness and Growth in the Internal Market' (2015) 38 *J Consum Policy* 380

Rule, C., 'AAA Chooses ODR for Its Largest Volume Case Load' (2014) 1(1) *Int J Online Disp Resol* 97

'How the Internet Is Changing the Way Disputes Are Resolved' *Wire Innovation Insights* (24 June 2014). Available at http://insights.wired.com/profiles/blogs/how-the-internet-is-changing-the-way-disputes-are-resolved#axzz39bcSIGVK

'Making Peace on eBay', ACResolution (Fall 2008)

Online Dispute Resolution for Businesses. B2B, E-Commerce, Consumer, Employment, Insurance, and Other Commercial Conflicts (Jossey Bass, 2002)

'Quantifying the Economic Benefits of Effective Redress: Large E-Commerce Data Sets and the Cost-Benefit Case for Investing in Dispute Resolution' (2012) 34 *Univ of Ark Little Rock Law Rev* 767

Rule, C. and Del Duca, L., 'From Lex Mercatoria to Online Dispute Resolution: Lessons From History in Building Cross-Border Redress Systems' (2011) 43(3) *Uniform Commercial Code Law J* 1–15

Rule, C. and Nagarajan, C., 'Leveraging the Wisdom of Crowds: The eBay Community Court and the Future of Online Dispute Resolution', AC Resolution (2010)

Rutherglen, G., 'Wal-Mart, AT&T Mobility, and the Decline of the Deterrent Class Action' (2012) 98 *Virginia Law Rev* 24

Samuel, A., 'Consumer Financial Services in Britain: New Approaches to Dispute Resolution and Avoidance' (2002) 3(3) *Eur Bus Organ Law Rev* 649–694

Sander, F., 'Varieties of Dispute Resolution' National Conference on the Causes of Popular Dissatisfaction with the Administration of Justice 7–9 April 1976 Pound Conference (1976) 79 *FRD* 111

Sander, F. and Goldberg, S., 'Fitting the Forum to the Fuss: A User-Friendly Guide to Selecting an ADR Procedure' (1994) 10(1) *Negot J* 49–68

Sapp, W., 'Creating an Online Property Guide and Resolution Center' Fair and Equitable (April 2014)

Scannicchio, N., 'L'Adeguamento dell' Ordinamento Italiano alla Nuova Disciplina Europea sulla Risolutzione Alternativea Delle Controversie di Consumo' in F. Esteban de la Rosa (ed.), *La Resolución Alternativa De Litigios De Consumo En Los Estados Miembros De La UE: Impacto Del Nuevo Derecho Europeo* (Tirant, 2015)

Schmitz, A., '"Drive-Thru" Arbitration in the Digital Age: Empowering Consumers through Regulated ODR' (2010) 62 *Baylor Law Rev* 178–244

'Introducing the "New Handshake" to Expand Remedies and Revive Responsibility in eCommerce' (2014) 26 *St. Thomas Law Rev* 522

'Legislating in the Light: Considering Empirical Data in Crafting Arbitration Reforms' (2010) 15 *Harv Negot Law Rev* 194

Schoenberger, C., 'Computers' Reasoning Skills to Equal Humans by 2029' (26 June 2012). Available at www.wsj.com/articles/SB10001424052702303640804577490681107864926

Schulte-Nölke, H., 'EC Law on the Formation of – From Common Frame of Reference to the 'Blue Button'" (2007) 3 *Eur Rev Contract Law* 332

Schultz, T., 'Does Online Dispute Resolution Need Governmental Intervention? The Case for Architectures of Control and Trust' (2004) 6 *N C J Law Technol* 71

'Internet Disputes, Fairness in Arbitration and Transnationalism: A Reply to Julia Hörnle' (2011) 19(2) *Int J Law Inf Technol* 156

'Private Legal Systems: What Cyberspace Might Teach Legal Theorists' (2007) 10 *Yale J Law Techol* 159

'The Roles of Dispute Settlement and ODR' in Ingen-Housz (ed.), *ADR in Business: Practice and Issues Across Countries and Cultures* (Kluwer, 2011) p. 135

Sela, A., 'The Effect of Online Technologies on Online Dispute Resolution System Design: Antecedents, Current Trends and Future Directions' (2017) 21(3) *Lewis Clark Law Rev* 1–48

Shackelford, S. and Raymond, A., 'Building the Virtual Courthouse: Ethical Considerations for Design, Implementation, and Regulation in the World of ODR' (2014) *Wis Law Rev* 616

Síndic de Greuges de Catalunya, 'The Catalan Ombudsman and General Interest Companies' (February 2014)

Smith, S. and Martinez, J., 'An Analytical Framework for Dispute System Design' (2009) 14(4) *Harv Negot Law Rev* 1401

Sorkin, D. E., 'Payment Methods for Consumer-to-Consumer Online Transactions' (2001) 35(1) *Akron Law Rev* 1

Special Eurobarometer 381, E-Communication Household Survey (June 2012)

Special Eurobarometer 395, European Small Claims Procedure (April 2013). Available at http://ec.europa.eu/public_opinion/archives/ebs/ebs_395_en.pdf

Speer, T. 'They Complain Because They Care' (1996) 18 *Am Demogr* 13

Sternlight, J. 'In Defense of Mandatory Arbitration (If Imposed on the Company)' (2007) 8 *Nevada Law J* 82

'Is Alternative Dispute Resolution Consistent With the Rule of Law' (2006) 56 *DePaul Law Rev* 569

Sternlight, J. and Jensen, E., 'Using Economic Arbitration to Eliminate Consumer Class Actions: Efficient Business Practice or Unconscionable Abuse?' (2004) 67 *Law Contemp Probl* 75

Stewart, K. and Matthews, J., 'Online Arbitration of Cross-Border, Business to Consumer Disputes' (2002) 56 *Univ Miami Law Rev* 1119

Stipanowich, T., 'The Arbitration Penumbra: Arbitration Law and the Rapidly Changing Landscape of Dispute Resolution' (2007) 8 *Nevada Law J* 427

Stone, M., 'A Paradox in the Theory of Commercial Arbitration' (1966) 21(3) *Arbitration J* 156–163

Stuhmcke, A., 'The Corporatisation and Privatisation of the Australian Telecommunications Industry: The Role of the Telecommunications Industry Ombudsman' (1998) 21(3) *Univ N S W Law J* 807

Stürner, M., Gascón Inchausti, F. and Caponi, R., *The Role of Consumer ADR in the Administration of Justice – New Trends in Access to Justice under EU Directive 2013/11* (Selp, 2015)

Stuyck, J., Terryn, E., Colaert, V., Van Dyck, T., Peretz, N., Hoekx, N. and Tereszkiewicz, P., *Study on Alternative Means of Consumer Redress Other Than Redress through the Ordinary Judicial Proceedings* (Catholic University of Lueven, 14 January 2007)

Susskind, R., *The End of Lawyers? Rethinking the Nature of Legal Services* (Oxford University Press, 2008)

Tomorrow's Lawyers: An Introduction to Your Future (Oxford University Press, 2013)

The Economist, 'The Truly Personal Computer' (28 February 2015)

The Irish Department of Jobs, Enterprise and Innovation 'Consultation on the Implementation of the EU Directive on Consumer Alternative Dispute Resolution and the EU Regulation on Consumer Online Dispute Resolution' (June 2014)

Thompson, D., 'Addressing Leveraging Technology in Civil Justice ODR' *Comput Law* (6 October 2014)

'Online Dispute Resolution Expansion in the EU' (2012) *Comput Law* 31 (3 December 2011)

Tulibacka, M., 'Europeanization of Civil Procedures: In Search of a Coherent Approach' (2009) 46 *Common Mark Law Rev* 1527–1565

UK Office for National Statistics, 'Statistical bulletin: Internet Access – Households and Individuals, 2013'. Available at www.ons.gov.uk/ons/rel/rdit2/internet-access–households-and-individuals/2013/stb-ia-2013.html

University of Lincoln, Lincoln Law School 'Representative Actions and Restorative Justice' (2008). Available at www.bis.gov.uk/files/file51559.pdf

Ury, W., Brett, J. and Goldberg, S., *Getting Disputes Resolved: Designing Systems to Cut the Costs of Conflicts* (Jossey-Bass, 1988)

US Department of Health and Human Services, 'Policy Issues Related to Patient Reported Data' (8 June 2012) p. 8, available at http://tinyurl.com/jsc42oz

Van Boom, W. and Loos, M. (eds.), *Collective Enforcement of Consumer Law: Securing Compliance in Europe through Private Group Action and Public Authority Intervention* (Europa Law Publishing, 2007)

Vilalta, E., 'ODR and E-Commerce' in M. Wahab, E. Katsh and D. Rainey (eds.), *Online Dispute Resolution: Theory and Practice* (Eleven International Publishing, 2012) pp. 113–138

Vilalta Nicuesa, A. E., *Mediación y Arbitraje Electrónicos* (Aranzadi, 2013)

Vreeswijk, G.A.W. and Lodder, A.R., 'Gearbi: Towards an Online Arbitration Environment Based On The Design Principles Simplicity, Awareness, Orientation, And Timeliness' (2005) 13(2) *Artif Intell Law* 297

Wagner, G., 'Private Law Enforcement Through ADR: Wonder Drug Or Snake Oil?' (2014) 51(1) *Common Mark Law Rev* 165–194

Wahab, M., Katsh, E. and Rainey, D., *Online Dispute Resolution: Theory and Practice* (Eleven International Publishing, 2012)

Weatherill, S., 'The Consumer Rights Directive: How and Why a Quest for "Coherence" Has (Largely) Failed' (2012) 49 *Common Mark Law Rev* 1279

EU Consumer Law and Policy (Edward Elgar, 2014)

Weatherill, S. and Bernitz, U. (eds.), *The Regulation of Unfair Commercial Practices under Directive 2005/29: New Rules and New Techniques* (Hart, 2007)

Webb, L. 'Brainstorming Meets Online Dispute Resolution' (2004) 15 *Am Rev Int Arb* 337

'International BBB Ratings á la eBay: A Proposal for an Improved Online Better Business Bureau to Facilitate International Business Transactions' (2004) 35 *Calif West Int Law J* 127

Which?, 'Millions experience problems with online purchases' (7 March 2014)

Williams, J. and Gill, C., 'A Dispute System Design Perspective on the Future Development of Consumer Dispute Resolution' in P. Cortés (ed.), *The European Framework for Consumer Dispute Resolution* (OUP, 2016) pp. 371–392

Winston, K., 'Introduction to the Revised Edition' in K. Winston (ed.), *The Principles of Social Order: Selected Essays of Lon L. Fuller* (Hart, 2001)

Yuthayotin, S., *Access to Justice in Transnational B2C E-Commerce* (Springer, 2015)

Zickuhr, K. *'Who's Not Online and Why' Pew Research* (25 September 2013)

INDEX